Modern Critical Views P9-EJO-739

Chinua Achebe
Henry Adams
Aeschylus
S. Y. Agnon
Edward Albee
Raphael Alberti
Louisa May Alcott
A. R. Ammons
Sherwood Anderson
Aristophanes
Matthew Arnold
Antonin Artaud
John Ashbery
Margaret Atwood
W. H. Auden
Jane Austen
Isaac Babel
Sir Francis Bacon
James Baldwin
Honoré de Balzac
John Barth
Donald Barthelme
Charles Baudelaire
Simone de Beauvoir
Samuel Beckett
Saul Bellow
Thomas Berger
John Berryman
The Bible
Elizabeth Bishop
William Blake
Giovanni Boccaccio
Heinrich Böll
Jorge Luis Borges
Elizabeth Bowen
Bertolt Brecht
The Brontës
Charles Brockden Brown
Sterling Brown
Robert Browning
Martin Buber
John Bunyan
Anthony Burgess
Kenneth Burke
Robert Burns
William Burroughs
George Gordon, Lord
  Byron
Pedro Calderón de la Barca
Italo Calvino
Albert Camus
Canadian Poetry: Modern
  and Contemporary
Canadian Poetry through
  E. J. Pratt
Thomas Carlyle
Alejo Carpentier
Lewis Carroll
Willa Cather
Louis-Ferdinand Céline
Miguel de Cervantes

Geoffrey Chaucer
John Cheever
Anton Chekhov
Kate Chopin
Chrétien de Troyes
Agatha Christie
Samuel Taylor Coleridge
Colette
William Congreve & the
  Restoration Dramatists
Joseph Conrad
Contemporary Poets
James Fenimore Cooper
Pierre Corneille
Julio Cortázar
Hart Crane
Stephen Crane
e. e. cummings
Dante
Robertson Davies
Daniel Defoe
Philip K. Dick
Charles Dickens
James Dickey
Emily Dickinson
Denis Diderot
Isak Dinesen
E. L. Doctorow
John Donne & the
  Seventeenth-Century
  Metaphysical Poets
John Dos Passos
Fyodor Dostoevsky
Frederick Douglass
Theodore Dreiser
John Dryden
W. E. B. Du Bois
Lawrence Durrell
George Eliot
T. S. Eliot
Elizabethan Dramatists
Ralph Ellison
Ralph Waldo Emerson
Euripides
William Faulkner
Henry Fielding
F. Scott Fitzgerald
Gustave Flaubert
E. M. Forster
John Fowles
Sigmund Freud
Robert Frost
Northrop Frye
Carlos Fuentes
William Gaddis
Federico García Lorca
Gabriel García Márquez
André Gide
W. S. Gilbert
Allen Ginsberg
J. W. von Goethe

Nikolai Gogol
William Golding
Oliver Goldsmith
Mary Gordon
Günther Grass
Robert Graves
Graham Greene
Thomas Hardy
Nathaniel Hawthorne
William Hazlitt
H. D.
Seamus Heaney
Lillian Hellman
Ernest Hemingway
Hermann Hesse
Geoffrey Hill
Friedrich Hölderlin
Homer
A. D. Hope
Gerard Manley Hopkins
Horace
A. E. Housman
William Dean Howells
Langston Hughes
Ted Hughes
Victor Hugo
Zora Neale Hurston
Aldous Huxley
Henrik Ibsen
Eugène Ionesco
Washington Irving
Henry James
Dr. Samuel Johnson and
  James Boswell
Ben Jonson
James Joyce
Carl Gustav Jung
Franz Kafka
Yasonari Kawabata
John Keats
Søren Kierkegaard
Rudyard Kipling
Melanie Klein
Heinrich von Kleist
Philip Larkin
D. H. Lawrence
John le Carré
Ursula K. Le Guin
Giacomo Leopardi
Doris Lessing
Sinclair Lewis
Jack London
Robert Lowell
Malcolm Lowry
Carson McCullers
Norman Mailer
Bernard Malamud
Stéphane Mallarmé
Sir Thomas Malory
André Malraux
Thomas Mann

Modern Critical Views

Katherine Mansfield
Christopher Marlowe
Andrew Marvell
Herman Melville
George Meredith
James Merrill
John Stuart Mill
Arthur Miller
Henry Miller
John Milton
Yukio Mishima
Molière
Michel de Montaigne
Eugenio Montale
Marianne Moore
Alberto Moravia
Toni Morrison
Alice Munro
Iris Murdoch
Robert Musil
Vladimir Nabokov
V. S. Naipaul
R. K. Narayan
Pablo Neruda
John Henry Newman
Friedrich Nietzsche
Frank Norris
Joyce Carol Oates
Sean O'Casey
Flannery O'Connor
Christopher Okigbo
Charles Olson
Eugene O'Neill
José Ortega y Gasset
Joe Orton
George Orwell
Ovid
Wilfred Owen
Amos Oz
Cynthia Ozick
Grace Paley
Blaise Pascal
Walter Pater
Octavio Paz
Walker Percy
Petrarch
Pindar
Harold Pinter
Luigi Pirandello
Sylvia Plath
Plato

Plautus
Edgar Allan Poe
Poets of Sensibility & the
    Sublime
Poets of the Nineties
Alexander Pope
Katherine Anne Porter
Ezra Pound
Anthony Powell
Pre-Raphaelite Poets
Marcel Proust
Manuel Puig
Alexander Pushkin
Thomas Pynchon
Francisco de Quevedo
François Rabelais
Jean Racine
Ishmael Reed
Adrienne Rich
Samuel Richardson
Mordecai Richler
Rainer Maria Rilke
Arthur Rimbaud
Edwin Arlington Robinson
Theodore Roethke
Philip Roth
Jean-Jacques Rousseau
John Ruskin
J. D. Salinger
Jean-Paul Sartre
Gershom Scholem
Sir Walter Scott
William Shakespeare
    Histories & Poems
    Comedies & Romances
    Tragedies
George Bernard Shaw
Mary Wollstonecraft
    Shelley
Percy Bysshe Shelley
Sam Shepard
Richard Brinsley Sheridan
Sir Philip Sidney
Isaac Bashevis Singer
Tobias Smollett
Alexander Solzhenitsyn
Sophocles
Wole Soyinka
Edmund Spenser
Gertrude Stein
John Steinbeck

Stendhal
Laurence Sterne
Wallace Stevens
Robert Louis Stevenson
Tom Stoppard
August Strindberg
Jonathan Swift
John Millington Synge
Alfred, Lord Tennyson
William Makepeace Thackeray
Dylan Thomas
Henry David Thoreau
James Thurber and S. J.
    Perelman
J. R. R. Tolkien
Leo Tolstoy
Jean Toomer
Lionel Trilling
Anthony Trollope
Ivan Turgenev
Mark Twain
Miguel de Unamuno
John Updike
Paul Valéry
Cesar Vallejo
Lope de Vega
Gore Vidal
Virgil
Voltaire
Kurt Vonnegut
Derek Walcott
Alice Walker
Robert Penn Warren
Evelyn Waugh
H. G. Wells
Eudora Welty
Nathanael West
Edith Wharton
Patrick White
Walt Whitman
Oscar Wilde
Tennessee Williams
William Carlos Williams
Thomas Wolfe
Virginia Woolf
William Wordsworth
Jay Wright
Richard Wright
William Butler Yeats
A. B. Yehoshua
Emile Zola

Modern Critical Views

VIRGINIA WOOLF

Modern Critical Views

VIRGINIA WOOLF

Edited with an introduction by

Harold Bloom

Sterling Professor of the Humanities
Yale University

CHELSEA HOUSE PUBLISHERS
New York
Philadelphia

PROJECT EDITORS: Emily Bestler, James Uebbing
ASSOCIATE EDITOR: Maria Behan
EDITORIAL COORDINATOR: Karyn Gullen Browne
EDITORIAL STAFF: Perry King, Bert Yaeger
DESIGN: Susan Lusk

Cover by Robin Peterson

10   9   8   7   6   5   4   3   2

Library of Congress Cataloging in Publication Data

Virgina Woolf.
      (Modern critical views)
      Bibliography: p.
      Includes index.
      Summary: Eighteen critical essays on the works of
the English writer who experimented with stream-of-
consciousness and other innovative techniques.
      1. Woolf, Virgina, 1882–1941–Criticism and
interpretation–Addresses, essays, lectures.
[1. Woolf, Virgina, 1882–1941–Criticism and
interpretation–Addresses, essays, lectures. 2. English
literature–History and criticism–Addresses, essays,
lectures]   I. Bloom, Harold.   II. Series.
PR6045.072Z8918   1986   823'.912   85-25518
ISBN 0–87754–673–8

Contents

Editor's Note   ix

Introduction . . . . . .*Harold Bloom*   1

Something Central Which Permeated:
   Mrs. Dalloway . . . . . .*Reuben Brower*   7

The Brown Stocking . . . . . .*Erich Auerbach*   19

Virginia's Web . . . . . .*Geoffrey Hartman*   41

"Death Among the Apple Trees":
   The Waves and the World of Things
   Frank D. McConnell   53

Nature and History in *The Years* . . . . . .*James Naremore*   67

Enigmas of Imagination: *Orlando*
   Through the Looking Glass . . . . . .*Paul West*.   83

The Waves . . . . . .*Hermione Lee*. 101

An Uncertain Balance: *Night and Day* . . . . . .*T. E. Apter* 119

Virginia Woolf and Walter Pater . . . . . .*Perry Meisel*. 129

Between the Acts: The Play of Will . . . . . .*Maria DiBattista*. . . . 137

Toward the Far Side of Language:
   The Voyage Out . . . . . .*E. L. Bishop*. 153

Mrs. Dalloway: Repetition as the
   Raising of the Dead . . . . . .*J. Hillis Miller*. 169

Irreconcilable Habits of Thought in *A Room of*
   One's Own and *To the Lighthouse* . . . . . .*John Burt*. 191

Jacob's Room: A Study in Still Life . . . . . .*Robert Kiely* 207

The Musical Style of *The Waves* . . . . . .*Gerald Levin*. 215

The Politics of Holiday: *Orlando* . . . . . .*Judy Little*. 223

Narrative Voice and the Female Perspective
   in *The Voyage Out* . . . . . .*Virginia Blain*. 231

Narrative Structure(s) and Female Development:
   The Case of *Mrs. Dalloway* . . . . . .*Elizabeth Abel* 243

Chronology 265
Contributors 267
Bibliography. 269
Acknowledgments. 275
Index 277

Editor's Note

This volume gathers together a representative selection of the best criticism devoted to the work of Virginia Woolf. The essays and excerpts range from 1951 to the present, and are arranged here in the chronological order of their publication. Without the erudition of Ms. Susan Laity, the editor would have been unaware of many of these essays.

The "Introduction" emphasizes an interplay in Woolf's novels between her Paterian aestheticism, with its focus upon perception and sensation in a universe of death, and her developing feminism, which subtly modifies and corrects her literary tradition without overthrowing it, despite her larger ambitions. With Reuben Brower's reading of *Mrs. Dalloway*, and Erich Auerbach's of *To the Lighthouse*, the chronological sequence begins strongly, as these have become the classic accounts of her two most admired novels.

An overview by Geoffrey Hartman follows, centering on Woolf's ingenuity in trying to solve the representational problems of modern fiction. This is succeeded by Frank D. McConnell on *The Waves*, and James Naremore on *The Years*, each meditating upon the different relation, in Woolf, between time and the object world.

The essays of the later 1970s—Paul West on *Orlando*, Hermione Lee on *The Waves* and T. E. Apter on *Night and Day*—necessarily also investigate this relation, for it is Woolf's prevalent concern, as it was Pater's. Like Pater, Woolf is a theorist of belatedness in the Romantic tradition, still working out the enigmas of self, skepticism and vision bequeathed by Wordsworth and Shelley. Perry Meisel, like the editor, makes this his subject, as he directly ponders the concealed debt of Woolf to Pater.

All the remaining essays, constituting the second half of this book, stem from the intense Woolf renewal of the early 1980s, which shows no sign of abating, based as it is both on a public obsession with the Bloomsbury set, and the spiritual reliance of feminist literary criticism upon *A Room of One's Own* and other Woolfian polemics. Something of the aura of these interests surrounds the interesting juxtaposition of Maria DiBattista's reading of Woolf's final novel, *Between the Acts*, and E. L. Bishop's analysis of her first, *The Voyage Out*.

With J. Hillis Miller on *Mrs. Dalloway* and John Burt on *To the Lighthouse*, we are given critical descriptions of the most sophisticated and advanced kind, informed as they are by both deconstructive and feminist insights. The emphasis changes to allied arts in Robert Kiely's study of the relation of *Jacob's Room* to painting, and Gerald Levin's analysis of the musical style of *The Waves*.

This book ends with three very varied essays that represent the ongoing feminist criticism of Woolf. Judy Little on *Orlando*, Virginia Blain on *The Voyage Out* and Elizabeth Abel on *Mrs. Dalloway* engage issues of feminist politics, narrative perspective and psychic development. Their differences are an indication, happily, of the vast field implicit in the still-emerging cosmos of what is called feminist criticism.

Introduction

I

In May 1940, less than a year before she drowned herself, Virginia Woolf read a paper to the Worker's Educational Association in Brighton. We know it as the essay entitled "The Leaning Tower," in which the Shelleyan emblem of the lonely tower takes on more of a social than an imaginative meaning. It is no longer the point of survey from which the poet Athanase gazes down in pity at the dark estate of mankind, and so is not an image of contemplative wisdom isolated from the mundane. Instead, it is "the tower of middle-class birth and expensive education," from which the poetic generation of W. H. Auden and Louis MacNeice stare sidelong at society. Woolf does not say so, but we can surmise that she preferred Shelley to Auden, while realizing that she herself dwelt in the leaning tower, unlike Yeats, to whom the lonely tower remained an inevitable metaphor for poetic stance.

It is proper that "The Leaning Tower," as a speculation upon the decline of a Romantic image into belatedness, should concern itself also with the peculiarities of poetic influence:

> Theories then are dangerous things. All the same we must risk making one this afternoon since we are going to discuss modern tendencies. Directly we speak of tendencies or movements we commit ourselves to the belief that there is some force, influence, outer pressure which is strong enough to stamp itself upon a whole group of different writers so that all their writing has a certain common likeness. We must then have a theory as to what this influence is. But let us always remember—influences are infinitely numerous; writers are infinitely sensitive; each writer has a different sensibility. That is why literature is always changing, like the weather, like clouds in the sky. Read a page of Scott; then of Henry James; try to work out the influences that have transformed the one page into the other. It is beyond our skill. We can only hope therefore to single out the most obvious influences that have formed writers into groups. Yet there are groups. Books descend from books as families descend from families. Some descend from Jane Austen; others from Dickens. They resemble their parents, as human children resemble their parents; yet they differ as children differ, and revolt as children revolt. Perhaps it will be easier to understand living writers as we take a quick look at some of their forbears.

A critic of literary influence learns to be both enchanted and wary when such a passage is encountered. Sensibility is indeed the issue, since without "a different sensibility" no writer truly is a writer. Woolf's sensibility essentially is Paterian, as Perry Meisel accurately demonstrated. She is hardly unique among the great Modernist writers in owing much to Pater. That group includes Wilde, Yeats, Wallace Stevens, Hart Crane, as well as Pound and Eliot. Among the novelists, the Paterians, however involuntary, include Scott Fitzgerald, the early Joyce, and in strange ways both Conrad and Lawrence, as well as Woolf. Of all these, Woolf is most authentically Pater's child. Her central tropes, like his, are personality and death, and her ways of representing consciousness are very close to his. The literary ancestor of those curious twin sensibilities—Septimus Smith and Clarissa Dalloway—is Pater's Sebastian Van Storck, except that Woolf relents, and they do not go into Sebastian's "formless and nameless infinite world, quite evenly grey."

Mrs. Dalloway (1925), the fourth of Woolf's nine novels, is her first extraordinary achievement. Perhaps she should have called it The Hours, its original working title. To speak of measuring one's time by days or months, rather than years, has urgency, and this urgency increases when the fiction of duration embraces only hours, as Mrs. Dalloway does. The novel's peculiar virtue is the enigmatic doubling between Clarissa Dalloway and Septimus Smith, who do not know one another. We are persuaded that the book is not disjointed because Clarissa and Septimus uncannily share what seem a single consciousness, intense and vulnerable, each fearing to be consumed by a fire perpetually about to break forth. Woolf seems to cause Septimus to die instead of Clarissa, almost as though the novel is a single apotropaic gesture on its author's part. One thinks of the death died for Marius by Cornelius in Pater's Marius the Epicurean, but that is one friend atoning for another. However unified, does Mrs. Dalloway cogently link Clarissa and Septimus?

Clearly the book does, but only through its manipulation of Pater's evasions of the figure or trope of the self as the center of a flux of sensations. In a book review written when she was only twenty-five, Woolf made a rough statement of the stance towards the self she would take throughout her work-to-come, in the form of a Paterian rhetorical question: "Are we not each in truth the centre of innumerable rays which so strike upon one figure only, and is it not our business to flash them straight and completely back again, and never suffer a single shaft to blunt itself on the far side of us?" Here is Clarissa Dalloway, at the novel's crucial epiphany, not suffering the rays to blunt themselves on the far side of her:

What business had the Bradshaws to talk of death at her party? A young man had killed himself. And they talked of it at her party—the Bradshaws talked of death. He had killed himself—but how? Always her body went through it first, when she was told, suddenly, of an accident; her dress flamed, her body burnt. He had thrown himself from a window. Up had flashed the ground; through him, blundering, bruising, went the rusty spikes. There he lay with a thud, thud, thud in his brain, and then a suffocation of blackness. So she saw it. But why had he done it? And the Bradshaws talked of it at her party!

She had once thrown a shilling into the Serpentine, never anything more. But he had flung it away. They went on living (she would have to go back; the rooms were still crowded; people kept on coming). They (all day she had been thinking of Bourton, of Peter, of Sally), they would grow old. A thing there was that mattered; a thing, wreathed about with chatter, defaced, obscured in her own life, let drop every day in corruption, lies, chatter. This he had preserved. Death was defiance. Death was an attempt to communicate; people feeling the impossibility of reaching the centre which, mystically, evaded them; closeness drew apart; rapture faded, one was alone. There was an embrace in death.

The evasiveness of the center is defied by the act of suicide, which in Woolf is a communication and not, as it is in Freud, a murder. Earlier, Septimus had been terrified by a "gradual drawing together of everything to one centre before his eyes." The doubling of Clarissa and Septimus implies that there is only a difference in degree, not in kind, between Clarissa's sensibility and the naked consciousness or "madness" of Septimus. Neither needs the encouragement of "Fear no more the heat o' the sun," because each knows that consciousness is isolation and so untruth, and that the right worship of life is to defy that isolation by dying. J. Hillis Miller remarks that: "A novel, for Woolf, is the place of death made visible." It seems to me difficult to defend *Mrs. Dalloway* from moral judgments that call Woolf's stance wholly nihilistic. But then, *Mrs. Dalloway*, remarkable as it is, is truly Woolf's starting-point as a strong writer, and not her conclusion.

II

Critics tend to agree that Woolf's finest novel is *To the Lighthouse* (1927), which is certainly one of the central works of the modern imagination, comparable to Lawrence's *The Rainbow* or Conrad's *Victory*, if not quite of the range of *Women in Love* or *Nostromo*. Perhaps it is the only novel in which Woolf displays all of her gifts at once. Erich Auerbach, in his *Mimesis*, lucidly summing up Woolf's achievement in her book, could be expounding Pater's trope of the privileged moment:

> What takes place here in Virginia Woolf's novel is . . . to put the emphasis on the random occurrence, to exploit it not in the service of a planned continuity of action but in itself. And in the process something new and elemental appeared: nothing less than the wealth of reality and depth of life in every moment to which we surrender ourselves without prejudice. To be sure, what happens in that moment—be it outer or inner processes—concerns in a very personal way the individuals who live in it, but it also (and for that very reason) concerns the elementary things which men in general have in common. It is precisely the random moment which is comparatively independent of the controversial and unstable orders over which men fight and despair; it passes unaffected by them, as daily life. The more it is exploited, the more the elementary things which our lives have in common come to light. The more numerous, varied, and simple the people are who appear as subjects of such random moments, the more effectively must what they have in common shine forth.

The shining forth is precisely Pater's secularization of the epiphany, in which random moments are transformed: "A sudden light transfigures a trivial thing, a weathervane, a windmill, a winnowing flail, the dust in the barn door; a moment—and the thing has vanished, because it was pure effect." Woolf, like Pater sets herself "to realize this situation, to define, in a chill and empty atmosphere, the focus where rays, in themselves pale and impotent, unite and begin to burn . . . " To realize such a situation is to set oneself against the vision of Mr. Ramsay (Woolf's father, the philospher Leslie Stephen), which expresses itself in the grimly empiricist maxim that: "The very stone one kicks with one's boot will outlast Shakespeare." Against this can be set Lily Briscoe's vision, which concludes the novel:

> Quickly, as if she were recalled by something over there, she turned to her canvas. There it was—her picture. Yes, with all its greens and blues, its lines running up and across, its attempt at something. It would be hung in the attics, she thought; it would be destroyed. But what did that matter? she asked herself, taking up her brush again. She looked at the steps; they were empty; she looked at her canvas; it was blurred. With a sudden intensity, as if she saw it clear for a second, she drew a line there, in the centre. It was done; it was finished. Yes, she thought, laying down her brush in extreme fatigue, I have had my vision.

"An attempt at something" postulates, for Woolf, a center, however evasive. The apotheosis of aesthetic or perceptive principle here is Woolf's beautifully poised and precarious approach to an affirmation of the difficult possibility of meaning. *The Waves* (1931) is a large-scale equivalent of Lily Briscoe's painting. Bernard, the most comprehensive of the novel's six first-person narrators, ends the book with a restrained exultation, profoundly representative of Woolf's feminization of the Paterian aesthetic stance:

> "Again I see before me the usual street. The canopy of civilisation is burnt out. The sky is dark as polished whale-bone. But there is a kindling in the sky whether of lamplight or of dawn. There is a stir of some sort— sparrows on plain trees somewhere chirping. There is a sense of the break of day. I will not call it dawn. What is dawn in the city to an elderly man standing in the street looking up rather dizzily at the sky? Dawn is some sort of whitening of the sky; some sort of renewal. Another day; another Friday; another twentieth of March, January, or September. Another general awakening. The stars draw back and are extinguished. The bars deepen themselves between the waves. The film of mist thickens on the field. A redness gathers on the roses, even on the pale rose that hangs by the bedroom window. A bird chirps. Cottagers light their early candles. Yes, this is the eternal renewal, the incessant rise and fall and fall and rise again.
>
> "And in me too the wave rises. It swells; it arches its back. I am aware once more of a new desire, something rising beneath me like the proud horse whose rider first spurs and then pulls him back. What enemy do we now perceive advancing against us, you whom I ride now, as we stand pawing this stretch of pavement? It is death. Death is the enemy. It is death against whom I ride with my spear couched and my hair flying back like a young man's, like Percival's, when he galloped in India. I strike spurs into my horse. Against you I will fling myself, unvanquished and unyielding, O Death!"
>
> *The waves broke on the shore.*

"Incessant rise and fall and fall and rise again," though ascribed to Bernard, has in it the fine pathos of a recognition of natural harshness that does not come often to a male consciousness. And for all the warlike imagery, the ride against death transcends aggressivity, whether against the self or against others. Pater had insisted that our one choice lies in packing as many pulsations of the artery, or Blakean visions of the poet's work, into our interval as possible. Woolf subtly hints that even Pater succumbs to a male illusion of experiential quantity, rather than to a female recognition of gradations in the quality of possible experience. A male critic might want to murmur, in defense of Pater, that male blindness of the void within experience is very difficult to overcome, and that Pater's exquisite sensibility is hardly male, whatever the accident of his gender.

Between the Acts (1941), Woolf's final novel, can be read as a covert and witty subversion of late Shakespeare, whose romances Woolf attempts to expose as being perhaps more male than universal in some of their implications. Parodying Shakespeare is a dangerous mode; the flat-out farce of Max Beerbohm and Nigel Dennis works more easily than Woolf's allusive deftness, but Woolf is not interested in the crudities of farce. *Between the Acts* is her deferred fulfillment of the polemical program set forth in her marvelous polemic *A Room of One's Own* (1929), which is still the most persuasive of all feminist literary manifestos. To me the most powerful and unnerving stroke in that book is in its trope for the enclosure that men have forced upon women:

> For women have sat indoors all these millions of years, so that by this time the very walls are permeated by their creative force, which has, indeed, so overcharged the capacity of bricks and mortar that it must needs harness itself to pens and brushes and business and politics. But this creative power differs greatly from the creative power of man . . . .

That last assertion is becoming a kind of shibboleth in contemporary feminist literary criticism. Whether George Eliot and Henry James ought to be read as instances of a gender-based difference in creative power is not beyond all critical dispute. Is Dorothea Brooke more clearly the product of a woman's creative power than Isabel Archer would be? Could we necessarily know that Clarissa Harlow ensues from a male imagination? Woolf, at the least, lent her authority to provoking such questions. That authority, earned by novels of the splendour of *To the Lighthouse* and *Between the Acts*, becomes more formidable as the years pass.

REUBEN BROWER

Something Central Which Permeated: "Mrs. Dalloway"

The best preparation for understanding *Mrs. Dalloway* is to read *The Tempest*, or *Cymbeline*, or, better still, *A Winter's Tale*. One might go further and say that in her singleness of vision and in her handling of words, Virginia Woolf has a Shakespearean imagination. If that sounds like nonsense—and it may—perhaps by the end of this [essay], the reader will agree that it sounds "so like sense, that it will do as well."

Mrs. *Dalloway* has a story and some characters—by conventional standards, a fragmentary dramatic design—but the fragments of which the novel is composed would not seem elated or particularly significant without another sort of connection. The dramatic sequences are connected through a single metaphorical nucleus, and the key metaphors are projected and sustained by a continuous web of subtly related minor metaphors and harmonizing imagery.

Once we have seen this design and the vision of experience it implies, we shall understand why *Mrs. Dalloway* takes the form it does, why as a story it has properly no beginning or ending. It opens one morning with Clarissa Dalloway in the midst of preparing for a party; it closes in the early hours of the next morning with Clarissa very much involved in giving the party. The major event of her day is the return of Peter Walsh, the man she had almost married instead of Richard Dalloway, a successful

From *The Fields of Light: An Experiment in Critical Reading*. Copyright © 1951 by Oxford University Press.

M.P. Clarissa and Richard have a daughter, Elizabeth, who is temporarily attached to a religious fanatic, a woman with the Dickensian name of Miss Kilman. There is also in the novel another set of characters who at first seem to have no connection with Clarissa and her world: Septimus Smith, a veteran of the First World War, and his Italian wife, Rezia, a hatmaker by trade. Septimus, who is suffering from shell shock, is being treated—somewhat brutally—by a hearty M.D., Dr. Holmes. During the day of Clarissa's preparations, Septimus visits Sir William Bradshaw, an eminent psychiatrist, who recommends rather too firmly that Septimus should be taken to a sanatorium. In the late afternoon, as Dr. Holmes comes to take him away, Septimus jumps from the balcony of his room and kills himself. That evening, Sir William Bradshaw reports the story of his death at Clarissa's party.

Readers of the novel will recognize this outline as more or less accurate, but they will want to add that the impression it gives is very remote from their remembered experience of *Mrs. Dalloway*. For the peculiar texture of Virginia Woolf's fiction has been lost. The ebb and flow of her phrasing and the frequent repetition of the same or similar expressions, through which her characteristic rhythmic and metaphorical designs are built up, have completely disappeared.

No one needs to be shown that the novel is full of odd echoes. The Shakespearean tag, "Fear no more," occurs some six or seven times; certain words turn up with surprising frequency in the various interior monologues: "life," "feel," "suffer," "solemn," "moment," and "enjoy." Less obvious, and more peculiar to Virginia Woolf is the recurrence in the individual monologues of expression for similar visual or aural images. Some of these images—the aeroplane and the stopped motorcar are examples—connect separate dramatic sequences in a rather artificial way; but others, such as Big Ben's striking and the marine images, often connect similar qualities of experience and so function as symbolic metaphors. There are many repeated words, phrases, and sentences in the novel, besides those already quoted, which gradually become metaphorical: "party," "Holmes and Bradshaw," "there she was," "plunge," "wave," and "sea," "sewing," "building" and "making it up," "Bourton," et cetera. Almost innumerable continuities, major and minor, may be traced through the various recurrent expressions; but as compared with Shakespeare's practice in *The Tempest*, the continuities are less often built up through the use of explicit metaphors. The repeated word does not occur in a conventional metaphorical expression, and its metaphorical value is felt only after it has been met in a number of contexts. Virginia Woolf's most characteristic metaphors are purely symbolic.

I can indicate from the adjective "solemn" how a recurrent expression acquires its special weight of meaning. By seeing how metaphor links with metaphor, the reader will also get a notion of the interconnectedness of the entire novel. The word appears on the first page of *Mrs. Dalloway*:

> How fresh, how calm, stiller than this of course, the air was in the early morning; like the flap of a wave; the kiss of a wave; chill and sharp and yet (for a girl of eighteen as she then was) solemn, feeling as she did, standing there at the open window, that something awful was about to happen . . .

It is echoed at once, on the next page, in the first account of Big Ben's striking (an important passage in relation to the whole novel):

> For having lived in Westminister—how many years now? over twenty,— one feels even in the midst of the traffic, or waking at night, Clarissa was positive, a particular hush, or solemnity; an indescribable pause; a suspense (but that might be her heart, affected they said, by influenza) before Big Ben strikes. There! Out it boomed. First a warning, musical; then the hour, irrevocable. The leaden circles dissolved in the air.

"Solemn," which on our first reading of the opening page had only a vague local meaning of "something awful about to happen," is now connected with a more particularized terror, the fear of a suspense, of a pause in experience. Each time that "solemn" is repeated in subsequent descriptions of Big Ben, it carries this additional meaning. The word recurs three times in the afternoon scene in which Clarissa looks across at an old woman in the next house:

> How extraordinary it was, strange, yes, touching, to see the old lady (they had been neighbours ever so many years) move away from the window, as if she were attached to that sound, that string. Gigantic as it was, it had something to do with her. Down, down, into the midst of ordinary things the finger fell making the moment solemn.

And a little further on:

> . . . Big Ben . . . laying down the law, so solemn, so just . . . on the wake of that solemn stroke which lay flat like a bar of gold on the sea.

In the early morning scene near the end of the book, Clarissa goes to the window, again sees the old lady, and thinks, "It will be a solemn sky . . . it will be a dusky sky, turning away its cheek in beauty." In all but the last passage there is some suggestion in the imagery of Big Ben's stroke coming down and marking an interruption in the process of life. By the end of the book we see the significance in the use of "solemn" on the first page in a passage conveying a sharp sense of freshness and youth. The terror symbolized by Big Ben's "pause" has a connection with early life, ". . . one's parents giving it into one's hands, this life, to be lived to the end." The "something awful . . . about to happen" was associated with "the flap of a wave, the kiss of a wave"; the "solemnity" of life is a kind of "sea-terror" (so Shakespeare might express it in *The Tempest*). Wave and water images recur in other "solemn" passages: "the wave," "the wake," "the leaden circles dissolved in the air." So, through various associations, "solemn" acquires symbolic values for the reader: some terror of entering the sea of experience and of living life and an inexplicable fear of a "suspense" or interruption.

While following a single symbolic adjective in Mrs. *Dalloway*, we have seen that it was impossible to interpret one continuity apart from several others. Various expressions—"solemn," "wave," "Big Ben," "fear," and "pause"—kept leading us toward the key metaphor of the book. The metaphor that links the continuities and gives unity to the dramatic design of Mrs. *Dalloway* is not a single, easily describable analogy, but two complementary and extremely complex analogies which are gradually expressed through recurrent words and phrases and through the dramatic pattern of the various sequences. Though they are salient in the sequences of nearly all the main characters, they are best interpreted from Clarissa's, since her experience forms the center of attention for the reader.

One of the two metaphorical poles of the novel emerges in a passage that comes just after the first account of Big Ben's striking:

> Such fools we are, she thought, crossing Victoria Street. For Heaven only knows why one loves it so how one sees it so, making it up, building it round one, tumbling it, creating it every moment afresh; but the veriest frumps, the most dejected of miseries sitting on doorsteps (drink their downfall) do the same; can't be dealt with, she felt positive, by Acts of Parliament for that very reason: they love life. In people's eyes, in the swing, tramp, and trudge; in the bellow and the uproar; the carriages, motor cars, omnibuses, vans, sandwich men shuffling and swinging; brass bands; barrel organs; in the triumph and the jingle and the strange high singing of some aeroplane overhead was what she loved; life; London; this moment of June.

The key phrase here is "they love life," and what is meant by "life" and "loving it" is indicated by the surrounding metaphors—"building it," "creating it every moment," "the swing, tramp, and trudge"—and also by the various images of sights, sounds, and actions.

"Life" as expressed in Mrs. Dalloway's morning walk (and in the walks of Peter and of her daughter Elizabeth) consists first in the doings of people and things and in the active perception of them. To meet Clarissa's approval, people "must do something," as she did in "making a world" in her drawing room, in "assembling" and "knowing" all sorts of individuals, in running her house, and in giving "her parties," which were for her "life." But the perception, the savoring of these doings of oneself and of others is itself a creation. For Mrs. Dalloway, "enjoying" and "loving" is "creating" and "building up," not passive enjoyment. Life is experienced in successively created "moments"; the sense of succession, of process, is inseparable from Clarissa's feeling about life; it is implicit in her movement along the streets, "this astonishing and rather solemn progress with the rest of them, up Bond Street." She thinks of "all this" as "*going on* without her." ("This" and "all this" also become metaphors for life.) Later, in Elizabeth's experience of going up Fleet Street, all these metaphors are explicitly combined: "this van; this life; this procession." To live, then, is to enter into the process of action and active perception, to be absorbed in the successive moments: " . . . yet to her it was absolutely absorbing; all this."

But the sense of being absorbed in the process is inseparable from a fear of being excluded, from the dread that the process may be interrupted. The progress is a "solemn" one, the adjective suggesting (as elsewhere) the terror of "plunging" into experience. The sense of being *in* experience is inseparable from the sense of being *outside* of it:

> She sliced like a knife through everything; at the same time was outside, looking on. She had a perpetual sense, as she watched the taxi cabs, of being out, out, far out to sea and alone; she always had the feeling that it was very, very dangerous to live even one day.

Though the terror lies in having to go through with life, paradoxically the escape from terror lies in building up delight and sharing in the process:

> Even now, quite often if Richard had not been there reading the *Times*, so that she could crouch like a bird and gradually revive, send roaring up that immeasurable delight, rubbing stick to stick, one thing with another, she must have perished.

The central metaphor of Clarissa's narrative (and of the novel) is thus twofold: the exhilarated sense of being a part of the forward moving process and the recurrent fear of some break in this absorbing activity, which was symbolized by the "suspense" before Big Ben strikes. We are to feel all sorts of experiences qualified as at once "an absorbing progression" and "a progression about to be interrupted." Such in crudely schematic terms are the two analogies which make up the metaphorical nucleus of the novel. As my analysis has indicated, this complex metaphor is expressed through countless variant minor metaphors and images.

Both of the major aspects of the metaphor are intricately linked in the wonderful sewing scene in which Clarissa's old lover, Peter Walsh, returns to announce his plans for a second marriage:

> Quiet descended on her, calm, content, as her needle, drawing the silk smoothly to its gentle pause, collected the green folds together and attached them, very lightly, to the belt. So on a summer's day waves collect, overbalance, and fall; collect and fall; and the whole world seems to be saying "That is all" more and more ponderously, until even the heart in the body which lies in the sun on the beach says too, That is all. Fear no more, says the heart. Fear no more, says the heart. committing its burden to some sea, which sighs collectively for all sorrows, and renews, begins, collects, lets fall. And the body alone listens to the passing bee; the wave breaking; the dog barking, far away barking and barking.

Through the wave simile the opening statement expands in a metaphorical bloom which expresses in little the essence of the novel. The quiet, calm, and content (Clarissa's absorption in what she is doing) and the rhythmic movement of the needle are the points in the immediate situation from which the two main meanings of the key metaphor grow. The comparison between sewing and wave movements draws in these further levels of meanings, thanks to the nice preparation of earlier scenes and the delicate adjustment of those that follow. There are the wave and sea images which have been appearing when Clarissa recalls the terror of early life or when she hears Big Ben's solemn stroke. Much later in the novel, here is Clarissa at her party in her "silver-green mermaid's dress . . . lolloping on the waves." Here, in the scene with Peter, as in the final party scene, the waves mainly symbolize Clarissa's complete absorption in her life: "That is all"—the phrase she had used twice while shopping and which had come back in her musings on "the solemn progress up Bond Street." There is for the heart at this moment nothing but the process, and the individual becomes a mere percipient body, intensely aware of the immediate sensation. But the moment has a dual value, as has been suggested by the oblique allusions to solemnity and terror ("waves," "ponderously," "That is all"). So the reader is perfectly prepared for the return of "Fear no more," which it is now clear suggests both freedom from fear and the fear of interruption, meanings which are dramatized in the scene that immediately follows.

Clarissa's quiet is rudely shaken by the sound of the front-door bell:

"Who can—what can," asked Mrs. Dalloway (thinking it was outrageous to be interrupted at eleven o'clock on the morning of the day she was giving a party), hearing a step on the stairs. She heard a hand upon the door. She made to hide her dress, like a virgin protecting chastity, respecting privacy.

The nature of the interruption, the return of her former lover, Peter Walsh, and her gesture, "like a virgin protecting chastity, respecting privacy," point to another analogy in *Mrs. Dalloway*, which is simply a special aspect of the "life" metaphor. We might call it the "destroyer" theme. Peter's coming in temporarily destroys Clarissa's domesticity, even her marriage. As a lover Peter had allowed her no independence, and as a husband he would have been intolerable, leaving her no life of her own. Clarissa reasserts herself and her life by calling after him as he leaves, "Remember my party tonight!" Peter is one of those who would cut her off from her way of living by making her into another person; he is one of the "destroyers of the privacy of the soul." Compulsion of this sort is a special form of the "suspense" in life's exhilarating process. The "suspense" may be fear itself, or the sense of time's passing, or death, or a failure in personal relationships, or, finally, the loss of independence which results from love or hatred or officiousness.

We shall now see to what a remarkable extent the central metaphor penetrates and organizes the novel. The dramatic sequences of the principal characters are all linked with Clarissa's through a shuttling pattern of verbal reminiscences. (Curious readers may amuse themselves by finding dozens more than can be cited here.) Although "life" is peculiarly the key figure in Clarissa's experience, it is important in that of other characters, including Septimus and Miss Kilman, who are unable to "live" as Clarissa does.

We may begin with Peter Walsh, who as a lover has the role of one of the "interrupters" and "destroyers." But in the two accounts of his walks through London, he shows much of Clarissa's eager experience of life. He sets off on his morning walk, speaking rhythmically her parting words, "Remember my party, remember my party." He then "marches up Whitehall" as she has gone "up Bond Street," and he too "makes up" life (his mild "escapade with the girl"). During his evening walk, he expresses Clarissa's sense of enjoyment:

Really it took one's breath away, these moments . . . absorbing, mysterious, of infinite richness, this life.

Elizabeth also shares her mother's perceptiveness, and in her bus ride has an experience closely paralleling Clarissa's morning walk. As all three char-

acters pass through the "procession" of experience, they savor life as a series
of exquisite moments, a sensation summed up by the motif of the scene in
which Richard brings Clarissa the roses: "Happiness is this."

The crude parallel between the roles of Mrs. Dalloway and Septimus
is obvious; the finer relations and how they are expressed may be best seen
by tracing the links made through the "life" metaphor. While Clarissa
usually feels her inclusion *in* everything and only occasionally feels *outside*,
Septimus is almost always "alone" and unable to connect with the world
about him. He had "felt very little in the war," and "now that it was all
over, truce signed, and the dead buried, he had, especially in the evening,
these thunder-claps of fear. He could not feel." Rezia, his wife, is his refuge
from fear, though like Mrs. Dalloway she too has moments of panic when
she cries, "I am alone; I am alone!" But she is shown as having some of
Mrs. Dalloway's gift for active enjoyment, and through her Septimus is for
once able to recover his power of feeling and to enter into the real life
around him. The moment comes near the end of his narrative, in the late
afternoon, as he lies on a sofa while Rezia is making a hat. The writing in
this scene shows wonderfully the way in which Virginia Woolf moves from
one narrative plane to another via image and metaphor. (The parallel with
Shakespeare is obvious.)

Immediately preceding the scene comes the episode of Elizabeth's
bus ride, with "this van; this life; this procession." These metaphors are
then echoed in a long description of cloud movements which cast changing
lights on the moving buses; the transition to Septimus takes place as he
watches the "goings and comings" of the clouds. The movements and colors
referred to and the verbal rhythm ("watching watery gold glow and fade")
prepare us easily for the return of the wave and sea imagery of Clarissa's
and Peter's monologues:

> Outside the trees dragged their leaves like nets through the depths of the
> air; the sound of water was in the room and through the waves came the
> voices of birds singing. Every power poured its treasures on his head, and
> his hand lay there on the back of the sofa, as he had seen his hand lie
> when he was bathing, floating, on the top of the waves, while far away
> on shore he heard dogs barking and barking far away. Fear no more, says
> the heart in the body; fear no more.

The last words anticipate the next phrase of the scene. Septimus, watching
Rezia sew a hat, temporarily loses himself in his interest in her activity:
"She built it up, first one thing, then another, she built it up, sewing."
(The "building" is an echo of the "life" metaphor, and the sewing is now
symbolic.) Septimus begins to note actual objects around him, as Rezia
gives him assurance that real things are real: "There she was, perfectly

natural, sewing." The words, "There she was" (also the concluding sentence of the novel) are an exact repetition of one of Peter's earlier remarks about Clarissa, where they signifed her "extraordinary gift, that woman's gift, of making a world wherever she happened to be." Septimus' participation in life is interrupted, as was Clarissa's, by one of the compellers, Dr. Holmes. His suicide is a protest against having his life forcibly remade by others.

In the figure of Sir William Bradshaw we get an almost allegorical representation of a "destroyer." His talk of keeping a "sense of proportion" and his tactful questions are a screen for his firm intention of getting patients to do what he thinks best. There is a close relation, we are told, between preaching proportion and being a converter, for Proportion has a sister, Conversion, who "feasts on the wills of the weakly." Clarissa also is pursued by a compeller of this less lovely type, the horrendous if pious spinster, Miss Kilman. She ruins Clarissa's enjoyment of life and is shown as having herself no capacity for delight (if we overlook her perverse fondness for chocolate éclairs!). In the mock-heroic tea-table scene she fails in her attempt to exert a negative influence over Elizabeth, who leaves to go to her mother's party. As Miss Kilman questions Elizabeth, the reader recalls that Mrs. Dalloway's parting words to Miss Kilman and her daughter had been those she had used to Peter: "Remember my party!" Her words are symbolic of defiance.

Just after this episode the mysterious old lady makes the first of her two appearances, the value of which can now be seen. The old lady, Clarissa says, was "merely being herself." "There was something solemn in it—but love and religion would destroy that, whatever it was, the privacy of the soul." "Solemn" connects this "privacy" theme, symbolized by the old lady, with the attitudes expressed through the key metaphor of the novel, especially with the precarious and terrifying sense of enjoyment. To experience life, terror and all, we must be left alone.

All of the related analogies that make up the key metaphor are combined near the end of the novel, at the point when Bradshaw tells Clarissa of Septimus' death and when Clarissa, reflecting on its meaning, looks out of the window at the old lady going to bed. Bradshaw, a man "capable of some indescribable crime—forcing your soul, that was it—," momentarily ruins her party ("in the middle of my party, here's death, she thought . . ."). But Clarissa immediately recognizes that Septimus' death has a further meaning in relation to his life and hers. By killing himself Septimus had defied the men who make life intolerable, and though he had "thrown it away," he had not lost his independence of soul. This (in so far as we can define it) is "the thing" he had preserved. By contrast Clarissa had sacrificed some of this purity. She had made compromises for the sake of social success, "She had schemed; she had pilfered." But she had not given in to Peter, and by marrying Richard she had been able to make a life of her own. The delight, though impure, remained. The old lady, in her second appearance as in her first, symbolizes the quiet maintenance of one's own life, which is the only counterbalance to the fear of "interruption" whether by death or compulsion.

This scene shows in the highest degree the concentration of various dramatic relationships through a central metaphor. What we would emphasize here is Virginia Woolf's literary feat in achieving this result—literary in the primitive sense of Frost's pun, "feat of words." The unity of her design depends on the building up of symbolic metaphors through an exquisite management of verbal devices: through exact repetitions, reminiscent variations, the use of related eye and ear imagery, and the recurrence of similar phrase and sentence rhythms. The novel has as a result a unique closeness of structure which is only slightly dependent on story, though also supported by the time patterns which David Daiches has chosen to emphasize. What is most remarkable is the way in which so many different experiences have been perceived through a single metaphorical vision: the lives of Clarissa, Peter, Richard, Septimus, and Rezia as glimpsed at various periods, and of Elizabeth at the moment of growing up. Most of the characters are seen, too, in some relation to the persons who "make life intolerable": Miss Kilman, Holmes, Bradshaw, and Peter in his role as lover. Experience, rich and various in its range, has struck the mind of the novelist at a single angle and been refracted with perfect consistency. This singleness in reception and expression, as evidenced in the metaphorical design, is what we mean by integrity of imagination in Virginia Woolf.

But there are certainly points in the novel at which this singleness of vision shows signs of strain. Philistine readers have observed that the men of the novel are not full-blooded or are barely "men" at all—a type of criticism that could be applied with disastrous results to Tom Jones, or Emma, or The Portrait of a Lady. But the strain that is truly a sign of weakness appears in the relating of dramatic elements through the central metaphorical nucleus. That Peter is no man—whether we mean not lifelike or not masculine—is a relevant comment only because of the symbolic role in which he is sometimes cast. As a lover he stands in Clarissa's thoughts for one of the dark "forcers of the soul"; but in much of his behavior he is described as a womanish sort of person who has little power to manage himself or to move others. In one rather embarrassing episode, Peter's half-imaginary pursuit of a young girl, Virginia Woolf is apparently attempting to present his passionate side. The lack of lively sensuous detail in this narrative contrasts very badly with the glowing particularity of Mrs. Dalloway's walk though Bond Street or with the vividness of Peter's impressions of a London evening, while by way of a poor compensation there is a good deal of generalized emotional language: "vast philanthropy," "exquisite delight," "mournful tenderness," "laughing and delightful," et cetera. Peter calls this "making up" an "exquisite amusement," which is in this instance a painfully accurate label. The metaphor ceases to be an instrument through which experience is connected for us in a new relation and remains a simple declaration of a connection never made.

On occasion Virginia Woolf becomes so fascinated with this instrument that she elaborates the metaphor out of all proportion to its expressive value. (*The Waves* is a kind of metaphorical monster of this sort.) The purest and most interesting example of such elaboration in *Mrs. Dalloway* comes just after Peter's imaginary flirtation, the interlude of "the solitary traveller." The passage—which is not a dream, though it covers the time while Peter is sleeping—is an enlarged symbolic version of Peter's experience with the girl and in part an expression of his desire for a more satisfactory relationship with Clarissa. As various echoes show, it is, like the experience on the street, a grand example of "making up," a vision of the consolatory woman who gives the kind of understanding which Peter had attributed to the girl and which he had not found in Clarissa. It is in a picturesque sense a beautiful passage, but merely beautiful, a piece which could be detached with little loss. The detailed picture of the woman, the evening, the street, and the adorable landlady does not increase or enrich our knowledge of Peter or of anyone else in the book.

Perhaps the most obvious examples of metaphorical elaboration for its own sake are the super-literary, pseudo-Homeric similes which adorn various pages of *Mrs. Dalloway*. Whether they are in origin Proustian or eighteenth-century Bloomsbury, we could wish that they might be dropped. Here is a relatively short example from the scene following the sewing passage:

> "Well, and what's happened to you?" she said. So before a battle begins, the horses paw the ground; toss their heads; the light shines on their flanks; their necks curve. So Peter Walsh and Clarissa, sitting side by side on the blue sofa, challenged each other. His powers chafed and tossed in him. He assembled from different quarters all sorts of things; praise; his career at Oxford; his marriage, which she knew nothing whatever about; how he had loved; and altogether done his job.

The contrast between such a literary pastiche and the wave-sewing simile shows us in part what is wrong. The particular sense images, "paw," "toss," "light shines," are not grounded on the dramatic and narrative level, since there is no preparation for this Homeric horseplay in the account of Clarissa's and Peter's talk and gestures. (By contrast the wave motion was anticipated through describing Clarissa's movements as she sewed.) So the reader is unprepared to take the further jump to the psychological levels of the metaphor. The efforts to show any similarity in Peter's internal "chafings" and "tossings" come too late. The metaphor is crudely explained; but it doesn't work. Such simulations—like Peter's escapade and the solitary traveller's vision—are verbally inert matter, sending no radiations through the reader's experience of the novel.

But what is vital in the writing of Mrs. Dalloway is both more nearly omnipresent and more unobtrusive. To say, as I did at the beginning of this, that Virginia Woolf creates a Shakespearean pattern of metaphor tells us something, of course; but to see how she connects diverse moments of experience by playing on a single analogy, or on a single word, tells us much more. As Clarissa is thinking of the death of Septimus Smith, she says to herself: "But this young man who had killed himself—had he plunged holding his treasure?" She has just recalled that he had "plunged" by "throwing himself from a window," which in turn echoes his earlier agonies ("falling through the sea, down, down") and his actual death ("flung himself vigorously, violently down"). But Septimus' "plunge" recalls experiences of a very different sort in Clarissa's social life:

> . . . as she stood hesitating one moment on the threshold of her drawing-room, an exquisite suspense, such as might stay a diver before plunging while the sea darkens and brightens beneath him . . .

"Darkens" suggests that "plunge" has also a more fearful significance, as we saw on the first page of the novel:

> What a lark! What a plunge! For so it had always seemed to her, when, with a little squeak of the hinges, which she could hear now, she had burst open the French windows and plunged at Bourton into the open air. How fresh, how calm, stiller than this of course, the air was in the early morning; like the flap of a wave; the kiss of a wave; chill and sharp and yet (for a girl of eighteeen as she then was) solemn, feeling as she did, standing there at the open window, that something awful was about to happen . . .

Septimus' plunge from the window is linked with those earlier windows and "the triumphs of youth" and thereby with the exhilarating and "solemn" sense of delight in life's process (the "treasure"). This twofold sense of life is constantly being expressed through the central metaphor of Mrs. Dalloway. The recurrence of a single word is a quiet indication of the subtlety and closeness of the structure which Virginia Woolf was "building up" as she wrote this novel.

ERIC AUERBACH

The Brown Stocking

"And even if it isn't fine to-morrow," said Mrs. Ramsey, raising her eyes to glance at William Bankes and Lily Briscoe as they passed, "it will be another day. And now," she said, thinking that Lily's charm was her Chinese eyes, aslant in her white, puckered little face, but it would take a clever man to see it, "and now stand up, and let me measure your leg," for they might go to the Lighthouse after all, and she must see if the stocking did not need to be an inch or two longer in the leg.

Smiling, for an admirable idea had flashed upon her this very second—William and Lily should marry—she took the heather mixture stocking, with its criss-cross of steel needles at the mouth of it, and measured it against James's leg.

"My dear, stand still," she said, for in his jealousy, not liking to serve as measuring block for the Lighthouse keeper's little boy, James fidgeted purposely; and if he did that, how could she see, was it too long, was it too short? she asked.

She looked up—what demon possessed him, her youngest, her cherished?—and saw the room, saw the chairs, thought them fearfully shabby. Their entrails, as Andrew said the other day, were all over the floor; but then what was the point, she asked herself, of buying good chairs to let them spoil up here all through the winter when the house, with only one old woman to see to it, positively dripped with wet? Never mind: the rent was precisely twopence halfpenny; the children loved it; it did her husband good to be three thousand, or if she must be accurate, three hundred miles from his library and his lectures and his disciples; and there was room for visitors. Mats, camp beds, crazy ghosts of chairs and tables whose London life of service was done—they did well enough here; and a photograph or two, and books. Books, she thought, grew of themselves. She never had time to read them. Alas! even the books that had been given her, and inscribed by the hand of the poet himself: "For her whose wishes must be obeyed . . ." "The happier Helen of our days . . ." disgraceful to say, she had never read them. And Croom on the Mind and Bates on the Savage Customs of Polynesia ("My dear, stand still," she said)—neither of those could one send to the Lighthouse. At a certain moment, she supposed, the house would become so shabby that something must be done. If they could be taught to wipe their feet and not bring the beach in with them—that would be something. Crabs, she had to allow, if Andrew really wished to dissect them, or if Jasper believed that one could make soup from seaweed, one could not prevent it; or Rose's objects—shells, reeds, stones; for they were gifted, her children, but all in quite different ways. And the result of it was, she sighed, taking in the whole room from floor to ceiling, as she held the stocking against James's leg, that things got shabbier and got shabbier summer after summer. The mat was fading; the wall-paper was flapping. You couldn't tell any more that those were roses on it. Still, if every door in a house is left perpetually open, and no lockmaker in the whole of Scotland can mend a bolt, things must spoil. What was the use of flinging a green Cashmere shawl over the edge of a picture frame? In two weeks it would be the colour of pea soup. But it was the doors that annoyed her; every door was left open. She listened. The drawing-room door was open; the hall door was open; it sounded as if the bedroom doors were open; and certainly the window on the landing was open, for that she had opened herself. That windows should be open, and doors shut— simple as it was, could none of them remember it? She would go into the maids' bedrooms at night and find them sealed like ovens, except for Marie's, the Swiss girl, who would rather go without a bath than without fresh air, but then at home, she had said, "the mountains are so beautiful." She had said that last night looking out of the window with tears in her eyes. "The mountains are so beautiful." Her father was dying there, Mrs. Ramsay knew. He was leaving them fatherless. Scolding and demonstrating (how to make a bed, how to open a window, with hands that shut and spread like a Frenchwoman's) all had folded itself quietly about her, when the girl spoke, as, after a flight through the sunshine the wings of a bird fold themselves quietly and the blue of its plumage changes from bright steel to soft purple. She had stood there silent for there was nothing to be said. He had cancer of the throat. At the recollection—how she had stood there, how the girl had said "At home the mountains are so beautiful," and there was no hope, no hope whatever, she had a spasm of irritation, and speaking sharply, said to James:

"Stand still. Don't be tiresome," so that he knew instantly that her severity was real, and straightened his leg and she measured it.

The stocking was too short by half an inch at least, making allowance for the fact that Sorley's little boy would be less well grown than James.

"It's too short," she said, "ever so much too short."

Never did anybody look so sad. Bitter and black, half-way down, in the darkness, in the shaft which ran from the sunlight to the depths, perhaps a tear formed; a tear fell; the waters swayed this way and that, received it, and were at rest. Never did anybody look so sad.

But was it nothing but looks? people said. What was there behind it—her beauty, her splendour? Had he blown his brains out, they asked, had he died the week before they were married—some other, earlier lover, of whom rumours reached one? Or was there nothing? nothing but an incomparable beauty which she lived behind, and could do nothing to disturb? For easily though she might have said at some moment of intimacy when stories of great passion, of love foiled, of ambition thwarted came her way how she too had known or felt or been through it herself, she never spoke. She was silent always. She knew then—she knew without having learnt. Her simplicity fathomed what clever people falsified. Her singleness of mind made her drop plumb like a stone, alight exact as a bird, gave her, naturally, this swoop and fall of the spirit upon truth which delighted, eased, sustained—falsely perhaps.

("Nature has but little clay," said Mr. Bankes once, hearing her voice on the telephone, and much moved by it though she was only telling him a fact about a train, "like that of which she moulded you." He saw her at the end of the line, Greek, blue-eyed, straight-nosed. How incongruous it seemed to be telephoning to a woman like that. The Graces assembling seemed to have joined hands in meadows of asphodel to compose that face. Yes, he would catch the 10:30 at Euston.

"But she's no more aware of her beauty than a child," said Mr. Bankes, replacing the receiver and crossing the room to see what progress the workmen were making with an hotel which they were building at the back of his house. And he thought of Mrs. Ramsay as he looked at that stir among the unfinished walls. For always, he thought, there was something incongruous to be worked into the harmony of her face. She clapped a deerstalker's hat on her head; she ran across the lawn in goloshes to snatch a child from mischief. So that if it was her beauty merely that one thought of, one must remember the quivering thing, the living thing (they were carrying bricks up a little plank as he watched them), and work it into the picture; or if one thought of her simply as a woman, one must endow her with some freak of idiosyncrasy; or suppose some latent desire to doff her royalty of form as if her beauty bored her and all that men say of beauty, and she wanted only to be like other people, insignificant. He did not know. He did not know. He must go to his work.)

Knitting her reddish-brown hairy stocking, with her head outlined absurdly by the gilt frame, the green shawl which she had tossed over the edge of the frame, and the authenticated masterpiece by Michael Angelo, Mrs. Ramsay smoothed out what had been harsh in her manner a moment before, raised his head, and kissed her little boy on the forehead. "Let's find another picture to cut out," she said.

COMMENTARY

This piece of narrative prose is the fifth section of part I in Virginia Woolf's novel, *To the Lighthouse*, which was first published in 1927. The situation in which the characters find themselves can be almost completely deduced from the text itself. Nowhere in the novel is it set forth systematically, by way of introduction or exposition, or in any other way than as it is here. I shall, however, briefly summarize what the situation is at the beginning of our passage. This will make it easier for the reader to understand the following analysis; it will also serve to bring out more clearly a number of important motifs from earlier sections which are here only alluded to.

Mrs. Ramsay is the wife of an eminent London professor of philosophy; she is very beautiful but definitely no longer young. With her youngest son James—he is six years old—she is sitting by the window in a good-sized summer house on one of the Hebrides islands. The professor has rented it for many years. In addition to the Ramsays, their eight children, and the servants, there are a number of guests in the house, friends on longer or shorter visits. Among them is a well-known botanist, William Bankes, an elderly widower, and Lily Briscoe, who is a painter. These two are just passing by the window. James is sitting on the floor busily cutting pictures from an illustrated catalogue. Shortly before, his mother had told him that, if the weather should be fine, they would sail to the lighthouse the next day. This is an expedition James has been looking forward to for a long time. The people at the lighthouse are to receive various presents; among these are stockings for the lighthouse-keeper's boy. The violent joy which

James had felt when the trip was announced had been as violently cut short by his father's acid observation that the weather would not be fine the next day. One of the guests, with malicious emphasis, has added some corroborative meteorological details. After all the others have left the room, Mrs. Ramsay, to console James, speaks the words with which our passage opens.

The continuity of the section is established through an exterior occurrence involving Mrs. Ramsay and James: the measuring of the stocking. Immediately after her consoling words (if it isn't fine tomorrow, we'll go some other day), Mrs. Ramsay makes James stand up so that she can measure the stocking for the lighthouse-keeper's son against his leg. A little further on she rather absent-mindedly tells him to stand still—the boy is fidgeting because his jealousy makes him a little stubborn and perhaps also because he is still under the impression of the disappointment of a few moments ago. Many lines later, the warning to stand still is repeated more sharply. James obeys, the measuring takes place, and it is found that the stocking is still considerably too short. After another long interval the scene concludes with Mrs. Ramsay kissing the boy on the forehead (she thus makes up for the sharp tone of her second order to him to stand still) and her proposing to help him look for another picture to cut out. Here the section ends.

This entirely insignificant occurrence is constantly interspersed with other elements which, although they do not interrupt its progress, take up far more time in the narration than the whole scene can possibly have lasted. Most of these elements are inner processes, that is, movements within the consciousness of individual personages, and not necessarily of personages involved in the exterior occurrence but also of others who are not even present at the time: "people," or "Mr. Bankes." In addition other exterior occurrences which might be called secondary and which pertain to quite different times and places (the telephone conversation, the construction of the building, for example) are worked in and made to serve as the frame for what goes on in the consciousness of third persons. Let us examine this in detail.

Mrs. Ramsay's very first remark is twice interrupted: first by the visual impression she receives of William Bankes and Lily Briscoe passing by together, and then, after a few intervening words serving the progress of the exterior occurrence, by the impression which the two persons passing by have left in her: the charm of Lily's Chinese eyes, which it is not for every man to see—whereupon she finishes her sentence and also allows her consciousness to dwell for a moment on the measuring of the stocking: we may yet go to the lighthouse, and so I must make sure the stocking is long enough. At this point there flashes into her mind the idea which has been prepared by her reflection on Lily's Chinese eyes (William and Lily ought to marry)—an admirable idea, she loves making matches. Smiling, she begins measuring the stocking. But the boy, in his stubborn and jealous love of her, refuses to stand still. How can she see whether the stocking is the right length if the boy keeps fidgeting about? What is the matter with James, her youngest, her darling? She looks up. Her eye falls on the room—and a long parenthesis begins. From the shabby chairs of which Andrew, her eldest son, said the other day that their entrails were all over the floor, her thoughts wander on probing the objects and the people of her environment. The shabby furniture . . . but still good enough for up here; the advantages of the summer place; so cheap, so good for the children, for her husband; easily fitted up with a few old pieces of furniture, some pictures and books. Books—it is ages since she has had time to read books, even the books which have been dedicated to her (here the lighthouse flashes in for a second, as a place where one can't send such erudite volumes as some of those lying about the room). Then the house again: if the family would only be a little more careful. But of course, Andrew brings in crabs he wants to dissect; the other children gather seaweed, shells, stones; and she has to let them. All the children are gifted, each in a different way. But naturally, the house gets shabbier as a result (here the parenthesis is interrupted for a moment; she holds the stocking against James's leg); everything goes to ruin. If only the doors weren't always left open. See, everything is getting spoiled, even that Cashmere shawl on the picture frame. The doors are always left open; they are open again now. She listens: Yes, they are all open. The window on the landing is open too; she opened it herself. Windows must be open, doors closed. Why is it that no one can get that into his head? If you go to the maids' rooms at night, you will find all the windows closed. Only the Swiss maid always keeps her window open. She needs fresh air. Yesterday she looked out of the window with tears in her eyes and said: At home the mountains are so beautiful. Mrs. Ramsay knew that "at home" the girl's father was dying. Mrs. Ramsay had just been trying to teach her how to make beds, how to open windows. She had been talking away and had scolded the girl, too. But then she had stopped talking (comparison with a bird folding its wings after flying in sunlight). She had stopped talking, for there was nothing one could say; he has cancer of the throat. At this point, remembering how she had stood there, how the girl had said at home the mountains were so beautiful— and there was no hope left—a sudden tense exasperation arises in her (exasperation with the cruel meaninglessness of a life whose continuance she is nevertheless striving with all her powers to abet, support, and secure). Her exasperation flows out into the exterior action. The parenthesis suddenly closes (it cannot have taken up more than a few seconds; just now she was still smiling over the thought of a marriage between Mr. Bankes and Lily Briscoe), and she says sharply to James: Stand still. Don't be so tiresome.

This is the first major parenthesis. The second starts a little later, after the stocking has been measured and found to be still much too short. It starts with the paragraph which begins and ends with the motif, "never did anybody look so sad."

Who is speaking in this paragraph? Who is looking at Mrs. Ramsay here, who concludes that never did anybody look so sad? Who is expressing these doubtful, obscure suppositions?—about the tear which—perhaps—forms and falls in the dark, about the water swaying this way and that, receiving it, and then returning to rest? There is no one near the window in the room but Mrs. Ramsay and James. It cannot be either of them, nor the "people" who begin to speak in the next paragraph. Perhaps it is the author. However, if that be so, the author certainly does not speak like the one who has a knowledge of his characters—in this case, of Mrs. Ramsay—and who, out of his knowledge, can describe their personality and momentary state of mind objectively and with certainty. Virginia Woolf wrote this paragraph. She did not identify it through grammatical and typographical devices as the speech or thought of a third person. One is obliged to assume that it contains direct statements of her own. But she does not seem to bear in mind that she is the author and hence ought to know how matters stand with her characters. The person speaking here, whoever it is, acts the part of one who has only an impression of Mrs. Ramsay, who looks at her face and renders the impression received, but is doubtful of its proper interpretation. "Never did anybody look so sad" is not an objective statement. In rendering the shock received by one looking at Mrs. Ramsay's face, it verges upon a realm beyond reality. And in the ensuing passage the speakers no longer seem to be human beings at all but spirits between heaven and earth, nameless spirits capable of penetrating the depths of the human soul, capable too of knowing something about it, but not of attaining clarity as to what is in process there, with the result that what they report has a doubtful ring, comparable in a way to those "certain airs, detached from the body of the wind," which in a later passage move about the house at night "questioning and wondering." However that may be, here too we are not dealing with objective utterances on the part of the author in respect to one of the characters. No one is certain of anything here: it is all mere supposition, glances cast by one person upon another whose enigma he cannot solve.

This continues in the following paragraph. Suppositions as to the meaning of Mrs. Ramsay's expression are made and discussed. But the level of tone descends slightly, from the poetic and non-real to the practical and earthly; and now a speaker is introduced: "People said." People wonder whether some recollection of an unhappy occurrence in her earlier life is hidden behind her radiant beauty. There have been rumors to that effect. But perhaps the rumors are wong: nothing of this is to be learned directly from her; she is silent when such things come up in conversation. But supposing she has never experienced anything of the sort herself, she yet knows everything even without experience. The simplicity and genuineness of her being unfailingly light upon the truth of things, and, falsely perhaps, delight, ease, sustain.

Is it still "people" who are speaking here? We might almost be tempted to doubt it, for the last words sound almost too personal and thoughtful for the gossip of "people." And immediately afterward, suddenly and unexpectedly, an entirely new speaker, a new scene, and a new time are introduced. We find Mr. Bankes at the telephone talking to Mrs. Ramsay, who has called him to tell him about a train connection, evidently with reference to a journey they are planning to make together. The paragraph about the tear had already taken us out of the room where Mrs. Ramsay and James are sitting by the window; it had transported us to an undefinable scene beyond the realm of reality. The paragraph in which the rumors are discussed has a concretely earthly but not clearly identified scene. Now we find ourselves in a precisely determined place, but far away from the summer house—in London, in Mr. Bankes's house. The time is not stated ("once"), but apparently the telephone conversation took place long (perhaps as much as several years) before this particular sojourn in the house on the island. But what Mr. Bankes says over the telephone is in perfect continuity with the preceding paragraph. Again not objectively but in the form of the impression received by a specific person at a specific moment, it as it were sums up all that precedes—the scene with the Swiss maid, the hidden sadness in Mrs. Ramsay's beautiful face, what people think about her, and the impression she makes: Nature has but little clay like that of which she molded her. Did Mr. Bankes really say that to her over the telephone? Or did he only want to say it when he heard her voice, which moved him deeply, and it came into his mind how strange it was to be talking over the telephone with this wonderful woman, so like a Greek goddess? The sentence is enclosed in quotation marks, so one would suppose that he really spoke it. But this is not certain, for the first words of his soliloquy, which follows, are likewise enclosed in quotation marks. In any case, he quickly gets hold of himself, for he answers in a matter-of-fact way that he will catch the 10:30 at Euston.

But his emotion does not die so quickly. As he puts down the receiver and walks across the room to the window in order to watch the work on a new building across the way—apparently his usual and characteristic procedure when he wants to relax and let his thoughts wander freely—he continues to be preoccupied with Mrs. Ramsay. There is always something strange about her, something that does not quite go with her beauty (as for instance telephoning); she has no awareness of her beauty, or at most only a childish awareness; her dress and her actions show that at times. She is constantly getting involved in everyday realities which are hard to reconcile with the harmony of her face. In his methodical way he tries to explain her incongruities to himself. He puts forward some conjectures but cannot make up his mind. Meanwhile his momentary impressions of the work on the new building keep crowding in. Finally he gives it up. With the somewhat impatient, determined matter-of-factness of a methodical and scientific worker (which he is) he shakes off the insoluble problem "Mrs. Ramsay." He knows no solution (the repetition of "he did not know" symbolizes his impatient shaking it off). He has to get back to his work.

Here the second long interruption comes to an end and we are taken back to the room where Mrs. Ramsay and James are. The exterior occurrence is brought to a close with the kiss on James's forehead and the resumption of the cutting out of pictures. But here too we have only an exterior change. A scene previously abandoned reappears, suddenly and with as little transition as if it had never been left, as though the long interruption were only a glance which someone (who?) has cast from it into the depths of time. But the theme (Mrs. Ramsay, her beauty, the enigma of her character, her absoluteness, which nevertheless always exercises itself in the relativity and ambiguity of life, in what does not become her beauty) carries over directly from the last phase of the interruption (that is, Mr. Bankes's fruitless reflections) into the situation in which we now find Mrs. Ramsay: "with her head outlined absurdly by the gilt frame" etc.—for once again what is around her is not suited to her, is "something incongruous." And the kiss she gives her little boy, the words she speaks to him, although they are a genuine gift of life, which James accepts as the most natural and simple truth, are yet heavy with unsolved mystery.

Our analysis of the passage yields a number of distinguishing stylistic characteristics, which we shall now attempt to formulate.

The writer as narrator of objective facts has almost completely vanished; almost everything stated appears by way of reflection in the consciousness of the dramatis personae. When it is a question of the house, for example, or of the Swiss maid, we are not given the objective information which Virginia Woolf possesses regarding these objects of her creative imagination but what Mrs. Ramsay thinks or feels about them at a particular moment. Similarly we are not taken into Virginia Woolf's confidence and allowed to share her knowledge of Mrs. Ramsay's character; we are given her character as it is reflected in and as it affects various figures in the novel: the nameless spirits which assume certain things about a tear, the people who wonder about her, and Mr. Bankes. In our passage this goes so far that there actually seems to be no viewpoint at all outside the novel from which the people and events within it are observed, any more than there seems to be an objective reality apart from what is in the consciousness of the characters. Remnants of such a reality survive at best in brief references to the exterior frame of the action, such as "said Mrs. Ramsay, raising her eyes . . . " or "said Mr. Bankes once, hearing her voice." The last paragraph ("Knitting her reddish-brown hairy stocking . . . ") might perhaps also be mentioned in this connection. But this is already somewhat doubtful. The occurrence is described objectively, but as for its interpretation, the tone indicates that the author looks at Mrs. Ramsay not with knowing but with doubting and questioning eyes—even as some character in the novel would see her in the situation in which she is described, would hear her speak the words given.

The devices employed in this instance (and by a number of contemporary writers as well) to express the contents of the consciousness of the dramatis personae have been analyzed and described syntactically. Some of them have been named (*erlebte Rede*, stream of consciousness, *monologue intérieur* are examples). Yet these stylistic forms, especially the *erlebte Rede*, were used in literature much earlier too, but not for the same aesthetic purpose. And in addition to them there are other possibilities—hardly definable in terms of syntax—of obscuring and even obliterating the impression of an objective reality completely known to the author; possibilities, that is, dependent not on form but on intonation and context. A case in point is the passage under discussion, where the author at times achieves the intended effect by representing herself to be someone who doubts, wonders, hesitates, as though the truth about her characters were not better known to her than it is to them or to the reader. It is all, then, a matter of the author's attitude toward the reality of the world he represents. And this attitude differs entirely from that of authors who interpret the actions, situations, and characters of their personages with objective assurance, as was the general practice in earlier times. Goethe or Keller, Dickens or Meredith, Balzac or Zola told us out of their certain knowledge what their characters did, what they felt and thought while doing it, and how their actions and thoughts were to be interpreted. They knew everything about their characters. To be sure, in past periods too we were frequently told about the subjective reactions of the characters in a novel or story; at times even in the form of *erlebte Rede*, although more frequently as a monologue, and of course in most instances with an introductory phrase something like "it seemed to him that . . . " or "at this moment he felt that . . . " or the like. Yet in such cases there was hardly ever any attempt to render the flow and the play of consciousness adrift in the current of changing impressions (as is done in our text both for Mrs. Ramsay and for Mr. Bankes); instead, the content of the individual's consciousness was rationally limited to things connected with the particular incident being related or the particular situation being described. . . . And what is still more important: the author, with his knowledge of an objective truth, never abdicated his position as the final and governing authority. Again, earlier writers, especially from the end of the nineteenth century on, had produced narrative works which on the whole undertook to give us an extremely subjective, individualistic, and often eccentrically aberrant impression of reality, and which neither sought nor were able to ascertain anything objective or generally valid in regard to it. Sometimes such works took the form of first-person novels; sometimes they did not. As an example of the latter case I mention Huysman's novel *A rebours*. But all that too is basically different from the modern procedure here described on the basis of Virginia Woolf's text, although the latter, it is true, evolved from the former. The essential characteristic of the technique represented by Virginia Woolf is that we are given not merely one person whose consciousness (that is, the impressions it receives) is rendered, but many persons, with frequent shifts from one to the other—in our text, Mrs. Ramsay, "people," Mr. Bankes, in brief interludes James, the Swiss maid in a flash-back, and the nameless ones who speculate over a tear. The multiplicity of persons suggests that we are here after all confronted with an endeavor to investigate an objective reality, that is, specifically, the "real" Mrs. Ramsay. She is, to be sure, an enigma and such she basically remains, but she is as it were encircled by the content of all the various consciousnesses directed upon her (including her own); there is an attempt to approach her from many sides as closely as human possibilities of perception and expression can succeed in doing. The design of a close approach to objective reality by means of numerous subjective impressions received by various individuals (and at various times) is important in the modern technique which we are here examining. It basically differentiates it from the unipersonal subjectivism which allows only a single and generally a very unusual person to make himself heard and admits only that one person's way of looking at reality. In terms of literary history, to be sure, there are close connections between the two methods of representing consciousness—the unipersonal subjective method and the multipersonal method with synthesis as its aim. The latter developed from the former, and there are works in which the two overlap, so that we can watch the development. . . .

Another stylistic peculiarity to be observed in our text—though one that is closely and necessarily connected with the "multipersonal representation of consciousness" just discussed—has to do with the treatment of time. That there is something peculiar about the treatment of time in modern narrative literature is nothing new; several studies have been published on the subject. These were primarily attempts to establish a connection between the pertinent phenomena and contemporary philosophical doctrines or trends—undoubtedly a justifiable undertaking and useful for an appreciation of the community of interests and inner purposes shown in the activity of many of our contemporaries. We shall begin by describing the procedure with reference to our present example. We remarked earlier that the act of measuring the length of the stocking and the speaking of the words related to it must have taken much less time than an attentive reader who tries not to miss anything will require to read the passage— even if we assume that a brief pause intervened between the measuring and the kiss of reconciliation on James's forehead. However, the time the narration takes is not devoted to the occurrence itself (which is rendered rather tersely) but to interludes. Two long excursuses are inserted, whose relations in time to the occurrence which frames them seem to be entirely different. The first excursus, a representation of what goes on in Mrs. Ramsay's mind while she measures the stocking (more precisely, between the first absent-minded and the second sharp order to James to hold his leg still) belongs in time to the framing occurrence, and it is only the representation of it which takes a greater number of seconds and even minutes than the measuring—the reason being that the road taken by consciousness is sometimes traversed far more quickly than language is able to render it, if we want to make ourselves intelligible to a third person, and that is the intention here. What goes on in Mrs. Ramsay's mind in itself contains nothing enigmatic;

these are ideas which arise from her daily life and may well be called
normal—her secret lies deeper, and it is only when the switch from the
open windows to the Swiss maid's words comes, that something happens
which lifts the veil a little. On the whole, however, the mirroring of Mrs.
Ramsay's consciousness is much more easily comprehensible than the sort
of thing we get in such cases from other authors (James Joyce, for example).
But simple and trivial as are the ideas which arise one after the other in
Mrs. Ramsay's consciousness, they are at the same time essential and significant. They amount to a synthesis of the intricacies of life in which her
incomparable beauty has been caught, in which it at once manifests and
conceals itself. Of course, writers of earlier periods too occasionally devoted
some time and a few sentences to telling the reader what at a specific
moment passed through their characters' minds—but for such a purpose
they would hardly have chosen so accidental an occasion as Mrs. Ramsay's
looking up, so that, quite involuntarily, her eyes fall on the furniture. Nor
would it have occurred to them to render the continuous rumination of
consciousness in its natural and purposeless freedom. And finally they would
not have inserted the entire process between two exterior occurrences so
close together in time as the two warnings to James to keep still (both of
which, after all, take place while she is on the point of holding the unfinished stocking to his leg); so that, in a surprising fashion unknown to earlier
periods, a sharp contrast results between the brief span of time occupied
by the exterior event and the dreamlike wealth of a process of consciousness
which traverses a whole subjective universe. These are the characteristic
and distinctly new features of the technique: a chance occasion releasing
processes of consciousness; a natural and even, if you will, a naturalistic
rendering of those processes in their peculiar freedom, which is neither
restrained by a purpose nor directed by a specific subject of thought; elaboration of the contrast between "exterior" and "interior" time. The three
have in common what they reveal of the author's attitude: he submits,
much more than was done in earlier realistic works, to the random contingency of real phenomena; and even though he winnows and stylizes the
material of the real world—as of course he cannot help doing—he does
not proceed rationalistically, nor with a view to bringing a continuity of
exterior events to a planned conclusion. In Virginia Woolf's case the exterior events have actually lost their hegemony, they serve to release and
interpret inner events, whereas before her time (and still today in many
instances) inner movements preponderantly function to prepare and mo-
tivate significant exterior happenings. This too is apparent in the random-
ness and contingency of the exterior occasion (looking up because James

does not keep his foot still), which releases the much more significant inner process.

The temporal relation between the second excursus and the framing occurrence is of a different sort: its content (the passage on the tear, the things people think about Mrs. Ramsay, the telephone conversation with Mr. Bankes and his reflections while watching the building of the new hotel) is not a part of the framing occurrence either in terms of time or of place. Other times and places are in question; it is an excursus of the same type as the story of the origin of Odysseus' scar. . . . Even from that, however, it is different in structure. In the Homer passage the excursus was linked to the scar which Euryclea touches with her hands, and although the moment at which the touching of the scar occurs is one of high and dramatic tension, the scene nevertheless immediately shifts to another clear and luminous present, and this present seems actually designed to cut off the dramatic tension and causes the entire footwashing scene to be temporarily forgotten. In Virginia Woolf's passage, there is no question of any tension. Nothing of importance in a dramatic sense takes place; the problem is the length of the stocking. The point of departure for the excursus is Mrs. Ramsay's facial expression: "never did anybody look so sad." In fact several excursuses start from here; three, to be exact. And all three differ in time and place, differ too in definiteness of time and place, the first being situated quite vaguely, the second somewhat more definitely, and the third with comparative precision. Yet none of them is so exactly situated in time as the successive episodes of the story of Odysseus' youth, for even in the case of the telephone scene we have only an inexact indication of when it occurred. As a result it becomes possible to accomplish the shifting of the scene away from the window-nook much more unnoticeably and smoothly than the changing of scene and time in the episode of the scar. In the passage on the tear the reader may still be in doubt as to whether there has been any shift at all. The nameless speakers may have entered the room and be looking at Mrs. Ramsay. In the second paragraph this interpretation is no longer possible, but the "people" whose gossip is reproduced are still looking at Mrs. Ramsay's face—not here and now, at the summer-house window, but it is still the same face and has the same expression. And even in the third part, where the face is no longer physically seen (for Mr. Bankes is talking to Mrs. Ramsay over the telephone), it is nonetheless present to his inner vision; so that not for an instant does the theme (the solution of the enigma Mrs. Ramsay), and even the moment when the problem is formulated (the expression of her face while she measures the length of the stocking), vanish from the reader's memory. In terms of the exterior event the three parts of the excursus have nothing to do with one another. They have no common and externally coherent development, as have the episodes of Odysseus' youth which are related with reference to the origin of the scar; they are connected only by the one thing they have in common—looking at Mrs. Ramsay, and more specifically at the Mrs. Ramsay who, with an unfathomable expression of sadness behind her radiant beauty, concludes that the stocking is still much too short. It is only this common focus which connects the otherwise totally different parts of the excursus; but the connection is strong enough to deprive them of the independent "present" which the episode of the scar possesses. They are nothing but attempts to interpret "never did anybody look so sad"; they carry on this theme, which itself carries on after they conclude; there has been no change of theme at all. In contrast, the scene in which Euryclea recognizes Odysseus is interrupted and divided into two parts by the excursus on the origin of the scar. In our passage, there is no such clear distinction between two exterior occurrences and between two presents. However insignificant as an exterior event the framing occurrence (the measuring of the stocking) may be, the picture of Mrs. Ramsay's face which arises from it remains present throughout the excursus; the excursus itself is nothing but a background for that picture, which seems as it were to open into the depths of time—just as the first excursus, released by Mrs. Ramsay's unintentional glance at the furniture, was an opening of the picture into the depths of consciousness.

The two excursuses, then, are not as different as they at first appeared. It is not so very important that the first, so far as time is concerned (and place too), runs its course within the framing occurrence, while the second conjures up other times and places. The times and places of the second are not independent; they serve only the polyphonic treatment of the image which releases it; as a matter of fact, they impress us (as does the interior time of the first excursus) like an occurrence in the consciousness of some observer (to be sure, he is not identified) who might see Mrs. Ramsay at the described moment and whose meditation upon the unsolved enigma of her personality might contain memories of what others (people, Mr. Bankes) say and think about her. In both excursuses we are dealing with attempts to fathom a more genuine, a deeper, and indeed a more real reality; in both cases the incident which releases the excursus appears accidental and is poor in content; in both cases it makes little difference whether the excursuses employ only the consciousness-content, and hence only interior time, or whether they also employ exterior shifts of time. After all, the process of consciousness in the first excursus likewise includes shifts of time and scene, especially the episode with the Swiss maid. The important point is that an insignificant exterior occurrence releases ideas and chains of ideas which cut loose from the present of the exterior occurrence and range freely through the depths of time. It is as though an apparently simple text revealed its proper content only in the commentary on it, a simple musical theme only in the development-section. This enables us also to understand the close relation between the treatment of time and the "multipersonal representation of consciousness" discussed earlier. The ideas arising in consciousness are not tied to the present of the exterior occurrence which releases them. Virginia Woolf's peculiar technique, as exemplified in our text, consists in the fact that the exterior objective reality of the momentary present which the author directly reports and which appears as established fact—in our instance the measuring of the stocking—is nothing but an occasion (although perhaps not an entirely accidental one). The stress is placed entirely on what the occasion releases, things which are not seen directly but by reflection, which are not tied to the present of the framing occurrence which releases them. . . .

The distinctive characteristics of the realistic novel of the era between the two great wars . . . —multipersonal representation of consciousness, time strata, disintegration of the continuity of exterior events, shifting of the narrative viewpoint (all of which are interrelated and difficult to separate)—seem to us indicative of a striving for certain objectives, of certain tendencies and needs on the part of both authors and public. These objectives, tendencies, and needs are numerous; they seem in part to be mutually contradictory; yet they form so much one whole that when we undertake to describe them analytically, we are in constant danger of unwittingly passing from one to another.

Let us begin with a tendency which is particularly striking in our text from Virginia Woolf. She holds to minor, unimpressive, random events; measuring the stocking, a fragment of a conversation with the maid, a telephone call. Great changes, exterior turning points, let alone catastrophes, do not occur; and though elsewhere in *To the Lighthouse* such things are mentioned, it is hastily, without preparation or context, incidentally, and as it were only for the sake of information. The same tendency is to be observed in other and very different writers, such as Proust or Hamsun. In Thomas Mann's *Buddenbrooks* we still have a novel structure consisting of the chronological sequence of important exterior events which affect the Buddenbrook family; and if Flaubert—in many respects a precursor—lingers as a matter of principle over insignificant events and everyday circumstances which hardly advance the action, there is nevertheless to be sensed throughout *Madame Bovary* (though we may wonder how this would have worked out in *Bouvard et Pécuchet*) a constant slow-moving chronological approach first to partial crises and finally to the concluding catastrophe, and it is this approach which dominates the plan of the work as a whole. But a shift in emphasis followed; and now many writers present minor happenings, which are insignificant as exterior factors in a person's destiny, for their own sake or rather as points of departure for the development of motifs, for a penetration which opens up new perspectives into a milieu or a consciousness or the given historical setting. They have discarded presenting the story of their characters with any claim to exterior completeness, in chronological order, and with the emphasis on important exterior turning points of destiny. [*Ulysses*,] James Joyce's tremendous novel—an encyclopedic work, a mirror of Dublin, of Ireland, a mirror too of Europe and its millennia—has for its frame the externally insignificant course of a day in the lives of a schoolteacher and an advertising broker. It takes up less than twenty-four hours in their lives—just as *To the Lighthouse* describes portions of two days widely separated in time. (There is here also, as we must not fail to observe, a similarity to Dante's Comedy.) Proust presents individual days and hours from different periods, but the exterior events which are the determining factors in the destinies of the novel's characters during the intervening lapses of time are mentioned only incidentally, in retrospect or anticipation. The ends the narrator has in mind are not to be seen in them; often the reader has to supplement them. The way in which the father's death is brought up in the passage cited above— incidentally, allusively, and in anticipation—offers a good example. This shift of emphasis expresses something that we might call a transfer of confidence: the great exterior turning points and blows of fate are granted less importance; they are credited with less power of yielding decisive information concerning the subject; on the other hand there is confidence that in any random fragment plucked from the course of a life at any time the totality of its fate is contained and can be portrayed. There is greater confidence in syntheses gained through full exploitation of an everyday occurrence than in a chronologically well-ordered total treatment which accompanies the subject from beginning to end, attempts not to omit anything externally important, and emphasizes the great turning points of destiny. It is possible to compare this technique of modern writers with that of certain modern philologists who hold that the interpretation of a few passages from *Hamlet*, *Phèdre*, or *Faust* can be made to yield more, and more decisive, information about Shakespeare, Racine, or Goethe and their times than would a systematic and chronological treatment of their lives and works. . . . But to return to those modern writers who prefer the exploitation of random everyday events, contained within a few hours and days, to the complete and chronological representation of a total exterior continuum—they too (more or less consciously) are guided by the consideration that it is a hopeless venture to try to be really complete within the total exterior continuum and yet to make what is essential stand out. Then too they hesitate to impose upon life, which is their subject, an order which it does not possess in itself. He who represents the course of a human life, or a sequence of events extending over a prolonged period of time, and represents it from beginning to end, must prune and isolate arbitrarily. Life has always long since begun, and it is always still going on. And the people whose story the author is telling experience much more than he can hope to tell. But the things that happen to a few individuals in the course of a few minutes, hours, or possibly even days—these one can hope to report with reasonable completeness. And here, furthermore, one comes upon the order and the interpretation of life which arise from life itself: that is, those which grow up in the individuals themselves, which are to be discerned in their thoughts, their consciousness, and in a more concealed form in their words and actions. For there is always going on within us a process of formulation and interpretation whose subject matter is our own self. We are constantly endeavoring to give meaning and order to our lives in the past, the present, and the future, to our surroundings, the world in which we live; with the result that our lives appear in our own conception as total entities—which to be sure are always changing, more or less radically, more or less rapidly, depending on the extent to which we are obliged, inclined, and able to assimilate the onrush of new experience. These are the forms of order and interpretation which the modern writers here under discussion attempt to grasp in the random moment—not one order and one interpretation, but many, which may either be those of different persons or of the same person at different times; so that overlapping, complementing, and contradiction yield something that we might call a synthesized cosmic view or at least a challenge to the reader's will to interpretive synthesis.

Here we have returned once again to the reflection of multiple consciousness. It is easy to understand that such a technique had to develop gradually and that it did so precisely during the decades of the first World War period and after. The widening of man's horizon, and the increase of his experiences, knowledge, ideas, and possible forms of existence, which began in the sixteenth century, continued through the nineteenth at an ever faster tempo—with such a tremendous acceleration since the beginning of the twentieth that synthetic and objective attempts at interpretation are produced and demolished every instant. The tremendous tempo of the changes proved the more confusing because they could not be surveyed as a whole. They occurred simultaneously in many separate departments of science, technology, and economics, with the result that no one—not even those who were leaders in the separate departments—could foresee or evaluate the resulting overall situations. Furthermore, the changes did not produce the same effects in all places, so that the differences of attainment between the various social strata of one and the same people and between different peoples came to be—if not greater—at least more noticeable. The spread of publicity and the crowding of mankind on a shrinking globe sharpened awareness of the differences in ways of life and attitudes, and mobilized the interests and forms of existence which the new changes either furthered or threatened. In all parts of the world crises of adjustment arose; they increased in number and coalesced. They led to the upheavals which we have not weathered yet. In Europe this violent clash of the most heterogeneous ways of life and kinds of endeavor undermined not only those religious, philosophical, ethical, and economic principles which were part of the traditional heritage and which, despite many earlier shocks, had maintained their position of authority through slow adaptation and transformation; nor yet only the ideas of the Enlightenment, the ideas of democracy and liberalism which had been revolutionary in the eighteenth century and were still so during the first half of the nineteenth; it undermined even the new revolutionary forces of socialism, whose origins did not go back beyond the heyday of the capitalist system. These forces threatened to split up and disintegrate. They lost their unity and clear definition through the formation of numerous mutually hostile groups, through strange alliances which some of these groups effected with non-socialist ideologies, through the capitulation of most of them during the first World War, and finally through the propensity on the part of many of their most radical advocates for changing over into the camp of their most extreme enemies. Otherwise too there was an increasingly strong factionalism—at times crystallizing around important poets, philosophers, and scholars, but in the majority of cases pseudo-scientific, syncretistic, and primitive. The temptation to entrust oneself to a sect which solved all problems with a single formula, whose power of suggestion imposed solidarity, and which ostracized everything which would not fit in and submit—this temptation was so great that, with many people, fascism hardly had to employ force when the time came for it to spread through the countries of old European culture, absorbing the smaller sects.

As recently as the nineteenth century, and even at the beginning of the twentieth, so much clearly formulable and recognized community of thought and feeling remained in those countries that a writer engaged in representing reality had reliable criteria at hand by which to organize it. At least, within the range of contemporary movements, he could discern certain specific trends; he could delimit opposing attitudes and ways of life with a certain degree of clarity. To be sure, this had long since begun to grow increasingly difficult. Flaubert (to confine ourselves to realistic writers) already suffered from the lack of valid foundations for his work; and the subsequent increasing predilection for ruthlessly subjectivistic perspectives is another symptom. At the time of the first World War and after—in a Europe unsure of itself, overflowing with unsettled ideologies and ways of life, and pregnant with disaster—certain writers distinguished by instinct and insight find a method which dissolves reality into multiple and multivalent reflections of consciousness. That this method should have been developed at this time is not hard to understand.

But the method is not only a symptom of the confusion and helplessness, not only a mirror of the decline of our world. There is, to be sure, a good deal to be said for such a view. There is in all these works a certain atmosphere of universal doom: especially in *Ulysses*, with its mocking *odi-et-amo* hodgepodge of the European tradition, with its blatant and painful cynicism, and its uninterpretable symbolism—for even the most painstaking analysis can hardly emerge with anything more than an appreciation of the multiple enmeshment of the motifs but with nothing of the purpose and meaning of the work itself. And most of the other novels which employ multiple reflection of consciousness also leave the reader with an impression of hopelessness. There is often something confusing, something hazy about them, something hostile to the reality which they represent. We not infrequently find a turning away from the practical will to live, or delight in portraying it under its most brutal forms. There is hatred of culture and civilization, brought out by means of the subtlest stylistic devices which culture and civilization have developed, and often a radical and fanatical urge to destroy. Common to almost all of these novels, is haziness, vague indefinability of meaning: precisely the kind of uninterpretable symbolism which is also to be encountered in other forms of art of the same period.

But something entirely different takes place here too. Let us turn again to the text which was our starting-point. It breathes an air of vague and hopeless sadness. We never come to learn what Mrs. Ramsay's situation really is. Only the sadness, the vanity of her beauty and vital force emerge from the depths of secrecy. Even when we have read the whole novel, the meaning of the relationship between the planned trip to the lighthouse and the actual trip many years later remains unexpressed, enigmatic, only dimly to be conjectured, as does the content of Lily Briscoe's concluding vision which enables her to finish her painting with one stroke of the brush. It is one of the few books of this type which are filled with good and genuine love but also, in its feminine way, with irony, amorphous sadness, and doubt of life. Yet what realistic depth is achieved in every individual occurrence, for example the measuring of the stocking! Aspects of the occurrence come to the fore, and links to other occurrences, which, before this time, had hardly been sensed, which had never been clearly seen and attended to, and yet they are determining factors in our real lives. What takes place here in Virginia Woolf's novel is precisely what was attempted everywhere in works of this kind (although not everywhere with the same insight and mastery)—that is, to put the emphasis on the random occurrence, to exploit it not in the service of a planned continuity of action but in itself. And in the process something new and elemental appeared: nothing less than the wealth of reality and depth of life in every moment to which we surrender ourselves without prejudice. To be sure, what happens in that moment—be it outer or inner processes—concerns in a very personal way the individuals who live in it, but it also (and for that very reason) concerns the elementary things which men in general have in common. It is precisely the random moment which is comparatively independent of the controversial and unstable orders over which men fight and despair; it passes unaffected by them, as daily life. The more it is exploited, the more the elementary things which our lives have in common come to light. The more numerous, varied, and simple the people are who appear as subjects of such random moments, the more effectively must what they have in common shine forth. In this unprejudiced and exploratory type of representation we cannot but see to what an extent—below the surface conflicts—the differences between men's ways of life and forms of thought have already lessened. The strata of societies and their different ways of life have become inextricably mingled. There are no longer even exotic peoples. A century ago (in Mérimée for example), Corsicans or Spaniards were still exotic; today the term would be quite unsuitable for Pearl Buck's Chinese peasants. Beneath the conflicts, and also through them, an economic and cultural leveling process is taking place. It is still a long way to a common life of mankind on earth, but the goal begins to be visible. And it is most concretely visible now in the unprejudiced, precise, interior and exterior representation of the random moment in the lives of different people. So the complicated process of dissolution which led to fragmentation of the exterior action, to reflection of consciousness, and to stratification of time seems to be tending toward a very simple solution. Perhaps it will be too simple to please those who, despite all its dangers and catastrophes, admire and love our epoch for the sake of its abundance of life and the incomparable historical vantage point which it affords. But they are few in number, and probably they will not live to see much more than the first forewarnings of the approaching unification and simplification.

GEOFFREY HARTMAN

Virginia's Web

Transitions may well be the hardest part of a writer's craft: Virginia Woolf shows that they are also the most imaginative. One remembers, from *Mrs. Dalloway*, the inscrutable motor car proceeding toward Piccadilly, and the way it serves to move the plot with it. Or, in the next episode, how the skywriting plane moves different minds, each guessing at the slogan being dispensed and then dispersed. The wind stealing the smoky letters before any guess is confirmed is the same that, fifteen years later, miscarries the players' words in *Between the Acts*. Suppose now that these letters or words or glimpses are divided by years, by some indefinite or immeasurable gap. We know that years pass, that words are spoken or spelled, and that cars reach their destination; yet the mystery lies in space itself, which the imaginative mind must fill, perhaps too quickly. The dominant issues in the study of Virginia Woolf have been her solipsism and her treatment of time and character; I propose to suspend these and to see her novels as mirrors held up primarily to the imagination.

Let us consider a fairly simple passage from *To the Lighthouse*. To look at it closely requires a concern, a prior interest: in our case, how the novelist goes from one thing to another. The context of the passage is as follows. Mr. Ramsay and his two children, Cam and James, are being ferried to the Lighthouse. The weather is calm, and it seems the boat will never get there; Cam and James, moreover, do not want it to get there, resenting the tyrannous will of their father. In the first section of the novel, with Mrs. Ramsay still alive, it is he who dampens the childish eagerness of James to go to the Lighthouse; and now (many years later) he insists on this outing as a commemorative act.

From *Chicago Review* 14 (Spring 1961). Copyright © 1970 by Geoffrey Hartman.

The sails flapped over their heads. The water chuckled and slapped the sides of the boat, which drowsed motionless in the sun. Now and then the sails rippled with a little breeze in them, but the ripple ran over them and ceased. The boat made no motion at all. Mr. Ramsay sat in the middle of the boat. He would be impatient in a moment, James thought, and Cam thought, looking at her father who sat in the middle of the boat between them (James steered; Cam sat alone in the bow) with his legs tightly curled. He hated hanging about.

The continuity is kept on the verbal as well as visual plane by echo and repetition (flapped, slapped, drowsed, them, them, boat, boat). This is an intensifying device any writer might use, but one is hardly aware with what skill the sentences lead inward, to that parenthesis and fine slowing-up that encompasses boat, man, and children. Mrs. Woolf's style is here at its best, and the continuities going from the freest to the stillest part of the scene (from the sail to the middle of the boat) do so with an almost humorous resistance. It is interesting to think that the rhythm should be generated by an avoidance; there is, in any case, a stop and go pattern to it, magnified perhaps by the subject of the passage. In terms of plot or subject we have a pause; in terms of the prose that describes it, a sustained if not augmented interest in continuity. As the description reaches the inside of the boat, and then the inside of the mind, the rhythm slows, and as the rhythm slows the continuity is made more obvious as if to counterpoint the pausing. This pattern, however, may be found elsewhere too and cannot be purely an intensifying or descriptive device. It may originate in the writer prior to the particular subject.

I am suggesting that continuity is a deeper matter here than craft or style. In his first important essay Valéry remarked that the extension of continuity by means of metaphor, language, or other means was the common gift of genius. His thesis implied two things: that there is "space" or apparent discontinuity, and that the genial inventor can project his mind into it. If we identify this ability to project (or better, interpolate) with imagination, then the crucial question is what this space may be. There can be only one answer which is not a gross generalization, and this is— anything. We are dealing, it must be remembered, with appearances, and there is nothing that may not succumb to blankness. Art respects appearances so much that everything may become questionably blank, even the continuities firmly established by science. For though science has shown them to exist, it has not shown why they should exist so unapparently, and the formula that proves them also proves the coyness of nature.

To the Lighthouse begins with a sense of fullness and continuous life as we are led in and out of Mrs. Ramsay's mind. There are few apparent pauses to threaten the continuity of thought or existence. The dark space between the beams of the Lighthouse does, however, penetrate consciousness. "A shutter, like the leathern eyelid of a lizard, flickered over the intensity of his gaze and obscured the letter R. In that flash of darkness he heard people saying—he was a failure—that R was beyond him. He would never reach R. On to R, once more. R—" Mr. Ramsay's intellectual ambitions are described, and there are other fine sequences of the same kind.

These darker intervals, rare in the first part, consolidate as the encroaching and live darkness of the second part, which traces the gradual abandonment of the Ramsay house and its last minute rescue from oblivion. Then, in the last section of the novel, a horrid calm moves directly into the heart of the characters. The becalming of the boat is part of a larger sequence, in which all are involved with death, present as distance or the sea's calm or the absence of Mrs. Ramsay. Each person is compelled by a stilling glance, like the wedding guest by the Mariner. They must suffer the suspense, endure the calm, and ultimately resist it—its intimations of peace and of a happy death of the will.

Resistance is the major theme of this novel. The Lighthouse itself is a monitory object, warning off, centered in hostile elements. Mr. Ramsay, an enemy of the sea that becalms his boat, is a stronger resister than Mrs. Ramsay, who lives toward the sea. Resistance is a matter of imagination which can either actively fill space or passively blend with it and die. Imagination could also die to itself and become pure will, as in the case of Mr. Ramsay, who wishes to cross the sea, or from Q to R, by force. He denies space and violates the privacy of others. Yet to keep imagination alive involves staying alive to space, to the horrid calms of Virginia Woolf's ocean.

The imagination itself neither acknowledges nor denies space: it lives in it and says to every question "Life, life, life," like Orlando's little bird or Blake's cricket. Affirmation, not meaning, is basic to it, and the problem of meaning cannot even be faced without considering the necessity or fatality of some primary affirmation. Religious belief is such a primary act, but a special form of it. The founding of fictional world is such a primary act. Fiction reveals something without which the mind could not be, or could not think. The mind needs a world, a substantialized Yes.

Yet every great artist rebels against this, and today his rebellion is conventional. By beginning to question the necessity of fiction, i.e., the inherently affirmative structure of imagination, he joins the philosopher who seeks a truth greater than that arbitrary Yes. The more Henry James seeks the definitive word, the more his mind shrinks from affirmation. It is, similarly, Mrs. Woolf's resistance, her continuous doubting of the continuity she is forced to posit, that we are interested in. At the end of *To the Lighthouse*, Lily Briscoe's "It is finished," referring in turn to the reaching of the Lighthouse and to her picture, is deeply ironic. It recalls a sufferance greater than the object attained by this last term, by any term. Each artist resists his own vision.

This resistance, however, cannot take place except in the space of fiction and requires the creation of a work of art which is its own implicit critique. The reason that an artist's critique cannot be discursive, or purely so, is that it still involves an affirmation—the new work of art. It is therefore quite proper to put our question in strictly literary terms: What kind of novel does Mrs. Woolf write? And how does it criticize its origin in the affirmative impulse?

I shall try to define Virginia Woolf's novel as the product of a certain kind of prose and a certain kind of plot. This dyad should justify itself as we proceed, but what I say is experimental and may lead to some undue generalizing. The reason for omitting character should also appear: there is only one fully developed character in Mrs. Woolf's novels, and that is the completely expressive or androgynous mind.

Her concern for the novel is linked everywhere with that for prose style. She often remarks that prose, unlike poetry, is still in its infancy, and her first experimental novel, *Mrs. Dalloway*, matures it via the peregrinations of a woman's mind. It may be said with some truth that the novel is, for Virginia Woolf, simply the best form of presenting a completely expressive prose.

A Room of One's Own (1928) illustrates in slow motion how this mature prose came to be. Mrs. Woolf's "sociological essay" is about the future of fiction and woman's part in it. But we are not given a straight essay. She refuses to separate her thought from certain imaginary accidents of time and place and writes something akin to the French *récit*. Her mind, porous to the world even during thought, devises a prose similar to that of *To the Lighthouse*, which makes continuities out of distractions. It is as if a woman's mind were linked at its origin, like the novel itself, to romance; and one is quite happy with this natural picaresque, the author walking us and the world along on the back of her prose.

Still, prose in a novel is different from prose in some other form. Its function can be determined only within a particular structure, and a novel or story requires some finite series of events necessary to produce suspense and move the reader toward the resolving point. This raises the question of the relation of plot and prose.

In the modern novel there are at least two significant ways of making prose subsume the suspense previously offered by plot. One is to structure it as highly as the verse of the seventeenth-century classical drama in France, so that even the simplest conversation becomes dramatic. Henry James's prose has affinities to this. The other is to have the plot coincide with the special perspective of a character. Faulkner and many others (including James) may use this method, which creates a kind of mystery story, the mystery being the mind itself. Mrs. Woolf's prose has some affinities here, but it is not made to issue from a mind limited or peculiar enough to make us suspect the darkness it circles.

The curious fact is that neither the prose nor the plot of Mrs. Woolf's novels can explain the suspense we feel. Perhaps suspense is the wrong word, since we are not avid for what happens next but fascinated by how the something next will happen. To understand this let us take *Mrs. Dalloway*. Its plot is simple and realistic, as is always the case with Virginia Woolf (*Orlando* is only an apparent exception). The suspense or fascination cannot come from that source. Nor does it come, in isolation, from the rich prose woven by Clarissa's mind, since the plot often parts from her to present other people or views, yet our attention does not flag at those points. But if Mrs. Woolf goes at will beyond Clarissa's consciousness, it is on condition that some line of continuity be preserved. There are no jumps, no chapters; every transition is tied to what precedes or has been introduced. The first line of the novel, "Mrs. Dalloway said she would buy the flowers herself," presupposes some immediate prior fact already taken up in consciousness and is emblematic of the artist's mood throughout the novel. Our fascination is involved with this will to continuity, this free prose working under such strict conditions.

The plot, however, does play an important role. Clarissa waiting to cross the street, then crossing, is part of the plot; her thoughts while doing so effect many finer transitions. A tension is thus produced between the realistic plot and the expressive prose; the latter tends to veil or absorb the former, and the former suggests a more natural continuity, one less dependent on mind. We know that certain things happen in sequence, that a play will go on, that people fall in love or cross streets, that a day moves from dawn to dusk. The simpler continuity of the plot tempts the mind forward, as a relief from the essential prose, or as a resting place in something solid.

This tension between two types of continuity also makes the mind realize the artificial or arbitrary character of both. It is moved to conceive the void they bridge. A void is there, like the pauses or thoughts of death in Mrs. Dalloway. But the mind conceives it joyfully, rather than in terror, because of the constant opening up of new perspectives, and the realization through this of its connective power. The continuities we have labeled "plot" and "prose" are, moreover, not unrelated or without special value. I would now like to show that they stand to each other dialectically as major types of affirmation, the plot line coinciding mostly with what we call nature, and the prose line intimating something precarious but also perhaps greater—the "Nature that exists in works of mighty Poets." To do so I return to *A Room of One's Own,* in which Mrs. Woolf (or her persona) is thinking about women writers, and the last of her thought sequences suggests the structure of her novels in microcosm.

Mrs. Woolf looks from her window at London waking for the day's business in the fall of '28. She looks out, not in, allowing herself to be distracted. The city seems to be indifferent to her concerns, and she records the fact strongly:

> Nobody, it seemed, was reading *Antony and Cleopatra* . . . Nobody cared a straw—and I do not blame them—for the future of fiction, the death of poetry or the development by the average woman of a prose style completely expressive of her mind. If opinions upon any of these matters had been chalked on the pavement, nobody would have stooped to read them . . . Here came an errand-boy; here a woman with a dog on a lead.

Something is wrong. Can a writer be so calm about indifference, especially when it threatens art? But Mrs. Woolf is hastening the end. Not her own, but the end of a civilization which had exalted one part of the soul at the expense of the rest. The twenties are reaching their close; the first world war is not forgotten; Proust, Bergson, and Freud have advertised human possessiveness and male arbitrariness, the subtlest workings-out of the patriarchal will. The bustle she welcomes has, at least, the arbitrariness of life rather than of the will: an errand boy here, a funeral there, business men, idlers, shoppers, each going his way.

But her thought does not stop at this point; she lets it found its dialectic. The mind, to begin with, accepts a life indifferent to itself. The affirmative movement is not overcome, though what Virginia Woolf affirms is life rather than her will. Yet she is less interested in life as such than in the life of the mind, which can only appear if thought is left as apparently free as the goings and comings beneath her window.

That this freedom may be an illusion does not matter. It is still a window to the truth and, in any case, lasts a short time. As Mrs. Woolf continues to look, the life disappears, and only the indifference remains: "There was a complete lull and suspension of traffic. Nothing came down the street; nobody passed. A single leaf detached itself from the plane tree at the end of the street, and in that pause and suspension fell." Her mind, however, will not accept this pause, this emptiness. The affirmative movement attaches itself the more strongly to the slightest sign. "Somehow it was like a signal falling, a signal pointing to a force in things which one had overlooked."

What the mind has overlooked seems at first to be nature, an impersonally and constantly active principle of life. This certainly has a presence in Mrs. Woolf's novels. It is much more important to her than the spice of illusionistic realism. In her wish for a purer affirmation, one which does not merely go toward the male will, she often has her characters go toward nature. Their direct relationships are diverted by a second one: "human beings not always in their relations to each other but in their relation to reality; and the sky too, and the trees or whatever it may be in themselves." No human being, she adds, should shut out the view.

Yet it becomes clear, as Mrs. Woolf continues, that the mind had also overlooked something in itself. The falling leaf reminds her, it is true, of a natural force—but in the artist. It is the artist, the person at the window, who affirms a world where there is none. She imagines that the signal points to "a river, which flowed past, invisibly round the corner, down the street, and took people and eddied them along." In *Mrs. Dalloway* the author's consciousness is precisely this: a stream of prose that moves people together and apart, entering at will this mind and that. Nature, as she now conceives it, is one in which the artist participates, so that Shakespeare, poetry, and the finding of a new prose style become once again vital issues.

The artist, at this point, is clearly a Prospero figure. She stages an illusion whose object is a marriage: the mind coming together outside of itself by means of the world or the stage. Nature and art conspire for this illusion or prothalamion; the river, we notice, is a natural and artificial image of rhythm and leads directly to the closing event. As if the river had eddied them together, a girl in patent leather boots and a young man in a maroon raincoat meet a taxi beneath Virginia Woolf's window and get in. "The sight was ordinary enough," she remarks; "what was strange was the rhythmical order with which my imagination had invested it."

Only now does she withdraw from the window, reflecting on the mind. Because of her topic—the woman as writer—she had been thinking intensely of one sex as distinct from the other. But, seeing the couple, the mind felt as if after being divided it had come together again in a natural fusion. Perhaps, she goes on, a state of mind exists in which one could continue without effort, because nothing is required to be repressed and no resistance develops. Interpreting the event literally as well as analogically, she concludes that the fully functioning mind is androgynous.

There is much fantasy in this. What remains is a sustained act of thought, a dialectic that comprises certain distinct types of affirmation. *Dialectic* is not, at first glance, the right word, since all we see is an affirmative movement increasing in scope. There comes, however, a critical pause, a moment of discontinuity, in which the *negative* almost appears. "Nothing came down the street; nobody passed." Such "power failures" are not rare in Virginia Woolf and not always so lightly overcome. They assume a cosmic proportion in her last novel. Miss La Trobe, the illusionist, cannot sustain her country pageant. The wind is against her, life is against her, the rhythm breaks. She learns the depth of space between her and her creation; the vacuum, also, between it and the audience. "Miss La Trobe leant against the tree, paralyzed. Her power had left her. Beads of perspiration broke on her forehead. Illusion had failed. 'This is death,' she murmured, 'death.' " At this very moment, as in the scene beneath Virginia Woolf's window, nature seems to take over and reestablish the rhythm in an expressionistic passage revealing the complicity of art and nature: "Then, suddenly, as the illusion petered out, the cows took up the burden. One had lost her calf. In the very nick of time she lifted her great moon-eyed head and bellowed. All the great moon-eyed heads laid themselves back. From cow after cow came the same yearning bellow. . . . The cows annihilated the gap; bridged the distance; filled the emptiness and continued the emotion."

Between the Acts reveals the same voracious desire for continuity as *Mrs. Dalloway* and *To the Lighthouse*, yet in this last work the novelist has dropped all pretense as to the realism of her transitions. She is outrageously, sadly humorous. "Suddenly the cows stopped; lowered their heads, and began browsing. Simultaneously the audience lowered their heads, and read their programmes." This is how she gets from the cows to the audience, with the result, of course, that one feels the space she bridges more intensely. Yet does not the whole novel turn on what is between the acts, on the interpolations of the novelist who continually saves the play for Miss La Trobe? As in the example from *A Room of One's Own*, it is finally irrelevant whether the continuities discovered by Mrs. Woolf are in nature or in the artist.

Our question as to the kind of novel Virginia Woolf writes can now be answered. There is a line of development which goes from the realism of *The Voyage Out* (1915) to the expressionism of *Between the Acts* (1941), and passes through the experimental period of 1925–31 containing *Mrs. Dalloway, To the Lighthouse, Orlando,* and *The Waves.* Mrs. Woolf sought to catch the power of affirmation in its full extent, and her effort to do so includes this shuttling between realistic and expressionistic forms of style. She never abandoned realism entirely because it corresponds to an early phase of affirmation. It is realism of the simple and illusionistic kind which guides our powers of belief toward the world we see, when we see it most freely. We can call this world nature, understanding by that a continuous yet relatively impersonal principle of life, even when (as in the bustle beneath Virginia Woolf's window) it assumes a more human shape. The next phase, more complex, raises the problem of "interpolation." The falling leaf is a signal from Nature, but it points to the artist who sees or affirms a nature persisting through the negative moment. Art, therefore, becomes interpolation rather than mimesis. Though Mrs. Woolf retains a realistic plot, everything of importance tends to happen between the acts, between each finite or external sign. *Mrs. Dalloway* and *To the Lighthouse* are distinguished by this indefinite expansion of the interval, of the mind-space, for example, between the beams of the Lighthouse. The realistic plot is sustained by an expressionistic continuity.

Let us provisionally omit *The Waves* and go to Virginia Woolf's last novel. Though its plot is as realistic as ever, we cannot any longer tell with complete certainty what really happens between the acts that make up the action. The novel has a movement like that of Zeno's arrow: we know it flies continuously, and will reach some end, yet are still amazed it does not break in mid-flight. The author, another La Trobe, might fail the continuity, and history, the subject of the play, might fail likewise and not reach the present moment. But life and the novel continue in the same country manner because the artist's interpolations are imaginative enough.

In the case of *The Waves* we cannot even tell what happens. It is not that the plot line is unclear, but now everything is interpolation, even the characters who are simply their speeches, and these speeches interpret acts that might and might not have been. What happens is what the speeches make happen. The purple prefaces alone, describing a day from dark to dark, seem to be founded in reality, or rather nature: the human parts are pushed between as a supreme interpolation standing against the impersonal roll of time.

Considered as notes toward a supreme fiction the novels of Virginia Woolf say "It must be affirmative." They suppose a mind with an immense, even unlimited, power to see or build continuities. It is almost as if the special attribute of the unconscious, that it does not know the negative, belonged also to mind in its freest state. The artist is either not conscious of the negative (i.e., his unconscious speaks through him), or fiction is generically the embodiment of the negative—and whatever dialectic characterizes mind—in purely affirmative terms. The reader, of course, may reconstitute the negative; this task is one of the principal aims of interpretation. We have done a similar thing by pointing to the precarious and interpolative character of Virginia Woolf's continuities. In parts of *To the Lighthouse,* in the last chapter of *Orlando,* and in *The Waves,* the novel is brought to the limit of its capacity to show death, decay, repression, and discontinuity in terms of thought, speech, and prose rhythm. Irony is no longer a device; art becomes irony, and the reader sees that the extreme eloquence of *The Waves* hides silence and incommunicability, or that Mrs. Ramsay thinking to affirm life really affirms death.

I wish to make this irony more cogent by a last glance at Mrs. Ramsay. The first section of *To the Lighthouse* is called "The Window." Mrs. Ramsay (like her creator in *A Room of One's Own*) sits near a window and knits. Her hands knit—so does her mind. Every strain that comes from without is absorbed by the regularity of her hands and the continuity of her mind. The strains are endless; she is besieged by eight children, by memory, by nature, and above all by a husband who constantly if surreptitiously demands her attention. Yet, as if another Penelope, apart from the clamoring suitors, she sits and weaves an interminable garment.

Is it a dress or a shroud? A reddish brown stocking, of course, in expectation of visiting the Lighthouse Keeper and his son, though we will not see her arrive. She dies suddenly one night, and her death reveals what she has woven. Darkness and decay creep over the house, which even now is none too tidy. Mrs. Ramsay alive keeps the disorder vital and prevents it from overrunning. She is the natural center, the sun, and however confused relationships get, all come back to her and are resolved into simplicity by her word or presence. But when she dies, impersonality, waste, and vagueness flood the house like a delayed judgment.

The second part of the novel, "Time Passes," describes the near-ruin of the House of Ramsay. It reverts to the sea, to nature; and the human events breaking that slope are reported parenthetically, as interpolations. The structure of *The Waves* comes directly out of this second part. What can the author be saying but that there existed a strange (perhaps unavoidable) correspondence between the mind of Mrs. Ramsay and the will of nature? Although most open to life, sitting by the window, knitting every impulse into a fabric of thought and feeling, what she worked proved finally to be a shroud. But the male will survives in the form of Mr. Ramsay, a sparse, old, domineering man still feeding on the sympathy of others.

It is, therefore, a tragic choice which confronts us. Mrs. Ramsay is the feminine part of the soul, with its will to bypass the will, its desire to let things be and grow in their own time, and above all with its frightening power for mystical marriage, that refusal to sustain the separateness of things in an overly great anticipation of final unity. This last is her most profound trait (she is also literally a matchmaker), and it reveals her identification with death:

> Not as oneself did one find rest ever, in her experience (she accomplished here something dexterous with her needles) but as a wedge of darkness. Losing personality, one lost the fret, the hurry, the stir; and there rose to her lips always some exclamation of triumph over life when things came together in this peace, this rest, this eternity; and pausing there she looked out to meet that stroke of the Lighthouse, the long steady stroke, the last of the three, which was her stroke, for watching them in this mood always at this hour one could not help attaching oneself to one thing, especially of the things one saw; and this thing, the long steady stroke, was her stroke. Often she found herself sitting and looking, sitting and looking, with her work in her hands until she became the thing she looked at—that light for example. And it would lift up on it some little phrase or other which had been lying in her mind like that—"Children don't forget, children don't forget"—which she would repeat and begin adding to it. It will end, it will end, she said. It will come, it will come, when suddenly she added, We are in the hands of the Lord.

This is Mrs. Ramsay's mind knitting, and she knows she has gone too far, hypnotized by her own rhythm. It was not she who said, "We are in the hands of the Lord." "She had been trapped into saying something she did not mean." It is curious how at this moment Mrs. Ramsay echoes a mood which breaks into Shakespeare's tragedies imminently before the end. Do we not hear Desdemona's "All's one" and Hamlet's "If it be now, 'tis not to come; if it be not to come, it will be now; if it be not now, yet it will come"? Despite her great longing for privacy, she cannot but help the reconciliation of all things—she plots to marry off Paul and Minta, William Bankes and Lily Briscoe, subdues her judgment, and always finally gives in to her husband, betraying her soul and others for the sake of peace.

Virginia Woolf's use of a realistic plot and an expressionistic continuity seems to me as deep a solution to the structural problems of prose fiction as that found in *Ulysses*. Though the form cannot be said to originate with her, she gave it a conscious and personal perfection, and it remains a vital compromise with the demands of realism. She learned, of course, a great deal from (and against) Joyce, and to mention her in that company is itself a judgment. Her weakness, bound up with her virtues, lies less in any formal conception than in her subject, which is almost too specialized for the novel. I suspect that it is her subject, not her form, which is poetic, for she deals always with a part of the mind closest to the affirmative impulse. We do not find in her great scenes, passionate and fatal interviews with the characters restricted to and revolving about each other. For however complex her characters may be, they are caught up essentially in one problem and are variations of the "separatist" or "unifier" type. The one lives by doubting, and the other by affirming, the illusion of a divine or childhood nature. Poetry gives us this nature more vividly than Virginia Woolf, but it is she who makes us aware of its daily necessity and deception.

FRANK D. McCONNELL

"Death Among the Apple Trees": "The Waves" and the World of Things

And what were thou, and earth, and stars, and sea, If to the human mind's imaginings Silence and solitude were vacancy?

—from MONT BLANC

Shelley's final question in the Vale of Chamouni, like the apparent cliché which concludes the *Ode to the West Wind*, is not so triumphantly rhetorical as a simple reading suggests. In context, both questions reveal an uncertainty about the relative primacy, in this world, of the human imagination, with its endless train of rich and apparently holy impressions, on the one hand, and the "everlasting universe of things" which, as inhuman and possibly mindless power, presents a chillingly negative version of the Intellectual Beauty in which the mind craves to believe, on the other hand. If the apocalyptic wind of change and revolution, like the "Necessity" of Shelley's tutor Godwin, is in fact *not* a power benign to and consonant with the mind's imaginings, then a humane Spring may be very far indeed behind the Winter it brings on. The questions reverberate in the silence they impose with that curious and profound self-criticism which is characteristic of Shelley's best poetry. But of course they are only an extreme manifestation of one of the most per-

From *Bucknell Review* 16 (December 1968). Copyright © 1968 by *Bucknell Review*.

manent dilemmas of the romantic imagination: the terrible ambiguity, Col-
eridgean in origin, implied by the autonomy of the creative mind, the fear
that what seems an imaginative transfiguration of the world of matter may
in the end be only the vaudeville trick Edward Bostetter calls it: ventriloquism.

Virginia Woolf, writing about Shelley in 1927, at about the time
she envisioned the novel that was to become *The Waves*, seems to have
been aware of this distinctively romantic problem:

> He loved the clouds and the mountains and the rivers more passionately
> than any other man loved them; but at the foot of the mountain he always
> saw a ruined cottage; there were criminals in chains, hoeing up the weeds
> in the pavement of St. Peter's Square; there was an old woman shaking
> with ague on the banks of the lovely Thames . . . The most ethereal of
> poets was the most practical of men.

It is an odd conflation of Shelley with Wordsworth and with Virginia Woolf
herself; for certainly the "ruined cottage" is an unconscious reminiscence
of *The Excursion*, and the old woman on the banks of the Thames seems
remarkably like the grimly prophetic figure, "a tall quivering shape, like a
funnel, like a rusty pump, like a wind-beaten tree for ever barren of leaves,"
Peter Walsh encounters in *Mrs. Dalloway*. But as an evaluation of Shelley
it is enlightened, accurate, and, for the era of the "New Criticism," courageously generous. And by one of those tricks which literary history seems
delighted to play on authors, it ironically anticipates the critical fate of
Virginia Woolf's own work, particularly her strangest and richest novel,
The Waves. For while criticism, both enthusiastic and dyslogistic, of Virginia
Woolf has taken it more or less for granted that she is "the most ethereal
of novelists," indications have been rare—if indeed there have been any—
that she is also "the most practical of women": that the aestheticism of her
"stream of consciousness" includes the qualifying and fulfilling counter-
movement which is an essential energy of the profoundest romantic and
modern literature.

The reasons for Virginia Woolf's reputation as ethereal are, of
course, both apparent and inevitable, with a perverse kind of inevitability.
The very violence with which she inveighed against a double critical standard for women writers, and her vast scorn for the characterization of herself
as "lady novelist," have insured for her an enduring attractiveness to people
who hold precisely the values she contemned: a hypersensitive feminist
apartheid, a concern for the obsessively "mystical" element in literature,
and a kind of narrative introspectionism which has less to do with the
mainstream of twentieth-century fiction than with the neurasthenia of the

suffragette who insists on the vote but swoons at the editorial page. The inaccuracy of such a view finally results in the domesticated "Mrs. Woolf" of a book like Dorothy Brewster's *Virginia Woolf*, a mixture of the tough-minded narrator with her own heroines, a book much like one that would result if one were to take as the final authoritative voice in *The Rape of the Lock* Belinda rather than Pope; or the Virginia Woolf-guru of N.C. Thakur's *The Symbolism of Virginia Woolf*, which in an access of mystagogy identifies as analogues for *The Waves* the Persian mystic Malauna Rumi, the Christian Trinity, the Hindu Trimurti, a misreading of Shelley's "Hymn to Intellectual Beauty," and the sayings of Buddha—in a single page.

It is finally "mysticism," as a kind of exalted subjectivity, which is the *ignis fatuus* for Virginia Woolf's commentators, and particularly for commentators on *The Waves*. For *The Waves*, as both Miss Brewster and Mr. Thakur inform us, was the novel which the author called her "abstract mystical eyeless book," her "playpoem." The reference is to a 1928 entry in Virginia Woolf's diary, one of the earliest pertaining to *The Waves*, at that time still to be called *The Moths*. But the passage, read more fully, puts a significant bias on the aura of "mysticism." Virginia Woolf writes:

> Yes, but *The Moths*? That was to be an abstract mystical eyeless book: a playpoem. And there may be affectation in being too mystical, too abstract; saying Nessa and Roger and Duncan and Ethel Sands admire that: it is the uncompromising side of me; therefore I had better win their approval . . . I rather think the upshot will be books that relieve other books: a variety of styles and subjects: for after all, that is my temperament, I think, to be very little persuaded of the truth of anything—what I say, what people say—always to follow, blindly, instinctively with a sense of leaping over a precipice—the call of—the call of—now, if I write *The Moths* I must come to terms with these mystical feelings.

It was, in fact, in one sense precisely the "coming to terms" with the mystical feelings that accounted for the long and complex growth of the book and its transformation from *The Moths* to *The Waves*. An earlier entry, from 1927, in Virginia Woolf's diary explains the relevance of the first title as she again mentions "the play-poem idea; the idea of some continuous stream, not solely of human thought, but of the ship, the night, etc., all flowing together; intersected by the arrival of the bright moths." She obviously thought of this book as the *chef d'oeuvre* of her distinctive fictional talents, and obviously identified the initial impulse of its writing as a quasi-mystical revelation of what the completed whole would be like—the prophetic "fin in a waste of waters" which finds its way into Bernard's Roman vision. But in the very writing of the book, in the "coming to terms" with its subjectivist origin, it seems to have grown into something which Virginia Woolf herself could not have recognized at the beginning, something both tougher and more profoundly relevant to her own best gifts than the triumph of affectiveness the book has often been thought to be—something whose insignia is in fact the difference between the bright and evanescent moths who were first to "intersect" the book's plot and the inhuman, terrifying neutral waves which have the last inarticulate "word" in the final novel and give their ambiguous benediction to the human sense of a personal immortality.

"Coming to terms" with mysticism—at least in the English imaginative mainstream—is precisely a matter of translation, which implies necessarily eradication of the full subjective flower of mysticism, of *writing it down*, turning contemplation into verbalization, vision into version. From Walter Hilton's medieval *Scale of Perfection*, which in making the mystic's way a ladder refuses to leave out the lower rungs of unrefined experience, to Wesley's "methodizing" of the Evangelical Inner Light; and from the Red Cross knight's descent from the mount of vision to the self-conscious and quizzical apocalypse of *Prometheus Unbound*, the massive commonplacing bias of the English mainstream is clear: a mainstream to which Virginia Woolf irrevocably belongs, as her earliest diary entries indicate, with their unflattering comparison of Christina Rossetti to the Byron of *Don Juan*.

One of the most important "translations" of the mystic into the fictive is the passage already referred to, describing Bernard's experience in Rome:

> These moments of escape are not to be despised. They come too seldom. Tahiti becomes possible. Leaning over this parapet I see far out a waste of water. A fin turns. This bare visual impression is unattached to any line of reason, it springs up as one might see the fin of a porpoise on the horizon. Visual impressions often communicate thus briefly statements that we shall in time to come uncover and coax into words. I note under F., therefore, "Fin in a waste of waters." I, who am perpetually making notes in the margin of my mind for some final statement, make this mark, waiting for some winter's evening.

There is something remarkably Wordsworthian about this passage, not only in the gratuitousness with which the vision, the moment of escape, comes, but also in its spareness, the deliberate and nearly abstract simplicity of it. What gives it its peculiar force, however, is the determination of Bernard to "coax into words" the phenomenon whose irrational, unawaited appearance defeats his present effort at description. The fin, he says, springs up suddenly, like a fin in a waste of waters. And with the romantic phrase-maker's characteristic faith in his own failures, he duly notes the phenom-enon in his mental chap-book for later working into the story he is trying to make of his life and the lives of his friends.

It is, in fact, precisely the befuddlement of the vision which makes it important to Bernard. For if the vision of the fin in a waste of waters is a "moment of escape," the escape is *from* words themselves, with their implicit "plotting" of human life and with their pretensions to causality and coherence. Bernard simultaneously welcomes and forestalls the defeat of his language since this defeat, by revealing a tension between word and world, insures his liberation from the possible "mysticism," or absolute subjectivity, of his perpetual storytelling. He is the most pretentious and self-conscious of catalogers, noting this purely phenomenological and non-human revelation under "F" for "fin"; but it is just this pretension, anxious to take risks with experience yet willing to be made absurd by the experience itself, which is his imaginative salvation.

Is there a story to tell at all? asks Bernard a moment before he has the vision of the fin. Confronted with the teeming and massively undif-ferentiated sight of a Roman street, he realizes that he could isolate any figure or grouping within range and "make it a story":

> Again, I could invent stories about that girl coming up the steps. She met him under the dark archway . . . "It is over," he said, turning from the cage where the china parrot hangs. Or simply, "That was all." But why impose my arbitrary design? Why stress this and shape that and twist up little figures like the toys men sell in trays in the street? Why select this, out of all that—one detail?

It is a question directly relevant, not only to the internal coherence of *The Waves* and, indeed, of all fiction, but to the specific situation in which Bernard finds himself. For his Roman monologue is, among other things, his first speech after the death of Percival, the strange, mute seventh figure about whom the other six characters of *The Waves* weave so much of their discourse. And whatever the similarity between Percival and Virginia Woolf's brother Thoby Stephen, his importance for the novel cannot be mistaken.

If Percival's death is a rupture in the hopes and sensibilities of the other characters, it is equally a rupture in the serial organization of their monologues: a delicate and highly subtle instance of imitative form. In the manner of serial music, each set of monologues by the six characters begins with a speech by Bernard and runs through the speeches of the other five before Bernard initiates a new "movement." But at the beginning of the fifth large section of the novel, the section introducing the news of Percival's death, Bernard for the first and only time does not begin the series: the first speaker is Neville, the closest of the six to Percival: " 'He is dead,' " said Neville. 'He fell. His horse tripped. He was thrown. The sails of the world have swung round and caught me on the head. All is over. The lights of the world have gone out. There stands the tree which I cannot pass.' " Throughout the fifth and sixth sections, Bernard does not appear, and the order of speakers is Neville—Rhoda—Louis—Susan—Jinny—and again Neville. Six speakers, but no Bernard. With that kind of mathematical aesthetic puzzlement which is common to *The Waves* and serial music, we can ask whether Bernard when he begins section six with his Italian monologue is initiating a new series or ending the previous one; whether he is reacting to Percival's death or continuing (subsisting) in Percival's absence; whether, in fact, this most articulate of the six has overcome or been overcome by the sheer datum of the body's end. The narrative placement of his voyage to Rome imposes on the reader the same kind of casuistry he imposes upon himself in his crucial vision of the fin. And in forcing us to ask, with and about Bernard and his friends, Is there a story?—or, Does the form hold?—the book also forces us to question, again with Bernard, the subjectivity which is its own inmost structure.

All this, of course, depends upon Percival, the silent, physically impressive character whose nearly Sartrean role in *The Waves* is *to be present* and *to be seen* by the others. "But look," says Neville, seeing Percival in the school chapel, "he flicks his hand to the back of his neck. For such gestures one falls hopelessly in love for a lifetime." And the lonely Louis, in his vision of fields and grass and sky, sees that "Percival destroys it, as he blunders off, crushing the grasses, with the small fry trotting subservient after him. Yet it is Percival I need; for it is Percival who inspires poetry." As the figure who is, resplendently, *there*, both conscious and yet definitely the object of all the other consciousness in the book, Percival is necessarily the inspirer of poetry as transaction between the inner and outer worlds. He is also necessarily mute since the fullness of his presence in his own body is a plenum of self-consciousness which does not require the kind of speech the others constantly perform: their continual effort at pontification, or bridge-building between consciousness and experience. Neville notes this essential "in-himselfness" of Percival at the crucial dinner party in section four of *The Waves*. "Without Percival," he says, "there is no solidity. We are silhouettes, hollow phantoms moving mistily without a background." And Bernard, least affected yet most perceptive about Percival, puts the matter in the precise terms, not only of the characters' experience but of the book's own highly self-conscious structure:

> "Here is Percival," said Bernard, "smoothing his hair, not from vanity (he does not look in the glass), but to propitiate the god of decency. He is conventional; he is a hero. The little boys trooped after him across the playing-fields. They blew their noses as he blew his nose, but unsuccessfully, for he is Percival. Now, when he is about to leave us, to go to India, all these trifles come together. He is a hero."

Much in the manner of the window-turned-mirror in the first chapter of *To the Lighthouse*, Percival by his presence organizes the other six into a "party" in the fourth section of *The Waves*, and again organizes them—this time by his absence—in the final gathering in section eight. For the unity he represents, the impossible—for the six and for the book itself—full transaction between subject and object, is a unity no less primary in its negation than in its assertion. Susan realizes this when she addresses the dead Percival: "You have gone across the court, further and further, drawing finer and finer the thread between us. But you exist somewhere. Something of you remains. A judge. That is, if I discover a new vein in myself I shall submit it to you privately. I shall ask, 'What is your verdict?' You shall remain the arbiter."

Percival is a "hero" of acclimatization, of that at-homeness in both the world of things and the world of self-awareness whose loss is the creative trauma of the Romantic imagination. He represents in his self-containment, his absolute visibility, the sense which the other characters can never quite attain or resign themselves to, the sense that "I am (rather than I have) this body" which implies that "I am of (as well as in) this world." Bernard's summing-up of the final gathering of the six at Hampton Court is, in this context, an immensely poignant coda to the book's career: "We saw for a moment laid out among us the body of the complete human being whom we have failed to be, but at the same time, cannot forget." For the body is at once the body of the dead Percival, impossible of attainment for these modern children, the stunted corpses of each one's potential self, and of course the shattered and diminishing continuity of the six sensibilities taken as a single *gestalt*.

That the six speaking characters do form a kind of *gestalt*, not only in their common relationship to Percival, but in their sustained effort to see clearly the world around them and each other, has long been a commonplace of commentary on *The Waves*. But we must not confuse the *gestalt*-narrative with either lyricism or allegory; we must not assume, with

Jean Guiguet, that the monologues of *The Waves* are a sustained single voice only factitiously differentiated by character names, or, with Dorothy Brewster, that the six characters are a code for different aspects of a single massive human personality. Both interpretations, which end by more or less totally "subjectivizing" the book, fail to take account of the range of complexity and phenomenological subtlety of the grouping of the six.

Perhaps the most useful commentary on the organization of *The Waves* is Virginia Woolf's brief sketch, "Evening Over Sussex: Reflections in a Motor Car," published posthumously in *The Death of the Moth*. In this remarkable performance, Virginia Woolf not only projects a set of six "personalities"—six separate yet complementary reactions to the world of things—but explicitly links them to the central Romantic and modern problem of breaking out of the subjective into a real resonance with the phenomenal: the selves are "six little pocket knives with which to cut up the body of a whale" and although she may not have had Melville in mind at the time, the "whale" involved is obviously of the same mysterious and absolute objectivity, terrible in its purity, as Moby Dick. Driving through Sussex at evening, when incipient darkness has obliterated all but the most permanent rock-face of the landscape, Virginia Woolf notes (again in noticeably Wordsworthian terms) that: "One is overcome by beauty extravagantly greater than one could expect . . . one's perceptions blow out rapidly like air balls expanded by some rush of air, and then, when all seems blown to its fullest and tautest, with beauty and beauty and beauty, a pin pricks; it collapses."

The pin prick, the sense of despair at the fecund exuberance of the world, introduces the first of the "selves": for "it was allied with the idea that one's nature demands mastery over all that it receives; and mastery here meant the power to convey . . . so that another person could share it." Such despair, however, generates the second self whose counsel is to "relinquish . . . be content . . . believe me when I tell you that it is best to sit and soak; to be passive; to accept . . . ." As these two selves hold colloquy, a third self is detached, and observing the other two aloofly, reflects that: "While they are thus busied, I said to myself: Gone, gone; over, over; past and done with, past and done with. I feel life left behind even as the road is left behind. We have been over that stretch, and are already forgotten . . . Others come behind us." The first three selves seem to have reached a point of exhaustion in each other's counsel and in the melancholy at imminent death which the third self articulates. But suddenly a fourth self, which "jumps upon one unawares . . . often disconnected with what has been happening," say, " 'Look at that.' It was a light;

brilliant, freakish; inexplicable." It is a star; and as soon as the star is named as such, a new self attempts to find the "meaning" of the star in its prospects for human progress: "I think of Sussex in five hundred years to come. I think much grossness will have evaporated. Things will have been scorched up, eliminated. There will be magic gates. Draughts fan-blown by electric power will cleanse houses. Lights intense and firmly directed will go over the earth, doing the work."

With this, the sunset is complete, and a sixth self, presumably dormant all the time, arises to coordinate the other five:

> Now we have got to collect ourselves: . . . Now I, who preside over the company, am going to arrange in order the trophies which we have all brought in. Let me see; there was a great deal of beauty brought in today: farmhouses; cliffs standing out to sea; marbled fields; mottled fields; red feathered skies; all that. Also there was disappearance and the death of the individual. . . . Look, I will make a little figure for your satisfaction; here he comes.

The "bringing in" of beauty, with its homey touch of "bringing in" produce at the end of the day, strikes precisely the right note: for this extended *gestalt* activity of assimilation, energetic as it is, is still a kind of factitious "bringing in" whose origin is the insuperable otherness of the phenomenal and whose end-product is the deliberately ambiguous *placebo* of the "little figure."

Working back from the sixth "self" of "Evening Over Sussex," it is a fairly simple matter to see in each of the selves a close parallel to the six speaking characters of *The Waves*. The sixth, making his little figure against the onset of night, is obviously very like Bernard, the inveterate phrase-maker who "sums up," or attempts to, in the last section of the novel. The fourth self, with its quick and inarticulate cry of "Look!" resembles Jinny, who says of herself, "Every time the door opens I cry 'More!' But my imagination is the bodies. I can imagine nothing beyond the circle cast by my body." And the fifth, who in reaction to the fourth attempts to describe and to project into the future the world of appearances, is like Louis, the man of business, ashamed of his past and his father, the banker in Brisbane, who imagines himself forging in iron rings the world to come. Rhoda, the most ethereal of the characters, for whom life is "the emerging monster" and whose career is a calculated disappearing act, is the full-blown version of the third self, in love with death and the approaching dark. The second self, with its counsel to resign and accept, is like the country-bred, self-contained Susan, probably the most chthonic of Virginia Woolf's characters. And the first self, whose need to master and to articulate sets off the procession of the other selves, is like Neville, the poet and precisian whose terrible need for communication seems almost to skirt a desperate homosexuality.

But more important than these striking parallels of mood is the light thrown by "Evening Over Sussex" on the basic phenomenological impulse of *The Waves*, which, as I have tried to indicate, is a compelling effort to subvert the subjective or the comfortably "mystical." For as it is the discomfort—highly Wordsworthian or Shelleyan—of the first self at the *intransigence* of the non-human world which necessitates the procession of "selves," so Neville's crucial version in the first chapter of the man with his throat cut seems to "begin" the movement of the novel. The version must be quoted at length:

> His blood gurgled down the gutter. His jowl was white as a dead codfish. I shall call this structure, this rigidity, "death among the apple trees" for ever. There were the floating, pale-grey clouds; and the immitigable tree; the implacable tree with its greaved silver bark. The ripple of my life was unavailing. I was unable to pass by. There was an obstacle. "I cannot surmount this unintelligible obstacle," I said. And the others passed on. But we are doomed, all of us by the apple trees, by the immitigable tree which we cannot pass.

The tone of this passage is inescapably related to one of the most important apprehensions of things in the English language, Wordsworth's despairing sight of the *Intimations Ode*:

> —But there's a Tree, of many one,
> A single Field which I have looked upon,
> Both of them speak of something that is gone:
> The Pansy at my feet
> Doth the same tale repeat:
> Whither is fled the visionary gleam?
> Where is it now, the glory and the dream?
>   (ll.51–57)

The doom is, of course, the doom of consciousness-in-the-body, the "dying animal" of Yeats or the "ghost in the machine" of Gilbert Ryle. And this is the essential context for the italicized passages describing the waves, the house, and the birds at the beginning of each chapter. For these passages are not simply, as Joan Bennett and others have described them, compelling prose-poems paralleling human life with the cycle of the day and of nature. They are, on the other hand, deliberate and highly effective attempts to present a phenomenal world without the intervention of human consciousness, a world of blind things which stands as a perpetual challenge to the attempts of the six monologists to seize, translate, and "realize" their world. And although full of lyrical and "anthropomorphic" metaphors, it is difficult not to see in these passages an anticipation of the concerns and predispositions of contemporary novelists like Alain Robbe-Grillet and Nathalie Sarraute:

> The sun fell in sharp wedges inside the room. Whatever the light touched became dowered with a fanatical existence. A plate was like a white lake. A knife looked like a dagger of ice. Suddenly tumblers revealed themselves upheld by streaks of light . . . The veins on the glaze of the china, the grain of the wood, the fibres of the matting became more and more finely engraved. Everything was without shadow.

The sense of preternatural (or preconscious) clarity, the way in which the precision with which things appear actually jeopardizes their stability as "this" thing—everything Robbe-Grillet most desires for the so-called "new novel" is there, and profoundly assimilated to the central theme of The Waves. In fact, the obvious parallel between the "day" of these descriptions and the lives of the characters may well be quite too obvious. The connection is such a ready commonplace that the ease with which we adopt it may be a deliberately planted instance of our own willingness to assume an overeasy mastery of the universe of things. Certainly the very end of the book is disturbingly ambiguous: Bernard's final ecstatic resolve to assert the human, to fling himself, "unvanquished and unyielding" against death itself is followed by the chilling line: "The waves broke on the shore." To ask whether this is an affirmation or a denial of Bernard's resolve is nugatory: it is simply and sublimely irrelevant to Bernard, as Bernard to it, and therein lies its enormous power. For the "nature" of the italicized passages is neither the anthropomorphic and sympathetic nature of the pastoral nor its malevolent but equally anthropomorphic contrary in a view like Gloucester's: "As flies to wanton boys, are we to th' Gods;/ They kill us for their sport." It is rather the nature of sublime and self-sufficient unhumanity which finds articulation in the dirge from Cymbeline (an important "hidden theme" for both Mrs. Dalloway and The Waves), in Shelley's confrontation with Mont Blanc, or in Sartre's conception of the forbidding and impenetrable être en-soi.

Each of the characters, in lifelong quest of a fully articulate existence, reflects in one way or another the inherent tension between the words of subjective consciousness and the irrecoverable otherness of both things and other people. Only Bernard, in a moment of vision near the end of his final summing-up, achieves a perception which "redeems" him and his five friends precisely by bringing the terms of their failure to full consciousness: "For one day as I leant over a gate that led into a field, the rhythm stopped: the rhymes and the hummings, the nonsense and the poetry. A space was cleared in my mind. I saw through the thick leaves of habit. Leaning over the gate I regretted so much litter, so much accomplishment and separation, for one cannot cross London to see a friend, life being so full of engagements." As the life of intrasubjectivity, "so full of engagements," grows finally to the proportions where it chokes off the possibility of even the most minimal actions, Bernard momentarily shunts off personality and sees "the world without a self":

> But how describe the world seen without a self? There are no words. Blue, red—even they distract, even they hide with thickness instead of letting the light shine through. How describe or say anything in articulate words again?—save that it fades, save that it undergoes a gradual transformation, becomes, even in the course of one short walk, habitual—this scene also. Blindness returns as one moves and one leaf repeats another. Loveliness returns. . . . But for a moment I had set on the turf somewhere high above the flow of the sea and the sounds of the woods, had seen the house, the garden, and the waves breaking. The old nurse who turns the pages of the picture-book had stopped and had said, "Look. This is the truth."

It is a vision of absolute phenomenality, where "there are no words" or, in Bernard's earlier terms, "there is no story." And as such it is not an absolutely beautiful vision, since "beauty" is a product of the affective consciousness. "Loveliness" and "blindness" return together as the vision fades and becomes habitual—literally as it again becomes a vision subject to the *use* of language. But what is most startling about this passage is what Bernard does see in his moment of enlightenment. What "the old nurse" (who may very well be a reminiscence of the foster-mother Nature of the *Intimations Ode*) *shows* Bernard is precisely the world of the italicized chapter-heads, "the house, the garden, and the waves breaking'—precisely, that is, the world of unobserved, nonconscious things in the full ambivalence of its relationship to the characters of *The Waves* so that in a moment of almost perfect representative form, Bernard simultaneously breaks out of subjectivity into a phenomenological perception, and breaks into *The Waves* in its inmost structure. Her lyrical tough-mindedness will not allow Virginia Woolf to take the way either of aestheticism or of "objectivism," but insists even here that narrative form and formless world mutually condition each other. The way out and the way in, like the way up and the way down, are one and the same.

Finally, what *The Waves* gives us is something very like the world of Jorge Luis Borges' fable, "Tlön, Uqbar, Orbis Tertius," where an attempt to project a fictive, totally Berkeleyan and subjective world ends by taking over and transforming the "real" world. Virginia Woolf's mystical and eyeless book achieves a subjectivity so total and so self-conscious that it finally becomes a radical criticism of "mysticism" and of the subjective eye itself in the face of sheer phenomenalism. It is a kind of Hegelian paradox of "purity" whereby the subjective carries itself through a mirror reversal, entering a new and strange style of the insuperably nonhuman and "other":

> People go on passing; they go on passing against the spires of the church and the plates of ham sandwiches. The streamers of my consciousness waver out and are perpetually torn and distressed by their disorder. I cannot therefore concentrate on my dinner. "I would take a tenner. The case is handsome; but it blocks up the hall." They dive and plunge like guillemots whose feathers are slippery with oil.

> Soon unfortunately time will no longer be master. Wrapped in their aura of doubt and error, this day's events, however insignificant they may be, will in a few seconds begin their task, gradually encroaching upon the ideal order, cunningly introducing an occasional inversion, a discrepancy, a confusion, a warp, in order to accomplish their work: a day in early winter without plan, without direction, incomprehensible and monstrous.

The first passage is Louis's monologue in a London restaurant; the second is Robbe-Grillet's description of a day in a French café. The remarkable resemblance between these passages, from novels normally assumed to represent polar schools of contemporary literature, is an index not only of the substantiality of a "modern tradition" of narrative but also of the profound contemporaneity of Virginia Woolf's greatest novel. Far from being the *sui generis* masterpiece of a hyper-aesthetic "lady novelist," *The Waves* is a tough-minded and sobering examination of the chances for the shaping intellect to shape meaningfully at all. And far from being a "dead end" for fiction, it is a novel whose penetration to the roots of a distinctly modern and crucially humanistic problem is human and humanizing as few other books can claim to be.

JAMES NAREMORE

Nature and History in
"The Years"

To understand Woolf's attitude to-
ward social change or indeed to understand her politics in general, it is
necessary to read *The Years* in conjunction with *Three Guineas* (1938), the
long polemical essay which, as she herself suggested, serves as a companion
to her novel. Her original intention was to make *The Years* an "essay novel,"
but *Three Guineas* appears to have absorbed much of the analysis and
rhetoric which might have found its way into the fiction. Unfortunately,
however, *Three Guineas* has been the most undervalued of Woolf's writings
and until recently has been neglected almost as much as the book it illuminates. From the beginning it was not much liked, and became the subject
of the most vitrolic of all the attacks by the *Scrutiny* group: Q.D. Leavis'
"Caterpillars of the Commonwealth Unite," an influential essay which
maintained, among other things, that Woolf was "quite insulated by class,"
that she was "silly and ill-informed," and that she had written a tract
characterized by a "deliberate avoidance of any argument." Woolf's friends
and admirers were not much more sympathetic. One of her most scholarly
critics has called *Three Guineas* a "neurotic" book; and Quentin Bell has
said that it failed because Woolf attempted to discuss two issues which
seemed at the time to have only a tenuous connection: women's rights and
the war against fascism.

But in fact there is a profound connection between these two issues,
a connection Woolf brought out with great lucidity. Unlike most of her

From *Virginia Woolf: Revaluation and Continuity*, edited by Ralph Freedman. Copyright ©
1980 by the Regents of the University of California.

critics, Woolf was no conventional liberal, and she did not view the rise of fascist dictatorships in the thirties as a simple aberration or as a case of the "good" British versus the "bad" Germans. Though she confessed a deep, nonrational loyalty toward England like that of a child for a parent, she looked beyond the old European patriotisms, seeking the causes of war at a deeper level—in the very structure of middle-class, liberal democracy. To Woolf the treatment of women under such a democracy was symptomatic of the society's basic contradictions, its inability to live up to the ideals it professed; furthermore, she argued that the Spanish Civil War, and the dictators of the right who were the immediate cause of that war, were the direct outgrowth of the very system the British were trying to preserve. Such a perception naturally left her feeling uneasy. British democracy was preferable to fascism, but it maintained the same sexual and class divisions, the same proprietary modes of thought, the same masculine militarism which had given rise to the fascists in the first place.

Caught in a dilemma, Woolf ultimately gave a guinea to a barrister who had written asking her advice and support in preventing war, and she contributed two more guineas to support women's colleges and women's entry into the profession. But at the same time she pointed out that all the committees to prevent war, all the colleges and all the professions, were either beside the point or themselves a part of the problem; the society and its values would have to be radically changed before humane goals could be achieved. Under present circumstances, she wrote, people were forced to choose between bad institutions and an essentially private life as "outsiders." This split between public and private worlds—a split which is embodied throughout modernist literature and in all of Woolf's novels— was ultimately destructive. "For such will be our ruin," Woolf said, "if you in the immensity of public abstractions forget the private figure, or if we in the intensity of our private emotions forget the public world. Both houses will be ruined . . . the material and the spiritual, for they are inseparably connected." What was needed, and what at present could be found only in the voices of the poets, was "that capacity of the human spirit to overflow boundaries and make unity out of multiplicity." But such a unity is only a dream, Woolf said, "the recurring dream that has haunted the human mind since the beginning of time."

In writing The Years, Woolf tried to give a concrete demonstration of the split between private and public worlds, the conflict between a timeless, transpersonal human nature and a divisive, changing social struc- ture. She also provided intimations of that "dream" of unity which haunts the mind, and envisioned history moving toward a potential resolution of people's inner conflicts. Interestingly, however, she chose to write a book which was superficially similar to the family chronicles of John Galsworthy himself, and that may explain why a few of her critics have wrongly described *The Years* as one of her more conventional works. In fact the novel is strikingly unorthodox, and in every respect serves to undermine the assumptions of traditional "realist" fiction.

Although history is one of the book's manifest subjects, *The Years* subordinates public events to a series of domestic scenes or dinner parties, taking us into people's cell-like homes or rented rooms, where sounds can be heard drifting in through windows, or where characters repeatedly gaze outside, noting symbolic details in the environment. The novel is never tendentious, and it does not offer a comprehensive view of social classes; Woolf's progress from chapter to chapter is determined simply by the passing of time, and while Eleanor Pargiter comes close to being a central personage, she hardly qualifies as the agent of the basic change or *parapataea* which gives shape to most plots. The story arises not out of action or exposition but out of a web of family relationships and the collective memories of various characters. We are given not so much a narrative history as a montage, an irregular succession of meaningful but undramatic moments which reveal the quality of daily life.

In her typical fashion, Woolf organizes the material according to a roughly musical form, repeating certain motifs (such as a pigeon cry heard throughout), and establishing thematic echoes between chapters. And yet despite the rigor with which it is executed, *The Years* has a somewhat diffuse surface. Compared to other novels by Woolf, such as *The Waves*, it is striking in its lack of symmetry, its refusal to present an obvious pattern; even the nature discriptions which preface each chapter are not given a sequential rhythm. Such features of the novel may account for the remarks of Basil de Senancourt, whose early review pleased Woolf a great deal. Senancourt noted especially the writer's "instinct . . . towards disjunction," together with a "poetical" movement of consciousness which seemed to pull unity out of chaos. This double tendency is indeed the basis of Woolf's later writings, where she is always challenging her view of unity and continuity in human experience by choosing to render the dislocations caused by passing time, by death, or by the mind's conversations with itself. In *The Years*, her problem is posed explicitly by Eleanor, who wonders if there is a "pattern" to life, "a theme, recurring, like music; half remembered, half forseen? . . . But who makes it? Who thinks it?" Ironically, the same idea has just been rejected by Eleanor's niece Peggy, who bitterly contemplates the chatter of her relatives and feels that even if there were a pattern it would be meaningless, like a "habit," or a "kitten catching its tail."

Throughout *The Years* Woolf's mood seems to waver precariously between Eleanor's turn-of-the-century optimism and Peggy's "present day" pessimism, so that feelings of unity, communion, and significant form are always threatened. The threat is felt not simply at the level of content—as in those passages where characters mediate inconclusively upon the meaning of life—but in the technique itself; the blank spaces between scenes act as signifiers of some gap, some fissure in experience which the imagination of both author and reader seeks to close up.

The Years therefore shares with *Between the Acts* a fragmented, asymmetrical form, and it also has in common with Woolf's last novel a constantly shifting tone, moving effortlessly between lyricism, satire, and perverse ugliness, rather like Eliot in his *Waste Land* period. Clearly the atmosphere of political engagement in thirties' literature affected *The Years* profoundly, even though the book takes place in a private sphere and does not give much sense of an industrial England. In none of Woolf's previous works is there so powerful a sense of urban poverty and violence, or of economic disparities within and between the social classes. These qualities persist throughout the novel, even at the close, when the Edwardian culture is in ruins and Woolf has a clear sense of what the new world ought to be like; Woolf even predicts, through Eleanor, the possible advent of that world, but she has been so unremittingly honest in confronting the capitalist wasteland of the present that she leaves the novel poised, reflecting the tension of doubt. Because she is writing out of a deep knowledge of injustice, her vision of unity and meaning in life is not easily won.

Woolf's uneasiness about the ultimate meaning of history is reflected not only in individual episodes, but in the whole shape of the book. At first glance even the years themselves seem to have been chosen randomly, with little regard to historical significance or official importance to the characters' lives. Except for the death of Mrs. Pargiter in 1880, the dramatic events take place offstage; the first and last years of the world war are given, but the 1914 section takes place in spring, a little in advance of hostilities, whereas the very brief 1918 section is meant to indicate the meaninglessness of "victory"—the Pargiters' ex-servant Crosby simply pauses to hear the guns booming in the distance, then queues up at the grocer's shop as usual. The novel alludes to historical incidents (including the deaths of Parnell and King Edward, the Irish Civil War, the emancipation movement, the rise of Mussolini, and so on), but people seldom comment on the relation between their lives and these events. Even the narrator of the book, that ghostly persona so common to Virginia Woolf's work, tries to direct attention away from social or political facts. The evocative but generalized descriptions of landscape at the opening of each chapter suggests that nature has transcended both history and the unsatisfactory conditions of individual lives, the weather becoming more significant than social change.

The descriptions of landscape, however, are not so much a negation of history as an attempt to give the novel a firm grounding in what I have already described as the "eternal" natural process. Thus the consciousness of the characters is influenced not only by their social class and their economic needs, but also by their natural instincts and their desire for communion. Nearly all the people in the novel are powerfully affected by the conflict between social institutions and some deeper human nature; and the corollary to such a proposition is that true happiness can be attained only when civilization is brought into harmony with *bios*, or with what Lawrence, in another context, called the "deepest self." In the society as Woolf perceives it, however, this harmony is continually frustrated; especially in the earlier parts of the novel, one senses a battle between the characters' instincts and the social forms which dictate their behavior. Here, for example, is the scene where Delia Pargiter watches her mother's burial:

> Earth dropped on the coffin; three pebbles fell on the hard shiny surface; and as they dropped she was possessed by a sense of something everlasting; of life mixing with death, of death becoming life. For as she looked she heard the sparrows chirp quicker and quicker; she heard wheels in the distance sound louder and louder; life came closer and closer . . .
>
> "We give thee hearty thanks," said the voice, "for that it has pleased thee to deliver this our sister out of the miseries of this sinful world—"
>
> What a lie! she cried to herself. What a damnable lie! He had robbed her of the one feeling that was genuine; he had spoilt her one moment of understanding.

Obvious as these social impediments to Delia's "understanding" may be, they are not commented upon until fairly late in the book, when Eleanor and Nicholas Pomjalovsky have a conversation during a blackout in World War I:

> "I was saying," he went on, "I was saying we do not know ourselves, ordinary people; and if we do not know ourselves, how then can we make religions, laws, that—" he used his hands as people do who find language obdurate, "that—"
>
> "That fit—that fit," she said, supplying him with a word that was shorter, she felt sure, than the dictionary word foreigners always used . . .

". . . that fit," she repeated. She had no idea what they were talking about. Then suddenly, as she bent to warm her hands over the fire, words floated together in her mind and made one intelligible sentence. It seemed to her that what he had said was, "We cannot make laws and religions that fit because we do not know ourselves."

"How odd that you should say that!" she said, smiling at him, "because I've so often thought it myself!"

"Why is that odd?" he said. "We all think the same things; only we do not say them."

Nicholas and Eleanor are able to achieve a tentative, halting perception, a shared insight, because they are both "outsiders." Eleanor is one of those "daughters of educated men" who do not participate as full members of the society, whereas Nicholas is a foreigner and a homosexual who, as Sara ironically puts it, "ought to be in prison." We are asked, however, to regard these two as "ordinary people," because Virginia Woolf is suggesting that at the deepest levels of biological necessity we all share the same needs, feel the same discontent, "think the same things." Nicholas elaborates on this issue, arguing that under present conditions there is no way to achieve harmony and wholeness, no way for what he calls "the soul" to express itself:

"The soul—the whole being," he explained. He hollowed his hands as if to enclose a circle. "It wishes to expand; to adventure; to form—new combinations?"

"Yes, yes," she said, as if to assure him that his words were right.

"Whereas now,"—he drew himself together; put his feet together; he looked like an old lady who is afraid of mice—"this is how we live, screwed up into one hard little, tight little—knot?"

"Knot, knot—yes, that's right," she nodded.

"Each is his own little cubicle; each with his own cross or holy book; each with his fire, his wife . . . "

Significantly, Nicholas' vision of a selfish, proprietary society is centered not in public institutions, but in the same private realm of family life that Virginia Woolf's novel has sought to describe. As Woolf had said in *Three Guineas*, "the public and the private worlds are inseparably connected . . . the tyrannies and servilities of the one are the tyrannies and servilities of the other." Indeed, the suppression of the "soul" by social forms is nowhere more evident than in Woolf's depiction of people's "own little cubicle" of marriage, which in *Three Guineas* is called "the one great profession open to [women] since the dawn of time."

Every chapter of *The Years* contains some reference to marriages of property or to unrequited loves. The first, most vividly satiric example of the latter theme is in the early episodes involving Abel Pargiter's niece Kitty Malone, a handsome young woman who is the daughter of an Oxford don. Kitty's conservative, snobbish father is a man who, "had a frame been set round him, might have hung over the fireplace," whereas her mother is contrasted unfavorably with the American visitor Mrs. Fripp, a lady who wears makeup and eats ices instead of making the customary tourist's visit to the Bodleian. Kitty feels frustrated and imprisoned in Oxford, where it always seems to be raining and where she is being forced to read Dr. Andrews's "The Constitutional History of England." (We are told that she once inadvertently spilled ink over one of her father's manuscripts—a history of the college—obliterating "five generations of Oxford men." Dr. Malone's only reply had been, "Nature did not intend you to be a scholar, my dear.") Kitty's mother intends her to marry a suitable man, and cannot understand her daughter's unhappiness; after all, her own convenient marriage has represented an escape of sorts from the tedious country life of Yorkshire. The irony is that Kitty would actually prefer an empty countryside to the college. She contemplates the "barber's block," Edward Pargiter, with distaste, and her only impression of one of the famous scholars who has visited the house is the "damp feel of a heavy hand on her knee." Her attraction to Jo Robeson becomes the one moment when her life holds out the possibility of romantic liberation, but just when her story seems to be taking a hopeful turn Virginia Woolf concludes the chapter, leaping over several years and casually remarking that Kitty has made a prosperous marriage with Lasswade, a mate approved by her mother.

Actually, the theme of frustrated, misplaced, or hypocritical alliances has been introduced even earlier, and Kitty's essential loneliness is echoed in the lives of nearly everyone we meet. Somewhat in the manner of Eliot, Woolf is describing a sexual wasteland, but unlike Eliot she implies that the causes of love's failure are more social than metaphysical. Thus the book opens with Abel Pargiter's clandestine, grotesque visit to his mistress in a street of "dingy little houses" near Westminster. As his amputated fingers fumble at the neck of his lover, Woolf calls attention to sordid details: an eczemous dog; a creaking staircase; the sounds of children outside jumping in and out of "white chalk marks on the pavement"—this last a recurrent motif in the early parts of the novel, and an image used in *Three Guineas* to signify "a monstrous male . . . childishly intent upon scoring the floor of the earth with chalk marks, within whose mystic boundaries human beings are penned, rigidly, separately, artificially."

Meanwhile, Abel Pargiter's wife Rose lies dying in their huge house in Abercorn Terrace, where the children of the family, particularly the females, are quite literally "penned, rigidly . . . artificially," becoming virtual prisoners of Edwardian respectability. Here we are introduced to the four Pargiter daughters: Rose, the adventurous little girl who grew up to become a suffragette, and who will one day have painful memories of "a certain engagement" when "her happiness, it seemed . . . had fallen"; Delia, the romantic, rebellious teenager who daydreams about Parnell, and who will reject the Pargiter household only to end her life married to a conservative Anglo-Irish landlord; Milly, a self-conscious, unremarkable young woman, who will marry a rustic Devonshire gentleman and live contentedly producing his children; and Eleanor, the eldest and most sympathetic, who neither marries nor rebels against her father, but who wishes for one painful moment in her old age that she had been able to find a companion: "I should like to have married," she thinks suddenly, almost surprising herself, resenting "the passage of time and the accidents of life which had swept her away."

Companionship is obviously a necessity for all these characters, but in the world of *The Years* marriage is rarely presented as a satisfactory alternative to isolation. The daughters of Digby Pargiter, Maggie and Sara, seem to represent the two possible extremes in life: because their side of the family is relatively poor, they grow up to share a shabby apartment in Hyams Place; Maggie ultimately finds a relatively happy, unconventional marriage with a foreigner, and Sara, who is frequently compared to Antigone, becomes totally isolated and harmlessly insane—indeed, her speeches are examples of what Woolf, in the context of *Mrs. Dalloway*, called the "mad truth."

The Pargiter sons, on the other hand, have the advantage of "Arthur's Education Fund," that money which throughout British history had been set aside for the education of males. Edward Pargiter becomes a classical scholar at Oxford, Morris enters the law, and Martin joins the army—three institutions Woolf had taken special pains to attack in *Three Guineas*. In *The Years* we see just enough of this public world to understand how it is related to the domestic lives of the characters. The deadly Oxford environment, with its prejudice against women and its complacent snobbishness, is treated in some detail in the Kitty Malone section of the first chapter; the horrors of militarism and war are suggested at various places, most obviously in the 1917 chapter; and the courts of law are depicted in an early scene when Eleanor goes to see Morris perform. At first she admires the wise looks of the presiding judge, but then remembers having met him socially: "And it was a sham. She wanted to laugh." But even though

Woolf points to the social inequity between men and women, she does not suggest that the men have fuller lives; on the contrary, a profound feeling of frustration and lost possibility is felt equally by both sexes. Morris makes a prosperous marriage to a daughter of the Chinnery family and lives on their estate, but he grows old before his time, and Eleanor at one point feels guilty because she urged him to go to the bar. Martin wishes he had been an architect, "but they sent me into the Army instead, which I loathed." Even Edward, the vain but successful scholar, becomes supercilious, reserved, and secretly homosexual; his nephew North tries to speak with him at Delia's party, but ends up thinking "It's no go . . . He can't say what he wants to say; he's afraid."

"When shall we be free?" Eleanor wonders as she listens to Nicholas, "When shall we live adventurously, wholly, not like cripples in a cave?" The book never answers this question and none of the years marks a liberating change in either society or character. Even when Woolf records events from 1910, they are less momentous than we might expect. The announcement of King Edward's death, which Maggie Pargiter hears out the window of her flat, is clearly a symbolic event and is followed closely by an important moment in the lives of the Abel Pargiter family: in the 1913 chapter, Eleanor sells the house in Abercorn Terrace, and Martin thinks back on his childhood. "It was an abominable system . . . family life," he notes, "there all those different people had lived, boxed up together, telling lies." But the collapse of the old Edwardian order does not seem to have created a healthy new day. The years are still pervaded with an atmosphere of futility and lost opportunity; every level of the Pargiter family, from the poor rooms at Hyams Place to the Lasswade seats at the opera, has been shown suffering in quiet desperation. People are still "boxed up," unable to express their feelings, and the death of the king seems merely in keeping with the theme of mortality which is found everywhere in the novel.

If *The Years* has a most important year, it is not 1910 but a date which is never inscribed in the text. We are shown the lives of the Pargiter family between 1880 and 1918, and then Woolf leaps into the "present day," leaving 1919 as an unstated boundary between old and new. The significance of that year is apparent in *Three Guineas*, where it is repeatedly cited as a watershed in the history of women's emancipation; for in 1919, as Woolf notes, women were admitted legally to the professions. This event, however, tended only to liberalize British life, not to change it fundamentally. Although Woolf believed 1919 was an important date, she regarded the new power of women with some irony, pointing out the dangers of being admitted to equal partnership in an evil system.

> Now that the Civil Service is open to us we may well earn from one thousand to three thousand a year; now that the Bar is open to us we may well earn 5,000 a year as judges, and any sum up to forty or fifty thousand a year as barristers. When the Church is open to us we may draw salaries of fifteen thousand . . . When the Stock Exchange is open to us we may die worth as many millions as Pierpont Morgan, or as Rockefeller himself . . . In short, we may change our position from being the victims of the patriarchal system . . . to being the champions of the capitalist system.

The playfulness of these remarks does not conceal the seriousness of Woolf's convictions. She admits that women seeking to enter the universities might think her arguments niggling, but she cautions that her readers should look at the photographs of dead bodies and ruined houses that the Spanish government sends almost weekly. In her view, as we have seen, there is a direct connection between patriarchy, capitalism, and fascist dictatorship; indeed the historical period covered by *The Years* shows the society moving from the first of these stages into the second, with the third brooding on the horizon as the book closes. Woolf therefore opposed any compromise which would allow women to participate even marginally in the British system while at the same time preserving its unjust features. And it is precisely such a compromised social condition that we find in the "Present Day" section of *The Years*. Peggy, the daughter of Morris Pargiter, has become a doctor, but this important change in the status of women does not lead to personal happiness, nor does it heal the split between old and young, between social classes, between individuals and the community. The last section does suggest the dawning of some new world, as indeed throughout the novel we have been given the sense that the movement of history might ultimately redeem everyday life from its sadness and futility. But the new day is not yet arrived as the novel ends, and the chief representatives of the "Present Day" are just as dissatisfied as their forebears had been.

Clearly certain hopeful changes have taken place in the texture of middle-class relationships: Delia Pargiter's elaborate family reunion, which is the setting for most of the action of the final chapter, takes place not in a home, but in a flower-bedecked estate agent's office, with people sitting on stools or on the floors, dining off every kind of table. Delia thinks that this "had always been her aim . . . to do away with the absurd conventions of English life." But her attempt to dissolve the old formalities and bring people together has not been completely successful. North remarks sardonically to himself that everyone present makes a good income, and both he and his sister feel a sharp division between their own generation and Delia's. Of the two younger Pargiters, Peggy is especially isolated and embittered; now thirty-seven years old and beginning to turn grey, she lives what she herself calls a "suppressed" life, a frustrated existence different in kind but not in quality from the one we saw earlier in the daughters of Abel. Bored and distressed by the habitual chatter of her older relatives, she is equally upset by the conversation of an egotistical young man. She does not participate in the dancing, and spends much of the evening brooding alone. She is made especially uncomfortable by the difference between herself and her aunt, and notes sourly that Eleanor can still believe in "freedom" and "justice," "the things that man had destroyed."

Peggy's dissatisfaction is given its most vivid and painful expression early in the chapter, when, en route to the party, she and Eleanor take a cab through London's entertainment district. Peggy is struck by the grotesquerie of the streets:

> The light fell on broad pavements; on white, brilliantly lit-up public offices; on a pallid, hoary-looking church. Advertisements popped in and out. There was a bottle of beer: it poured: then stopped: then poured again . . . Cabs were wheeling and stopping. Their own taxi was held up. It stopped dead under a statue: the lights shown on its cadaverous pallor.
> "Always reminds me of an advertisement of sanitary towels," said Peggy, glancing at the figure of a woman in a nurse's uniform holding out her hand.

The remark shocks Eleanor, who momentarily feels that a knife has sliced her skin. But Peggy's description of the "figure of a woman in a nurse's uniform" is still more unsettling if we recognize the London landmark to which it refers, a monument that Woolf has carefully avoided naming. We are told simply that the figure makes Eleanor think of Peggy's brother, "a nice . . . boy who had been killed."

> "The only fine thing that was said in the war," she said aloud, reading the words cut on the pedestal.
> "It didn't come to much," said Peggy sharply.
> The cab remained fixed in the block.

The statue which evokes this brief exchange is dedicated to Nurse Cavell and in 1937 was one of the four best-known monuments to women in London. Erected in St. Martin's Place in 1920, the Cavell statue was given an inscription by the Labor government in 1924; the words on the pedestal read "Patriotism is not enough." Typically, Eleanor has read the motto as a kind of lesson learned in the war, whereas Peggy regards it cynically. Hence at a later point in the novel Eleanor will comment that things have changed for the better: "We've changed in ourselves," she says, "We're happier—we're freer." But Peggy can only wonder what "freedom" and happiness" mean.

At Delia's party, Peggy tries to explain to North that she perceives a "state of being" in which there might be real happiness; but then she insults him by predicting that he will marry and "make money" instead of "living differently." Actually, North is almost as isolated as she, and has begun his drift toward marriage only because he cannot find a satisfactory alternative. Having spent years in the army and then on an African sheep farm, he returns to London feeling oddly out of place, a stranger to his relatives, his thoughts during the day and evening turning around the problem "Society or solitude, which is best?"—a topic he has heard Nicholas Pomjalovsy discussing at Eleanor's apartment.

North's own feelings seem to pull him toward solitude. His favorite poem, for example, is Marvell's *The Garden,* and he enjoys quoting the lines, "Society is all but rude / to this delicious solitude." At the same time, however, his bachelorhood has grown oppressive, and he has come to London partly out of a vague longing for a mate. While in Africa, he wrote a letter to Sara containing the message that "this is Hell. We are the damned." But now that he has returned to London, he shares an almost surreal luncheon with Sara in her apartment at 52 Milton Street, "near the Prison Tower," and he seems not much happier. In one of the more comic passages of the final chapter, he sits at Delia's party and meditates on the marriage between Hugh Boggs and Milly. An overweight, bovine couple, they make sounds like the "munching of animals in a stall," and North wonders if this is what marriage comes to, where the men go out to hunt and the women "break off into babies." For a moment he contemplates revolution and dynamite, wondering if his sister Peggy could invent a potion that would exterminate the Gibbses of the world. "They're not interested in other people's children," he observes, "Only in their own, their own property . . . How then can we be civilized?" While Eleanor comments on the "miracle" of life, which she calls "a perpetual discovery," North can only say, "I don't know what I want."

Even more clearly than Peggy, North perceives the split between his desires and the objective conditions of the society. Looking about Delia's party, he thinks, "What do they mean by Justice and Liberty? . . . all these nice young men with two or three hundred a year. Something's wrong . . .

there's a gap, a dislocation, between the word and the reality." Gazing into his champagne glass, he imagines what life ought to be and unknowingly echoes Nicholas' and Eleanor's thoughts from an earlier chapter:

> For them it's all right, he thought; they've had their day; but not for him, not for his generation . . . Why not down barriers and simplify? But a world, he thought, that was all one jelly, one mass, would be a rice pudding world, a white counterpane world. To keep the emblems and tokens of North Pargiter—the man Maggie laughs at; the Frenchman holding his hat; but at the same time spread out, make a new ripple in human consciousness, be the bubble and the stream, the stream and the bubble—myself and the world together—he raised his glass. Anonymously, he said, looking at the clear yellow liquid. But what do I mean, he wondered—I, to whom ceremonies are suspect, and religion's dead; who don't fit, as the man said, don't fit in anywhere? He paused. There was the glass in his hand; in his mind a sentence. And he wanted to make other sentences. But how can I, he thought—he looked at Eleanor, who sat with a silk handkerchief in her hands—unless I know what's solid, what's true; in my life, in other people's lives?

North's meditation in this passage is crucial not only to an understanding of *The Years*, but in a more general way to appreciation of Virginia Woolf's entire work. For at virtually every level of her writing she is preoccupied with the distinction she feels between the inner self and the outer world, between solitude and society, between "the bubble and the stream." Like North, she wishes to harmonize two kinds of existence: on the one hand are the timeless recesses of being, where one feels a loss of personal identity and a communion with nature; on the other hand is the time-bound social world of day-to-day relationships, where people assert their identity and relish their differences. The difficulty presented in *The Years*—and by implication in all of Woolf's novels—is that the two kinds of existence will not "fit," partly because the society will not allow people to translate their private dreams of unity into public relationships. As a result the characters feel torn between two worlds, doomed if they choose either one exclusively.

As a novelist, Virginia Woolf seems to have faced a similar difficulty. In "Mr. Bennett and Mrs. Brown," for example, she confronts the problem of reconciling the inward essence of character with the outer shell; as Peggy says when she tries to describe Eleanor, "Where does she begin, and where do I end? . . . two sparks of life enclosed in two separate bodies." Always Woolf tried to capture some transpersonal human essence, some "spark of life" which unites individuals. In passages like the "Time Passes" section of *To the Lighthouse*, she actually attempted to write about a pure life process, a stream without bubbles, where unity has become so complete that there is no distinction between seeing and seen. In most cases, however, she felt torn between a visionary mode of writing and a more public approach, which she identified with the hated orthodoxies of the society. She recognized the ultimate unsatisfactoriness of these alternatives, which forced her to experience life purely at extremes, and she often felt compelled to choose between what she called the novel of "vision" as opposed to the novel of "fact." Hence in *The Waves* she attempted a purely visionary work, but she was no sooner finished than she felt a positive need to write about an opposite kind of experience, to make a solid, "factual" counterpart such as *The Years*.

What makes the later novels like *The Years* and *Between the Acts* so interesting, however, is that they will not settle for one mode of existence over another. Woolf was actually seeking a synthesis of extremes, a dialectic between "female" and "male," between "thou" and "I," between "stream" and "bubble." As North Pargiter recognizes, a world of pure unity and vision would be a " rice pudding world, a white counterpane world," whereas a world of pure individuality must inevitably make people feel that they are "boxed in," cut off from essences. The problem is to develop a human consciousness and a manner of writing which is able to express both kinds of existence simultaneously. In *The Years* Woolf suggests that this problem has social and historical causes and will not be solved by an act of individual will. The split between the two kinds of existence is related to all those artificial boundaries set up between people, all those petty tyrannies of the household, all those economic inequities which have been shown indirectly throughout the novel; and the reconciliation is not possible until the society itself is fundamentally changed.

This dissociation between public and private worlds helps explain why characters in *The Years* have so much difficulty expressing their feelings to one another, or even to themselves. Repeatedly, especially in the last chapter, people experience North's difficulty of trying to "make other sentences," an anxiety Woolf the novelist must have felt as strongly as her imagined characters. The problem is most obvious when the characters try to ask large questions. When Peggy asks if there is any "standard" for human behavior, the issue is dropped while Eleanor tries to recall something she wanted to say; when North asks whether society or solitude is best, Sara's reply is washed away by the chaotic sounds outside her window; when Nicholas tries to make a significant speech at Delia's party, his comments become slightly drunken and incoherent. "Directly something got together, it broke," Peggy thinks, and her observation is reinforced when Nicholas accidentally shatters a champagne glass while he is trying to make his most important statement.

And yet, underneath these elliptical, unfinished attempts to give life meaning, underneath the apparently random fragments of the text, Virginia Woolf suggests a kind of unity, a potential for harmony. This unity is expressed partly by the fact that, despite their surface differences, the characters in the novel at least feel the same discontent across generations—indeed, the elder Pargiters do not conform to the easy stereotypes given them by Peggy and North in the final section. Given this possibility of human community, Woolf is able to provide the novel with a conclusion which strikes a balance between hope and irony. In the last scene, Eleanor looks out the doorway of the estate agent's office, echoing all those times before when characters have looked out unhappily on the streets, and sees a young couple entering the house across the way, a symbol for the sexual accord and fulfillment which has been denied nearly everyone else: " 'There,' Eleanor murmured . . . 'There,' she repeated, as the door shut with a little thud behind them."

Like the couple Woolf notices out the window in *A Room of One's Own*, the man and woman in this scene represent "a force in things which one had overlooked," a potential for unity in life. At the same time, however, they are going inside a house, where the door shuts with a little thud. Are they not "boxed in," like so many of the characters we have seen elsewhere in the novel? Clearly the image is not a satisfactory representation of happiness, beause it returns us to the same kind of domesticity which has been a center of trouble throughout. As if in compensation for this final scene, Woolf closes the novel with an explicitly optimistic statement: We are told that "the sky above the houses wore an air of extraordinary beauty, simplicity, and peace." Understandably, some critics have felt that the exaltation in these lines is not congruent with the tone of the novel as a whole. But it seems to me that we are not intended to read Woolf's last words as a sort of "Happy ever after"; she is not saying that the problems of the novel have been solved, only that a certain natural harmony is potentially within the grasp of humanity.

Actually, Woolf does not know what the future will bring, and in the moment when she tries to predict tomorrow, her essential optimism is tinged with fear. Only a few pages before the conclusion of the novel, Delia's party is interrupted by the entry of a group of children of the building's "caretaker," who are not members of the class who make up the party. "Speak!" Martin Pargiter commands, taking up the role of his father before him, and when they do not reply Peggy remarks sardonically that the younger generation "don't mean to speak." Instead, the children nudge one another and break into song:

> Etho passo tanno hai,
> Fai donk to tu do,
> Mai to, kai to, lai to see
> Toh dom to tuh do—

It is a new and strange language, understood by none of the adults. One of the more conservative members of the party suggests it is a "Cockney accent," but no one is quite sure. We are told that the "distorted sounds rose and sank as if they followed a tune" and there was "something horrible in the noise they made. It was so shrill, so discordant, and so meaningless." Typically, only Eleanor can find something good to say about the performance:

> "But it was . . . " Eleanor began. She stopped. What was it? As they stood there they had looked so dignified; yet they had made this hideous noise. The contrast between their faces and voices was astonishing; it was impossible to find one word for the whole. "Beautiful?" she said, with a note of interrogation, turning to Maggie.
>
> "Extraordinarily," said Maggie.
>
> But Eleanor was not sure that they were thinking of the same thing.

The curious mixture of admiration and sinister terror in this episode is rather like the final scene in *Between the Acts*, where a husband and wife approach one another across the darkness, about to commit an "act" which will determine the future. We may safely assume that Virginia Woolf herself felt such emotions when, in the late thirties, she tried to think about the movement of history. Unlike T.S. Eliot, she did not cling to a tradition, but at the same time she was appalled at what liberal democracy (identified with the masculine ego) had done to the human spirit. She was therefore fearful: Would the inevitable changes to come lead humanity toward some higher plane, or were the years moving in a downward spiral, each stage as frustrating as the one before? Her novel leaves us waiting for the answer, poised for an apocalypse. And yet what is so remarkable about *The Years* is the tenacity with which it keeps faith in "beauty, simplicity, and peace," despite so much social and sexual frustration. Although Woolf is not in league with Blake or Lawrence, she does suggest that a radical change in human consciousness is due; by offering the vision of a peaceful landscape, even if tentatively, she partly overcomes the feelings of despair and solitude which are characteristic of so much modernist literature, helping us believe that human nature might eventually triumph over history.

PAUL WEST

Enigmas of Imagination: "Orlando" Through the Looking Glass

Bad and strange as it may sound, if Virginia Woolf were alive today she would almost certainly feel obliged to resume the aesthetic war which, in *Mr. Bennett and Mrs. Brown,* published fifty years ago, she declared on the circumstantial and unreal realism of Arnold Bennett, John Galsworthy and H.G. Wells; against the belief that, if imagination has to exist, it had best behave itself like any half-decent foreign camera; against what I might call Babbiturates, which sedate sensibility to the point of philistine funk. (In retrospect, both Bennett and Galsworthy merited the C– she gave them, whereas Wells perhaps deserved better, especially on the strength of his romances and fantasias, much admired, one gathers, by Vladimir Nabokov.) Her indictment still holds good anyway, against all literary greengrocers, furniture dealers, and quantity surveyors, perhaps even against those obsessive literary philatelists who conjured into being the novel of *chosisme.* And yet, through some perverse ambiguity of favor, attributable no doubt to forces of reaction that endure in the literary world like colonial marine coelenterates—calcarious skeletons massed in a wide variety of shapes, and often forming reefs or islands in New York or London—she has been grudgingly admitted into literature without, however, being taken seriously. Dubbed precious by the ignorant,

From *The Southern Review* 3, vol. 13 (July 1977). Copyright © 1977 by Louisiana State University.

and obscure by some who ought to know better, her novels remain on the library shelves, taken out only under duress or the influence of a movement that intends to change the status of women. As for her ideas, these impress too many—among those who have even heard of them—as hyper-exquisite aberrations to be looked away from, as if a genteel butterfly had vomited. The plain fact is that, as a creative artist, she has been tolerated (in other words, she is not George Eliot or Sylvia Plath), while, as a thinker, she has been popped into the same oubliette as Bergson and William James; those fervently creative ideas of hers, having to do with character and spirit, with the mercuriality of consciousness and the open-endedness of the universe, have by and large failed to register in the heads of publishers, editors, critics and reviewers, not to mention that hardboiled, malodorous egg, out of Bennett by Michener, the reading public. The unappetizing answer to Edward Albee's meretriciously lupine question is that far too many *are* afraid of her, as of her predecessor Laurence Sterne. They both consternate, just as Samuel Beckett's fiction does, just as each month's issue of *Scientific American* does, as does one's first (and maybe one's fiftieth) sight of a star-nosed mole.

According to another distinguished and comparably neglected practitioner of complex prose, John Hawkes (although less flow-conscious than Woolf), a fiction writer composes in order to create the future. I share that feeling, and I see Virginia Woolf as a literary counterpart of Max Planck, whose 1900 quantum theory recast nature as a flux and virtually junked the neotic truss that held together cause and effect, and of Einstein, who five years later merged space with time, and energy with mass and velocity. In her scientifically uninitiated way, she was thinking herself into the future—the not-yet-known—intuiting just as finely in her nimble words as, say, Eddington, Jeans, and Whitehead in the more sibylline of their formulas of the twenties. It is worth pointing out, however, that inasmuch as Woolf made herself a neighbor of their disciplines, they came pretty close to hers. For example, here is Sir Arthur Eddington, in *Stars and Atoms* (1927): "I am afraid the knockabout comedy of modern atomic physics is not very tender to our aesthetic ideals. The stately drama of stellar evolution turns out to be more like the hair-breadth escapades on the films. The music of the spheres has almost a suggestion of —jazz?" Another of his observations, just as winning, seems almost to imply an episode from a novel: "When an atom is excited, we may picture its electron as a guest in an upper story of an old-fashioned hotel with many alternative and interlacing staircases; he has to make his way down to the lounge—the normal unexcited condition." Sir James Jeans, in *The Mysterious Universe*

(1933), is just as vivid, and if anything even pithier in his analogies: "The shadows which reality throws onto the wall of our cave might *a priori* have been of many kinds. They might conceivably have been perfectly meaningless to us, as meaningless as a cinematograph film shewing the growth of microscopic tissues would be to a dog who had strayed into a lecture-room by mistake." He follows up with an image more dignified and more decorous: "The motions of electrons and atoms do not resemble those of the parts of a locomotive so much as those of the dancers in a cotillion." If we do not like either dismay through Terpsichore or alienation through the image of a canine intruder, we might settle for the more delicate relegation of our unconquerable mind to this: "our consciousness is like that of a fly caught in a dusting-mop which is being drawn over the surface of the picture. . . ." Alfred North Whitehead is dourer then Eddington and Jeans, but he too has his moments. He can be slyly obvious, as in his Page-Barbour Lecture entitled *Symbolism* (1927): "Mankind had gained a richness of experiential content denied to electrons." And, in the same lecture, prudently seditious: "Language and algebra seem to exemplify more fundamental types of symbolism than do the Cathedrals of Medieval Europe." Or, in *Science and the Modern World* (1925), iconoclastic in a quite unfussy way: "My theory involves the entire abandonment of the notion that simple location is the primary way in which things are involved in space-time. In a certain sense, everything is everywhere at all times. For every location involves an aspect of itself in every other location. Thus every spatio-temporal standpoint mirrors the world." I find that very Woolfian indeed; but my purpose in assembling a few jewels from these salient thinkers is not so much to suggest, as I well might, that they and Woolf coincide in many things, as it is to liken their assault on an obsolete world view to hers.

Not only was Virginia Woolf on nodding terms with the *Zeitgeist*; she had opened herself up to it, as to the whole of Jeans's mysterious universe; and her effort seems almost comparable to that of Einstein who, in devoting himself after 1920 to the hunt for a unified field theory, risked looking just as deluded as did she—to some folk at any rate—in asking her contemporaries, in her famous essay, "Modern Fiction," (written in 1919) to "record the atoms as they fall upon the mind in the order in which they fall . . . trace the pattern, however disconnected and incoherent in appearance, which each sight or incident scores upon the consciousness. Let us not take it for granted," she went on, "that life exists more fully in what is commonly thought big than in what is commonly thought small." From stars to atoms indeed! Hers was very much a voyage out, an experimental foray, a piece of high phenomenological honesty. Where Einstein was hoping for a theory, a teleological cornerstone, and persisted in that hope right up to his death, she was being undogmatically receptive, on the *qui vive* for cosmic surprise. Had she, through some happy recombination of her atoms, been able to sample the astronomical theology of Professor John Wheeler of Princeton, she might have responded without the prejudice of some scientists to his notion of the black hole, past whose so-called absolute event horizon there begins a condition called "singularity," in which all conventional physics goes by the board and the cosmic joker runs wild. I do not think it would even bother her, any more than it does Wheeler, that thus far no one has actually found a black hole (unless it is the invisible half of the binary star called Cygnus X–I); rather than dismiss the theory as noetic snakes-and-ladders, she might extol its quality as a phenomenon, its role as a challenge to imaginative agility. Whenever I think of certain characteristic images of hers, among the orchestrated copiousness of her manner at its most affable—fish and snail, river and sea, lighthouse and Kew Gardens, flamingo sunsets and Big Ben, Jacob's Ladder and a piece of glass, the steel blue feather of an airplane, an Orlando who is thirty-six or 336 years old—I sense a longing for mosaic, an apprehension of the One although she can convey it only through being an eclectic of the Many. For her, the universe keeps on adding to itself, but it does not add up; the sign for "equals" is only for someone who does not relish catalogues or lists.

In the long run, she sees that nothing can fall out of the universe, although no one's notion of that universe is likely to be complete or accurate. Not only is Mrs. Brown, passenger in the train from Richmond to Waterloo, incapable of being known outright; by the same token, and coincidentally by the same name, there is Brownian Motion, the quantitative explanation of which came in 1905 from Einstein when he suggested that a body surrounded by a gas or liquid would acquire an energy of agitation equal to the average kinetic energy of a molecule of what surrounded it: for example, Mrs. Brown's body in the air of her compartment or Mrs. Woolf's in the water of the River Ouse. These analogies evince, I hope, the motions of her mind, which was more a piece of the main than even she knew. One need not envoke Indeterminacy or Complementarity in order to establish her almost innate modernity; one need only collect samples of her preferred idiom. Anyone who thought so naturally of flow and immersion, of duration and concentricity, of above all "this varying, this unknown and uncircumscribed spirit, whatever aberration or complexity it may display," meant not just the stream of—but an *extreme* of—consciousness, and, rather than being an over-fastidious Bloomsbury brahmin, was relativity's M. Jourdain, who had been talking scientific incertitudes all along without knowing it. Literary cousin of James Joyce she may have been, and certainly in his debt, she in fact had fewer affinities with him than with those open-minded and untimid scientists of her own day, whose disabused attentiveness to the universe—not asking it to be anything that it was not and amazedly finding it stranger than they could even imagine—provides a model for creative artists for all time. In the words of Plotinus: "If a man were to inquire of Nature the reason for her creative activity, and if she were willing to give ear and answer, she would say: 'Ask me not, but understand in silence, even as I am silent and am not wont to speak.' " Indeed, Woolf's books, like those scientists' findings, are reservoirs of mental silence, silent mentality: thought-crowded, impression-crammed, rich with the kinesis of agitated pensiveness, yes; but more intended to evince than to argue, more acts of attentiveness than of initiative, and given over more to the joys of being disabused than to those of (as André Malraux would say) carving a scar on the universe. I offer her as a superb example of negative capability. Sufficient to say that, in trapping her in a moving railway carriage with Eddington, Jeans, Whitehead, Einstein and Company—quanta surveyors all—I am also trying to dramatize my hunch that an itinerant from another galaxy, slumming around a bit in our solar suburb, would be amazed to notice how little fiction has changed between 1905 and now, as if twentieth-century innovations in thought had never taken place. I mean the fiction of the English-speaking world in particular, and I am not ignoring science fiction, so-called; what I have in mind, and even more so after re-reading Woolf, is the extraordinary omission from serious, articulate, mainstream fiction of the almost unthinkably mysterious auspices under which we lead our societal lives, of the human spectrum in which our technological society is merely one gray flannel shade. The novel still has its head buried in the kitty-litter of Arnold Enoch Bennett, even though, behind the ostrich's behind, so to speak, there has come into view, as any merely casual reader of the New York *Times* will know, the identifiable edge of the universe. I cannot think that Woolf would not have responded to such a juxtaposition, built it into her prose and made her prose move toward it. After all, what concerned her most was not how the weather was (that animal-shooter's red badge of lyricism), or a Building Society Secretary's dream of a mortgaged paradise—nurseries, fountains, libraries, dining rooms, drawing rooms, marriages, or even miraculous barges that "bring tropical fruit to Camberwell by eight o'clock in the morning." What mattered most was the amazingness of being alive in the total context; and that is something one never gets over in the same way as one can get over being rich, say, or neurotic, or bad at arithmetic. In this, she comes close to another novelist who, expert with surfaces, images, and words themselves, has often been thought unfeeling or suavely aloof: Nabokov, who as a matter of fact writes this in *Speak, Memory*:

> Whenever I start thinking of my love for a person, I am in the habit of immediately drawing radii from my love—from my heart, from the tender nucleus of a personal matter—to monstrously remote points of the universe. Something impels me to measure the consciousness of my love against such unimaginable and incalculable things as the behavior of nebulae (whose very remoteness seems a form of insanity), the dreadful pitfalls of eternity, the unknowledgeable beyond the unknown, the helplessness, the cold, the sickening interpenetrations of space and time. It is a pernicious habit, but I can do nothing about it. It can be compared to the incontrollable flick of an insomniac's tongue checking a jagged tooth in the night of his mouth and bruising itself in doing so but still persevering.

He goes on:

> I have to have all space and all time participate in my emotion, in my mortal love, so that the edge of its mortality is taken off, thus helping me to fight the utter degradation, ridicule, and horror of having developed an infinity of sensation and thought within a finite existence.

Virginia Woolf's version of that superhuman tenderness (in all its senses) can be found in what she says just after coming up with the phrase "the inconclusiveness of the Russian mind," which she compares with the English bent for energetic euphoria. Her main point is this: "It is the sense that there is no answer, that if honestly examined life presents question after question which must be left to sound on and on after the story is over in hopeless interrogation that fills us with a deep, and finally it may be with a resentful, despair." One has only to halt at that comma ("fills us with a deep,") to receive the full vastation before she spells it out. Yet, there is nothing else—the novelist can only, in his quick inventory of the universe he's in, "convey this varying, this unknown annd uncircumscribed spirit, whatever aberration it may display, with as little mixture of the alien and external as possible." No frills. No teddy bears. No distractions (such as, say, cricket, the weather, the stock market) from the underlying existential surd. And none of those "sleek, smooth novels, those portentous and ridiculous biographies," as she calls them, "that milk and watery criticism, those poems melodiously celebrating the innocence of roses and sheep which pass so plausibly for literature at the present time." Ultimately she hits on that nightmare of the ecumenical thinker: the apparent redundancy of the mind itself; and all that can be done is to report on minds to minds, tolerating "the spasmodic, the obscure, the fragmentary, the failure," because these are part of everyone's whole. It is a mature, harsh, and seemingly unhappy conclusion to have to come to, and upon which to base an invitation to the novelists of her own day. In the main, she accepted it herself, better than almost anyone; but she did so, not in the miser's verbal pellets of those who like their English plain, but in a complex, rippling prose that reproduces the mind's own motion amid a universe in which it feels beside the non-point. Her words, indeed, are the outpatients of a mind always, as minds are, in isolation.

II

Not only, then, is it not enough to recognize that she was attuned to the spirit of the age, as to a universe whose mathematics has something incalculable about it, we should be glad that at least one of the writers ordinarily dubbed genteel or whimsical had a mind subtle and unprejudiced enough to envision life as a total process inseparable from a radiant universe whose very fabric, as Orlando says, "is magic," whether in the red and hairy bulbs thrust into the humus of Kew Gardens in October or in light now reaching us that left Berenice's Hair before even the Sun and the Earth had formed. It is indeed possible, for us as well as Orlando, to observe how the mind becomes "a fluid that flow[s] round things and enclose[s] them completely," so much so that what she called "the narrow plank of the present" gives way to the Max Planck of timeless quanta. Connoisseur of social surfaces that Virginia Woolf was, she never lost sight of, or sense of, the mysteries that Creation—with its big-league capital C—and creation, with its lower-berth small c, irrefragably are.

That is what is so modern about her, as about Lucretius, say, whereas the ostentatiously modish stuff of so many science fiction writers has a vapidly obsolescent air: its prose is as dull as its cult. A quality of Woolf's, a rare and hardly imitable one, transcends even the significance of her writings on financial and intellectual freedom for women; I mean her uncategorical sense of wonder, her perpetual sense of the imminence of new forms, her being perpetually at her own disposal—what André Gide called disponibility. Let me exemplify. Looking the other day at an extraordinary composite photograph of the Milky Way, made by all-sky cameras, I saw a long, corrugated, transparent sausage crammed with planetary nebulae, dust clouds, and diffraction haloes: the peristalsis of a cosmic gut, both awesome and oddly homely. Yet it was Woolf, and not Beckett or Borges or even Joyce, of modern authors, that came to mind: not because she was overtly scientific, or professedly exobiological, in avocation; indeed, she insists less on nothingness than Beckett does, less on runic pattern than Borges, less on relativistic fission-fusion than Joyce. In fact, what brought her to mind was, to borrow Coleridge's word, her casually esemplastic power which transforms the many into the one, partly by discovering that everything is partly something else anyway: a particle a wave, a door a tree, a bush a bear, a sheep even in part a tall Mayfair house; partly by submitting herself to a process neatly expressed by Husserl when he writes in *Cartesian Meditations* that "Daily practical living is naïve. It is immersion in the already-given world, whether it be experiencing, or thinking, or valuing, or acting." I mean, and I think he means, something anonymous, almost impersonal: one is invaded; one achieves a naïvety of a higher level. Put shortly, this special gift of hers is a unifying innocence which, far from being uneducated or uncivil, both educates and civilizes; puts us on nodding terms with the infinite, on ecumenical terms with the finite, and gives us a *pied à terre* in the hinterland of harmony: the condition in which everything belongs.

An exhaustive devotee, with mind's eye perfectly adjusted for her deliberate and inadvertent tokens, would track her all the way from the Forsterian *The Voyage Out* (1915) to death by water in 1941: from the poignant figure-ground recognitions of Rachel the ewe-lamb, against a busy fresco of those *sui generis* misfits known as British tourists, to the noumenal quadrille done by four young Londoners, overlapping and withdrawing, in the Dostoyevskian *Night and Day* (1919); from the empty-centered ring nebula of minds in *Jacob's Room* (1922) to the organic complementarity of Septimus and Mrs. Dalloway of three years later; from the split and multiplied awareness of Mr. Ramsey in that diachronic Fingal's Cave of the Hebrides, *To the Lighthouse* (1927), the finesse of whose sea-music eludes Mr. Ramsay's inductive *geometrie*, to the three-century-long Moebius strip of reciprocal identities that is festively twisted together in *Orlando* (1928); from the magistrally intuitive brain chorus of *The Waves* (1931) to the generational overlaps of *The Years* (1937) and the visionary pageant that succeeds by including within itself a visionary pageant that flops, in *Between the Acts* (1941). What a consistent yet minimally repetitious invigilation of consciousness it is, this *oeuvre*, a tide of long fictions coming in again and again upon the one-hundred billion brain cells of each and every one of us, a prose corpus in which, and in response to which, metaphors no longer can be said to be mixed, whereas the mix is certainly metaphorical for *rizomata panton:* the all of created things, in which in a cosmic sense, just as amid the characteral permutations in an accomplice sense, we see ourselves (our *selves*) and perhaps enlightenedly fail to recognize *who* we are while discovering *what.*

III

I would like now to restrict myself, and my view of Woolf's vision, to what many think her most extravagant, most exuberant novel, *Orlando,* published at the midpoint of her career. Born male in the Elizabethan age to wealth and status, as the benign paraphrast of one blurb puts it, Orlando through fingersnap androgyny and a well-tempered time machine turns into a Victorian woman of thirty at the bottom of page 137 of the Harvest paperback edition: a transsexual without benefit of surgery. Reading her twentieth-century adventures, one wonders why Woolf didn't adjust her character into Orland*a*, or even neuter her into a mutant of the twenty-first century, Orland*on*, as well. Beyond that dysgenic hypothesis the mind spins dizzily under Woolf's impetus, reminting Orlando(a)(on) as the first and subsequent person forms of the verb for not just changing sex, but for Ovidian metamorphoses of all kinds: *orlando, orlandeis, orlandei, orlandoume, orlandete, orlandoun.* Very irregular, of course, because the results include, I don't doubt, one Elizabethan Gregor Samsa, a Victorian griffin or manticore, and a twentieth-century nymphet who, an apparent mermaid, ingests ectoplasm while living in sin in a Hampstead motel with H.G. Wells. The possibilities, as Woolf's limited permutation reveals, are endless, and it is an invincibly solemn reader of this novel who does not respond to its ebullient playfulness with gratuitous pantomime of his, her, own, and does not recognize how close Woolf came to the Borges who is the impresario of imaginary beings, the Calvino who in *Cosmicomics* upsets the laws of physics for intergalactic jollifications, the Beckett whose Watt miscellaneously talks backward and walks in the same way, whose Mahood is an aged fetus, whose Belacqua is a Dublin fugitive from the *Purgatorio.* If by now we have not accustomed our minds to doubleness, anachronism, sea-changes, and compound ghosts, we should not be reading twentieth-century literature, or even literature at all. For Woolf, what is imagined exists, has been irrevocably added to the sum of created things, thus reaffirming and proving the notion of an open-ended universe.

But her scope was wider than imaginative play for the sake of exercise. I think she saw too the element of play in the universe at large: the sheer foison, if I may use an old word, of the supposed, uncatalogable All; the web, the variety, the chancy interrelatedness of things, including the accident that human life possibly is. Unlike some writers who inspect the edifice of convention and find it intact, she inspected the flux of the universe and found it tactless. Especially in *Orlando*, that sample of available options, a novel whose mindscape is worth, just briefly, reducing to just the kind of scheme which it exists to dissipate.

Quite early on, Orlando metaphorically ties his heart to an oak tree and lies there by it, so still that the deer step nearer, the rooks wheel round him, and the swallows dip and circle, and the dragonflies shoot past, "As if," runs Woolf's simile, "all the fertility and amorous activity of a summer's evening were woven web-like about his body." An Orlando may indeed thus link himself to the universe, feeling both enclosed and supported by it. That is the close, hemmed-in version, but there is another as unlike it as web is unlike pod, and this is open, incalculably contingent coincidence: "Thus, the most ordinary movement in the world, such as sitting down at a table and pulling the inkstand towards one, may agitate a thousand odd, disconnected fragments, now bright, now dim, hanging and bobbing and dipping and flaunting, like the underlinen of a family of fourteen on a line in a gale of wind." Visibly, no body, no sensibility, can be out of touch with the field it is in, whether the operant forces, or stimuli, be visible or not. There is an ineluctable ground for each figure, and each figure helps to compose the ground for something else. Thus, one is just as ultimately related to the inkstand manufacturer as to the oak tree, the deer, the birds, the dragonflies, and by implicaiton to, say, silversmiths,, miners, convulsions of earth's mantle, and so by causality to whichever cosmogony one happens to favor. All that, for needing to ink a pen's nib; or for, however, shortly, fancying one has a heart of oak. Implicit in both purlieus, of course, there is the rheumatism that afflicts the English bucolic lounger as much as the penman. You ache when you stand up; your arm aches as you reach for the inkstand. These are, however remotely initiated, effects of the universe, complexer than any neurology; earnests of involuntary membership that can be indefinitely extrapolated to link us up with quasars receding at 82 percent of the speed of light, the musculature of the flea, the suicide of Virginia Woolf. Call it repercussive identity, or first-cause resonance, this vision of hers, quite abolishing compartments and categories, takes its impetus from her quite uncasuistically accepting the *uni*-ness of the universe. She has enough of the unknown to go on: what she knows she knows affects her; what she knows she doesn't know affects her too. It all ends up in the mind, in which no mosaic is arbitrary, in which no random juxtaposition of items cannot be cogently interrelated, all the way from Mary Queen of Scots's prayerbook, which she held on the scaffold, in which Orlando finds a bloodstain, a lock of hair, and a crumb of pastry, contributing a flake of tobacco of her own—all the way from that "humane jumble" to her irritated recognition that a sight of her ankles may cause a sailor to fall from a masthead.

Of course, too sensitive an attunement to this connectedness of things can paralyze. Contemplative excess misses trains, pays no taxes, never quite gets down the first word, "He———"of the novel *Orlando*. In Woolf's work and life, of course, the vision became almost competitive, combative even. Confronted by the enigma of Creation, she nodded, and invented enigmas of her own: not symbols, or allegorical emblems, but combinations just as odd and as beguiling as the universe itself, full of conflicts and dissonance. In the opening pages of *Orlando* we find "such a welter of opposites—of the night and the blazing candles, of the shabby poet and the great Queen, of silent fields and the clatter of serving men— that he could see nothing; or only a hand." A mild version, to be sure, it anticipates the much later and much more imposing welter that appears as a pyramid, or hecatomb, or trophy, "a conglomeration at any rate of the most heterogeneous and ill-assorted objects, piled higgledy-piggledy in a vast mound where the statue of Queen Victoria now stands!" Brought into being by a sunbeam, this bizarre miscellany deserves to be itemized in full, in the very words that imbricate it, and then I can wheel something, or several things, up to it, as to something as commanding as a ziggurat of skulls, or the crucifixion, or the pyramid into which the dying in the gas chambers of the extermination camps involuntarily arranged themselves. The passage follows:

> Draped about a vast cross of fretted and floriated gold were widow's weeds and bridal veils; hooked on to other excrescences were crystal palaces, bassinettes, military helmets, memorial wreaths, trousers, whiskers, wedding cakes, cannon, Christmas trees, telescopes, extinct monsters, globes, maps, elephants and mathematical-instruments—the whole supported like a gigantic coat of arms on the right side by a female figure clothed in flowing white; on the left, by a portly gentleman wearing a frock-coat and sponge-bag trousers. The incongruity of the objects, the association of the fully clothed and the partly draped, the garishness of the different colors and their plaid-like juxtapositions afflicted Orlando with the most profound dismay. She had never, in all her life, seen anything at once so indecent, so hideous, and so monumental. It might, and indeed it must

be, the effect of the sun on the water-logged air; it would vanish with the first breeze that blew; but for all that, it looked, as she drove past, as if it were destined to endure for ever. Nothing, she felt, sinking back into the corner of her coach, no wind, rain, sun, or thunder, could ever demolish that garish erection. Only those noses would mottle and the trumpets would rust; but there they would remain, pointing east, west, south, and north, eternally. She looked back as her coach swept up Constitution Hill. Yes, there is was, still beaming placidly in a light which—she pulled her watch out of her fob—was, of course, the light of twelve o'clock midday. None other could be so prosaic, so matter of fact, so impervious to any hint of dawn or sunset, so seemingly calculated to last for ever. She was determined not to look again.

Reading that passage, and re-reading it with the contributive complicity of one who salutes a kindred spirit, I am reminded of nothing so much as Antonin Artaud's appeal for "a fabricated Being . . . entirely invented, corresponding to nothing yet disquieting by nature, capable of reintroducing on the stage a little breath of . . . metaphysical fear." Woolf's passage does all of that and more, being the concocted version of what De Quincey called an "involute" and spelled out, in *Suspiria de Profundis*, as follows: "Far more of our deepest thoughts and feelings pass to us through perplexed combinations of *concrete* objects, pass to us as *involutes* (if I may coin that word) in compound experiences incapable of being disentangled, than ever reach us *directly*, and in their own abstract shapes." How awkwardly constructed that sentence of De Quincey's is; yet I think he hits on something profound: a surdic or irrational element in experience, an element which resists—indeed prohibits—the half-clarifications of symbolism and can best be exemplifed through the kind of "fabricated Being," on page as on stage, that Artaud described.

In this dimension, of surdic improvisation, Woolf excels, and her capacity for creating something unforgettable yet not altogether meaningful is expressionism raised to its highest power. Of course, there are other examples in *Orlando*: I think of the park-size space that suddenly opens in the flank of a sunbaked hill near Constantinople and reveals an English summer's day that turns to snow, and of Eusebius Chubb, in whose disordered imagination cucumbers accost him, cauliflowers grow higher than the trees, and hens incessantly lay "eggs of no special tint." Mindful of the thirty-five folio pages he has written only that morning, "all about nothing," and of his wife in the throes of her fifteenth confinement, he notes the sky above the British Isles, a "vast feather bed" reproducing the "undistinguished fecundity of the garden, the bedroom, and the henroost," goes indoors, writes "the passage quoted above," and lays his head in a gas oven.

Predictably, too, Woolf's eminent lighthouse flashes into mind, plain as a pikestaff to the heirs of Freud, yet puzzling to several, including my onetime mentor William York Tindall, who in the chapter entitled "The Forest of Symbols" in his *Forces in Modern British Literature 1885–1956* observes, not without leprechaun malice, that: "What this stark erection embodies, as we might expect by now, is far from simple. Suggesting God, death, eternity, any absolute, and the goal of all endeavors, this solitary tower amid the flux provokes, without altogether satisfying, our curiosity as it informs us."

The more it seems to inform us, the more curiosity it arouses, as if epistemology were merely the fur on a forked tongue. One thinks of Sir James Jeans, in *The Mysterious Universe*, spelling out that magnetism depends on the peculiar properties of the twenty-six, twenty-seven, and twenty-eight-electron atoms, or that radioactivity is confined almost entirely to atoms having from eighty-three to ninety-two electrons, yet having to add in each case "we do not know why." Can it be that his mathematical universe is the graffito of a hare-brained numerologist? The fact is, Woolf knew in her heart, and knew by heart, that explicability is always at least one step away from definitive contact with Being. Twenty-six, twenty-seven, twenty-eight atoms make a magnet; Orlando's thirty-six and three hundred at 12:00 midnight on October 11, 1928, make a wild goose chase, much as 365 bedrooms in her ancestral home, or the sixty-eight or seventy-two years allotted on tombstones, or the "seventy-six different times all ticking in the mind at once" and the "say two thousand and fifty-two" optional selves "all having lodgement at one time or another in the human spirit." Neither statistician, nor numerologist, Woolf shares Kandinsky's question of 1910: "To discuss mysteries by means of the mysterious—is not that the meaning?" In short, she counters God's enigmas with enigmas of her own making: reifications that echo deification without the faintest touch of dogma.

IV

Having said this much; having credited Virginia Woolf with an antihermeneutic poieisis in which negative capability partners a deep relish of creative evolution; having installed at least a couple of her conglomerative edifices alongside such other invented enigmas as Kafka's Great Wall of China, Jarry's Ubu Roi, Mallarmé's Faun, Breton's Nadja, Genet's Miracle of the Rose, the piano tuners in Beckett's *Watt*, the rhinoceros of Ionesco, the *Schmurz* of Boris Vian's play *The Empire-Builders* (a big inflatable-looking whipping boy), I must, almost redundantly, but not quite, draw attention to an entire idiom of the arbitrary. *Orlando* teems with it. When there is nothing left to do, for example, send to Norway for elkhounds. Why? Why not? The gypsies think Orlando's four- or five-hundred years of descent "the meanest possible," going back themselves two or three thousand. Mistaken for coal, a black cat gets shovelled on the fire. The phrase "the biscuits ran out" comes to represent "kissing a negress in the dark when one has just read Bishop Berkeley's philosophy for the tenth time." "Life literature Greene toady," runs Orlando's wire to Shel, ending, "Rattigan Glumphoboo," which was her own cipher language for "a very complicated spiritual state—which if the reader puts all his intelligence at our service he may discover for himself." In every human being, we learn from this novel, "a vacillation from one sex to the other takes place," which fact may or may not fortify us for the catadioptric moment when Orlando cries, "You're a woman, Shel!" and Shel cries back, "You're a man, Orlando!" Since the gypsies have no word for beautiful, Woolf cunningly obliges Orlando to exclaim "How good to eat!" when praising the sunset.

If these textural insinuations will not convert the reader to relativism, perhaps Orlando's winged and whiskered ink blot will, "something between a bat and a wombat," a modifiable trouvaille like the piece of glass in the story "Solid Objects" or the mark on the wall which turns out to be a real snail amid the Bayeux tropistry of moorhens, water beetles, and fish "balanced against the stream like flags blown out." It was at just such marks that Leonardo da Vinci counselled his students to peer in the hope of "arousing the mind to various inventions." Such was hopeful phenomenology in the late fifteenth and early sixteenth centuries. Enticed by that creative perceivership, Orlando thinks: "What a phantasmagoria the mind is and meeting-place of dissemblables," only to be kibitzed by her novelist-proprietor, who adds "and so bewildered as usual by the multitude of things which call for explanation and imprint their message without leaving any hint as to their meaning upon the mind, she threw her cheroot out of the window and went to bed."

If the reader protests that he cannot "understand" this protean novel—this "biography," this auto-fiction, this concentric textural opera, this chaosmos—he can hardly pretend he has not been warned. Remember, Woolf instructs him (though late in Orlando's rainbow career), "we are dealing with the most obscure manifestations of the human spirit." The entire thing is miasma, mirage, illusion, but then, as she insists, "illusions are the most valuable and necessary of all things"; the illusionist is among the supreme benefactors, whichever day he chooses to sleep or wake upon

(Orlando *wakes* on the seventh); and "he who robs us of our dreams robs us of our life." Anyone who believes that has an abidingly profound respect for the mind in its own right. And Woolf had.

Addressing herself to the often disparaged activity of "sitting in a chair and thinking," or imagining, Woolf leaves the reader to recite the calendar for himself, initiating him into a special semicreative uneasiness through devices or tricks that look backward to Sterne, and forward to the various practitioners of the so-called *nouveau roman*. The copious roll call of the preface is a cheek in which she can lodge her native tongue. A time-travelling vaudeville, the eight illustrations have a surreptitious blatancy, as if to pun through visual obbligato: *ars longa*, Vita Sackville-West *brevis?* (Never!) Our index, all the way from Lord A. to Christopher Wren, happens to be something we truly need when re-reconnoitering the book, yet it seems a pert travesty of both the scholarly apparatus and of the fictional mode; it is a concordance to a plot which is actually a plot against the reader, who must cope as best he can with the antic brio of the whole: especially when, for example, Woolf suggests he can probably "imagine the passage which should follow": or when, like some bellettristic coastguard, she enforces the six-line limit on Orlando's conclusions about Victorian literature; or when she draws the "said nothing" curtain over a three-hour conversation and, for the talk of Alexander Pope, refers us to sources outside the text. Needless to say, in such a context, it is no breach of any imagined civility to have expendable material included but "properly enclosed in square brackets" (indeed, one thinks of the optional chapters at the back of Julio Cortázar's *Hopscotch* and the Addenda to Beckett's *Watt:* "precious and illuminating material. . . . Only fatigue and disgust prevented its incorporation.") Arguably, such methods, for those who can abide them, send the mind on a chase and provide a sprightliness the reader must match with one of his own.

There are those, of course, who insist upon the purity of fiction, upon some ostensible underivedness, who do not relish invitations to suspend belief, who find such alienation effects not endearing but boorishly cute. I have never been among them, which is why I like the performative affair entitled *Orlando* as much as, say, Claude Simon's *Histoire* or Evan S. Connell's *Points for A Compass Rose*, rather than any product of those antiquarians who keep on trying to invent the nineteenth-century novel in the age of quasars. Woolf's sideshows, bagatelles, optical illusions and elasticated mosaics assist, rather than disrupt, the words ("the thinnest integument for our thoughts"). What keeps on coming through the prose of *Orlando* is the paramountcy of thought as it assimilates, and alters, the spirit of the age—a transaction, as Woolf says, of infinite delicacy, neither combative nor submissive. Orlando him-her-self makes a series of rapid adjustments in the presence of that abiding, fixed entity, the poem entitled "The Oak Tree," while Woolf herself, moving to and from, and through and past Orlando, entertains the relativism of all that can be thought, whether or not the sum of it can be interpreted. As she warns us early in chapter 2, concerning Orlando's week-long sleep, "there is no explaining it. Volumes might be written in interpretation of it; whole religious systems founded upon the signification of it. Our simple duty is to state the facts as far as they are known, and so let the reader make of them what he may." And, embarrassed or confused or (I would hope) intolerably stimulated by the book, he will do just that, with a frown, or with a vengeance, or with complicitous relish.

V

That there is such a thing as the spirit of the age, I do not doubt: or that it forces itself upon us, as Heisenberg says in *Steps Across the Frontiers*, while we are "proceeding as conservatively as possible." Picasso's cubism and Einstein's special theory of relativity appeared in the same year, 1905, not because the two of them were involved in some telepathic symbiosis, but because a certain phase in the European imagination was over: some old shibboleths were done for; some new recognitions were in. Almost a quarter of a century later, *Orlando* epitomized the new indeterminateness of things, not through psychological analysis but through re-creating the almost anonymous sensations that precede, accompany, and often smudge thought: the jazz of consciousness, not so very different from Eddington's jazz of the spheres. Woolf had put it well in a Cambridge lecture of 1928, mentioning reality as "something very erratic, very undependable—now to be found in a dusty road, now in a scrap of newspaper in the street, now in a daffodil in the sun." (Note how she says where each thing is, as if the figure's ground might come as a surprise.) It was to this undependability of things that she addressed herself, willing to seem subjective and diffuse, untidy and incoherent, rather than remain in thrall to the tyranny of an old epistemics or of a defunct societal realism. Sneered at by Nathalie Sarraute, whose imagination came from the Jardin des Plantes—whereas Woolf's seems to have come from Harrod's—Woolf nonetheless invented subconversation long before the era of suspiciousness; in fact, if *Orlando* doesn't make the reader suspicious, it hasn't worked at all. To Rilke's "It submerges us. We organize it. It falls to pieces. We organize it again and fall to pieces ourselves," she adds the transcendent punch line: We are meant to. Whatever one fails to learn from Woolf, one does learn gratitude for the senses five, for innumerable felicities of combination from within the permeable bubble of Woolfian rudiments: the red, thick stream of life; the unreliable kingfisher; the joyful treadmilling of "She wrote. She wrote. She wrote"; and the imperative repetition, " 'Ecstasy, ecstasy,' as she stood waiting to cross." As Woolf says so well at her most Daedalian-Promethean, "the nerve which controls the pen winds itself about every fibre of our being, threads the heart, pierces the liver." Through the pen, as Orlando drives fast along the Old Kent Road and out of London, it all falls to pieces, anticipating unconsciousness and death, and then it comes together again as the "green screen"(s) of the countryside show up on both sides of her trajectory. It's all in the mind, as coercive optimists tell us, whereas the All never is; but, in Woolf's case, enough of the All, mentally skirmished with, does conjure up the total, the symbol of whose teleology is one wild goose. Chase it or not.

It is instructive to note that, in a recent novel, *Neutre* (1972), by Hélène Cixous, a French spiritual descendant of Woolf, the title noun signifies *ne* plus *uter*, meaning *not either*: neither this sex nor that, neither sex nor non-sex, neither singular nor plural, neither now nor then, not even either categorizable or not, but a phoenix-like multiplicity of recognitions through which the personal one becomes an impersonal many. Or just a blur. What *Orlando* was for the late twenties, *Neutre* may well be for the early seventies.

Among all the permutations of creative guesswork, it is such autofictions as these, brain-orphans of Lewis Carroll, that overtly remind us of an ancient principle which, since relativity became a byword, we have rehonored: the hunt for teleology, across the ages, is the history of the mind's adventures in a looking glass. In a word, reflexive: the invitation to paradise is written by ourselves while *Logos* is just a word in the dictionary, a label denoting the best mathematician out of sight; and ultimately all human experience reduces itself to what Woolf called the "silent land," a zone of ineffable yet not unpleasurable bafflement, where "songs without words" (Woolf's phrase) prove as irresistible as indecipherable while, perhaps, answering a child's plea for reassurance: Yes Virginia, there *is* a saving clause—call it inquisitive imagination, which sponsors a stoicism based on the tenuousness of self itself.

At forty-five, in her diary, after an admiring note on her sister Vanessa's children, Woolf reiterated her own preference for art over maternity in face of "this ravaging sense of the shortness and feverishness of life." She saw each individual human life as a complex sentence, short even when at its lengthiest, meaningful only in evolutionary terms, but therefore a sample of a process she found "everlasting and perpetual." In such an agnostic, nonratiocinative dimension, one can only sympathize (or not) with her intuitings, her earth-ecstasy, her knowledge of the mind's exhilaration with itself, just for being available: something, at its least, to play with; something, at its most, with which to mimic the "microscopic eye" of aboriginal man. It is not often that we find so intricate a sense of wonder depressed to the level of diagnosis, or so granitic a vision made manifest in such radiant and, sometimes, bravura, sentences.

HERMIONE LEE

"The Waves"

O*rlando's* "ease and dash" only par-
tially expressed Virginia Woolf's state of mind after *To the Lighthouse*. Behind the "externality" of *Orlando* and *A Room of One's Own* another kind
of novel was being evolved from a "play-poem idea" of "some semi-mystic
very profound life of a woman" in which "time shall be utterly obliterated;
future shall somehow blossom out of the past." The difficult development
from that first mysterious hint of "The Moths" in 1926 to the triumphant
completion of *The Waves* in 1931 is thoroughly charted in the *Diary*,
enabling us to see that, although the form and the subject of the novel
were very much changed, the original conception remained. The life of a
woman against the background of flying moths became "a series of dramatic
soliloquies," but there was a consistent abstract idea behind these changing
forms:

> Now is life very solid or very shifting? I am haunted by the two contra-
> dictions. This has gone on for ever; will last for ever; goes down to the
> bottom of the world—this moment I stand on. Also it is transitory, flying,
> diaphanous. I shall pass like a cloud on the waves. Perhaps it may be that
> though we change, one flying after another, so quick, so quick, yet we
> are somehow successive and continuous we human beings, and show the
> light through.

The diary entry combines allusions to moths and waves in a passage which
recalls the language of "Modern Fiction," but with a slightly different
emphasis. The concepts of the "semi-transparent envelope" and the "shower
of innumerable atoms" shaping themselves "into the life of Monday or

Tuesday" are now applied to "human beings" rather than to "life." *The Waves*, more devoted to abstraction than any of the other novels, uses human beings as case histories to illustrate the nature of life. The concentration on abstract ends requires a further eradication of materialism from the novel; and the terms in which this is envisaged remind us, again, of the transition period between *Night and Day* and *Jacob's Room*:

> What I want now to do is to saturate every atom. I mean to eliminate all waste, deadness, superfluity: to give the moment whole: whatever it includes. Say that the moment is a combination of thought; sensation; the voice of the sea. Waste, deadness, come from the inclusion of things that don't belong to the moment; this appalling narrative business of the realist: getting on from lunch to dinner. It is false, unreal, merely conventional. Why admit anything to literature that is not poetry—by which I mean saturated?

Again, as in the passage describing her discovery of a "new form" for *Jacob's Room* in 1920, she expresses a desire to "enclose everything, everything." But the desire to exclude and eliminate is as powerful, and the emphasis is now on concentration and intensity rather than on "looseness and lightness." The tone of the 1928 diary entry is sterner and more definite, and suggests some disaffection with the methods tried out in *Jacob's Room* and perfected in *To the Lighthouse*. It augurs a radical departure from her previous achievements which seemed to her inevitable: "no other form of fiction suggests itself except as a repetition."

The third-person narrative which characterized the earlier novels is still found in the italicized passages in *The Waves*, the "interludes," but no longer in a fluid, malleable, chameleon style. Instead it is elaborately literary and impersonal, and carefully set apart from the bulk of the novel, a first-person narrative in which the six characters "speak" of themselves. This would suggest that Virginia Woolf is now, for the first and last time, writing what could be called a "stream of consciousness" novel, in which the minds of the characters flow on, as from the inside, with no authorial interpolations. And *The Waves* does seem to fulfil our criteria for such a novel. Apart from the interludes, the action, dialogue, description, factual information, do not exist autonomously, but only (if at all) within the characters' minds. The need for more than one point of view is satisfied, not as in the earlier novels by the chameleon activity of the third-person narrator, but simply by presenting six streams of consciousness rather than one.

The definition, however, is inadequate. If we set a passage from *The Waves* against some excerpts from twentieth-century novels which might be, and have been, described by the term "stream of consciousness," the effect is one of dissimilarity.

In this way, for two consecutive summers I used to sit in the heat of our Combray garden, sick with a longing inspired by the book I was then reading for a land of mountains and rivers, where I could see an endless vista of sawmills, where beneath the limpid currents fragments of wood lay mouldering in beds of watercress; and near by, rambling and clustering along low walls, purple flowers and red. And since there was always lurking in my mind the dream of a woman who would enrich me with her love, that dream in those two summers used to be quickened with the freshness and coolness of running water; and whoever she might be, the woman whose image I called to mind, purple flowers and red would at once spring up on either side of her like complementary colours.

(Marcel Proust, *Swann's Way*)

The far east. Lovely spot it must be: the garden of the world, big lazy leaves to float about on, cactuses, flowery meads, snaky lianas they call them. Wonder is it like that. Those Cinghalese lobbing around in the sun, in *dolce far niente*. Not doing a hand's turn all day. Sleep six months out of twelve. Too hot to quarrel. Influence of the climate. Lethargy. Flowers of idleness. The air feeds most. Azotes. Hothouse in Botanic gardens. Sensitive plants. Waterlilies. Petals too tired to. Sleeping sickness in the air. Walk on roseleaves.

(James Joyce, *Ulysses*)

First of all shall I have a haystack? Well idealized that might be quite good. First of all then we will consider the haystack. It stands up in a sunny field by the side of but out from a chestnut tree. So. The hay has been cut. Of course. It isnt imported hay in that stack. Well all the rest of the field, it is a very big field, it stretches away far and wide, and there on it are the swatches of white hay that have been left over. There it lies. So. There is a blue sky overhead and some white puff clouds bowling along in front of a summery wind. Not the sort you say as you crouch under the breakwater: "I will say this about Shrimpton-on-Strand you can always get out of the wind one side of the breakwater or the other, or under the bathing machine."

Well now into this picture empty of all human interest comes Pompey Casmilus. Here at last, she says, is the right haystack . . . So I lay back on my ivory haystack and there is nobody else in the whole wide world and so I fall asleep. No dreams. No dreams.

(Stevie Smith, *Novel on Yellow Paper*)

"I shall edge behind them," said Rhoda, "as if I saw someone I know. But I know no one. I shall twitch the curtain and look at the moon. Draughts of oblivion shall quench my agitation. The door opens; the tiger leaps. The door opens; terror rushes in; terror upon terror, pursuing me.

Let me visit furtively the treasures I have laid apart. Pools lie on the other side of the world reflecting marble columns. The swallow dips her wings in dark pools. But here the door opens and people come; they come towards me. Throwing faint smiles to mask their cruelty, their indifference, they seize me. The swallow dips her wings; the moon rides through blue seas alone. I must take his hand; I must answer. But what answer shall I give? I am thrust back into this clumsy, this ill-fitting body, to receive the shafts of his indifference and his scorn, I who long for marble columns and pools on the other side of the world where the swallow dips her wings."

(Virginia Woolf, *The Waves*)

Evidently the stream of consciousness novel in the first third of the century is a hybrid genre. The methods used by these four narrators for examining an exotic alternative to reality are very different. Marcel orders his child-hood sensations, with retrospective irony, into a completed picture designed like the illustration to a book. Bloom's fantasy, nourished by his accu-mulated perceptions and information, is immediate: the sentence structure, by avoiding the imposition of a verb tense, gives us the impression that we are hearing his mind as it works. Pompey Casmilus's present-tense narrative, which shows that her daydream is recurrent, creates the sound of a voice recounting a humorous anecdote. Rhoda's soliloquy resembles none of these. Like Marcel, she presents an elaborate, literary version of her thought process, but unlike him she is supposed to be thinking about a scene which is actually taking place. In spite of this, there is no attempt, as in Joyce, to evoke natural immediacy, no realistic representation of the jerks and twists of the mind as it is idly running along. Indeed, there is no sense of idleness or relaxation: the daydream and the public experience are pitched at the same level of intensity. There is no room for the humour available to the other three writers. The sound of the spoken voice is not simulated in order to create an ironic distance between the narrator and her own experience. Instead, a formal, rhythmic monologue subjugates the repre-sentation of personality or action to a series of physical images which are made to stand for a state of mind. The effect is that of a translation of life and consciousness into a rigid set of analogies, as though a character on stage were being represented by two actors, one carrying out a mime in slow motion while the other comments on the meaning of the actions. Coldness and intensity are strangely mixed; agony and fear are formalized, while they are being communicated, into rhythms and images. The rhythmic prose which is substituted for a naturalistic representation of speech or thoughts does not distinguish between descriptions, action, con-versation, reflections or recollection. Whether Rhoda is young or old, happy or sad, excited or despondent, it does not vary.

The style is the same of all the characters. It is characteristic of Susan to express herself in simple statements ("The meat is stood in the oven; the bread rises in a soft dome"), but the others may do this too. And Susan is not confined to words of one syllable—"I love, I hate". Describing how Bernard makes phrases, she makes one herself: "Now you mount like an air-ball's string, higher and higher through the layers of the leaves." She is as liable as the others to employ the Latinisms which are supposed to be Neville's idiosyncrasy: going to school, she says: "All here is false; all is meretricious." The tautology is there for the sake of the rhythm and is not in character. Parallelism is introduced throughout irrespective of who is speaking, patterned out of the repetition of certain parts of speech:

Bernard:	They too bubbled up, they also escaped.
Jinny:	The torments, the divisions of your lives.
Rhoda:	After all these callings [. . .] these pluckings and searchings
Neville:	I choose at random; I choose the obvious.
Louis:	People go on passing; they go on passing.
Susan:	Everything is now set; everything is fixed.

This rhythm creates a long prose-poem. Though recurrent rhythm has been an important ingredient of the earlier novels, nowhere else has it been consistent and insistent enough to suggest that the book should be read as lines of poetry rather than as lines of prose.

> How strange that people should sleep
> that people should put out the lights
>   and go upstairs.
> They have taken off their dresses,
> they have put out white night-gowns.
> There are no lights in any of these houses.
> There is a line of chimneypots against the sky;
> and a street lamp or two burning,
> as lamps burn when nobody needs them.
> The only people in the streets
> are poor people hurrying.
> There is no one coming or going in this street;
> the day is over.
> A few policemen stand at the corners.
> Yet night is beginning.

The effect is sustained with extraordinary ease throughout. *The Waves* is not difficult to read as poetry; its rhythm is agreeable and insidious. But it is difficult to read as a novel, in that its emphasis on rhythm overwhelms distinctions of character. Only the content enables us to distinguish between the voices. An idiosyncrasy of speech—Louis's Australian accent—can be described but not rendered, since, obviously, the formal framework of "said Louis," "said Bernard," is a sustained irony: real speech is not being represented.

Given a formal, undifferentiated style, distinctions can only be made on the basis of the images. This brings the novel dangerously close to a play of humours in which bits of the human personality are parcelled out among the different characters. Bernard's twisting of little toys, Neville's call to "one person," Rhoda's dreamland of swallows and pillars, Louis's vision of the Nile, Susan's screwed-up pocket-handkerchief and Jinny's yellow scarf seem at times like routine reminders of which "humour" is speaking. But there is a counterweight to this limiting technique of identification in the fact that many images are shared between the characters. The first utterances of the six as children immediately suggest how fluid is the relationship between individual and common experience. To some extent distinctions are made. Louis voices an image which will be a constant symbol of his insecurity, the great chained beast stamping on the shore. The metaphor suggests a vivid imagination and is in contrast to Susan's direct physical impressions—"I see a slab of pale yellow"—and her apprehension of concrete, ordinary objects—"Biddy has smacked down the bucket on the kitchen flags." Rhoda's images evoke the pressure of hostile or indifferent elements on unprotected things—the snail flattening the grass blades, the cold water running on the mackerel, the bird left singing alone. But the "first impressions" suggest the common experience of the six children as much as their differences. The mackerel in the bowl, the bucket on the kitchen flags and the scraping of fish scales might be noticed by the same voice. As they grow older, the voices become more distinct. But the narrative sustains their common consciousness through the general use of images like circles or waves, and through their participation in each other's private figures of speech, Neville and Susan, for instance, both thinking of Bernard as a loose, dangling thread (as he does himself), Jinny and Louis both associating Rhoda with the petals with which she herself identifies, and Bernard, finally, incorporating all their lives in himself:

> Here on my brow is the blow I got when Percival fell. Here on the nape of my neck is the kiss Jinny gave Louis. My eyes fill with Susan's tears. I see far away, quivering like a gold thread, the pillar Rhoda saw, and feel the rush of the wind of her flight where she leapt.

Percival, whose death Bernard here assimilates into his own experience, is the central, dominant example of an image shared by all the speakers. Images may become words, but they do not use words. Percival is silent, then absent, and then dead, so that he can be used as a catalyst for the feelings of the six narrators. None of them wants to think about Percival himself, only about Percival as a gauge by which to measure their own lives. This is so even when Percival is present:

> We are drawn into this communion by some deep, some common emotion. Shall we call it, conveniently, "love?" Shall we say 'love of Percival' because Percival is going to India?
>
> No, that is too small, too particular a name. We cannot attach the width and spread of our feelings to so small a mark.

After his death it is hard for them to concentrate on him. Once Percival's obsequies are done, Bernard and Jinny have to go back into the "machine" of ordinary life; it is an artificial effort to think of the dead, and after a time it becomes a false gesture, like covering him with lilies. His death is generalized by Louis ("all deaths are one death"), forgotten by Rhoda ("I seldom think of Percival now"), and merged with other experiences even by Neville: "You are you. That is what consoles me for the lack of many things [. . .] and the flight of youth and Percival's death [. . .]." Instead, the image of Percival's death gives birth, as it were, to an idea of youth and life: it is that which becomes memorable about Percival, as though he is resurrected in the continuing lives of his friends. This paradox is not only found in Bernard's last phrases, but, earlier, in the way that Susan and Jinny both turn the idea of going to India into an image of life and renewal:

> "His eyes will see when mine are shut," I think. "I shall go mixed with them beyond my body and shall see India."

> The activity is endless. And to-morrow it begins again; to-morrow we make Saturday. Some take train for France; others ship for India. [. . .] Life comes; Life goes; we make life.

Images are not only shared among the voices, but also overlap between the voices and the interludes. Interspersed with the expressions of personal consciousness from birth to death are the descriptions of an impersonal scene—a beach, a garden, a house—from dawn to dusk (which broadens out occasionally into more remote, exotic settings). Since the style of the two are different, the interludes being far more effusive, lyrical and alliterative, it is something of a shock to find the speakers appropriating details from a universe which is indifferent to them (Louis, for instance, comparing himself to "a warden" carrying "a lamp from cell to cell," an image which has been used for light on the hills in the fifth interlude). At such moments *the* world becomes *their* world, particularly at the end, when Bernard turns the scene of the interludes into his vision of truth, and confirms our supposition that the house of the interludes is the house where the children's lives began.

The overlap is made more plausible by the sustained anthropomorphism of the interludes. In the first one, every figure of speech is used to relate the processes of nature to those of human beings. Sea, air, waves and light, become a cloth, a veil, the sediment in an old wine bottle, the arm of a woman, a lamp, the blades of a fan and a bonfire. It is the same in the third, where we find a characteristically elaborate image for the rim of flotsam on the shore "as if some light shallop had foundered and burst its sides and the sailor had swum to land and bounded up the cliff and left his frail cargo to be washed ashore." The birds are characterized as companionable, fearful, apprehensive, emulous, aware, quizzical and savage. The waves are turbaned warriors with assegais (an image also used by Rhoda and Louis in the fourth section to describe those involved in the dance of life). The cruelty of maturing life is imaged by the vicious warfare in the undergrowth between birds and sluggy matter; and in the third section all the voices use birds as images. Obviously a consistent analogy is being made between non-human growth and decay and the human lifespan. But the effect of the anthropomorphism is peculiar; the inhuman scenes seem, because of it, to be bursting with active life, and to provide (like the activity of nature in the "Time Passes" section of *To the Lighthouse*) a threat to the individual human consciousness.

The mixture of analogy and opposition between nature and man is found particularly in the treatment of the waves themselves, where there is an unresolved ambiguity. Are the waves meant to suggest the human lives, or are they the detached, impersonal forces of fatality? The last sentence of the book, *"The waves broke on the shore,"* may suggest that Bernard's encounter with death is itself a wave, another inevitable part of existence; but it also implies that his individual effort is set against an arbitrary, uncaring universe. But the irony of the last line has to do with language as well as life. Bernard, in his last soliloquy, has used the images of the interludes as his own phrases, almost as though he were the author of *The Waves*. The world described in the interludes is that of "the house, the garden, and the waves breaking" which make up Bernard's vision of "the world seen without a self." At the moment of seeing the world as it really is, he realizes that his phrases are useless to him; only words of one syllable will serve. The criticism is not only of Bernard's phrase-making self, but also of the elaborately written interludes. And when Bernard stops

speaking, only words of one syllable are left: "*The waves broke on the shore.*"
Both narrators have had finally to resort to the simplest of terms.

The interweaving of images suggests that the book is about the
relationships between the six characters, who all, not only Bernard, measure
their own lives against the other five, bringing up in their "spoons" another
of those minute objects which we call optimistically "characters of our
friends." These lines of thought, netting the voices together like a "string
of six little fish that let themselves be caught while a million others leap
and sizzle," create the narrative links in a book without much plot. Twice
Susan thinks of Jinny in London and the next voice to speak is Jinny's, in
London. But, apart from two meetings in Percival's honour, the extent of
their involvement in adult life is uncertain. Bernard pays visits to Jinny
after Percival's death, to Susan in the country and to Neville in his room.
Rhoda and Louis are lovers for a time; Jinny prepares her room "in case
Bernard comes, or Neville or Louis." Their relationships, however, do not
seem vital or impassioned. The information that Susan has always loved
Bernard, or that Rhoda and Louis are lovers, seems to have little relevance
to the voices. The quality of the book is abstract, not personal.

In thus disallowing the emphasis on relationships which was an
important part of *Mrs Dalloway* and *To the Lighthouse,* in favour of an
emphasis on the essences of personality, Virginia Woolf deprives herself of
some of her most powerful qualities. She loses the fine tension between
outer and inner levels of experience which makes the party scenes of *Mrs
Dalloway* and *To the Lighthouse* more interesting than the dinner scenes in
The Waves. Denying her characters idiosyncrasies and social mannerisms,
she denies herself the kind of humour which energized her treatment of
Mr Ramsay. There are limited comic possibilities when the characters exist
at a level where they must take themselves seriously, though Jinny provides
comedy by virtue of being the most superficial "humour"—"Here is Percival
[. . .] he has not dressed"—and Bernard by being the wittiest, as in his
description of Percival's Indian triumphs:

> By applying the standards of the west, by using the violent language that
> is natural to him, the bullock-cart is righted in less than five minutes.
> The Oriental problem is solved.

Though the resistance of her chosen form to comedy may not seem
very important, it is part of the lack of distinction between different levels
of intensity which makes *The Waves* the most arduous of her novels. The
important points of climax—the vision of unity at the dinner for Percival,
the momentary fusion of separate selves at Hampton Court, Bernard's final

vision of truth and his ensuing encounter with death—are movingly and strenuously lyrical, but they do not stand out vividly from the rest of the writing.

Yet, in spite of the levelling effect of the style, her natural bent for characterization will not be suppressed. The outer life presses in through vivid anecdotes. Neville watches distastefully as Bernard mops up with his handkerchief the pool of tea running over *Don Juan*. Louis leaves his table in the steamy eating house, slipping a too large tip under the plate. Jinny writes a note and powders her nose giving "her body a flick with the whip." Though Bernard's wife, Susan's husband, and Jinny's and Neville's lovers hardly exist, the moments of active emotion they induce are as strongly and crudely presented as the ordinary material of conventional novels:

> You left me. The descent into the Tube was like death. We were cut up, we were dissevered by all those faces and the hollow wind that seemed to roar down there over desert boulders. I sat staring in my own room. By five I knew that you were faithless. I snatched the telephone and the buzz, buzz, buzz, of its stupid voice in your empty room battered my heart down, when the door opened and there you stood. That was the most perfect of our meetings. But these meetings, these partings, finally destroy us.
>
> (Neville)

> And then that rasping, dog-fish-skin-like roughness—those black arrows of shivering sensation, when she misses the post, when she does not come. Out rush a bristle of horned suspicions, horror, horror, horror—but what is the use of painfully elaborating these consecutive sentences when what one needs is nothing consecutive but a bark, a groan? And years later to see a middle-aged woman in a restaurant taking off her cloak.
>
> (Bernard)

But such activities, like the places described in the novel, are subsumed in the lyric rhythm of consciousness, and become images. Action and environment inevitably take on a universal quality when treated in this way, and this creates a difficulty about the novel's social assumptions.

Obviously all Virginia Woolf's novels deal—though not flatteringly or complacently—with a limited social mileu, and betray a lack of imaginative reach over the classes outside her own experience. Septimus Smith is convincingly portrayed (at least as well as Leonard Bast, Forster's comparable character in *Howards End*), but he is, after all, mad, which gives him a classless air. The charladies and women singing outside tube stations may act as potent symbols, but they are not characterized at any more convincing level than is found in "The mothers of Pimlico gave suck to their young" or "A woman of the lower classes was wheeling a perambulator." Such awkward excursions into foreign territory do not greatly matter if the central social group of the novel is vividly presented. The close-knit upper-middle-class society that dominates *Night and Day, Mrs Dalloway, To the Lighthouse* and *Between the Acts* is firmly in the tradition of the novel of social realism dealing with a particular class, from *Emma* to *The Egoist*. There can be no valid criticism of Virginia Woolf for staying within her own world, nor for turning working-class women like the singer in *Mrs Dalloway* and Mrs McNab in *To the Lighthouse* into mythical, subhuman figures. In *The Waves*, however, because of the determined rejection of realism, the class distinctions are, paradoxically, disturbing. The six characters are constantly talking about the proletariat. Rhoda fears and hates it:

> Oh, human beings, how I have hated you! [. . .] how hideous you have looked in Oxford Street, how squalid sitting opposite each other staring in the Tube!

Louis wishes he could "look like the rest" but, if he cannot be assimilated, he is determined to impose his will on the flux and disorder of the "average man's" life. Jinny is oblivious of any class but her own; Susan identifies the lives of country working people with the lives of animals:

> I [. . .] sit by the beds of dying women [. . .] frequenting rooms intolerable except to one born as I was and early acquainted with the farmyard and the dung-heap and the hens straying in and out, and the mother with two rooms and growing children. I have seen the windows run with heat, I have smelt the sink.

Neville uncompromisingly despises the world of "horsedealers and plumbers," saying in Cambridge: "Where there are buildings like these [. . .] I cannot endure that there should be shop girls." Bernard, supposedly in warm contrast to Neville as one who wants to absorb all the different lives he encounters, is in no doubt, however, of the cosmic difference between his perceptions and those of the "small shopkeepers":

> What a sense of the tolerableness of life the lights in the bedrooms of small shopkeepers give us! Saturday comes, and there is just enough to pay perhaps for seats at the Pictures. Perhaps before they put out the light they go into the little garden and look at the giant rabbit crouched in its wooden hut. That is the rabbit they will have for Sunday dinner. Then they put out the light. Then they sleep. And for thousands of people sleep is nothing but warmth and silence and one moment's sport with some fantastic dream. "I have posted my letter," the greengrocer thinks,

"to the Sunday newspaper. Suppose I win five hundred pounds in the football competition? And we shall kill the rabbit. Life is pleasant. Life is good. I have posted the letter. We shall kill the rabbit." And he sleeps.

Bernard and his five friends thus, in their different ways, write off the possibility that another class of people could share their perceptions. The very lack of realism makes this assumption unpalatable in *The Waves* where it would not have mattered in *To the Lighthouse*. Because the six characters are abstracted to their essences from those material envelopes (which in their case may be semi-transparent but in the case of the small shopkeepers are certainly opaque), they seem to be giving a definitive account of the quality of all experience. But the underlying details of their real lives, protected and privileged, suggest how relative their experience must in fact be. Though their individual weaknesses are described, the one, overall weakness—that not one of them ever considers whether sensibilities as interesting might not be found among the masses they fear and despise— is not perceived by their creator.

The six voices are not equally important and complex. The images that identify Jinny and Susan are less suggestive than those for Rhoda or Bernard, since characters whose lives are dominated by their bodies require physical images which can be literally applied. When Louis speaks of his body going down to the depths of the world, the image stands for his sense of history. But when Jinny describes herself as dancing like a fire, unfurling like a fern, rippling like a plant in a river, the image does not reach beyond itself: it only describes the bodily actions of one who lives in the "society of bodies." Her leitmotif—"The door opens. O come, I say"—is a literal description of the pattern of her life. Very occasionally Jinny makes a statement about herself which reaches towards a complex idea of personality: "I cannot follow any thought from present to past [. . .] I do not dream." The sentence deals, unusually for Jinny, with a state of mind rather than a physical sensation, though it is about her lack of mental subtlety. There is little room for complexity in the portrayal of an alluring society lady bravely facing up to the oncoming of old age, though some attempt is made to transform her interest in clothes, lipstick and facepowder into a moral stand against chaos:

This is the triumphant procession; this is the army of victory [. . .]
    Look how they show off clothes here even under ground in perpetual radiance. They will not let the earth even lie wormy and sodden. There are gauzes and silks illumined in glass cases and underclothes trimmed with a million close stitches of fine embroidery. Crimson, green, violet, they are dyed all colours. Think how they organize, roll out,

smooth, dip in dyes and drive tunnels blasting the rock. [. . .] I am a native of this world, I follow its banners.

In the opposition Jinny makes between civilization and prehistoric savagery there is an interesting antithesis to Louis's sense of the links between all ages of the world. But her praise of artifice goes only as far as the formula of life lived for the body can take one. And there are limits too within that formula. Jinny is a sensual creature, living from one orgasm to the next. But the physical images which describe her—the thin rippling body, the narrow throat—suggest a barren nerve-racked sexuality, rather like Lucy Tantamount's in *Point Counterpoint* (1928), not a rich, warm bodily life. There is no such thing in *The Waves*. Susan, whose bodily life is slow, maternal and earthbound, is in direct contrast to Jinny, but hers is a sinister and gloomy sensuality. Her empathy with things of the earth, leading (predictably) from wild rural adolescence to silent motherhood, is obscure and alarming:

> What I give is fell. I cannot float gently, mixing with other people. I like best the stare of shepherds met in the road; the stare of gipsy women beside a cart in a ditch suckling their children as I shall suckle my children. For soon in the hot midday when the bees hum round the hollyhocks my lover will come. He will stand under the cedar tree. To his one word I shall answer my one word. What has formed in me I shall give him. I shall have children; I shall have maids in aprons; men with pitchforks [. . .] I shall be like my mother, silent in a blue apron locking up the cupboards.

Susan, locking cupboard doors and netting fruit, "glutted with natural happiness" in a landscape heavy and rich with the perpetual breeding and ripening of "Those dying generations at their song," seems a bringer of death as much as of life. Her refusal of Percival suggests this: "She who had refused Percival lent herself to this, to this covering over."

By contrast with Jinny and Susan, every physical image associated with Rhoda points away from the body, towards a description of mental anguish:

> I must push my foot stealthily lest I should fall off the edge of the world into nothingness.

> I came to the puddle. I could not cross it. Identity failed me.

> Like a ribbon of weed I am flung far every time the door opens.

> The walls of the mind become transparent.

Rhoda's fearful instability, like Septimus's, is defined throughout by physical sensations. And, like Septimus, she combines a sense of the reality of the life of "Monday or Tuesday" with a desire to escape it. She knows that she is "a girl, here in this room" as well as being a ribbon of weed. Rhoda's is an irreconcilable position: she is stretched between an ideal vision of impersonality and serenity, evoked by her imaginary journeys and the satisfaction she finds in abstract shapes, and the torture of "here and now." Though she makes journeys away from the real world, she cannot separate herself entirely, nor does she really want to. Her real desire is to be included and to give herself—but "Oh, to whom?"—and her escapism is tempered by her reluctant allegiance to reality:

> But these pilgrimages, these moments of departure, start always in your presence, from this table, these lights, from Percival and Susan, here and now.

Rhoda expresses an extreme version of the tension between isolation and participation which dominates all Virginia Woolf's novels, and she is defeated by it. Her suicide is her judgement on the real world, with which she can never be reconciled. Should we be tempted, however, to draw a simplistic analogy between Rhoda's experience and that of her creator, Bernard's voice provides an important qualification of Rhoda's judgement: "Cruel and vindictive as we are, we are not bad to that extent."

Louis is a more interesting and complex voice than Rhoda in that, though he too fears the world, he wishes to impose order on it rather than to flee it; he is more frightening than frightened. His sense of insecurity and isolation in childhood results in an authoritarian and highly ordered public life which is always to be at odds with his secret loneliness. Thus, more emphatically than with the other characters, the images that define his personality are drawn from his childhood. His feelings of inadequacy are for ever evoked by the fat woman at the children's party who gave him, in pity, the Union Jack from the Christmas tree. His fear of untidy passionate relationships will always be imaged by Jinny's kiss on the back of the neck. His desire to impose order and make his way in a hostile world are already present in the blow he lands on the oak door at school and in his respect for Crane the headmaster. From the first, he feels himself to be part of an endless process of historical growth, his veins going down into the past, and this leads him to work at putting a ring of commerce round the world in his public life and, in his solitary attic room, to write poetry which will "forge [. . .] a ring of beaten steel." Like the flamboyant historical figures with whom he identifies, he wants to provide an element of the continuity of which he is so vividly aware:

> to mark this inch in the long, long history that began in Egypt, in the time of the Pharaohs, when women carried red pitchers to the Nile.

This recurrent image is a clear indication of the difference between Louis and Rhoda. Louis's imaginary pilgrimage to the Nile is not a terrified flight from the real world, but an implacable source of strength. In spite of his constant dread of death, of the great beast stamping, Louis is in the ranks: he is part of "the eternal procession" of working life and, as such, is rather the odd one out of the six.

Neville, like St John Hirst and William Dodge, a clever, passionate, unattractive homosexual, is a character who cannot well be summed up by such recurrent physical images as are used for Louis. Though his life is organized around physical comforts and intimacies, the "ordinary things" in which he finds his peace—"a table, a chair, a book with a paper-knife stuck between the pages"—are not symbols but descriptions of his life. His engrossment in personal relationships, which gives existence, for him, the flavour of a Shakespearian play, can only be communicated anecdotally and analytically. To some extent his life is summed up by the images of the headmaster's crucifix, the gardener raising his mallet, and the boys on deck squirting each other with hosepipes. From these figures we gather Neville's distaste for virile pomp and circumstance, and his yearning for a momentous, consuming personal intimacy. But the image of the naked boys is a pathetic one. Neville's refined scenes of intimacy are verbal rather than physical. Though he longs for a life of the body, like Jinny's, his is in fact a life of the mind.

In this passage, Neville's type, one well known to Virginia Woolf, is brilliantly portrayed. The physical images are introduced not as symbols of his personality, but as the material for his thoughts and relationships:

Now this room seems to me central, something scooped out of the eternal night. Outside lines twist and intersect, but round us, wrapping us about. Here we are centred. Here we can be silent, or speak without raising our voices. Did you notice that and then that? we say. He said that, meaning . . . She hesitated, and I believe suspected. Anyhow, I heard voices, a sob on the stair late at night. It is the end of their relationship. Thus we spin round us infinitely fine filaments and construct a system. Plato and Shakespeare are included, also quite obscure people, people of no importance whatsoever. I hate men who wear crucifixes on the left side of their waistcoats. I hate ceremonies and lamentations and the sad figure of Christ [. . .] Some spray in a hedge, though, or a sunset over a flat winter field, or again the way some old woman sits, arms akimbo, in an omnibus with a basket—those we point at for the other to look at.[. . .] And then not to talk. To follow the dark paths of the mind and enter the past, to visit books, to brush aside their branches and break off some fruit. And you take it and marvel, as I take the careless movements of your body and marvel at its ease, its power—how you fling open windows and are dexterous with your hands. For alas! my mind is a little impeded, it soon tires; I fall damp, perhaps disgusting, at the goal.

If one lives by the body, as Susan and Jinny do, and as Neville attempts to, the body will fail one. Two alternatives are provided in *The Waves*. One can be a visionary and look for "a reason," "a plot" behind "this ordinary scene," like Rhoda and Louis. To go in this direction is to go towards alienation, solitude and even suicide. Or one can commit oneself to an interest in "this ordinary scene," but treating it not as the arena of immediate gratification but as the material for art. This is no safer direction, in that words, like the body, may fail one. Bernard's stories and phrases, his "sense of what other people are like," frequently desert him. As a storyteller he is at the mercy of all his assumed identities, of his need for an audience, and of his chronic sense of imperfection. Growing old, he begins to wonder whether there are "stories" at all and whether there is any point in his life's activity:

> Why impose my arbitrary design? Why stress this and shape that and twist up little figures like the toys men sell in trays in the street? Why select this, out of all that—one detail?

He is assailed by the sense of making so many transitions and acting out so many different tales that "there is nothing to lay hold of. I am made and remade continually. Different people draw different worlds from me." He relies on being able to call upon the real Bernard, "you the usual partner in my enterprises," whom he thinks of as a "faithful, sardonic man." But he goes in fear of the moment when he will call upon his real self, like Orlando in her motor car, and no one will reply.

When this happens—when the fist does not form, the fin does not rise above the waste of waters—the story-making identity finds itself merged with an undifferentiated, "omnipresent, general life." Passive, undesiring, inarticulate, it becomes part of "the world seen without a self." It is paradoxical that Bernard, who is the most worldly, domestic and articulate of the voices, is the character who experiences this mystical abnegation of the self, "at the still point of the turning world."

At the end of *The Waves*, after summing up his life and the lives of his friends, he admits the limitations of being always an observer, a raconteur, a separate identity. He recognizes that his moments of merging, of becoming one with the others, were "a sort of death," and that to merge and become depersonalized is as necessary and inevitable as death. Through Bernard the six lives become one, and this suggests, as in *Mrs Dalloway* and *To the Lighthouse*, that the personality is not a discrete entity but can be subsumed into the general life flow of the universe. For all this, Bernard's mystical experience of a loss of personality is not the moral conclusion of the book. For Bernard (unlike the narrator of *Four Quartets*) the timeless moment without a self is not infinitely desirable. Though it gives one a vision of the truth, "to let oneself be carried on passively is unthinkable." Loath though Bernard is to suffer from the compulsions of daily life, of having to do one thing and then another because "Tuesday follows Monday: Wednesday, Tuesday," he nevertheless accepts that action must take place within that ordinary, sequential life:

> What are days for?
> Days are where we live.
> They come, they wake us
> Time and time over.
> They are to be happy in.
> Where can we live but days?
> (Philip Larken, "Days")

Bernard remembers the shape of his nose, he bangs his spoon on the table. He asserts the individual personality and the value of its struggle against the impersonal forces of flux and death. His childhood resilience to life's hostility, expressing itself intuitively in his explorings and his stories, becomes in later life a more conscious resistance:

> I jumped up. I said, "Fight! Fight!" I repeated. It is the effort and the struggle, it is the perpetual warfare, it is the shattering and piecing together—this is the daily battle, defeat or victory, the absorbing pursuit. The trees, scattered, put on order; the thick green of the leaves thinned itself to a dancing light. I netted them under with a sudden phrase. I retrieved them from formlessness with words.

In old age, Bernard faces death, like Mr Ramsay, with an individual effort which is translated into the physical image of Percival on horseback— Percival being the epitome of the life of action and effort. Ironic though this image is, Percival having been conquered by death, it ends the book firmly in a word *with* a self:

> the theme effort, effort, dominates; not the waves: and personality: and defiance.

T. E. APTER

An Uncertain Balance: "Night and Day"

Night and Day, despite the conventional form which disappointed Virginia Woolf's contemporary critics, offers a more profound study than does her first novel of the clash between the person society expects and believes one to be, and the scope of that self one most values. The aspects of society which impede individual thought and feeling are frequently presented in a comedy of manners where the emphasis is on the way self-importance and emotional greed serve ignorance in the creation of moral principles. The shock Katherine's aunt, Mrs Milvain, suffers at the discovery of cousin Cyril's mistress and illegitimate children is a symptom of her desire to intrude upon others' lives and to deny others the emotional life she has been denied. Her moral fastidiousness is presented as a lack of vision; towards the end of the book she is about to lose the sight of one eye. Katherine's father shares this fastidiousness, but his limitation is the result of laziness. Refusing to consider as relevant Cyril's feelings, he concludes that the young man has behaved wrongly because he has not behaved acceptably: Mr Hilbery "seemed to be looking through a telescope at little figures hundreds of miles in the distance."

The actual effects of this narrow social vision on Katherine are rather slight. She has freedom both in decision and action, and there is never any danger that society will punish her transgressions with more than a paternal scolding. The author, then, gives her character trumped-up praise

From *Virginia Woolf: A Study of Her Novels.* Copyright © 1979 by T. E. Apter. New York University Press.

when she says that in deciding to encourage her fiancé's love for the more suitable Cassandra, Katherine "let difficulties accumulate unresolved, situations widen their jaws unsatiated, while she maintained a position of absolute and fearless independence." This monumental pose is far less subtle than her actual task, which is not that of staving off intruding gossips, but of defining that valuable self which has no simple, social means of expression, and of discovering a bridge between that self and one's daily life.

The division between self and society in Ralph Denham's life is in many respects more pronounced than in Katherine's. His work, his family responsibilities, his ambition and his conscientiousness lie beside, though with an unbridgeable gap between, his dreams. However much he values those dreams, however convinced he is that they point to a profound yet unrealised dimension of himself, they have the invalidity and escapism of daydreams. Indeed, much of his behaviour confirms the adolescent implications of his fantasies. He sulks because his family refuse him the privacy necessary for the development of his finer nature; he comforts himself with the reminder that he can at least keep his thoughts to himself—almost as though he were punishing his family by so doing; and he exhibits the adolescent vanity and ambivalence implicit in this supposition when, hearing his sister stand by his door and, frightened that she will pass by, he opens the door, feigning irritation at the intrusion. Even his love for Katherine, which he believes points to the realisation of his finer self, has a recalcitrant element of fantasy in that he is most confident of his love in her absence, and his dreams of her are constituted by egoism: he sees the woman descending from her perch to crown him with glory.

Ralph Denham bears some resemblance to the childish, vain men in Virginia Woolf's later fiction; but though he resents Katherine's self absorption—her "lapses" as he calls them—his primary need is not for her sympathy and attention, but for his vision of her. The fact of her actual, physical humanity, separate from his dream, is only a distraction. When he stands by the Hilberys' house and watches her through the window, he does not see a figure of flesh but of light. When he tells her of her love he explains that he *sees* her everywhere, and when she does not respond to him he concludes there must be some "blankness in the heart of his vision." The fulfilment of love is marked by an ordering of vision. After seeing Katherine in the Strand, Ralph looks about, and the scene "wore that curious look of order and purpose which is imparted to the most heterogeneous things when music sounds." And as Katherine walks with Ralph "it seemed to her the immense riddle was answered: the problem had been solved; she held in her hands for one brief moment the globe which we spend our lives in trying to shape, round, whole, and entire from the confusion of chaos."

The emphasis is not on the need for love, but on the need for a coherent vision of life, a vision that is one's own and which is linked to that private sphere of sensibility which is generally ignored even by one's friends and family—partly because it is so difficult to find a language in which to express that sensibility. The first sentence of the novel introduces the type of problem involved. Katherine Hilbery is pouring out tea "in common with many other young ladies of her class," but only one-fifth of her mind is occupied in this way. This partial involvement is alienation from her environment, and it is enforced by her belief that if someone were to open the door, he would suppose that she was a perfect participant of the tea-party. Anyone looking at her, that is, would identify her with the one-fifth of her mind. Though this aggravates her loneliness, she tries to take advantage of the fact that people see such a small part of her. Even among her family she must guard herself: "Her mother always stirred her to feel and think quickly, and then she remembered that her father was there, listening with attention." This frustrating contradiction of stimulus and suppression results not only in the belief that her real feelings are unacceptable, but also in a desire to protect herself from others' views of her, which are bound to be both incomplete and critical. As she looks out the window into the dark city—as she looks, that is, through her individual eye into the chaos and darkness in which she might begin to find her way within her self—she remembers that William Rodney is thinking of her and "she wished that no one in the whole world would think of her." Katherine's private view cannot be sustained in the cold ignorance of another's reality.

Inevitably the suppression of her self makes her angry, but Katherine is unable even to express anger. The only way she can show her annoyance at her aunt's behaviour (and Mrs. Milvain's assessment of Cyril's predicament is a general denial of the right to individual emotion and behaviour) is to let the window shade up with a little snap. Her restricted means of expression are linked to her decision to marry William. By a vicious logic, it seems to her that she would have more freedom by conforming to society's expectations. To marry William would be to disguise further the broader scope of her self; then others would find her acceptable, and leave her alone. Yet her decision co-exists with a longing for an emotion which would sweep away the dominating falsehood of her daily life:

Splendid as the waters that drop with resounding thunder from high ledges of rock, and plunge downwards into the blue depths of night, was the presence of love she dreamt, drawing into it every drop of the force of life [. . .] in which everything was surrendered, and nothing might be reclaimed.

As in *The Voyage Out*, the desire for release and dissolution is couched in the language of Romanticism, and the very excess of the language underlines Katherine's own sense that her desire is bound to be defeated. Her desires contain, moreover, a peculiar contradiction in that she both longs for perfect isolation and believes that this isolation can be achieved only with a heroic lover's aid. The acknowledgement of her desire's fantastical element and of the contradictions in her desires, does not lead her to integrate her self with reality but, rather, leads to an emotional paralysis. In Lincoln, when her disgust for her fiancé and her inability to break off the engagement act upon her with equal force, she rides in the carriage in a "state of gloomy self-suppression which resulted in complete apathy." (Mrs Hilbery, on the other hand, as she accompanies her daughter in the carriage, drops into a pleasant, inattentive state of mind in which she is conscious only of the passing countryside. She is a fore-runner of Mrs Dalloway in her ability to create a delightful world and to follow an individual flow of thought which at times makes her appear silly, but which gives her a respect for the individual differences of others.)

The need to discover and to confirm the reality of that four-fifths part of the mind not involved in the tea-party is in itself an acknowledgement of the reality of other people's responses; it is difficult to see things— even to see one's self—as different from others' views. When Mrs Milvain complains about Cassandra's and Rodney's behaviour Katherine suffers a loathing that makes her go rigid. It seems that however assured she is of her aunt's ignorance and shallowness, she must acknowledge it as a view with some kind of validity. For what she sees through her aunt's eyes is the indecent spectacle of "her own action beheld for the first time from the outside; her aunt's words made her realise how infinitely repulsive the body of life is without its soul." She must follow the wider implications of her aunt's view, and as she does so, it infects her own. After her conversation with her aunt everything seems poisoned: that is the effect of "objectivity" or of a viewpoint determined by convention rather than empathy.

Katherine's conclusion that "the only truth which she could discover was the truth of what she herself felt," clashes with the knowledge that her own view is "a frail beam when compared with the broad illumination shed by the eyes of all the people who are in agreement to see together."

The dichotomy between the value of her individual view and its frailty frequently results in paranoia and snobbishness: the knowledge that people will not, in general, confirm her thoughts and attitudes leads her to make a crude assessment of the general view, and she assumes that because people will be different from her, they will therefore be in opposition to her. As Katherine walks, trying to focus her thoughts, the expression on her face "would have made any passer-by think her reprehensibly and almost ridiculously detached from the surrounding scene," and only her beauty, the author explains, saves her from the worst fate that can befall a pedestrian: people looked at her, but did not laugh. This simplistic assumption, that all people one passes in the streets are cruel through limited imaginations, is enforced by Mrs Hilbery's pity for the workers, who cannot feel poetry as she and her daughter do.

This paranoic sensitivity to others' views becomes more discriminating with the development of Virginia Woolf's technique. As Katherine and Mary Datchet sit on the window ledge looking at the moon, someone in the crowded room makes a joke about star-gazing, thus destroying their privacy and their pleasure. This is precisely what Peter Walsh does to Clarissa and Sally when he finds them together in the garden at Bourton, but in Mrs Dalloway the reductive remark is not a symptom of people's general insensitivity. In the later novel Virginia Woolf focuses on the specific context. Peter's jealousy at the communion of the two women, and his desire to bring them back to his plane, are expressed by the query, "Star-gazing?," and it is Clarissa's particular vulnerability to Peter's opinion that makes his mockery so painful; so that we are given something more complex than a division between those characters who look out into the darkness of their minds and those who, representing the general mentality, demand that everyone participate in the shallow, lighted public gathering.

The limiting snobbishness of Night and Day is felt, too, in the attitude towards work which emerges in the novel. Though many critics have associated this flaw with all Virginia Woolf's fiction, it is in fact uncommon in her work (a few counter-examples to this charge would include Rezia's happiness as she sews the hat, Mrs Ramsay's concern for the welfare of her children and the running of the household, Mr Ramsay's need to have his work recognised, Lily Briscoe's need to get the painting right), and even in Night and Day it is partial and intermittent. Ralph Denham's view of his work as spiritual tedium might well be justified, but Katherine's depression upon visiting his home and realising that his family must work to earn their living, expresses a highly distasteful patronage. Certainly Katherine's reaction measures her own state; the defensive conversation of Mrs Denham strikes "upon a mind bereft of all defences, and, keenly conscious of the degradation which is the result of strife whether victorious or not, she thought gloomily of her loneliness, of life's futility, of the barren prose of reality, of William Rodney, of her mother, and the unfinished book." The focus is on the dreariness of Katherine's world, but the dreariness of the Denham's domestic life and the fact that these people are not even in the running for dignity and happiness, are revealed as the author's view. The scenes in the Denham home imply that the need to work to get by in the world oppresses the spirit without qualification.

In Mary Datchet's case, too—though the dignity and force of this character more than balances any negative conclusions the author reaches—work acts towards the destruction of individuality. In her office she must think of only one thing (in this case her thought is: how to catch the eye of a Cabinet Minister and deliver the old arguments in favour of women's rights with unexampled originality), and as soon as her thoughts begin to follow their individual course, the office atmosphere stifles them and brings her back to the task at hand. Moreover, it seems that any concentration, any singleness of purpose, is a type of soul-murder. Mary herself is afraid, above all things, of never changing, of always holding the same thought in her head; and the aggressive quality of repetition can be felt in the way Rodney reads his lifeless drama: he delivers each line with the same lilt in the voice which seemed to nail each line firmly on to the same spot in the hearer's brain.

Mary's attitude towards her colleagues supports the implication that her dignity as a worker is exceptional. They appear to her with some substantial part of them cut off; they are not in the running for life. Though the author shares this attitude, the subsequent change in her depiction of such characters can measure the change in her sympathy. Mrs Seal, the passionate suffragette who nonetheless suffers without protest man's vanity and presumption (Mr Clacton teases her about her lunch habits much as he would a pet dog who had convenient tricks), looks out the window and wishes that she could draw all the people in Russell Square and Southampton Row together, if only for five minutes. Then, she is sure, she could make them understand: "But they *must* see the truth some day . . . If only one could *make* them see it. . . ." The woman's faith in her truth and her desire to share it as a vision, makes her a fore-runner of Miss La Trobe in *Between the Acts*. There is, in the later character's struggle to express her vision, something both pathetic and valuable. Such effort, in *Between the Acts,* becomes part of the mind's means of self-expression, not a negation of it.

What remains valid in the fastidiousness that sometimes emerges as snobbishness or paranoia is the sense of oppression from the commonplace needs of life. This oppression arises from the confusion not only of the life round one but of one's own feelings and responses. Katherine's interest in mathematics is an escape from the frustrations of a reserved nature and from the muddle of her own emotions; the longing for a precise, clear world is also expressed in her fascination with the stars, though even this desire is accompanied by a blatantly contradictory desire:

> [. . .] after gazing for another second, the stars did their usual work upon the mind, froze to cinders the whole of our short human history, and reduced the human body to an ape-like, furry form, crouching amid the brushwood of a barbarous clod of mud. This stage was soon succeeded by another, in which there was nothing in the universe save stars and the light of stars; as she looked up the pupils of her eyes so dilated with starlight that the whole of her seemed dissolved in silver and split over the ledges of the stars for ever and ever indefinitely through space. Somehow simultaneously, though incongruously, she was riding with the magnanimous hero upon the shore or under forest trees. . . .

The squalid image of the human as ape-like and mud-inhabiting is less dominant here than in *The Years*, but it nonetheless functions as part of Katherine's reluctance to trust life and, also, it contributes to the author's presentation of vanity and self-importance (especially in William Rodney's case) as covering an ugly, pathetic nature. In face, then, of a fundamental human opposition to clarity and freedom, vision—the capacity, that is, to extend beyond our immediate reality and our immediate needs—offers a splendid release. Katherine is able to take into her self that which she sees ("the pupils of her eyes were so dilated with starlight that the whole of her seemed dissolved in silver and split over the ledges of the stars"); she becomes what she sees.

Mary Datchet, too, when—after losing Ralph—she becomes only a serviceable human being, when she decides that the world will not answer her more profound needs, can nonetheless discover the vitality and significance of personal vision:

> In the eyes of every single person she detected a flame; as if a spark in the brain ignited spontaneously at contact with the things they met and drove them on. The young women looking into the milliners' windows had that look in their eyes; and elderly men turning over books in the second-hand bookshops, and eagerly waiting to hear what the price was [. . .]

It is clear, then, that individual vision is not individual feeling of the type D.H. Lawrence, for example, emphasises. For individual vision can release one even from one's own emotions by extending and vivifying the impersonal, visual world. On the other hand, mood and emotion can also determine vision, though in this novel the association of vision and feeling is clumsily portrayed. When Ralph discovers Katherine's engagement to Rodney he feels the chilly fog obscuring the further bank, and he sees the ugliness and depravity of the streets: here the character's vision underlines his emotion with a three-inch brush, but does not explore it or define its specific qualities. The use of nature as symbol, too, is over-obvious: "The light of the late afternoon glowed green behind the straight trees, and became a symbol of her. The light seemed to expand his heart. She brooded over the grey fields, and was with him now in the railway carriage. . . ." Compare this cumbersome assertion of a landscape endowed with one's own thoughts to the ease and simplicity of Clarissa's—in *Mrs Dalloway*—awareness of Peter's presence: "Some days, some sights bringing him back to her calmly, without the old bitterness: which was perhaps the reward of having cared for people; they came back in the middle of St James's Park on a fine morning—indeed they did."

The heroic figure incongruously accompanying Katherine's celestial vision is not merely a comic reductive tag. It is necessary (as is the angelic figure of light in Ralph Denham's case) because the individual vision, and the individual self, are not assured. Nor are they stable, or even self-aware. Social and domestic demands do not entangle a self which would thrive without impediment. The larger part of the mind generally left out of account in "normal" life must be created, and in *Night and Day* this part of the mind clearly seeks a response from another person who shares the pain of division between personal and public reality. Katherine's love of mathematics is a desire for mental certainty and a revulsion against her mother's inability to concentrate on one thing, or to think logically and sequentially; yet this desire is not satisfied by her own nature, either. Frequently her responses and emotions conflict, and cancel out one another. As she rides on the omnibus with Ralph she begins to believe that she can sympathise with him and his attitudes, yet her present responses confuse her, for she had already placed him among people she does not want to know well: she runs "a bar through half her impressions, as one cancels a badly written sentence, having found the right one." When she writes to him to try to tell him how she feels, all her thoughts seem to flow to the tip of her pencil and to stop there: the reserve which protects the greater part of her mind from society's ignorance and assaults also impedes the development of the thoughts and feelings which belong to that part of the mind. Her dislike of literature is a dislike for discussions about emotions which always seem to her inadequate and fictitious; she has no faith that any language—even that of art—could express her deepest thoughts and feelings. When her feelings are couched in ordinary language, in an ordinary social setting, she becomes alienated from them. She shares with Ralph and Mary the sense that, should she explain her self to another person, she would be robbed of that self.

People become different beings when they are with different people—not because they behave differently with different people, but because they are seen in different ways. Ralph knows there are certain things about himself he can tell Mary; he knows there are certain feelings she draws from him like a magnet which are truly his, yet he knows, too, that he cannot give expression to his deepest feelings. The knowledge that a good part of one's self cannot be expressed in given circumstances impinges very sorely upon one's vanity. Certainly Ralph Denham's discomfort at the opening tea-party stems from his awareness that his more profound qualities will not be recognised in that setting. At times vanity can lead to a vicious impulse to assert one's self, to assault people in order to gain recognition. Among the crowd gathered in Mary's rooms to hear William Rodney's paper, Katherine feels that she is nothing because she does not have a profession: the attitude, that is, which she attributes to others, becomes her own. As a result, she would like to trample on their bodies and this violent reaction is due to her sense of what they are doing to her; in thinking her unimportant, or in some way insufficient, they are slighting her in a way that seems to her paranoically sensitive self like a type of murder. This paranoia is not totally exaggerated, because society does at times kill the self she most values. Even the sensible Mary feels, when Katherine comes to her office, that she represents another world, a world "therefore subversive of her world."

The alienation a character suffers from the knowledge that his most profound self has no recognition or expression in his social and interpersonal life, frequently makes it seem as though the character has no self. As Katherine is walking in Lincolnshire with Rodney, wishing she could tell him she does not want to marry him, she has the impression that all things round her are dimmed, and that she herself is incapable of passion: she feels herself to be insubstantial because she knows that she is not the person Rodney takes her to be, or the person he wants her to be. Since her real self is unknown, the people round her are strangers to her. She looks at William as though she were looking at someone on the opposite side of a window; she looks into the faces of passers-by and thinks only of their indifference to her, and of hers to them.

The vanity which makes one feel stifled at non-recognition can also, because it piques one's desire for self assertion, be a stimulus to communication. Mary, "When she found herself in talk with Katherine [. . .] began to feel rapid alternations of opinion about her, arrows of sensation striking strangely through the envelope of personality, which shelters us so conveniently from our fellows." The need of the women to justify themselves to one another becomes friendship. Moreover, Ralph's love for Katherine is a need for her to know him and to think well of him; and her desire for love is essentially a desire for "an echo, a sound"—that is, for some response to that self which is normally incommunicable.

Love, in this novel, is seen to be important to self-realisation because a stable emotion stabilises the self: "To seek a true feeling among the chaos of the unfeelings or half-feelings of life, to recognise it when found, and to accept the consequences of the discovery" quickens the light in the eyes, quickens one's vision. Love offers the only possibility of establishing the reality of the self while allowing one to function in society. Mary Datchet, who is unable to satisfy her love, suppresses her deeper self and directs her energy to a utilitarian goal: the public world eventually claims all of her. Ralph and Katherine, however, remain divided. Ralph feels that he has two bodies, one tied to the earth and one free. Initially, when at Kew Ralph offers friendship to Katherine, he proposed that friendship as a bridge between the private world, which is free, and the social world, which is constrained. Katherine, as she hears Ralph's idea, wonders why there should be

> this perpetual disparity between the thought and the action, between the life of solitude and the life of society, this astonishing precipice on one side of which the soul was active and in broad daylight, on the other side of which it was contemplative and dark as night? Was it not possible to step from one to the other, erect, and without essential change? Was this not the chance he offered her—the rare and wonderful chance of friendship?

The balance, however, between the "light" and "dark" sides of the soul is bound to be unsatisfactory when they remain totally unintegrated, and connected only by a bridge. The solution in this novel is simply to make the opposition tolerable by having one's non-social self recognised by one person. This is the last novel in which Virginia Woolf proposes such a crudely schematic solution, nor does she subsequently see love as a solution to the self's need for realisation and expression and communication. Love can at times stimulate or at others suppress the self; but it never again forms the focus of the creative vision.

PERRY MEISEL

Virginia Woolf and Walter Pater

"Stored . . . meanings" are what Woolf calls, in a chemical figure like Pater's, the "deposit" that "remains with us" when we read "a great book." What this deposit is composed of, then, are those layers of (unconsciously) retained or remembered meanings sedimented in the minds of writers and readers alike, with the figure of the "deposit" or sediment joining three figural systems at once—chemistry, geology, and textuality—each of which Woolf can deploy to represent a recovery of the process involved. The figure of the "fossilised" or inscribed trace is probably the most familiar one in Pater and Woolf alike: "There is, to speak metaphorically," says Woolf at the start of "Phases of Fiction," "some design that has been traced upon our minds which reading brings to light." The same figure emerges in A Room of One's Own, too, even though Woolf wishes there to put the burden on "Nature" rather than on language as such: "Nature, in her most irrational mood, has traced in invisible ink on the walls of the mind a premonition which these great artists confirm; a sketch which only needs to be held to the fire of genius to become visible."

Woolf's most graphic representation of the trace or deposit, however, comes, fittingly enough, in her essay on influence, "The Leaning Tower," written during her work on Between the Acts. What is particularly ironic about the essay is that here Woolf berates the writers of her own generation for being copiers, for being "the unconscious inheritors of a great tradition" and therefore "aristocrats" whose influences are too much in books and too little in life: "Put a page of their writing under the magnifying-glass"—for literary criticism is, after all, detective work—"and you will see, far away in the distance, the Greeks, the Romans; coming nearer, the Elizabethans; coming nearer still, Dryden, Swift, Voltaire, Jane Austen, Dickens, Henry James."

Woolf even has a term in "The Leaning Tower" for this common bed of memory and influence that stamps, inscribes, impresses readers and writers alike with a shared competence in language. It is a surprisingly Germanic term—"the under-mind"—and, like Pater's "under-texture," it signifies a textual unconscious that serves as that layer of residue, to use Pater's word for Woolf's "deposit," that allows signification itself to emerge.

The way the trace or residue functions, however, is made clearest in a late passage in *Between the Acts:*

> The tune began; the first note meant a second; the second a third. Then down beneath a force was born in opposition; then another. On different levels they diverged. On different levels ourselves went forward; flower gathering some on the surface; others descending to wrestle with the meaning; but all comprehending; all enlisted. The whole population of the mind's immeasurable profundity came flocking; from the unprotected, the unskinned; and dawn rose; and azure; from chaos and cacophony measure; but not the melody of surface sound alone controlled it; but also the warring battle-plumed warriors straining asunder: To part? No. Compelled from the ends of the horizon; recalled from the edge of appalling crevasses; they crashed; solved; united. And some relaxed their fingers; and others uncrossed their legs.

In this Paterian conceit of musical relationships, "not the melody of surface sound alone controlled it," of course, since for every "surface sound"—for every "first note"—there is a latent or murmuring sound against which the surface note positions itself as such, either harmonically or discordantly, although to tell which—to hear or read it at all—always requires a note already humming in the memory. This, in other words, is Woolf's version of Lucian's taxonomic exercise—there never can be, never was, a "first note" alone, a "surface sound" alone; there must always be a differential and deferring "under-texture" or "under-mind" functioning as a residue or permanent layer of memory against which every later utterance can be instantly compared so as to judge it syntactically appropriate or discordant, either in harmony or discord with what is already there.

Hence for Woolf, as for Pater, language signifies by means of the very residue that incandescence wishes to burn away. Woolf's "wholeness" and the "globe" that signifies it are as strictly impossible ideals as Pater's luminous crystal, founded as they are on the surplus they mean to refine out of existence. This residue or under-mind of language, moreover, is a paradigm for all those systems into which the individual emerges belatedly in Woolf's fiction, and the particular system into which a writer like Miss LaTrobe emerges in *Between the Acts.*

What makes the corrupt and belated nature of the writer's material doubly hazardous is that semantic discordance is built into the system, too. This is largely because, as Pater puts it, "figure . . . is rarely content to die to thought precisely at the right moment," but will also pick up "quite alien associations," leading to "the metaphor that is mixed in all our speech." Woolf's version of it comes in an essay on Turgenev: "the meaning goes on after the sound has stopped," and, as in the Tube, it will echo down "quite alien" pathways of association. Hence this semantic under-mind is to be located in those "regions," as Woolf puts it in "Phases of Fiction," "deep down in the mind where contradiction prevails."

What she has in mind here is less an unconscious pool of instinct, of course, than a linguistic or textual unconscious in which a word's semantic inventory, like a psychic memory trace, gets "stored." Here both semantic inventories and the various rhetorical devices that deploy their resources tend to cross and collide in their various ways of knowing the world thanks to "the strange way," as Woolf puts it in "The Narrow Bridge of Art," "in which things that have no apparent connection are associated in [the writer's] mind." And with the figure of physical depth difficult to mix persuasively with the figure of texts, among Woolf's principal mediatory representations for these unconscious and common pathways are the labyrinthine, and Paterian, corridors of the "vast building" of literature in "How It Strikes A Contemporary," and the "old house" of the English tradition in which the "most impressive" power of all is, like Chaucer's, the "shaping power, the architect's power."

With all its contingencies, Woolf's notion of the trace or under-mind also carries with it a prescriptive or evaluative standard akin to Pater's notion of the strong writer as "scholar," although her term for it is "rhythm," the "rhythm" (or really, harmony) by which the writer orchestrates the systematic hazards of the language in which he works in a reflection of the aesthetic virtues that *To the Lighthouse* discovers in repetition. Thus, with Chekhov:

> we need a very daring and alert sense of literature to make us hear the tune, and in particular those last notes which complete the harmony. Probably we have to read a great many stories before we feel, and the

feeling is essential to our satisfaction, that we hold the parts together, and that Tchekhov was not merely rambling disconnectedly, but struck now this note, now that with intention, in order to complete his meaning.

In Shakespeare, the successful juxtaposition of images is likewise figured as "striking two notes to make one chord," although here the context is really painting, since Woolf is writing on Walter Sickert, thus bringing to bear on writing the two principle Paterian analogues of music and the visual arts: "All great writers," says Woolf, "are great colourists, just as they are musicians into the bargain." Indeed, it is to the "best critics" that she grants these painterly and musical qualities, although their number here—Dryden, Hazlitt, Lamb—does not, of course, include Pater himself, even though what Woolf praises in her critics in particular is that they "were acutely aware of the mixture of elements"—the Paterian word for it is *Anders-streben*—"and wrote of literature with music and painting in their minds."

It is, moreover, rhythm, or really harmony, that accounts for the power of DeQuincey's "impassioned prose," too: "the train has been laid so deep beneath page after page and chapter after chapter that the single word when it is spoken is enough to start an explosion." Like the "train" or pathways of language, thought, and emotion in Woolf's novels, the train of DeQuincey's language provides his text with its own kind of (second-order) under-mind or under-texture against which particular words or phrases within it may, in a favorite word, "reverberate." Coleridge's words, too, "reverberate," and "buzz" in a "labyrinth" of prose like DeQuincey's which the "reader's net" will hope to catch by becoming coincident with it. And like Sterne, the writer may deploy (or the critic may hear) these reverberations "for some exquisite harmony or for some brilliant discord." Thus in great writing, says Woolf in "Phases of Fiction," "something is built up which is not the story itself," a "spectral architecture," as she puts it in Jane Austen's case, the "dome and column complete."

If a writer is strong, then, he will orchestrate the residue and discordances of the system in which he works, and, like a strong personality in Woolf's fiction, will strive to fortify and secure his position in the shifting flux of language and its perils. The wordsmith, in other words, needs to be tough-minded, almost a dictator, or at least an imperialist, in keeping his verbal constituency under control. For the Greeks, in fact, it is "only by collecting in companies"—already an implicitly military or imperial metaphor for their power—that "words . . . convey the meaning which each one separately is too weak to express." And in addition to the sign for literary power compact in "companies," there is also the recognition in it that literary language, like all language, cannot signify by the atom, by the single word, but only by its relations to other words (indeed, the same is true for the morpheme itself, although Woolf does not concern herself with this microscopic level of language). Thus by "the bold and running use of metaphor"—of that necessary relation of one term to another which gives each one its proper meaning and allows the poet to exploit the pathways that connect them—Aeschylus "will amplify," in a strictly stereophonic sense, "and give us, not the thing itself" (for words, like all the languages of life, are "impressions" of things rather than things themselves), "but the reverberation and reflection which, taken into his mind, the thing has made."

Despite the residue and the belatedness that are stipulated in the Greeks' very ability to deploy "reverberation" as a literary technique, Woolf, like Pater, has her myth of presence and beginnings in the Greeks, too. "The stable, the permanent, the original human being is to be found there," much as "Chaucer's pages" present us with the English equivalent, "the hardness and the freshness of an actual presence." "There are no schools," says Woolf in "On Not Knowing Greek," "no forerunners; no heirs." And yet the claim is also put into question by her equally Paterian insistence that behind Greek art there is, after all, an under-mind that forbids the retrospective belief in Greek originality and unmediated vision, "an ancient tradition of manners," even if there is not, as Pater himself insists in *Plato*, an ancient tradition behind it of literature and philosophy as well.

As we have already seen with Miss LaTrobe, of course, the notion of the artist's natural and original voice is an exceedingly problematic one given the under-mind and its common and already-given materials for self-making. When Woolf deploys the notion of "voice" to describe Meredith, for example, it is profoundly ironic: "to read Meredith is to be conscious of a packed and muscular mind; of a voice booming and reverberating with its own unmistakable accent." And yet just a few sentences earlier, Woolf has already ascribed the exuberance of Meredith's language—its very ability to reverberate as it does—to the "great ancestry behind it: we cannot," she says, "avoid all memory of Shakespeare." Thus Meredith's "unmistakable" personal "voice" is to be accounted for by its commerce with voices that are different from it. Unlike (the myth of) DeQuincey's language, which (supposedly) reverberates with the under-text of its own language alone, Meredith's reverberates with the under-text of texts not properly his own at all.

Hence the reoriginating modernist claim in "How It Strikes A Comtemporary" that "we are sharply cut off from our predecessors" is a preposterous one given the hum of a "cobweb of allusions" even denser in post-Renaissance culture than in the Greek. Indeed, when Woolf tries to account for her supposed rupture between present and past in the passage there which we have already examined under her modernist profile, her figures betray her into acknowledging, however unintentionally, a continuity in culture that is impossible to overlook: "A shift in the scale—the sudden slip of masses held in position for ages—has shaken the fabric from top to bottom, alienated us from the past and made us perhaps too vividly conscious of the present." Distant we surely are, but past and present are alike positioned in the weave of the same "fabric," in the first of a triply mixed metaphor for the history of culture. In the second metaphor, past and present are sounded, however discordantly, in or on the same "scale," channel, or measure by which utterances have always been sounded. Indeed, the third, geological figure ("slip of masses held in position for ages") even grants the qualities of culture a granite permanence more natural and abiding than those of nature itself.

It should be noted, too, that this "fabric" that represents history can also be folded in different ways by different interpreters, and so constitute the shape of history differently in the hands of each one. With residue a temporal necessity for the use of language, it is also a necessity for constituting the moment, and with a special consequence for the very making and coherence of history, whether the history of the individual or the history of literature. Writing again of Turgenev, Woolf notes that his "scene," as she puts it in a word synonymous with the moment in "A Sketch of the Past," "expands in the mind and lies there giving off fresh ideas, emotions, and pictures much as a moment in real life will sometimes only yield its meaning long after it has passed." Only "after it has passed," then, does the moment yield its meaning or become intelligible as such at all. Like the need for a second note to make the first one audible or syntactic in retrospect, the (prior) moment here becomes significant only later on, when some doubling or repetition of its elements provides access to the trace it has unknowingly left behind.

The impossibility of direct and immediate experience, however, is not the only consequence to be drawn from such deferred action. What is even more important is that what is early thereby comes into being through the action of what comes later on. If the moment occurs only "after it has passed," then one can rewrite or refold—indeed, one has no choice but to rewrite or rearrange—literary history to suit one's own belated needs.

If we wish to begin to draw conclusions about the way Woolf herself is inclined to rewrite literary history for personal purposes, let us see to what particular use she puts her theory of the common life or under-mind. With any writer a latecomer to the lineaments of a personality he fashions out of materials not his own, we have seen Woolf eager to insist, as she does in *Between the Acts,* on the writer's consequent lack of "voice," originality—indeed, of personality itself. And given the high price Woolf bestows upon personality elsewhere in her criticism, we can see how shocking and discordant a theory the under-mind is when it allows her to situate all individuals and all artists within so generalized a spectrum of influence that, as Miss LaTrobe and "A Sketch of the Past" have both indicated, it is hard to continue speaking of particular selves and particular authors at all in the process. What advantage such a theory gives Woolf in her struggle with Pater, however, emerges in "The Leaning Tower": "let us always remember—influences are infinitely numerous; writers are infinitely sensitive." And though Woolf is willing to claim that there are indeed "families" of influence, at the close of the essay she wishes to elide all such distinctions in favor of a view of literature and culture in its widest and most deindividuating profile:

> Let us trespass at once. Literature is no one's private ground; literature is common ground. It is not cut up into nations; there are no wars there. Let us trespass freely and fearlessly and find our own way for ourselves.

What is striking here is Woolf's sudden and cavalier endorsement of literary trespassing or poaching, although it seems entirely justified, of course, by the modest remark that influences are "numerous," and that, as Pater himself says through Heine, there can be, strictly speaking, no plagiarism. Indeed, from this point of view the very condition of literature is the condition of influence itself. And yet what Woolf seems to gain by her apparently benign and sincere—and decidedly Paterian—theory of the common life is the right to steal under cover of a collectivist and only secondary critical stance.

MARIA DiBATTISTA

"Between the Acts":
The Play of Will

In *Between the Acts*, her last novel, Woolf returns, in the face of immense historical pressures, to the time-honored and time-resistant figures of her native tradition. The novel traces the historical evolution as well as the permanent configurations of "Britannia," a cultural symbol more comprehensive than Percival, the figure in *The Waves* who evokes the English genius embodied in Arthurian romance, and more representative of national destiny than the family chronicle charted in *The Years*.

The historical pageant at the center of the novel reenacts and experiences the history of the world as an island history. The vast reaches of geological time that fascinate Lucy Swithin are aesthetically foreshortened to form a prologue memorializing that geomorphic, quasi-mythical event when England was "A child new born / Sprung from the sea" (Virginia Woolf, *Between the Acts*. New York: Harcourt Brace Jovanovich, 1969, p. 77. All further citations are to this edition). And even this cosmic drama serves as a prelude to that more engrossing, if perplexing spectacle which is human history. The pageant begins by acknowledging that "vast vacancy" between prehistorical and historical existence, between the wild child and the singing villagers who "Dug [themselves] in to the hill top . . . Ground roots between stones . . . Ground corn . . . till [they] too . . . lay under g–r–o–u–n–d . . ." (p. 78). The ellipses are Woolf's, denoting the gaps in

From *Virginia Woolf's Major Novels: The Fables of Anon.* Copyright © 1980 by Yale University Press.

time and leaps in consciousness that constituted the gradual, unrecorded advance from a state of nature to a state of culture. The multiple pun on "ground" which concludes the prologue announces the pageant's obsessive theme: the problematic relation of cultural figures to their native ground. Beginning with the heroic days of Anglo-Saxon warrior societies, the pageant proceeds to recreate the distinctive figurative identities of successive British cultures: Chaucer's "Merry England," Elizabethan majesty, Restoration and Augustan "Reason," Victorian marriage of messianic imperialism and the cult of Home. Only contemporary England is represented without its informing and presiding genius, its unifying spirit of the age. The playfully reconstructed myth of Britain's epic past and epic destiny, alternately celebrated and mocked in the refrain invoking "The valiant Rhoderick / Armed and valiant / Bold and blatant / Firm elatant," disintegrates into orts, scraps, and fragments.

While Woolf's historical perception of "Present time" as an epoch of cultural and personal disintegration was undoubtedly influenced by T. S. Eliot's theoretical and poetical pronouncements on the modernist crisis of disassociation, another figure, political rather than literary, insinuated itself into her thought and art in that crucial decade between 1930, when *The Waves* was written, and 1939, the crisis year in which *Between the Acts* is set: Fascist man. As described in *Three Guineas*, Fascist man represents human nature corrupted and emboldened by the blind absolutes of patriarchal culture:

> It is the figure of a man; some say, others deny, that he is Man himself, the quintessence of virility, the perfect type of which all the others are imperfect adumbrations. He is a man certainly. His eyes are glazed; his eyes glare. His body, which is braced in an unnatural position, is tightly cased in a uniform. Upon the breast of that uniform are sewn several medals and other mystical symbols. His hand is upon a sword.

The figure of Fascist man represents the quintessence of that sterile and aggressively destructive masculine will whose tyrannies, petty and titanic, Woolf had examined with ever finer precision since *Mrs. Dalloway* and *To the Lighthouse*. It confirms her intuition that "the public and the private worlds are inseparably connected; that the tyrannies and servilities of the one are the tyrannies and servilities of the other." Behind Fascist man, hand on sword, stands a long, and presently debased tradition of martial epic, with "as Herr Hitler puts it, the hero requiring recreation, or, as Signor Mussolini puts it, the wounded warrior requiring female dependents to bandage his wounds." Woolf's opposition to the mythologies that glorify martial virtues and legitimize the tyrannies and servilities of patriarchal states finds its rallying cry in the words of Antigone "worth all the sermons of all the archbishops": " 'Tis not my nature to join in hating, but in loving." Woolf repeatedly returns to the example of Antigone in *Three Guineas* and *The Years* to illustrate her moral and imaginative stance toward the tyrannies, servilities, and barbarities endemic to Fascist cultures, a stance epigrammatically rendered in the maxim—"Those also serve who remain outside."

Woolf's disassociation from patriarchal culture is no mere "experiment in passivity," as some critics suggest. Her act of withdrawal from the official culture, like Antigone's, permits her to exercise a natural and therefore superior right: to reenact the sanctified rituals that constitute the original ground of all human and natural law and, in doing so, to fulfill her own feminine nature to join in loving. The state of war, civil or global, preempts or abrogates those rights in the name of that martial law whose basis necessarily resides in hating. To end war, Woolf argued, culture and intellectual liberty must be protected against dictatorial wills and those totalitarian states that express the final, one might venture, the terminal form of their desires. Woolf defines this adversary, anterior culture as "the disinterested pursuit of reading and writing the English language," implying that for the modern Antigone the verbal rites are the objects of her disinterested love. Woolf's love, as intense as it is disinterested, perceives in British culture a rival literary tradition and rival genius whose visible and presiding spirit is Shakespeare: the English theater. In a world at war where the word theater came to connote the arenas of embattled armies, Woolf remained the purist, the outsider who recalled and preserved the creative and controlled denotations of an inherited vocabulary of form. And Woolf's own work, always straining to approximate the intensities of dramatic form, finally turns from the lyricism of *The Waves* and the essayistic, discursive, and episodic chronicle of *The Years*, to the perils and anxieties of public enactment—the play.

That the title of the novel is *Between the Acts* itself announces this ordering of priorities: time will be treated as an aesthetic occasion and the action of the drama to unfold will transpire in a self-insulated and self-enclosed aesthetic scene *outside* or *apart* from history's battlegrounds. Like Jane Austen writing during the Napoleonic Wars, Woolf rarely permits the chaos of history to perturb her own loving performances. Offstage, behind, not in the acts, yet inevitably shadowing Woolf's own performance, is the Nazi juggernaut, threatening to cross the channel, invade and occupy English ground. Lucy Swithin, who does not believe in history, thinks about the time when no channel separated England from the European continent, a thought that must have filled the contemporary reader with horror. Distance and natural division, the creation of aesthetic space of which the stage is the primary symbol, is as essential to Woolf's intention as the forging of community and the celebration of the "one world, one life" all men and women share. The walls of the stage, like the walls of civilization invoked at the pageant's conclusion, exclude as much life as they contain.

History in the making is never allowed onstage, for it would destroy the achieved sublimations in violence that distinguish the decorums of dramatic representation. The novel alludes and adheres to the "bienséances" of Racinian theater and the stylizations of Chinese drama in its historic reporting; an airplane flying overhead, like a dagger on the table, is sufficient to symbolize a bloody battle (p. 142). History as "present-time reality" proves too strong when allowed to flood the mind without the necessary mediations of art. To be comprehended history must be transmuted into text, dialogue, and symbolic gesture. What immediate historical reality is accommodated in the novel appears in its vivid presentness in the form of newspaper reports, what Woolf termed in *Three Guineas* "history in the raw." To shield her audience from the senseless, hideous, and stupefying chaos of contemporary history serves Woolf's ideological and aesthetic purpose, a purpose necessarily undermined, however, by Woolf's own ironic self-consciousness as an interpreter of history. *Between the Acts* is a war book of the most compelling and searching kind, a novel that makes history its subject matter in order to question the validity of art, the limits of the book, and the powers of illusion in a world absorbed in the work of destruction. Such self-questionings are the sign both of Woolf's "culture" and its disinterestedness.

The anxiety of art is the central problem of the novel and it is first posed by Isa, the aspiring poetess through whom all the anxieties of her generation are voiced. Isa is thirty-nine, the age of the century, an age book-shy and gun-shy, indicating that the two phobias are not unrelated. Unlike the "foolish, flattering lady" who naively held that "Books are the mirrors of the soul" (p. 16), Isa anxiously surveys both the ground and the figures of an art that foolishly flatters with its ennobling and consoling representations:

> In this case a tarnished, a spotted soul. For as the train took over three hours to reach this remote village in the very heart of England, no one ventured so long a journey without staving off possible mind-hunger, without buying a book on a bookstall. Thus the mirror that reflected the soul sublime, reflected also the soul bored. Nobody could pretend, as they

looked at the shuffle of shilling shockers that week-enders had dropped, that the looking glass always reflected the anguish of a Queen or the heroism of King Harry.

(p. 16)

The sublime pretendings of romantic fiction are chastised by the ennui of a shell-shocked present. Woolf suggests that her own art will mirror "English" nature and the village life that, though remote in time and space from war-torn London, still remains at the "heart" of British culture. The contemporary ennui and despair afflicting the British "soul" is reflected in the audience which both attends and participates in the performance of a village pageant. Woolf's implied aesthetic focus echoes George Eliot's prescription for literary realism:

There are few prophets in the world; few sublimely beautiful women; few heroes. I can't afford to give my love and reverence to such rarities.

But the dramatic year, 1939, is a world of extremes in which "to give the loving pains of a life to the faithful representing of commonplace things" is but to produce shilling shockers and newspaper dispatches which compose "the book of reality" for Isa and her generation. In a newspaper account in the *Times*, Isa accidentally discovers the narrative line that imitates the total action of the war:

"The troopers told her the horse had a green tail; but she found it was just an ordinary horse. And they dragged her up to the barrack room where she was thrown upon a bed. Then one of the troopers removed part of her clothing, and she screamed and hit him about the face. . . ."
    That was real; so real that on the mahogany door panels she saw the Arch in Whitehall; through the Arch the barrack room; in the barrack room the bed, and on the bed the girl was screaming and hitting him about the face, when the door (for in fact it was a door) opened and in came Mrs. Swithin carrying a hammer.

(p. 20)

Isa's imagination, like the victim's, is lured on by the fantastic (the horse with a green tail), encouraged by the romantic (the guard at Whitehall), only to be betrayed by the real. Abandoning the romantic, Isa traces the evidences of the real through the Arch in Whitehall, where councils of war convene, through the barrack room to the bed where war culminates, according to Woolf, where it begins, in sexual estrangement and violation. That love and war share the same strategies of deceit, dissimulation, disguise, but employ them toward different social and human ends is no mere feminist simplification, but an expression of the proverbial wisdom emerging from the collective experience of the race. Woolf's fearless literalization of this figurative analogy becomes the principle of her dramatic composition and yields her an authentic psychological, historical, and aesthetic insight. The love battles between men and women, the immemorial drama of love and hate naturally and necessarily center in the "act" of love, an act that may signal the fruition of that natural relation between the sexes out of which life issues or the violation of that relation by which life is betrayed and degraded. Woolf's insight into tragic form is essentially that of Georg Lukács when he argues that "The formal laws of drama arise out of the material of actual life," and that "the same inner laws of form" are "the laws of movement of life itself, of which the plays are artistic images." These dynamic images of historical and natural life, formalized by the collisions, climaxes, reversals, and resolutions that shape tragic action, are not "pure" or idealized representations, but generalizations and intensifications of what Lukács calls "a typical fact of life." For Woolf, of course, the facts of life derive primarily from the natural, rather than historical movement of life; her tragedy remains essentially a sexual tragedy. Between the acts of the village pageant the narrative suggests the presence of this unfolding sexual tragedy, a tragedy whose commanding temporal metaphor has traditionally been the ironic fruition of the past in the image of an aborted future. This sexual tragedy in turn yields an image of the tragedy of the war writ large: time and life cut short, destroyed, deprived of a future. *Between the Acts* begins with a discussion about a cesspool and from then on the novel seems mired in the murky, material reality of human waste and death that Woolf's own art seeks to mirror and transform.

If the sexual tragedy mirrors the larger action of world war, that mirror is itself the visible sign of unnatural or perverted vital energies. The barbaric energy unleashed by the war is psychologically registered in the sadism that infects the emotions dramatized in the novel, especially the emotions of the young and still passionate, those still capable of producing new life. Mrs. Haines, for example, the wife of the mysterious gentleman farmer Isa admires, yearns to disrupt the charged, illicit emotion generated by their unspoken flirtation in a singularly sadistic image: "In the car going home to the red villa in the cornfields, she would destroy it, as a thrush pecks the wings off a butterfly" (p. 6). The pressure of undischarged emotion, of the pandemic aggressiveness unleashed by the war, is relieved in the novel's moment of real violence, the moment when Giles squashes the snake with a toad in its mouth, the only time blood is drawn in the novel.

Giles's act dramatically discharges the irresistible desire to destroy, to inflict pain, to draw blood that infects all those whose future is shadowed by the war. Only Lucy Swithin seems free of this pandemic hatred, she who does not believe in history nor in the differences between the sexes, nations, or races that history makes evident. But she has not, as she herself intuits, yet touched earth: "Skimming the surface, she ignored the battle in the mud" (p. 203).

Ignoring the battle is not, however, synonymous with ignorance; keeping to the surface is a strategy, by custom become a habit, of the unifying imagination in Woolfian fiction. Mrs. Swithin, "Old Flimsy" or "Batty" as her maid prefers, is the incorrigible, perhaps anachronistic monist indigenous to Woolf's fictional world, a reminder of the effortless epiphanies—and certitudes—of the past. Through Lucy Swithin, whose first name recalls the translucent, innocent beings of romantic, Wordsworthian persuasions, Woolf comments on the visionary cadences of the style perfected in *To the Lighthouse* and *The Waves*. To Lucy she attributes the only panhistorical vision in the novel, a vision spanning from prehistoric man, half-human, half-ape, to modern man. Reading an Outline of History, thinking of the time "when the entire continent, not then she understood, divided by a channel, was all one." Lucy effortlessly envisions the evolutionary links connecting the iguanodon, the mammoth, and the mastodon with their human descendents:

> It took her five seconds in actual time, in mind time ever so much longer, to separate Grace herself, with blue china on a tray, from the leather-covered grunting monster who was about, as the door opened, to demolish a whole tree in the green steaming undergrowth of the primeval forest. Naturally, she jumped, as Grace put the tray down and said: "Good morning, Ma'am." "Batty," Grace called her, as she felt on her face the divided glance that was half meant for a beast in a swamp, half for a maid in a print frock and white apron.
>
> (p. 9)

Lucy's imaginative reconstruction of the past, directed by a supplied "outline" of evolutionary sequences, depends on her talent for "increasing the bounds of the moment" to accommodate the magnified images of the prehuman past within the homely, diminished confines of the present. Only the intercession of "Grace" recalls her to the disjunction between "actual" time, in all its remorseless chronicity, and "mind-time" with its synchronic fluidity. The shock of Lucy's recognition is comically rendered, thus deflating the potentially frightening distance separating the past from the present. "Batty," the mind-divided Lucy who could have been, Woolf reminds us at the end of the novel, "a tragic figure from another play" (p. 214), like the schizophrenic Septimus Smith, for example, is rescued by the comic rhythms and sanities of Woolf's play. Disruptions and deflations of Lucy's visionary moments never end with the terrifying alienations native to tragedy. With comic regularity, one thing succeeds, almost miraculously, in following another, just as Lucy quickly resituates herself in the present by venturing "How those birds sing!", which, certainly, the narrator comments, they were doing (p. 9).

For Woolf, the play of imagination, assisted, of course, by the timely entrance of "Grace," always yields a comic perception of resurgent life singing its own triumph, of nature obliging the mind with its own irrational intimations of continuity. War deranges the human perception of historical and natural time because it suggests more tragic images of the moment as occasions of apocalyptic or abortive finalities. To such images of the end, Woolf opposes the comic intuition of time as duration, a duration measured, as Locke taught and Sterne reminded us in *Tristram Shandy*, by the train or succession of ideas. Woolf relies on the associationalism endemic to British comic fiction as her authority in arguing for a form of succession that insures that one thing will follow another. The mechanical motions of Lucy's comically undisciplined mind in linking the iguanodon to the figure of intervening "Grace" may be a flimsy, yet still successful way to adjust to reality, to assimilate the discrete impressions, memories, and ideas confronting the mind. The random associations of Lucy's ideas, for example, never trail off into irrelevancy or inconsequentiality, but describe, through the circuitous digressions favored by comic imaginings, the circularity of thought and the essential integrity of all experience. Thus when Isa mentions her fears that the fish she had ordered would not be fresh, Lucy's mind moves effortlessly from the topic of fish, to the thought of the time when there was no sea between the continents, to Pharaohs, to dentists to false teeth to marriage between cousins to the Swithin and Oliver lineage and back, finally, to the problem at hand: "Oh yes, you were saying, Isa, you'd ordered fish; and you were afraid it wouldn't be fresh. And I said, 'That's the problem . . .' " (p. 31). Lucy's inability to fix her gaze on the problem at hand is precisely what permits the comic enlargement and comic assimilation of reality. Lucy's mind-time may be a breach in the unity, or rather the monotonous succession of actual time, but it is, as Sterne says, "the true scholastic pendulum." Woolf joins Sterne's Tristram in "abjuring and detesting the jurisdiction of all other pendulums whatever." Lucy's scholastic pendulum, which encompasses all the orts, scraps, and fragments

of her arcane archaeological and geological musings, composes another kind
of history, what Sterne, comically appropriating Locke, calls "a history of
what transpires in a man's mind." Lockean psychology, child of the British
empirical spirit, colors Lucy's all-too-human understanding of history. Nor
is the order articulated by "Batty's" meditative meanderings factitious. Her
mind is engaged throughout the novel in a comic, if relentless pursuit of
the originating "ground" for those very superstitions or irrational conjunctions of sensations which pass for ideas in her mind. It is she who proposes,
for example, the mythopoeic source for the superstition "touch wood":
"Antaeus, didn't he touch earth?" (p. 24).

If Lucy is the unifier who can never touch earth, but merely skims
the surface of her own randomly associating, unifying mind, her brother
Bartholomew is the separatist, her complementary opposite in the English
stock of comic characters. He is the rationalist who honors all the discriminations both nature and history produce in their separate, sometimes overlapping cycles. In the sibling love of Lucy and Bartholomew, the unifier
and the separatist, the mind-divided relations of the sexes finds a sublimated
expression of comic tolerance and conciliation: "Nothing changed their
affections; no argument; no fact; no truth. What she saw he didn't; what
he saw she didn't—and so on, *ad infinitum*" (p. 26). The irreconcilable
differences between the unifier who harbors a prayable being in her breast
and the agnostic who stoutly believes in history and the acts of representative men are never resolved. They are only mediated by the affection
through which sister and brother silently communicate. Between the lines
of their dialogue persists a rhythm of mechanical repetition that for Woolf,
as for Bergson, is a source of comic effects. The clash of their contrary
natures is contained by the comic predictability of their exchanges and the
comic regularity by which their differences are dissolved, like a mist, into
less impervious attitudes. Like all comic "relations," they achieve that
concord in discord and unity in dispersity by which society paradoxically
renews itself—*ad infinitum*.

But for the modern poet, Isa, the rhythms of comic plotting and
comic dialogue no longer repeat themselves in the same reassuring sequence
and the same reassuring register. She becomes impatient with the comic
litany of responses Mrs. Swithin rehearses and re-rehearses with her brother
about whether the "forecast" will be fine or not:

> Every summer, for seven summers now, Isa had heard the same words;
> about the hammer and the nails; the pageant and the weather. Every year
> they said, would it be wet or fine; and every year it was—one or the other.
> The same chime followed the same chime, only this year beneath the

chime she heard: "The girl screamed and hit him about the face with a hammer."

(p. 22)

Isa notices a break in the comic pattern of natural alternation between male and female, summer and winter, wet or fine. The dialogue in the human comedy remains the same, but a note of urgency and brutality disturbs the chime—or harmony—such alternations produce in the person who overhears. This is one of many instances in the novel in which the spectator or audience actively questions the set-piece played out before them. Such moments form a subplot of the drama that is played out between the acts. Spectators measure the artifices of order against the reality of disorder. Isa, too, has her own associations, tragically, not comically linked to the figure of Lucy and her hammer. Her thoughts do not follow each other in swift, mechanical succession, but are arrested and fixated on an image of traumatic and brutal violation. Isa brings to the drama of Pointz Hall a tragic perception of life despoiled, vanquished, and betrayed. Her vision of life at enmity with itself is internalized in the alternations of her own mind-divided glances between inner love and outer love, between love for her husband, the stockbroker, and love for the silent, romantic gentlemen farmer. She awaits for a *deus ex machina,* a miraculous intrusion of "Grace," to resolve the obscure and tangled emotions of her own erratic will: "O that our human pain could here have ending!" murmurs Isa near the conclusion of the pageant, hoping for deliverance.

Isa's sense of relation, then, is not one of comic contrast and concord, but of tragic entanglement. In the play of Isa's imagination, the dialogue between Lucy and Bartholomew provides moments of comic relief in the larger tragedy which seems to be her own life. Unlike Lucy, Isa can never keep to the surface, but casts her lines into the depths where they inevitably are entangled with the object of her love and her hate—Giles Oliver. Her love for Giles dates to their first meeting when "her line had got tangled" (p. 48), and the memory of that entanglement informs and qualifies her adulterous fantasies about herself and Haines as "swans floating downstream": "His snow-white breast was circled with a tangle of dirty duckweed; and she too, in her webbed feet was entangled, by her husband, the stockbroker" (p. 5).

The motif of entangled and obscure desire implies that Isa's potential tragedy does not proceed, as with classical tragic heroines, from an irrepressible will, an inalienable individuality. Isa is the modern tragicomic heroine in the tradition of Ibsen and Chekhov, a heroine whose will is incommensurate to her desire, whose actions are never complete expressions of her intention: " 'Abortive,' was the word that expressed her. "She never came out of a shop, for example, with the clothes she admired; nor did her figure, seen against the dark roll of trousering in a shop window, please her" (pp. 15–16). The "figure" Isa cuts is an object not of tragic awe, but of satiric observation, a figure Woolf consistently illuminates against a "novelistic" background of material and social facts: "She looked what she was: Sir Richard's daughter; and niece of the two old ladies at Wimbledon who were so proud, being O'Neils, of their descent from the Kings of Ireland" (p. 16). Woolf's careful characterization of Isa depends, finally, on the detailed circumstantial evidence of clothes, family lineage, and social surroundings—all those "ghosts of convention" by which the novel traditionally claimed to penetrate the being and explain the peculiar existence of its characters. Far from investigating the psychological depths of Isa's unhappy marriage, Woolf prefers to minimize and record her suffering in the rhetoric of novelistic cliché: "Their relations . . . were as people say in novels 'strained' " (p. 106).

Woolf's blend of satire and tragedy, in its larger generic configurations, culminates in another moment of abortive action and figurative illumination—Giles's killing of the snake with a toad in its mouth. The tragedies of Giles's life do not, like Isa's, slip "into the cliché conveniently provided by fiction" (p. 14). Rather they are displaced in another kind of imaginative play—a child's game, a game that allegorically expresses the moral typology by which human nature was once represented. Giles's is a game of controlled aggression in which a stone must be kicked to a goal in ten tries:

> The first kick was Manresa (lust). The second, Dodge (perversion). The third, himself (coward). And the fourth and the fifth and all the others were the same.
>
> (p. 99)

Giles's child's game is the vehicle for his own Dantesque allegorization of evil, for which his own experience provides both the text and the gloss. His allegory of selfhood traces the inevitable and, for him, eternally recurring declension from incontinence (excessive desire) to perversion (misdirected desire) to cowardice (shadow of desire). On reaching his goal, the allegorical figures of play are unexpectedly confirmed and replaced by a real image: "There, couched in the grass, curled in an olive green ring, was a snake. Dead? No, choked with a toad in its mouth. The snake was unable to swallow; the toad was unable to die" (p. 99). This figure of "monstrous inversion," with which nature mocks the despairing, incapacitated will, echoes Dante's portrait of Satan, the demonic agent whose own will is paralyzed, radiating evil from his frozen heart, held and bound in the frozen cesspool of the world. "There"—in the center of life, the heart of darkness, the bottom of the abyss—the tragedy of a soul that turns away from its spiritual sources combines with the satirical trope of inversion (*mundus inversus*) to produce a "mirror" of reality, but never the Love that animates it. Woolf's image of pure negation, an image provided by nature, of birth the wrong way round, of a deathless death, also combines satiric inversion with the tragic incapacity of the moral imagination, the moral will. Dante's paradoxical notion of freedom is imported into Woolf's fiction as a psychological truism: the will that acts out of hate, against the Love that moves the sun and the other stars, only secures its own self-bondage.

Woolf's own allegorization of figure, her reduction and compression of character into moral "types," and her identification of personalities through epithets (old Flimsy, Bossy) assimilates Giles's self-allegorizing play within the larger perspectives of her own human, historical, if not divine comedy. It is particularly through the artifice of the play within the novel that Woolf displays that analogical imagination which is alone capable of establishing a network of meanings and correspondences upon the unstable, chaotic materials of the self and its history. Through the pageant's allegorical presentation of history, in which various characters impersonate the ruling ideas of successive ages, the moral identity of Britannia is recovered and her present instability rationalized. At the center of the pageant within the novel, *there* is presented a Restoration play in which "Reason" is finally allowed to speak out against Unreason. The words of "Reason," which serve as an epilogue to a parodic treatment of Congreve's comedies, summarize the moral and imaginative vision of the pageant:

> And so to end the play, the moral is,
> The God of love is full of tricks;
> Into the foot his dart he sticks,
> But the way of the will is plain to see;
> Let holy virgins hymn perpetually:
> "Where there's a will there's a way."
> Good people all, farewell.
>
> (p. 148)

" 'God's truth!' cries Bartholomew, catching the inflection of the language, 'There's a moral for you!' " The inflection of language caught by Bartholomew's exclamation, like the infectious parodic rhetoric that informs Woolf's representation of scenes from British history, is double-edged: such playful mimicry chronicles the inevitable degeneration of figurative language into cliché, while simultaneously revitalizing and restoring cliché, the petrified expression of hereditary wisdom, to its pristine signification. "God's Truth" is precisely "Where there's a will there's a way." For Woolf, the will to life is allied to the will to comedy and conciliation, not the will to power and domination. The homely nature of her moral does not diminish the depth of her social and historical vision. As Freud argued, Eros, the God of Love, is full of tricks, but Eros is still War and Death's mighty antagonist. In "Why War" Freud proposes the same indirect methods of combatting war and hatred that Woolf suggested in Three Guineas—to join in loving:

> If willingness to engage in war is an effect of the destructive instinct, the most obvious plan will be to bring Eros, its antagonist, into play against it. Anything that encourages the growth of emotional ties between men must operate against war.

If, as Isa speculates, the basic plot of life is love and hate, it is the God of love who emerges triumphant—as long as there is a will to seek its own way. This is the moral of the Restoration comedy presented in the middle of pageant, a moral observed from the marriage of Reason and Love. As Avrom Fleishman has observed, at the center of the pageant is a moment of silence in which lovers embrace, signalling the renewal of nature's and society's creative cycles. "All that fuss for nothing!" (p. 138) a cynical, skeptical, but probably good-humored voice exclaims as Valentine and Flavinda rapturously embrace. But, of course, all the fuss is for something, and Woolf's insight is to see in the "fuss" of courtship and mating, the much ado about nothing, the very "something" which knits men and women, nature and culture together: the exchange of vows, the faithfulness of lovers to each other and to the life which will proceed from their union. The Restoration tableau concludes with a procession of lovers singing, often inaudibly, the strains of a comic song:

> . . . Summer and winter, autumn and spring return . . . All passes but we, all changes . . . but we remain forever the same.
>
> (p. 139)

The triumph of Eros is also the triumph of time the preserver and continuer over time the destroyer. As the processional song resumes, the lovers call out the catalogue of those ruins of time recorded in the book of life: "Babylon, Nineveh, Troy . . . And Caesar's great house . . . all fallen they lie. . . . " Only a few great names—Babylon, Nineveh, Clytemnestra, Agamemnon, Troy—survive time, haunting the present with their stories of passing civilizations, of family ties betrayed, of estranged lovers, of the falls of great houses. The ancestral memory of strife is never far from Woolf's consciousness in the tale of Pointz Hall, her own symbolic center for a civilization that is threatened by the enemy without and dissension within. It is this perception of the destructive passage of time that paralyzes La Trobe's imagination and imperils the comic rhythms of her play: "Illusion had failed. 'This is death,' she murmured, 'death' " (p. 140).

La Trobe's potentially fatal silence, her imaginative impotence in the presence of untransfigured historical time, is redeemed by one of the most daring comic reversals in Woolf's fiction. "In the very nick of time"—testimony to the comic faith in providential timing—Nature rescues Art with her own *deus ex machina*. The imagination's inability to resist the urge to death and destruction is rescued by the primeval voice of an outraged maternal nature. The herd instinct of dumb, yearning cows bellows its protest "as if Eros had planted his dart in their flanks and goaded them to fury." Nature brings Eros into play against death, annihilating the gap between past and present time, bridging the distance between illusion and the reality it denominates, filling the emptiness momentarily afflicting the mind, and continuing the emotion generated by the spectacles of the past.

Woolf's romantic appeal to Nature and its furious Eros to reinspirit the flagging, moribund energies of her imaginative play is both dramatically effective and historically reductive. Her vision of history is intentionally antipositivistic, antihistoricist, ignoring those complex and complicating convergences of accident, contingency, circumstance, human decision, and cultural change by which history is "made." History for Woolf *is* a process, but a process that primarily engages her imagination for its underlying generative rhythms, not for those surface discriminations of manners, dress, speech, class and economic organizations, cultural and philosophical beliefs that constitute the idiosyncratic, local and inalienable "style" of any given historical period. Woolf's project in her pageant is to de-idealize history by minimizing the importance of its plots, by underplaying the role of particular social, economic, or cultural determinants, and by denying to historical process any teleological or rational principle except the love and hate by which it, like Nature, is goaded and impelled to manifest itself:

> Did the plot matter? . . . The plot was only there to beget emotion. There were only two emotions: love; and hate. There was no need to puzzle out the plot. Perhaps Miss La Trobe meant that when she cut this knot in the centre?
>
> (pp. 90–91)

Woolf may be consciously playing on the word "denouement," that dramatic untying of the knot, that unravelling of "life's tangled skein" by which dramatic form imitates and comprehends the riddling complexities of life. The knot of reality, the puzzling "fuss" of life, is cut out of the pageant and displaced onto the intervals between the acts. The play within the novel dispenses with the complications and resolutions of an intricate plot, preferring to cut through the tense knot of dramatic exposition to expose its generating rhythms. The pageant reduces, through allegorical impersonation and symbolic condensation, all human history to an elemental conflict between love and hate. The primordial war between these two emotions, Woolf proposes, animates history and determines its emplotted forms—tragedy and comedy. Tragic form generates and is generated by the emotion of what Isa calls "hate." That Isa and Giles are the only central characters to feel this hate, and to feel it as a necessary component of their love, suggests that tragic hatred does not spring from a Satanic spirit of denial and negation, but from the aggrieved spirit of thwarted individuality, from the mistimed conjunctions of will and desire, from the intolerable passivity that is compensated by real or imagined acts of sadistic aggression. Comic form, on the other hand, is rooted in the vicissitudes of love, in the opportune and timely conjunctions of will and desire, in the final coincidence of love and its objects. The competition and interdependency of these two plots, traceable throughout all of Woolf's fiction, is sufficient to explain the vagaries and direction of human life and human history: " 'It was enough. Enough. Enough,' " Isa observes during the performance. "All else was verbiage, repetition" (p. 91).

What J. Hillis Miller has termed the skeletal "Ur-Drama" of *Between the Acts* is sufficient as a principle of historical explanation and aesthetic form because its resolution—or denouement—is classically and economically timed to coincide with a moment of recognition. As Isa is formulating her own theories about the meaning of the play presented by Miss La Trobe, she is nevertheless caught up in the immediacy of the climactic recognition scene that concludes the first major parodic tableau in the pageant. Theoretically committed to the notion that "the plot's nothing," Isa cannot forbear wondering "But what was happening?" (p. 91). On stage, what happens is a complex series of recognitions in which a withered beldame recognizes a young Prince thought lost and now found: "My child! My child!" she shrieks. This triumphant image of the rescued child prepares for the second major recognition, this time between lovers: "My love! My lord!" This double image of rescued child, whose birthmark links him to nature's cycles of generation, and of reunited lovers, whose pledge links them to society's rituals of regeneration, constitute a symbol, as Isa rightly interprets, of "Love embodied." The fruition of love through time marks

Woolf's most persistent symbol of human and natural creativity. All else pales to verbiage and repetition in the presence of that initial act of creation in which the midwife is Time.

The allegorical meaning of Woolf's historical vision can best be seen in the Restoration parody. That tableau also concludes with a complex recognition scene in which Valentine, the resourceful hero of "Where there's a Will there's a Way," is literally trapped in the entrails of a timepiece until the auspicious and inevitable moment of his deliverance. The allegorical significance of Valentine's—or Eros's—confinement within time is doubly referential. It refers to Valentine's own status within the play as a hero awaiting his love and his rightful inheritance, and it comments on the temporal mode of the allegorical situation in which he is placed. As Paul de Man has observed of allegory's temporality: "Allegory exists entirely within an ideal time that is never here and now, but always a past or endless future. It appears as a successive mode capable of engendering the illusion of continuity it knows to be illusionary." The allegorical experience of time as duration, of meaning suspended in its own process of engenderment and articulation, is Woolf's aesthetic defense against the demoralizing chronicity of contemporary history. The collective mind represented by the novel can never, in its despair, see beyond the here and now. Even those content with the here and now, like Lucy and her brother Bart, are representatives of a cycle coming to conclusion, not of a cycle continuing or about to begin again. It is Isa who represents the anxiety of contemporary history, for whom the present is not enough, not sufficient, "No, not for us, who've the future . . . the future disturbing our present" (p. 82). It is to assuage anxiety about the future that Woolf implements her allegory of love in which Eros, full of tricks, conspires *with* time to create a sustaining vision of love embodied *in* time. Woolf's comic vision of a love rescued in time is illusionary, a creation of the imagination's play, but, as Huizinga has noted, to maintain illusion is, etymologically speaking, to keep reality within the confines of the playing, active imagination. If the failure of illusion is, as Miss La Trobe says, Death, the triumph of illusion is, as Huizinga says, "in play."

E. L. BISHOP

Toward the Far Side of Language: "The Voyage Out"

One of Virginia Woolf's most eloquent statements on the role of language appears in her essay "On Not Knowing Greek" where she asserts that, in order to understand Aeschylus,

> it is not so necessary to understand Greek as to understand poetry. It is necessary to take that dangerous leap through the air without the support of words which Shakespeare also asks of us. . . . Connecting them in a rapid flight of the mind we know instantly and instinctively what they mean, but could not decant that meaning afresh into other words. The meaning is just on the far side of language.

The passage accurately describes the workings of Woolf's own mature art, yet even in her first novel, *The Voyage Out* (1915), language attains the concentration and suggestiveness of poetry. That this rather traditional work contains both thematic and stylistic intimations of her later, more experimental, novels has been remarked but never adequately explored. However, the novel rewards patient analysis, for in Rachel's restive questioning of the functions of language, Woolf introduces what will become a persistent theme in all her works: the problem of how words can encompass and communicate human experience. Further, it is in *The Voyage Out* that one discovers Woolf laboring to achieve what she would later effect with felicitous ease: a mode of discourse which compels the reader's active participation, guiding him to the point where he can make his own intuitive leap, to apprehend a reality that will not submit to denotative prose.

From *Twentieth Century Literature* 4, vol. 27 (Winter 1981). Copyright © 1982 by Hofstra University Press.

It was not until the spring of 1919, with the publication of "Modern Fiction" and "Kew Gardens" (manifestos in complementary modes), that she publicly announced her artistic intentions. However, in a letter to Clive Bell written in 1908 as she was beginning to shape "Melymbrosia," later *The Voyage Out*, she declared,

> I think a great deal of my future, and settle what book I am to write—how I shall re-form the novel and capture multitudes of things at present fugitive, enclose the whole, and shape infinite strange shapes. I take a good look at woods in the sunset, and fix men who are breaking stones with an intense gaze, meant to sever them from the past and the future—all these excitements last out my walk, but tomorrow I know, I shall be sitting down to the inanimate old phrases.

The young woman's bold plans of reform promise to lead her away from traditional concepts of plot and character, for her interest lies less in the variables of personality than in the radical character of human beings and things, both animate and inanimate, of the external world; she wants to "sever them from past and future," and she intends not merely to record but to "capture" and "shape" this elusive aspect of reality. But her enthusiasm for rejuvenating fiction is suddenly punctured by the thought of contending with the "inanimate old phrases." One notices throughout Woolf's writings a constantly fluctuating regard for language: it strikes her by turns as an almost magical force, as a mere necessary evil, and as a betrayer of life. These disparate attitudes inform *The Voyage Out*, and the work is both a groping exploration on Woolf's part of the connection between reality and language, and a dramatic portrayal of a corresponding exploration in the growth of the central character.

The novel traces Rachel Vinrace's voyage out: a journey from England to South America, an initiation into love, and finally a passage out of life into death. In a concurrent mental voyage that leads both inward and outward, Rachel awakens to the world at large and to her own consciousness. She discovers that life can seem very precarious and the world entirely desolate, only to decide later that the world is a most hospitable place and life something calm and certain. She finds it difficult to put either perception into words, and the problem arises as much from the uncertain nature of reality as it does from language. As it does for characters in Woolf's subsequent novels, Rachel's progress takes shape around "moments of being"—instants of almost visionary insight—in which her understanding of life is sharply, and somewhat disconcertingly, enhanced.

After their arrival in South America, Rachel's companion, the older and more worldly Helen Ambrose, desires "that Rachel should think, and for this reason offered books." Helen's prescription proves to be well-advised. The reading does make Rachel think—and in a manner that contrasts sharply both with the packrat-like cataloging of her fellow tourist, Mr. Pepper, and with the pedantry of Helen's husband, Ridley Ambrose. The books engender a curiosity about life itself: "What is the truth? What is the truth of it all?" she asks. Her new curiosity about "the truth of it all" derives as much from that sense of "wonder which always marks the transition from the imaginary world to the real world," as it does from the specific contents of the books. After reading she finds that "the landscape outside . . . now appeared amazingly solid and clear." The sensation of gazing upon or seeing the world, rather than merely looking at it, leaves Rachel ripe for the visionary experience that translates her disinterested curiosity into a vital personal concern. Here the side effects of reading act as the catalyst for a more intense and more disturbing apprehension of the phenomenal world:

> The morning was hot, and the exercise of reading left her mind contracting and expanding like the mainspring of a clock. The sounds in the garden outside joined with the clock, and the small noises of midday, which one can ascribe to no definite cause, in a regular rhythm. It was all very real, very big, very impersonal, and after a moment or two she began to raise her first finger and to let it fall on the arm of her chair so as to bring back to herself some consciousness of her own existence. She was next overcome by the unspeakable queerness of the fact that she should be sitting in an arm-chair, in the morning, in the middle of the world. . . . Her dissolution became so complete that she could not raise her finger any more, and sat perfectly still, listening and looking always at the same spot. It became stranger and stranger. She was overcome with awe that things should exist at all. . . . She forgot that she had any fingers to raise. . . . The things that existed were so immense and so desolate. . . . She continued to be conscious of these vast masses of substance for a long stretch of time, the clock still ticking in the midst of the universal silence.
>
> (first ellipsis mine)

Reading involves cognition that is both rational and perceptual, and whether or not Woolf had this in mind when she spoke of the "contracting and expanding" of Rachel's mind, it is the act of reading rather than the meaning of the words that triggers Rachel's experience. Further, the experience itself takes the form of a widening oscillation between sensory apprehension and conceptual analysis. Rachel moves deeper into a more radical mode of consciousness until, instead of discriminating among objects according to their individual qualities, she becomes aware only of "things," or "vast masses of substance." Now at the furthest possible remove from intellection, her question, "What is the truth of it all?" becomes something felt rather than entertained, replaced by a fundamental "awe that things should exist at all." This awe constitutes only the preliminary stage of Rachel's awakening, however, for she has perceived existence only, not the life of things nor the relations between them.

Immediately following her bleak vision, an invitation to a picnic affects her with unusual force: "The blood began to run in her veins; she felt her eyes brighten. 'We must go,' she said, rather surprising Helen by her decision. 'We must certainly go'—such was the relief of finding that things still happened, and indeed they appeared the brighter for the mist surrounding them." The "things that happen" are the bonds between human beings. Terence Hewet, who sent the note, underlines its significance: " 'Cows,' he reflected, 'draw together in a field; ships in a calm; and we're just the same when we've nothing else to do. But why do we do it—is it just to prevent ourselves from seeing to the bottom of things . . . or do we really love each other . . . ?' " It is communion, with others and with the external world, that separates the process of life from the stasis of pure existence. Rachel has begun to feel the necessity of love in its broadest sense.

Woolf extends the word "love" to include the complete and intimate knowing of anything outside the self. And human love is often (though not necessarily) a precursor to this larger sympathy, engaging the intuitive mode of perception through which one on rare occasions becomes immersed in the reality beneath the surfaces of life. Rachel's second brush with pure existence, which occurs after she has begun to fall in love, brings with it a sense of meaning. Filled with an "unreasonable exultation," she wanders aimlessly into the hills:

> So she might have walked until she had lost all knowledge of her way, had it not been for the interruption of a tree, which, although it did not grow across her path, stopped her as effectively as if the branches had struck her in the face. It was an ordinary tree, but to her it appeared so strange that it might have been the only tree in the world. Dark was the trunk in the middle, and the branches sprang here and there, leaving jagged intervals of light between them as distinctly as if it had but that second risen from the ground. Having seen a sight that would last her for a lifetime, and for a lifetime would preserve that second, the tree once more sank into the ordinary ranks of trees, and she was able to seat herself in its shade and to pick the red flowers with the thin green leaves which were growing beneath it. She laid them side by side, flower to flower and stalk to stalk, caressing them for walking alone. Flowers and even pebbles in the earth had their own life and disposition, and brought back the feelings of a child to whom they were companions.

At a dance the previous evening Rachel had declared, "I've changed my view of life completely"; and though Helen had scoffed, the occasion does mark the beginning of a new perception in Rachel. The present moment has none of the barrenness of her first vision of the world. Now Rachel's astonishment arises in response to the uniqueness of the tree, not to the indeterminate quality of existence. A moment to be preserved rather than escaped, it renews her appreciation of the individual "life and disposition" of each thing. She has momentarily become immersed in the life of something outside herself—yet without experiencing the complete "dissolution" of self that she had before. For Woolf, affinities exist not only among people but among all things, and to experience this web of relation is to be immersed in what she calls reality. This is precisely what was missing in Rachel's first vision. It brought her to an awareness of existence only, where her second granted her an apprehension of reality.

The communion with what lies outside the self occupies a central place in all Woolf's novels, and it is a mode of knowing that is invariably linked in some way to human (though not necessarily romantic) love. In *The Voyage Out* Woolf underlines the connection by presenting two minor characters who fall in love and who, like Rachel, experience a more profound response to the landscape. The young man, Arthur, haltingly describes how ". . . to-day, coming up that path, riding behind you, I seemed to see everything as if . . . As if it had a kind of meaning. . . . It's because I love you." On her part, "even while they had been saying commonplace things Susan had been conscious of the excitement of intimacy, which seemed not only to lay bare something in her, but in the trees and the sky. . . ." The very conventional love of Arthur and Susan not only provides the index for the more subtle states of emotion that distinguish Terence and Rachel's bond, it establishes that love can alert even unrefined sensibilities to the unity that underlies existence.

Rachel herself later analyzes the relation between human love and the empathy that one may establish with things. When Terence, irked with her ability to "cut herself adrift from him, and to pass away to unknown places where she had no need of him," charges her with "always wanting something else," she admits to herself that "what he was saying was perfectly true, and that she wanted many more things than the love of one human being—the sea, the sky." In this she anticipates Woolf's later protagonists, most of whom feel the attraction of the nonhuman realm. Upon entering Greece Jacob Flanders discovers "how tremendously pleasant it is to be alone. . . . to have—positively—a rush of friendship for stones and grasses, as if humanity were over. . . ." Peter Walsh feels the same lure in his dreams of the solitary traveler, the "desire for solace, for relief, for something outside these . . . craven men and women." That "solace" tempts Mrs. Ramsay at the beginning of the dinner when she wishes to avoid the effort of creating, to find instead "rest on the floor of the sea," and Lily watches her "drifting into that strange no-man's land." But just as Mrs. Ramsay gives herself a shake and turns to Bankes, so Rachel eventually, reluctantly, acknowledges that she cannot dispense with this imperfect and mutable world, and that the capacity for human love and the ability to penetrate what she calls the "curtain" of external reality are somehow linked. Near the close of the book she slips into a reverie that counterpoints her first vision of desolation. Life, which had seemed to be "only a light passing over the surface and vanishing," now through the agency of love has taken on a meaningful pattern:

> She felt herself amazingly secure as she sat in her arm-chair, and able to review not only the night of the dance, but the entire past. . . . one thing led to another and by degrees something had formed itself out of nothing, and so one reached at last this calm, this quiet, this certainty, and it was this process that people called living. . . . Why should this insight ever again desert her? The world was in truth so large, so hospitable, and after all it was so simple. "Love," St. John had said, "that seems to explain it all." Yes, but it was not the love of man for woman, of Terence for Rachel. . . . they had ceased to struggle and desire one another. There seemed to be peace between them. It might be love, but it was not the love of man for woman.

She argues to herself that the "love of man for woman" is relatively unimportant in reaching "this calm, this quiet, this certainty" in life's harmony. But, she finally concedes, maybe one cannot renounce it after all:

> . . . although she was going to marry him and to live with him for thirty, or forty, or fifty years, and to quarrel, and to be so close to him, she was independent of him; she was independent of everything else. Nevertheless, as St. John said, it was love that made her understand this, for she had never felt this independence, this calm, and this certainty until she fell in love with him, and perhaps this too was love.

She had begun to acquire the understanding that is Woolf's measure of true maturity: the knowledge that what seem to be polar opposites are most often complementary aspects of the same reality—that, as James Ramsay discovers of the lighthouse, "nothing was simply one thing."

The same paradoxical complexity proves characteristic of language as well, and Woolf explores the problem dramatically, incorporating it in the growth of Rachel's love for Terence. Just after her encounter with the tree, Rachel discovers that "the very words of books were steeped in radiance." As she reads a passage in Gibbon even the unexotic words become intensified:

> Never had any words been so vivid and so beautiful—Arabia Felix—Aethiopia. But those were not more noble than the others, hardy barbarians, forests, and morasses. They seemed to drive roads back to the very beginning of the world, on either side of which the populations of all times and countries stood in avenues, and by passing down them all knowledge would be hers, and the book of the world turned back to the very first page.

Before this time she had read "with the curious literalness of one to whom written sentences are unfamiliar, and handling words as though they were made of wood, separately of great importance, and possessed of shapes like tables or chairs." Now for the first time she has apprehended the essence of words: not just the import of Gibbon's prose, but of language itself. In a different connection D. H. Lawrence speaks of the "shape" as a "dead crust," and insists that the "shimmer" that is the "real living" resides within the shape. With the tree and with the words of Gibbon Rachel has perceived the shimmer where formerly she saw only the dead crust. Although at first glance it appears as if the events have little in common, other than a shared origin in her new love, the juxtaposition highlights their similarity. And in "A Sketch of the Past," recounting an experience that was probably the original for Rachel's, Woolf indicates that an intimate relation exists among moments of being, the process by which they are realized in language, and the kind of reading in which words become "experienced." Unfortunately she stops short of examining the precise nature of the connection between "being" and language. However, Ernst Cassirer, exploring the creation of language in his *Language and Myth*, deals with transactions strikingly similar to those Rachel participates in, and he provides illuminating commentary on the mental processes involved.

He suggests that there are two basic kinds of conception: logical and metaphorical. Logical thought, he says, ranges over the data of sensory and intuitive experience in order to relate them to each other. But metaphorical thought, far from making connections and comparisons, separates the given perception from ordinary experience. The mental view is not widened but narrowed to a single point, and the impression "compressed" and "distilled." When engaged in this kind of thought, one becomes utterly enthralled, while yet remaining completely independent. The object "confronts" one "in stark uniqueness and singleness . . . as something that exists only here and now, in one indivisible moment of experience." This could have been written with Rachel's encounter with the tree in mind.

The process of acute compression and intensification of sense experience is, Cassirer suggests, that which results in the generation of language. The "spiritual excitement" of the encounter is made manifest in the word:

> At this point, the word . . . is merged with its object in an indissoluble unity. The conscious experience is not merely wedded to the word, but is consumed by it. . . . The potential between "symbol" and "meaning" is resolved; in place of a more or less adequate "expression," we find a relation of identity, of complete congruence between "image" and "object," between the name and the thing.

> The word, like a god or a daemon, confronts man not as a creation of his own, but as something existent and significant in its own right, as an objective reality.

Because word and experience join in a bonding rather than a causal relation, we can expect the word-creating process to be reversible. When Rachel reads in her state of heightened sensitivity, the words release the intense impression of uniqueness which they consumed when they first sprang into being. Her sensation that the words "drive roads back to the beginning of the world" is well-founded: where logical thought would have enabled her to extract the denotative meaning of the passage, metaphorical thought takes her back to the sudden concentrated intuition of the object's nature that expressed itself in the original naming. Thus with both the tree and Gibbon Rachel engages the metaphorical, or intuitive, aspect of consciousness, apprehending the essence of the thing in a moment characterized by the acute heightening, compression, and distillation of the perception. Both are perceptual events of the same kind.

At the close of her walk through the countryside, after reading Gibbon, Rachel seeks the origins of the "exultation" which precipitated her visionary experience. She narrows the possible causes to Terence and his friend, St. John Hirst:

> Any clear analysis of them was impossible owing to the haze of wonder in which they were enveloped. . . . She then became haunted by a suspicion which she was so reluctant to face that she welcomed a trip and stumble over the grass. . . . "What is it to be in love?" she demanded, after a long silence; each word as it came into being seemed to shove itself out into an unknown sea.

Rachel emerges from her confusion as her emotions force themselves into language, almost against her will. As the metaphor suggests, to use language is to launch oneself on a voyage out, for once formulated the question reveals new implications: she is "awed by the discovery of a terrible possibility in life." She is also discovering that articulation may be heuristic as well as declarative. Yet later on, after she and Terence have become engaged, the word "love" frustrates precise definition of her feelings. Vexed with the platitudes of congratulation, she snaps, "I never fell in love, if falling in love is what people say it is, and it's the world that tells the lies and I tell the truth." But communicating this truth proves not to be a simple matter. In her replies "she produced phrases which bore a considerable likeness to those which she had condemned. She was struck by it herself, for she stopped writing and looked up . . . and was amazed at the gulf which lay between all that and her sheet of paper. Would there ever be a time when the world was one and indivisible?" In fact when reading Gibbon she had transcended the gulf between words and external reality; for a moment the world had seemed to be one and indivisible. However, such identity does not remain long intact, and if the word captures experience, yet in fixing and defining it also limits. Although the word begins by presenting immediate sensory experience to the intellect, it evolves into a cipher, losing the original sensory imprint as it becomes a vehicle for abstract thought. Language begins to constrict and distort that same experience which it brought to light.

One difficulty derives from the fact that emotions cannot be grasped by the lapel; as Woolf pointedly demonstrates, insight into the emotional state of oneself or another can best be achieved indirectly. Upon leaving Rachel after they have declared their love, Terence indulges in the rehearsal of their conversation that lovers can never resist and inevitably find excruciating:

> He ran his mind over the things they had said, the random, unnecessary things which had eddied round and round and used up all the time, and drawn them so close together and flung them so far apart, and left him in the end unsatisfied, ignorant still of what she felt and of what she was like. What was the use of talking, talking, merely talking?

Yet they have gained in intimacy. In later works Woolf will more emphatically affirm the generative value of "merely talking": Clarissa Dalloway feels that her parties are "an offering; to combine, to create," which provide the opportunity for individuals to "go much deeper" and thereby connect with "this thing she called life"; and at the outset of her dinner, Mrs. Ramsay deliberately resorts to her "social" language as the first step in

weaving the group into harmony around the Boeuf en Daube. The semantic
content may be minimal, but such exchanges create a tone, a mood, and
in fact for Terence and Rachel the "random unnecessary things" prove far
more effective than the formal biographical sketches that Hirst had de-
manded during an earlier meeting. They feel "more intimate because they
shared the knowledge of what eight o'clock in Richmond meant"; and their
discussion brings them to the point where they can make the leap of
understanding implicit in the highly charged though outwardly prosaic
exchange,

> "I like you; d'you like me?" Rachel suddenly observed.
> "I like you immensely," Hewet replied. . . .

The words here lose their colloquial vacuity and carry an emotional charge
disproportionate to their denotative meaning. They do so precisely because
neither party tries to fix the emotion, allowing the words instead to orient
the flow of understanding which takes place finally beyond language.

Although instances of genuine communion are infrequent and evanescent, to renounce the attempt is to wither spiritually. After his interview
with the insistent Evelyn Murgatroyd, Terence wonders querulously, "Why
was it that relations between different people were so unsatisfactory, so
fragmentary, so hazardous, and words so dangerous that the instinct to
sympathise with another human being was an instinct to be examined
carefully and probably crushed?" The alternative is to subscribe to Hirst's
belief that people are all types, that "you could draw circles around the
whole lot of them, and they'd never stray outside." Or one can simply
delude oneself as the guests do during the church service at the hotel. There
they slip into "a curious pleasant cloud of emotion," content with the
specious unity of mood: "As the childlike babble of voices rose, the congregation, many of whom had only met on the staircase, felt themselves
pathetically united and well-disposed towards each other." They attend to
the sermon with the same mindlessness: "From their faces it seemed that
for the most part they made no effort at all, and, recumbent as it were,
accepted the ideas that the words gave as representing goodness . . . ." To
attain communion one must exercise that "instinct to sympathise," not
pigeonhole people as Hirst advises, not slide into complacent oblivion as
Rachel feels the congregation does. And that instinct must function in part
through language, clumsy and dangerous though it is.

Further, Woolf demonstrates how continuously one must renew
whatever concord has been created. The day after their walk into the jungle
together, perhaps closer than they will be again until Rachel's death, the

lovers still struggle to put their emotions into words. Although "words were either too trivial or too large . . . it seemed necessary to bring themselves still more near, and to surmount a barrier which had grown up since they had last spoken": communing silently may become as awkward as communicating verbally. Moreover they do find that "with every word the mist which had enveloped them, making them seem unreal to each other, since the previous afternoon melted a little further, and their contact became more and more natural." Because human relations are not static a wordless harmony can be sustained only briefly, before one slides back into the realm of language. Although there exist only a few worn phrases to express love, Rachel and Terence both discover that even when the bond between them is unquestioned it must be reaffirmed in words. Language operates as an extension of the emotions, not a superfluous adjunct, and the logical quality of language forms an essential complement to the intuitive. For the word in evolving toward greater abstraction, from its initial fusion with sensory experience, enables one to consciously know the experience in a way that is impossible when one is immersed in it.

The ideal would be somehow to capture and communicate experience without reducing it to "inanimate phrases." This quintessential communication is what Terence (who speaks here for Woolf) hopes to achieve through art. He intends to convey the inner life, to present those things that cannot be baldly stated: his novel will be "about Silence . . . the things people don't say." Although his smugness might cause us to doubt his fitness for such a delicate task ("I'm good second rate; about as good as Thackeray"), he respects the fact that he will be working in an uncharted area: " 'I'm not like Hirst,' said Hewet, after a pause; he spoke meditatively; 'I don't see circles of chalk between people's feet. I sometimes wish I did. . . . We're all in the dark. We try to find out, but can you imagine anything more ludicrous than one person's opinion of another person?' " Yet literature can be a means of grasping the reality normally veiled both in human relations and in the external world. Echoing Woolf's letter in which she speaks of severing character from past and future, Terence asserts that the advantage of his projected "Stuart tragedy" is that "detached from modern conditions, one can make [characters] more intense and more abstract than people who live as we do." And of writing in general he observes:

> "What I want to do in writing novels is very much what you want to do when you play the piano, I expect," he began, turning and speaking over his shoulder. "We want to find out what's behind things, don't we?— Look at the lights down there," he continued, "scattered about anyhow. Things I feel come to me like lights. . . . I want to combine them. . . .

Have you ever seen fireworks that make figures? . . . I want to make figures."

(Woolf's ellipses)

In spite of his naïveté, in this image Terence expresses the discovery, ordering, and incandescent communication that takes place in the execution of a fully realized work of art.

Terence does not doubt the worth of his enterprise, although he concedes that it will not be easy:

> "The difficulty is immense. . . . And yet I sometimes wonder whether there's anything else in the whole world worth doing. These other people," he indicated the hotel, "are always wanting something they can't get. But there's an extraordinary satisfaction in writing, even in the attempt to write. What you said just now is true: one doesn't want to be things; one wants merely to be allowed to see them."

This conviction of the value of art, for oneself and for the human race, remains constant in Woolf's writings. In an essay written in 1925, "The Patron and the Crocus," she advises a hypothetical young writer on the proper relation between himself, his subject (the first crocus of spring), and his audience. She develops the thesis that a writer and his readers are bound "by more than maternal tie":

> It is futile to say, "Dismiss them all; think only of your crocus," because writing is a method of communication; and the crocus is an imperfect crocus until it has been shared. The first man or the last may write for himself alone, but he is an exception and an unenviable one at that, and the gulls are welcome to his works if the gulls can read them.

She reiterates this position in "A Sketch of the Past," where she echoes Terence's concern for the pattern behind things, and expresses with even greater force her belief in the importance of writing in creating and sustaining civilization:

> [My conception] is that there is a pattern hid behind the cotton wool. And this conception affects me every day. I prove this, now, by spending the morning writing, when I might be walking, running a shop, or learning to do something that will be useful if war comes. I feel that by writing I am doing what is far more necessary than anything else.

Art comes forth in response to that incorrigible "instinct to sympathise," kindling some light in that darkness in which Terence feels we all move. These three statements, spanning a quarter of a century, point to the work of art not as a means of resolving a personal need (although it is certainly that as well), but as something that creates communion: both by affording others a glimpse of the pattern of which we are all a part, and by expressing those things which we may sense but cannot express—"the things people don't say" and which, without the artist's guidance, we cannot articulate at all.

In *The Voyage Out* Woolf was already reaching toward the novel of silence; and in the account of Rachel's death, a scene paradigmatic of the work as a whole, the author succeeds in rendering experience beyond the usual reach of language. As Rachel slips out of life Terence hovers in the serene joy of their perfect union:

> An immense feeling of peace came over Terence, so that he had no wish to move or speak. The terrible torture and unreality of the last days were over, and he had come out now into perfect certainty and peace. . . . Once he held his breath and listened acutely; she was still breathing; he went on thinking for some time; they seemed to be thinking together; he seemed to be Rachel as well as himself; and then he listened again; no, she had ceased to breathe. So much the better—this was death. It was nothing; it was to cease to breathe. It was happiness, it was perfect happiness. They had now what they had always wanted to have, the union which had been impossible while they lived. Unconscious whether he thought the words or spoke them aloud, he said, "No two people have ever been so happy as we have been. No one has ever loved as we have loved."
>
> It seemed to him that their complete union and happiness filled the room with rings eddying more and more widely. He had no wish in the world left unfulfilled. They possessed what could never be taken from them.

Terence and Rachel's love will suffer no further alteration; it has transcended the "struggle and desire" she so abhorred, to reach, at last, perfect peace. But one confronts here the ironic conjunction of purity and sterility: this union, now far above all breathing human passion, exists only in the eternal separation of the lovers. Ironically, Terence's decisive, "It was happiness, it was perfect happiness," recalls the "more happy love! more happy, happy love!" of Keat's cold pastoral. Inevitably (because this moment is not etched in marble) the happiness shatters:

> As he saw the passage outside the room, and the table with the cups and the plates, it suddenly came over him that here was a world in which he would never see Rachel again.
>
> "Rachel! Rachel!" he shrieked, trying to rush back to her. But they prevented him and pushed him down the passage and into a bedroom far from her room. Downstairs they could hear the thud of his feet on the floor, as he struggled to break free; and twice they heard him shout, "Rachel! Rachel!"

Terence's cry expresses his loss and the heavy "thud" of his feet underscores the intransigent solidity of the world; but Woolf does not suggest that his desolation and sharp sense of absolute separateness negate the "perfect certainty and peace . . . [the] complete union" he has so recently felt. Both perceptions are valid, if contradictory, and neither can be denied on the strength of the other. One must hold them in suspension, without anxiously attempting a logical reconciliation. The nature of existence cannot be comprehended by either the logical or the intuitive mode of perception alone, and Woolf insures that both of Terence's states of being remain conjoined in our minds by taking leave of him at this point. During this passage Woolf quietly shifts from Terence's "they," which designates his friends ("they prevented him . . . "), to the authorial "they," which refers to the guests downstairs ("they heard him shout . . . "). Thus we slide out of his consciousness, and seem almost to hear his cries receding down the corridor. In the remaining two chapters he does not appear, nor are his later reactions recorded.

The scene also illustrates the distinction between describing and the realizing process of naming. After Rachel's death Terence thinks "No two people have ever been so happy as we have been. No one has ever loved as we have loved." Thus he describes their love, but the effect is slightly bathetic. His claim is that of all lovers, and it merely reminds the reader of how inadequate language is to express a complex of intense emotions, or to capture and convey an individual's character. Only with the anguished "Rachel! Rachel!," wrung from Terence in the transition to a world devoid of love, does the full meaning of their bond make itself felt. There could hardly be a more worn counter than a person's Christian name, and here distorted into a "shriek" and a "shout" one might expect to find it emptied of meaning. Yet most readers will feel on the contrary that Terence's howl is fraught with meaning—and that it transforms the name into much more than a label for the recently deceased individual in the other room. Through the name we feel the pressure of Terence's love for Rachel, and because that love has enabled him to become one with her, what is transmitted is all that Rachel has come to be, fulfilled as she is in their union. The cry, which effects and expresses the recognition of what has been lost, is an act of naming, in which word and essence fuse.

Woolf will more effectively focus later works on a single charged utterance—"Jacob! Jacob!"; "Mrs. Ramsay! Mrs. Ramsay!" "O Death!"—for the cry makes the experience intelligible even though that cry contains almost no logical import. Yet even here, it captures the experience and engages the reader with it in the same instant; the word, previously a sign, has become a channel for feeling. The distinction will make itself felt if one compares the charge here carried by "Rachel, Rachel!" with the relative flatness of "No one has ever loved as we have loved": the difference in intensity has little to do with the difference in spoken volume. The scene is the crisis point of the novel, a moment of recognition which brings a flash of meaning that irradiates the whole. The many loose ends in the book (Woolf herself later called it an "assortment of patches") prevent the scene from being entirely successful in this regard. Nonetheless the reader does grasp, in an instant and more completely, all that has been said so discursively about love and about the elusive nature of reality. And in appreciating this knowledge he suddenly sees what Terence and Rachel had so haltingly attempted to describe: how art can communicate the things people don't say, how it can afford one a vision of what is "behind things," and how it can (as Rachel says of music) "say all there is to say at once." For this scene, after much preparation, has done all those things.

On a holiday in September of 1908, a month after writing the letter to Clive Bell quoted above, a fresco in Perugia prompted Woolf to distinguish between the art of the painter and her own:

> I look at a fresco by Perugino. I conceive that he saw things grouped, contained in certain and invariable forms . . . all beauty was contained in the momentary appearance of human beings. . . . His fresco seems to me infinitely silent; as though beauty had swum up to the top and stayed there, above everything else, speech, paths leading on, relations of brain to brain don't exist.

> As for writing—I want to express beauty too—but beauty (symmetry?) of life and the world, in action. Conflict?—is that it? . . . I attain a different kind of beauty, achieve a symmetry by means of infinite discords, showing all the traces of the mind's passage through the world; achieve in the end, some kind of whole made of shivering fragments; to me this seems the natural process; the flight of the mind.

As Quentin Bell points out, these notes are rapid and disjointed, yet they embody some of the major concerns of *The Voyage Out* and of Woolf's yet unwritten canon. For Woolf no form was ever "certain and invariable"; the world always seemed to her, as to Rachel, capable of sudden unpredicated change. More than twenty years later she muses in her diary, "Now is life very solid or very shifting? I am haunted by the two contradictions." Until the end of her career she continued to examine the protean nature of reality, exploring it through the delicate and intricate processes of language. The broad concern of "speech, paths leading on, the relation of brain to brain"—whatever is connected with "the flight of the mind"—she takes as her special province. Indeed her own phrase "the flight of the mind" is probably the least misleading statement of what her works are "about." Physical event always remains peripheral: the "action" and "conflict" she speaks of is the clash between different modes of thought, the masculine and the feminine, the logical and the metaphorical. If after *The Voyage Out* we do not see the tension quite so patently discussed or meditated upon, it remains a governing factor in the relations of her characters. And the nature of words themselves continues to figure prominently as a theme in her work, culminating in Miss La Trobe's obsessed ruminations on language. For language bears the imprint of both logical and metaphorical thought, and it is through language that the flight of the mind can be made visible, and communion achieved.

"Some kind of whole made of shivering fragments" succinctly describes *The Waves*, and in a more general way it applies to the method of all her mature work. However, in *The Voyage Out* she has not yet fulfilled her boast to "re-form the novel and . . . enclose the whole." The reader sympathizes with Rachel's contention that, while "music goes straight for things . . . saying all there is to say at once," writing involves too much "scratching on the match box." One could point to much extraneous scratching in *The Voyage Out*. But in this first novel Woolf has demonstrated that she can bring language to the flash point, effecting a swift illumination which, like music, says many things at once. It is this musical quality (not the sonic or rhythmic effects that blatantly imitate music) that she strives for in her later work. In her endeavor to capture the essence of life, rather than the details of existence, Woolf continues the struggle begun in *The Voyage Out*: to restore language to its metaphorical intensity—to transform words from pellets of information into channels for perception—and thereby to net that elusive reality that lies just on the far side of language.

J. HILLIS MILLER

"Mrs. Dalloway": Repetition as the Raising of the Dead

The shift from the late Victorian or early modern Thomas Hardy to a fully modernist writer like Virginia Woolf might be thought of as the transition to a new complexity and a new self-consciousness in the use of devices of repetition in narrative. Critics commonly emphasize the newness of Virginia Woolf's art. They have discussed her use of the so-called stream-of-consciousness technique, her dissolution of traditional limits of plot and character, her attention to minutiae of the mind and to apparently insignificant details of the external world, her pulverization of experience into a multitude of fragmentary particles, each without apparent connection to the others, and her dissolution of the usual boundaries between mind and world. Such characteristics connect her work to that of other twentieth-century writers who have exploded the conventional forms of fiction, from Conrad and Joyce to French "new novelists" like Nathalie Sarraute. It might also be well to recognize, however, the strong connections of Woolf's work with the native traditions of English fiction. Far from constituting a break with these traditions, her novels are an extension of them. They explore further the implications of those conventions which Austen, Eliot, Trollope, and Thackeray exploited as the given conditions of their craft. Such conventions, it goes without saying, are elements of meaning. The most important themes of a given novel are likely to lie not in anything which is explicitly affirmed, but in significances

From *Fiction and Repetition: Seven English Novels.* Copyright © 1982 by J. Hillis Miller. Harvard University Press.

generated by the way in which the story is told. Among the most important of those ways is Woolf's organizing of her novels around various forms of recurrence. Storytelling, for Woolf, is the repetition of the past in memory, both in the memory of the characters and in the memory of the narrator. *Mrs. Dalloway* (1925) is a brilliant exploration of the functioning of memory as a form of repetition.

The novel is especially fitted to investigate not so much the depths of individual minds as the nuances of relationship between mind and mind. If this is so, then a given novelist's assumptions about the way one mind can be related to others will be a generative principle lying behind the form his or her novels take. From this perspective the question of narrative voice can be seen as a special case of the problem of relations between minds. The narrator too is a mind projected by a way of speaking, a mind usually endowed with special access to other minds and with special powers for expressing what goes on there.

The manipulation of narrative voice in fiction is closely associated with that theme of human time or of human history which seems intrinsic to the form of the novel. In many novels the use of the past tense establishes the narrator as someone living after the events of the story have taken place, someone who knows all the past perfectly. The narrator tells the story in a present which moves forward toward the future by way of a recapitulation or repetition of the past. This retelling brings that past up to the present as a completed whole, or it moves toward such completion. This form of an incomplete circle, time moving toward a closure which will bring together past, present, and future as a perfected whole, is the temporal form of many novels.

Interpersonal relations as a theme, the use of an omniscient narrator who is a collective mind rising from the copresence of many individual minds, indirect discourse as the means by which that narrator dwells within the minds of individual characters and registers what goes on there, temporality as a determining principle of theme and technique—these are, I have argued elsewhere, among the most important elements of form in Victorian fiction, perhaps in fiction of any time, in one proportion or another. Just these elements are fundamental to Virginia Woolf's work too. It would be as true to say that she investigates implications of these traditional conventions of form as to say that she brings something new into fiction. This can be demonstrated especially well in *Mrs. Dalloway*. The novel depends on the presence of a narrator who remembers all and who has a power of resurrecting the past in her narration. In *Mrs. Dalloway* narration is repetition as the raising of the dead.

"Nothing exists outside us except a state of mind"—this seemingly casual and somewhat inscrutable statement is reported from the thoughts of the solitary traveler in Peter Walsh's dream as Peter sits snoring on a bench in Regent's Park. The sentence provides an initial clue to the mode of existence of the narrator of *Mrs. Dalloway*. The narrator is that state of mind which exists outside the characters and of which they can never be directly aware. Though they are not aware of it, it is aware of them. This "state of mind" surrounds them, encloses them, pervades them, knows them from within. It is present to them all at all the times and places of their lives. It gathers those times and places together in the moment. The narrator is that "something central which permeate[s]," the "something warm which [breaks] up surfaces," a power of union and penetration which Clarissa Dalloway lacks. Or, to vary the metaphor, the narrator possesses the irresistible and subtle energy of the bell of St. Margaret's striking half past eleven. Like that sound, the narrator "glides into the recesses of the heart and buries itelf." It is "something alive which wants to confide itself, to disperse itself, to be, with a tremor of delight, at rest." Expanding to enter into the inmost recesses of each heart, the narrator encloses all in a reconciling embrace.

Though the characters are not aware of this narrating presence, they are at every moment possessed and known, in a sense violated, by an invisible mind, a mind more powerful than their own. This mind registers with infinite delicacy their every thought and steals their every secret. The indirect discourse of this registration, in which the narrator reports in the past tense thoughts which once occurred in the present moments of the characters' minds, is the basic form of narration in *Mrs. Dalloway*. This disquieting mode of ventriloquism may be found on any page of the novel. Its distinguishing mark is the conventional "he thought" or "she thought," which punctuates the narrative and reveals the presence of a strange one-way interpersonal relation. The extraordinary quality of this relation is hidden primarily because readers of fiction take it so much for granted. An example is the section of the novel describing Peter Walsh's walk from Clarissa's house toward Regent's Park: "Clarissa refused me, he thought"; "like Clarissa herself, thought Peter Walsh"; "It is Clarissa herself, he thought"; "Still the future of civilisation lies, he thought"; "The future lies in the hands of young men like that, he thought"—and so on, page after page. If the reader asks himself where he is placed as he reads any given page of *Mrs. Dalloway*, the answer, most often, is that he is plunged within an individual mind which is being understood from inside by an ubiquitous, all-knowing mind. This mind speaks from some indeterminate later point in time, a point always "after" anything the characters think or feel. The narrator's mind moves easily from one limited mind to another and knows them all at once. It speaks for them all. This form of language generates the local texture of *Mrs. Dalloway*. Its sequential structure is made of the juxtaposition of longer or shorter blocks of narrative in which the narrator dwells first within Clarissa's mind, then within Septimus Smith's, then Rezia Smith's, then Peter's, then Rezia's again, and so on.

The characters of *Mrs. Dalloway* are therefore in an odd way, though they do not know it, dependent on the narrator. The narrator has preserved their evanescent thoughts, sensations, mental images, and interior speech. She rescues these from time past and presents them again in language to the reader. Narration itself is repetition in *Mrs. Dalloway*. In another way, the narrator's mind is dependent on the characters' minds. It could not exist without them. *Mrs. Dalloway* is almost entirely without passages of meditation or description which are exclusively in the narrator's private voice. The reader is rarely given the narrator's own thoughts or shown the way the world looks not through the eyes of a character, but through the narrator's private eyes. The sermon against "Proportion" and her formidable sister "Conversion" is one of the rare cases where the narrator speaks for her own view, or even for Woolf's own view, rather than by way of the mind of one of the characters. Even here, the narrator catches herself up and attributes some of her own judgment of Sir William Bradshaw to Rezia: "This lady too [Conversion] (Rezia Warren Smith divined it) had her dwelling in Sir William's heart."

In *Mrs. Dalloway* nothing exists for the narrator which does not first exist in the mind of one of the characters, whether it be a thought or a thing. This is implied by those passages in which an external object— the mysterious royal motorcar in Bond Street, Peter Walsh's knife, the child who runs full tilt into Rezia Smith's legs, most elaborately the sky-writing airplane—is used as a means of transition from the mind of one character to the mind of another. Such transitions seem to suggest that the solid existing things of the external world unify the minds of separate persons because, though each person is trapped in his or her own mind and in his or her own private responses to external objects, nevertheless these disparate minds can all have responses, however different they may be, to the same event, for example to an airplane's skywriting. To this extent at least we all dwell in one world.

The deeper meaning of this motif in *Mrs. Dalloway* may be less a recognition of our common dependence on a solidly existing external world than a revelation that things exist for the narrator only when they exist for the characters. The narrator sometimes moves without transition out of the mind of one character and into the mind of another, as in the fourth paragraph of the novel, in which the reader suddenly finds himself transported from Clarissa's mind into the mind of Scrope Purvis, a character who never appears again in the novel and who seems put in only to give the reader a view of Clarissa from the outside and perhaps to provide an initial demonstration of the fact that the narrator is by no means bound to a single mind. Though she is bound to no single mind, she is dependent for her existence on the minds of the characters. She can think, feel, see only as they thought, felt, and saw. Things exist for her, she exists for herself, only because the others once existed. Like the omniscient narrators of *Vanity Fair*, *Middlemarch*, or *The Last Chronicle of Barset*, the omniscient narrator of *Mrs. Dalloway* is a general consciousness or social mind which rises into existence out of the collective mental experience of the individual human beings in the story. The cogito of the narrator of *Mrs. Dalloway* is, "They thought, therefore I am."

One implication of this relation between the narrator's mind and the characters' minds is that, though for the most part the characters do not know it, the universal mind is part of their own minds, or rather their minds are part of it. If one descends deeply enough into any individual mind one reaches ultimately the general mind, that is, the mind of the narrator. On the surface the relation between narrator and individual goes only one way. As in the case of those windows which may be seen through in a single direction, the character is transparent to the narrator, but the narrator is opaque to the character. In the depths of each individual mind, this one-way relationship becomes reciprocal. In the end it is no longer a relationship, but a union, an identity. Deep down the general mind and the individual mind become one. Both are on the same side of the glass, and the glass vanishes.

If this is true for all individual minds in relation to the universal mind, then all individual minds are joined to one another far below the surface separateness, as in Matthew Arnold's image of coral islands which seem divided, but are unified in the depths. The most important evidence for this in *Mrs. Dalloway* is the fact that the same images of unity, of reconciliation, of communion well up spontaneously from the deep levels of the minds of all the major characters. One of the most pervasive of these images is that of a great enshadowing tree which is personified, a great mother who binds all living things together in the manifold embrace of her leaves and branches. This image would justify the use of the feminine pronoun for the narrator, who is the spokeswoman for this mothering presence. No man or woman is limited to himself or herself, but each is joined to others by means of this tree, diffused like a mist among all the people and places he or she has encountered. Each man or woman possesses a kind of immortality, in spite of the abrupt finality of death: "did it not become consoling," muses Clarissa to herself as she walks toward Bond Street, "to believe that death ended absolutely? but that somehow in the streets of London, on the ebb and flow of things, here, there, she survived, Peter survived, lived in each other, she being part, she was positive, of the trees at home; of the house there, ugly, rambling all to bits and pieces as it was; part of people she had never met; being laid out like a mist between the people she knew best, who lifted her on their branches as she had seen the trees lift the mist, but it spread ever so far, her life, herself." "A marvellous discovery indeed—" thinks Septimus Smith as he watches the skywriting airplane, "that the human voice in certain atmospheric conditions (for one must be scientific, above all scientific) can quicken tree into life! . . . But they beckoned; leaves were alive; trees were alive. And the leaves being connected by millions of fibres with his own body, there on the seat, fanned it up and down; when the branch stretched he, too, made that statement." "But if he can conceive of her, then in some sort she exists," thinks the solitary traveler in Peter Walsh's dream, "and advancing down the path with his eyes upon sky and branches he rapidly endows them with womanhood; sees with amazement how grave they become; how majestically, as the breeze stirs them, they dispense with a dark flutter of the leaves charity, comprehension, absolution . . . let me walk straight on to this great figure, who will, with a toss of her head, mount me on her streamers and let me blow to nothingness with the rest." Even Lady Bruton, as she falls ponderously asleep after her luncheon meeting, feels "as if one's friends were attached to one's body, after lunching with them, by a thin thread."

This notion of a union of each mind in its depths with all the other minds and with a universal, impersonal mind for which the narrator speaks is confirmed by those notations in A Writer's Diary in which, while writing Mrs. Dalloway, Woolf speaks of her "great discovery," what she calls her "tunnelling process," that method whereby, as she says, "I dig out beautiful caves behind my characters: I think that gives exactly what I want; humanity, humour, depth. The idea is that the caves shall connect."

Deep below the surface, in some dark and remote cave of the spirit, each person's mind connects with all the other minds, in a vast cavern where all the tunnels end. Peter Walsh's version of the image of the maternal tree ends nevertheless on an ominous note. To reach the great figure is to be blown to nothingness with the rest. This happens because union with the general mind is incompatible with the distinctions, the limitations, the definite edges and outlines, one thing here, another thing there, of daylight consciousness. The realm of union is a region of dispersion, of darkness, of indistinction, sleep, and death. The fear or attraction of the annihilating fall into nothingness echoes through *Mrs. Dalloway*. The novel seems to be based on an irreconcilable opposition between individuality and universality. By reason of his or her existence as a conscious human being, each man or woman is alienated from the whole of which he or she is actually, though unwittingly or at best half-consciously, a part. That half-consciousness gives each person a sense of incompletion. Each person yearns to be joined in one way or another to the whole from which he or she is separated by the conditions of existence as an individual.

One way to achieve this wholeness might be to build up toward some completeness in the daylight world, rather than to sink down into the dark world of death. "What a lark! What a plunge!"—the beginning of the third paragraph of *Mrs. Dalloway* contains in miniature the two contrary movements of the novel. If the fall into death is one pole of the novel, fulfilled in Septimus Smith's suicidal plunge, the other pole is the rising motion of "building it up," of constructive action in the moment, fulfilled in Clarissa Dalloway's party. Turning away from the obscure depths within them, the characters, may, like Clarissa, embrace the moment with elation and attempt to gather everything together in a diamond point of brightness: "For Heaven only knows why one loves it so, how one sees it so, making it up, building it round one, tumbling it, creating it every moment afresh"; "what she loved was this, here, now, in front of her"; "Clarissa . . . plunged into the very heart of the moment, transfixed it, there—the moment of this June morning on which was the pressure of all the other mornings, . . . collecting the whole of her at one point." In the same way, Peter Walsh after his sleep on a park bench feels, "Life itself, every moment of it, every drop of it, here, this instant, now, in the sun, in Regent's Park, was enough." (This echoing from Clarissa to Peter, it is worth noting, is proof that Clarissa is right to think that they "live in each other.")

"The pressure of all the other mornings"—one way the characters in *Mrs. Dalloway* achieve continuity and wholeness is through the ease with which images from their past rise within them to overwhelm them with a sense of immediate presence. If the characters of the novel live according to an abrupt, discontinuous, nervous rhythm, rising one moment to heights of ecstasy only to be dropped again in sudden terror or despond- ency, nevertheless their experience is marked by profound continuities.

The remarkably immediate access the characters have to their pasts is one such continuity. The present, for them, is the perpetual repetition of the past. In one sense the moment is all that is real. Life in the present instant is a narrow plank reaching over the abyss of death between the nothingness of past and future. Near the end of the novel Clarissa thinks of "the terror; the overwhelming incapacity, one's parents giving it into one's hands, this life, to be lived to the end, to be walked with serenely; there was in the depths of her heart an awful fear." In another sense, the weight of all the past moments presses just beneath the surface of the present, ready in an instant to flow into consciousness, overwhelming it with the immediate presence of the past. Nothing could be less like the intermittencies and difficulties of memory in Wordsworth or in Proust than the spontaneity and ease of memory in Mrs. Dalloway. Repeatedly during the day of the novel's action the reader finds himself within the mind of a character who has been invaded and engulfed by a memory so vivid that it displaces the present of the novel and becomes the virtual present of the reader's experience. So fluid are the boundaries between past and present that the reader sometimes has great difficulty knowing whether he is en- countering an image from the character's past or something part of the character's immediate experience.

An example of this occurs in the opening paragraphs of the novel. Mrs. Dalloway begins in the middle of things with the report of something Clarissa says just before she leaves her home in Westminster to walk to the florist on Bond Street: "Mrs. Dalloway said she would buy the flowers herself." A few sentences later, after a description of Clarissa's recognition that it is a fine day and just following the first instance of the motif of terror combined with ecstasy ("What a lark! What a plunge!"), the reader is "plunged" within the closeness of an experience which seems to be part of the present, for he is as yet ignorant of the place names in the novel or of their relation to the times of Clarissa's life. Actually, the experience is from Clarissa's adolescence: "For so it had always seemed to her, when, with a little squeak of the hinges, which she could hear now, she had burst open the French windows and plunged at Bourton into the open air."

The word "plunge," reiterated here, expresses a pregnant ambiguity. If a "lark" and a "plunge" seem at first almost the same thing, rising and falling versions of the same leap of ecstasy, and if Clarissa's plunge into the open air when she bursts open the windows at Bourton seems to confirm this identity, the reader may remember this opening page much later when Septimus leaps from a window to his death. Clarissa, hearing of his suicide at her party, confirms this connection by asking herself, "But this young man who had killed himself—had he plunged holding his treasure?" If *Mrs. Dalloway* is organized around the contrary penchants of rising and falling, these motions are not only opposites, but are also ambiguously similar. They change places bewilderingly, so that down and up, falling and rising, death and life, isolation and communication, are mirror images of one another rather than a confrontation of negative and positive orientations of the spirit. Clarissa's plunge at Bourton into the open air is an embrace of life in its richness, promise, and immediacy, but it is when the reader encounters it already an image from the dead past. Moreover, it anticipates Septimus's plunge into death. It is followed in Clarissa's memory of it by her memory that when she stood at the open window she felt "something awful was about to happen." The reader is not surprised to find that in this novel which is made up of a stream of subtle variations on a few themes, one of the things Clarissa sees from the window at Bourton is "the rooks rising, falling."

The temporal placement of Clarissa's experiences at Bourton is equally ambiguous. The "now" of the sentence describing Clarissa's plunge ("with a little squeak of the hinges, which she could hear now"), is the narrator's memory of Clarissa's memory of her childhood home brought back so vividly into Clarissa's mind that it becomes the present of her experience and of the reader's experience. The sentence opens the door to a flood of memories which bring that faraway time back to her as a present with the complexity and fullness of immediate experience.

These memories are not simply present. The ambiguity of the temporal location of this past time derives from the narrator's use of the past tense conventional in fiction. This convention is one of the aspects of the novel which Woolf carries on unchanged from her eighteenth- and nineteenth-century predecessors. The first sentence of the novel ("Mrs. Dalloway said she would buy the flowers herself"), establishes a temporal distance between the narrator's present and the present of the characters. Everything that the characters do or think is placed firmly in an indefinite past as something which has always already happened when the reader encounters it. These events are resurrected from the past by the language of the narration and placed before the present moment of the reader's experience as something bearing the ineradicable mark of their pastness. When the characters, within this general pastness of the narration, remember something from their own pasts, and when the narrator reports this in that indirect discourse which is another convention of *Mrs. Dalloway*, she has no other way to place it in the past than some version of the past tense which she has already been using for the "present" of the characters' experience: "How fresh, how calm, stiller than this of course, the air was in the early morning." That "was" is a past within a past, a double repetition.

The sentence before this one contains the "had" of the past perfect which places it in a past behind that past which is the "present" of the novel, the day of Clarissa's party. Still Clarissa can hear the squeak of the hinges "now," and the reader is led to believe that she may be comparing an earlier time of opening the windows with a present repetition of that action. The following sentence is in the simple past ("the air was"), and yet it belongs not to the present of the narration, but to the past of Clarissa's girlhood. What has happened to justify this change is one of those subtle dislocations within the narration which are characteristic of indirect discourse as a mode of language. Indirect discourse is always a relationship between two distinguishable minds, but the nuances of this relationship may change, with corresponding changes in the way it is registered in words. "For so it had always seemed to her"—here the little word "had" establishes three identifiable times: the no-time or time-out-of-time-for-which-all-times-are-past of the narrator; the time of the single day of the novel's action; and the time of Clarissa's youth. The narrator distinguishes herself both temporally and, if one may say so, "spatially," from Clarissa and reports Clarissa's thoughts from the outside in a tense which she would not herself use in the "now" of her own experience. In the next sentence these distances between the narrator and Clarissa disappear. Though the text is still in indirect discourse in the sense that the narrator speaks for the character, the language used is much more nearly identical with what Clarissa might herself have said, and the tense is the one she would use: "How fresh, how calm, stiller than this of course, the air was in the early morning." The "was" here is the sign of a relative identity between the narrator's mind and the character's mind. From the point of view the narrator momentarily adopts, Clarissa's youth is at the same distance from the narrator as it is from Clarissa, and the reader is left with no linguistic clue, except the "stiller than this of course," permitting him to tell whether the "was" refers to the present of the narration or to its past. The "was" shimmers momentarily between the narrator's past and Clarissa's past. The subtly varying tense structure creates a pattern of double repetition in which three times keep moving together and then apart. Narration in indirect discourse, for Woolf, is repetition as distancing and merging at once.

Just as a cinematic image is always present, so that there is difficulty in presenting the pastness of the past on film (a "flashback" soon becomes experienced as present), so everything in a conventional novel is labeled "past." All that the narrator presents takes its place on the same plane of time as something which from the narrator's point of view and from the reader's is already part of the past. If there is no past in the cinema, there is no present in a novel, or only a specious, ghostly present which is generated by the narrator's ability to resurrect the past not as reality but as verbal image.

Woolf strategically manipulates in *Mrs. Dalloway* the ambiguities of this aspect of conventional storytelling to justify the power she ascribes to her characters of immediate access to their pasts. If the novel as a whole is recovered from the past in the mind of the narrator, the action of the novel proceeds through one day in the lives of its main characters in which one after another they have a present experience, often one of walking through the city, Clarissa's walk to buy flowers, Peter Walsh's walk through London after visiting Clarissa, Septimus and Rezia's walk to visit Sir William Bradshaw, and so on. As the characters make their ways through London the most important events of their pasts rise up within them, so that the day of *Mrs. Dalloway* may be described as a general day of recollection. The revivification of the past performed by the characters becomes in its turn another past revivified, brought back from the dead, by the narrator.

If the pressure of all the other moments lies on the present moment which Clarissa experiences so vividly, the whole day of the action of *Mrs. Dalloway* may be described as such a moment on a large scale. Just as Proust's *A la recherche du temps perdu*, a book much admired by Woolf, ends with a party in which Marcel encounters figures from his past turned now into aged specters of themselves, so the "story" of *Mrs. Dalloway* (for there is a story, the story of Clarissa's refusal of Peter Walsh, of her love for Sally Seton, and of her decision to marry Richard Dalloway), is something which happened long before the single day in the novel's present. The details of this story are brought back bit by bit for the reader in the memories of the various characters as the day continues. At the same time the most important figures in Clarissa's past actually return during the day, Peter Walsh journeying from India and appearing suddenly at her door, then later coming to her party; Sally Seton, now married and the mother of five sons, also coming to her party.

The passage in *A Writer's Diary* about Woolf's "discovery," her "tunnelling process," takes on its full meaning when it is seen as a description of the way *Mrs. Dalloway* is a novel of the resurrection of the past into the present of the characters' lives. The tunnelling process, says Woolf, is one "by which I tell the past by instalments, as I have need of it." The "beautiful caves" behind each of the characters are caves into the past as well as caves down into the general mind for which the narrator speaks. If in one direction the "caves connect" in the depths of each character's mind, in the other direction "each [cave] comes to daylight at the present moment," the present moment of Clarissa's party when the important figures from her past are present in the flesh.

Woolf has unostentatiously, even secretly, buried within her novel a clue to the way the day of the action is to be seen as the occasion of a resurrection of ghosts from the past. There are three odd and apparently irrelevant pages in the novel which describe the song of an ancient ragged woman, her hand outstretched for coppers. Peter hears her song as he crosses Marylebone Road by the Regent's Park Tube Station. It seems to rise like "the voice of an ancient spring" spouting from some primeval swamp. It seems to have been going on as the same inarticulate moan for millions of years and to be likely to persist for ten million years longer:

> ee um fah um so
> foo swee too eem oo

The battered old woman, whose voice seems to come from before, after, or outside time, sings of how she once walked with her lover in May. Though it is possible to associate this with the theme of vanished love in the novel (Peter has just been thinking again of Clarissa and of her coldness, "as cold as an icicle"; still the connection seems strained, and the episode scarcely seems to justify the space it occupies unless the reader recognizes that Woolf has woven into the old woman's song, partly by paraphrase and variation, partly by direct quotation in an English translation, the words of a song by Richard Strauss, "Allerseelen," with words by Hermann von Gilm. The phrases quoted in English from the song do not correspond to any of the three English translations I have located, so Woolf either made her own or used another which I have not found. Here is a translation more literal than any of the three published ones I have seen and also more literal than Woolf's version:

> Place on the table the perfuming heather,
> Bring here the last red asters,
> And let us again speak of love,
> As once in May.
>
> Give me your hand, that I may secretly press it,
> And if someone sees, it's all the same to me;

Give me but one of your sweet glances,
As once in May.

It is blooming and breathing perfume today on every grave,
One day in the year is free to the dead,
Come to my heart that I may have you again,
As once in May.

Heather, red asters, the meeting with the lover once in May, these are echoed in the passsage in *Mrs. Dalloway*, and several phrases are quoted directly: "look in my eyes with thy sweet eyes intently"; "give me your hand and let me press it gently"; "and if some one should see, what matter they?" The old woman, there can be no doubt, is singing Strauss's song. The parts of the song not directly echoed in *Mrs. Dalloway* identify it as a key to the structure of the novel. "One day in the year" is indeed "free to the dead," "Allerseelen," the day of a collective resurrection of spirits. On this day the bereaved lover can hope that the beloved will return from the grave. Like Strauss's song, *Mrs. Dalloway* has the form of an All Souls' Day in which Peter Walsh, Sally Seton, and the rest rise from the dead to come to Clarissa's party. As in the song the memory of a dead lover may on one day of the year become a direct confrontation of his or her risen spirit, so in *Mrs. Dalloway* the characters are obsessed all day by memories of the time when Clarissa refused Peter and chose to marry Richard Dalloway, and then the figures in those memories actually come back in a general congregation of persons from Clarissa's past. The power of narrative not just to repeat the past but to resurrect it in another form is figured dramatically in the action of the novel.

Continuity of each character with his own past, continuity in the shared past of all the important characters—these forms of communication are completed by the unusual degree of access the characters have in the present to one another's minds. Some novelists, Jane Austen or Jean-Paul Sartre, for example, assume that minds are opaque to one another. Another person is a strange apparition, perhaps friendly to me, perhaps a threat, but in any case difficult to understand. I have no immediate knowledge of what he is thinking or feeling. I must interpret what is going on within his subjectivity as best I can by way of often misleading signs—speech, gesture, and expression. In Woolf's work, as in Trollope's, one person often sees spontaneously into the mind of another and knows with the same sort of knowledge he has of his own subjectivity what is going on there. If the narrator enters silently and unobserved into the mind of each of the characters and understands it with perfect intimacy because it is in fact part of her own mind, the characters often, if not always, may have the same kind of intimate knowledge of one another. This may be partly because they share the same memories and so respond in the same way to the same cues, each knowing what the other must be thinking, but it seems also to be an unreflective openness of one mind to another, a kind of telepathic insight. The mutual understanding of Clarissa and Peter is the most striking example of this intimacy: "They went in and out of each other's minds without any effort," thinks Peter, remembering their talks at Bourton. Other characters have something of the same power of communication. Rezia and Septimus, for example, as he helps her make a hat in their brief moments of happiness before Dr. Holmes comes and Septimus throws himself out of the window: "Not for weeks had they laughed like this together, poking fun privately like married people." Or there is the intimacy of Clarissa and her servant Lucy: " 'Dear!' said Clarissa, and Lucy shared as she meant her to her disappointment (but not the pang); felt the concord between them."

In all these cases, there is some slight obstacle between the minds of the characters. Clarissa does after all decide not to marry Peter and is falling in love with Richard Dalloway in spite of the almost perfect communion she can achieve with Peter. The communion of Rezia and Septimus is intermittent, and she has little insight into what is going on in his mind during his periods of madness. Clarissa does not share with Lucy the pang of jealousy she feels toward Lady Bruton. The proper model for the relations among minds in *Mrs. Dalloway* is that of a perfect transparency of the minds of the characters to the mind of the narrator, but only a modified translucency, like glass frosted or fogged, between the mind of one character and the mind of another. Nevertheless, to the continuity between the present and the past within the mind of a given character there must be added a relative continuity from one mind to another in the present.

The characters in *Mrs. Dalloway* are endowed with a desire to take possession of these continuities, to actualize them in the present. The dynamic model for this urge is a movement which gathers together disparate elements, pieces them into a unity, and lifts them up into the daylight world in a gesture of ecstatic delight, sustaining the wholeness so created over the dark abyss of death. The phrase "building it up" echoes through the novel as an emblem of this combination of spiritual and physical action. Thinking of life, Clarissa, the reader will remember, wonders "how one sees it so, making it up, building it round one." Peter Walsh follows a pretty girl from Trafalgar Square to Regent Street across Oxford Street and Great Portland Street until she disappears into her house, making up a personality for her, a new personality for himself, and an adventure for them both together: "it was half made up, as he knew very well; invented, this escapade with the girl; made up, as one makes up the better part of life, he thought—making oneself up; making her up." Rezia's power of putting one scrap with another to make a hat or of gathering the small girl who brings the evening paper into a warm circle of intimacy momentarily cures Septimus of his hallucinations and of his horrifying sense that he is condemned to a solitary death: "For so it always happened. First one thing, then another. So she built it up, first one thing and then another . . . she built it up, sewing." Even Lady Bruton's luncheon, to which she brings Richard Dalloway and Hugh Whitbread to help her write a letter to the *Times* about emigration, is a parody version of this theme of constructive action.

The most important example of the theme is Clarissa Dalloway's party, her attempt to "kindle and illuminate." Though people laugh at her for her parties, feel she too much enjoys imposing herself, nevertheless these parties are her offering to life. They are an offering devoted to the effort to bring together people from their separate lives and combine them into oneness: "Here was So-and-so in South Kensington; some one up in Bayswater; and somebody else, say, in Mayfair. And she felt quite continuously a sense of their existence; and she felt what a waste; and she felt what a pity; and she felt if only they could be brought together; so she did it. And it was an offering; to combine, to create." The party which forms the concluding scene of the novel does succeed in bringing people together, a great crowd from poor little Ellie Henderson all the way up to the Prime Minister, and including Sally Seton and Peter Walsh among the rest. Clarissa has the "gift still; to be; to exist; to sum it all up in the moment."

Clarissa's party transforms each guest from his usual self into a new social self, a self outside the self of participation in the general presence of others. The magic sign of this transformation is the moment when Ralph Lyon beats back the curtain and goes on talking, so caught up is he in the party. The gathering then becomes "something now, not nothing," and Clarissa meditates on the power a successful party has to destroy the usual personality and replace it with another self able to know people with special intimacy and able to speak more freely from the hidden depths of the spirit. These two selves are related to one another as real to unreal, but when one is aware of the contrast, as Clarissa is in the moment just before she loses her self-consciousness and is swept up into her own party, it is impossible to tell which is the real self, which the unreal: "Every time she gave a party she had this feeling of being something not herself, and that every one was unreal in one way; much more real in another . . . it was possible to say things you couldn't say anyhow else, things that needed an effort; possible to go much deeper."

An impulse to create a social situation which will bring into the open the usually hidden continuities of present with past, of person with person, of person with the depths of himself, is shared by all the principal characters of Mrs. Dalloway. This universal desire makes one vector of spiritual forces within the novel a general urge toward lifting up and bringing together.

This effort fails in all its examples, or seems in part to have failed. It seems so implicitly to the narrator and more overtly to some of the characters, including Clarissa. From this point of view, a perspective emphasizing the negative aspect of these characters and episodes, Peter Walsh's adventure with the unknown girl is a fantasy. Lady Bruton is a shallow, domineering busybody, a representative of that upper-class society which Woolf intends to expose in her novel. "I want to criticise the social system," she wrote while composing Mrs. Dalloway, "and to show it at work, at its most intense." Rezia's constructive power and womanly warmth does not prevent her husband from killing himself. And Clarissa? It would be a mistake to exaggerate the degree to which she and the social values she embodies are condemned in the novel. Woolf's attitudes toward upper-class English society of the nineteen-twenties are ambiguous, and to sum up the novel as no more than negative social satire is a distortion. Woolf feared while she was writing the novel that Clarissa would not seem attractive enough to her readers. "The doubtful point," she wrote in her diary a year before the novel was finished, "is, I think, the character of Mrs. Dalloway. It may be too stiff, too glittering and tinselly." There is in fact a negative side to Clarissa as Woolf presents her. She is a snob, too anxious for social success. Her party is seen in part as the perpetuation of a moribund society, with its hangers-on at court like Hugh Whitbread and a Prime Minister who is dull: "You might have stood him behind a counter and bought biscuits," thinks Ellie Henderson, "—poor chap, all rigged up in gold lace."

Even if this negative judgment is suspended and the characters are taken as worth our sympathy, it is still the case that, though Clarissa's party facilitates unusual communication among these people, their communion is only momentary. The party comes to an end; the warmth fades; people return to their normal selves. In retrospect there seems to have been something spurious about the sense of oneness with others the party created. Clarissa's power to bring people together seems paradoxically related to her reticence, her coldness, her preservation of an area of inviolable privacy in herself. Though she believes that each person is not limited to himself, but is spread out among other people like mist in the branches of a tree, with another part of her spirit she contracts into herself and resents intensely any invasion of her privacy. It almost seems as if her keeping of a secret private self is reciprocally related to her social power to gather people together and put them in relationship to one another. The motif of Clarissa's frigidity, of her prudery, of her separateness runs all through *Mrs. Dalloway*. "The death of her soul," Peter Walsh calls it. Since her illness, she has slept alone, in a narrow bed in an attic room. She cannot "dispel a virginity preserved through childbirth which [clings] to her like a sheet." She has "through some contraction of this cold spirit" failed her husband again and again. She feels a stronger sexual attraction to other women than to men. A high point of her life was the moment when Sally Seton kissed her. Her decision not to marry Peter Walsh but to marry Richard Dalloway instead was a rejection of intimacy and a grasping at privacy. "For in marriage a little licence, a little independence there must be between people living together day in day out in the same house; which Richard gave her, and she him . . . But with Peter everything had to be shared; everything gone into. And it was intolerable." "And there is a dignity in people; a solitude; even between husband and wife a gulf," thinks Clarissa much later in the novel. Her hatred of her daughter's friend Miss Kilman, of Sir William Bradshaw, of all the representatives of domineering will, of the instinct to convert others, of "love and religion," is based on this respect for isolation and detachment: "Had she ever tried to convert any one herself? Did she not wish everybody merely to be themselves?" The old lady whom Clarissa sees so often going upstairs to her room in the neighboring house seems to stand chiefly for this highest value, "the privacy of the soul": "that's the miracle, that's the mystery; that old lady, she meant . . . And the supreme mystery . . . was simply this: here was one room; there another. Did religion solve that, or love?"

The climax of *Mrs. Dalloway* is not Clarissa's party but the moment when, having heard of the suicide of Septimus, Clarissa leaves her guests behind and goes alone into the little room where Lady Bruton has a few minutes earlier been talking to the Prime Minister about India. There she sees in the next house the old lady once more, this time going quietly to bed. She thinks about Septimus and recognizes how factitious all her attempt to assemble and to connect has been. Her withdrawal from her party suggests that she has even in the midst of her guests kept untouched the privacy of her soul, that still point from which one can recognize the hollowness of the social world and feel the attraction of the death everyone carries within him as his deepest reality. Death is the place of true communion. Clarissa has been attempting the impossible, to bring the values of death into the daylight world of life. Septimus chose the right way. By killing himself he preserved his integrity, "plunged holding his treasure," his link to the deep places where each man or woman is connected to every other man or woman. For did he not in his madness hear his dead comrade, Evans, speaking to him from that region where all the dead dwell together? "Communication is health; communication is happiness"—Septimus during his madness expresses what is the highest goal for all the characters, but his suicide constitutes a recognition that communication cannot be attained except evanescently in life. The only repetition of the past that successfully repossesses it is the act of suicide.

Clarissa's recognition of this truth, her moment of self-condemnation, is at the same time the moment of her greatest insight:

> She had once thrown a shilling into the Serpentine, never anything more. But he had flung it away. They went on living . . . They (all day she had been thinking of Bourton, of Peter, of Sally), they would grow old. A thing there was that mattered; a thing, wreathed about with chatter, defaced, obscured in her own life, let drop every day in corruption, lies, chatter. This he had preserved. Death was defiance. Death was an attempt to communicate; people feeling the impossibility of reaching the centre which, mystically, evaded them; closeness drew apart; rapture faded, one was alone. There was an embrace in death.

From the point of view of the "thing" at the center that matters most, all speech, all social action, all building it up, all forms of communication, are lies. The more one tries to reach this center through such means the further away from it one goes. The ultimate lesson of *Mrs. Dalloway* is that by building it up, one destroys. Only by throwing it away can life be preserved. It is preserved by being laid to rest on that underlying reality which Woolf elsewhere describes as "a thing I see before me: something abstract; but residing in the downs or sky; beside which nothing matters; in which I shall rest and continue to exist. Reality I call it." "Nothing matters"—compared to this reality, which is only defaced, corrupted, covered over by all the everyday activities of life, everything else is emptiness and vanity: "there is nothing," wrote Woolf during one of her periods of depression, "—nothing for any of us. Work, reading, writing are all disguises; and relations with people."

Septimus Smith's suicide anticipates Virginia Woolf's own death. Both deaths are a defiance, an attempt to communicate, a recognition that self-annihilation is the only possible way to embrace that center which evades one as long as one is alive. Clarissa does not follow Septimus into death (though she has a bad heart, and the original plan, according to the preface Woolf wrote for the Modern Library edition of the novel, was to have her kill herself). Even so, the words of the dirge in *Cymbeline* have been echoing through her head all day: "Fear no more the heat o' th' sun/ Nor the furious winter's rages." Clarissa's obsession with these lines indicates her half-conscious awareness that in spite of her love of life she will reach peace and escape from suffering only in death. The lines come into her mind for a last time just before she returns from her solitary meditation to fulfill her role as hostess. They come to signify her recognition of her kinship with Septimus, her kinship with death. For she is, as Woolf said in the Modern Library preface, the "double" of Septimus. In *Mrs. Dalloway*, Woolf said, "I want to give life and death, sanity and insanity." The novel was meant to be 'a study of insanity and suicide; the world seen by the sane and the insane side by side." These poles are not so much opposites as reversed images of one another. Each has the same elemental design. The death by suicide Woolf originally planned for Clarissa is fulfilled by Septimus, who dies for her, so to speak, a substitute suicide. Clarissa and Septimus seek the same thing: communication, wholeness, the oneness of reality, but only Septimus takes the sure way to reach it. Clarissa's attempt to create unity in her party is the mirror image in the world of light and life of Septimus's vigorous appropriation of the dark embrace of death in his suicide: "Fear no more the heat of the sun. She must go back to them. But what an extraordinary night! She felt somehow very like him—the young man who had killed himself. She felt glad that he had done it; thrown it away." For Woolf, as for Conrad, the visible world of light and life is the mirror image or repetition in reverse of an invisible world of darkness and death. Only the former can be seen and described. Death is incompatible with language, but by talking about life, one can talk indirectly about death.

Mrs. *Dalloway* seems to end in a confrontation of life and death as looking-glass counterparts. Reality, authenticity, and completion are on the death side of the mirror, while life is at best the illusory, insubstantial, and fragmentary image of that dark reality. There is, however, one more structural element in *Mrs. Dalloway*, one final twist which reverses the polarities once more, or rather which holds them poised in their irreconciliation. Investigation of this will permit a final identification of the way Woolf brings into the open latent implications of traditional modes of storytelling in English fiction.

I have said that Mrs. Dalloway has a double temporal form. During the day of the action the chief characters resurrect in memory by bits and pieces the central episode of their common past. All these characters then come together again at Clarissa's party. The narrator in her turn embraces both these times in the perspective of a single distance. She moves forward through her own time of narration toward the point when the two times of the characters come together in the completion of the final sentences of the novel, when Peter sees Clarissa returning to her party. Or should one say "almost come together," since the temporal gap still exists in the separation between "is" and "was"? "It is Clarissa, he said. For there she was."

In the life of the characters, this moment of completion passes. The party ends. Sally, Peter, Clarissa, and the rest move on toward death. The victory of the narrator is to rescue from death this moment and all the other moments of the novel in that All Souls' Day at a second power which is literature. Literature for Woolf is repetition as preservation, but preservation of things and persons in their antithetical poise. Time is rescued by this repetition. It is rescued in its perpetually reversing divisions. It is lifted into the region of death with which the mind of the narrator has from the first page been identified. This is a place of absence, where nothing exists but words. These words generate their own reality. Clarissa, Peter, and the rest can be encountered only in the pages of the novel. The reader enters this realm of language when he leaves his own solid world and begins to read Mrs. Dalloway. The novel is a double resurrection. The characters exist for themselves as alive in a present which is a resuscitation of their dead pasts. In the all-embracing mind of the narrator the characters exist as dead men and women whose continued existence depends on her words. When the circle of the narration is complete, past joining present, the apparently living characters reveal themselves to be already dwellers among the dead.

Clarissa's vitality, her ability "to be; to exist," is expressed in the present-tense statement made by Peter Walsh in the penultimate line of the novel: "It is Clarissa." This affirmation of her power to sum it all up in the moment echoes earlier descriptions of her "extraordinary gift, that woman's gift, of making a world of her own wherever she happened to be": "She came into a room; she stood, as he had often seen her, in a doorway with lots of people round her . . . she never said anything specially clever; there she was, however; there she was"; "There she was, mending her dress." These earlier passages are in the past tense, as is the last line of the novel: "For there she was." With this sentence "is" becomes "was" in the indirect discourse of the narrator. In that mode of language Clarissa along with all the other characters recedes into an indefinitely distant past. Life becomes death within the impersonal mind of the narrator and within her language, which is the place of communion in death. There the fragmentary is made whole. There all is assembled into one unit. All the connections between one part of the novel and another are known only to the agile and ubiquitous mind of the narrator. They exist only within the embrace of that reconciling spirit and through the power of her words.

Nevertheless, to return once more to the other side of the irony, the dirge in *Cymbeline* is sung over an Imogen who is only apparently dead. The play is completed with the seemingly miraculous return to life of the heroine. In the same way, Clarissa comes back from her solitary confrontation with death during her party. She returns from her recognition of her kinship with Septimus to bring "terror" and "ecstasy" to Peter when he sees her. She comes back also into the language of the narration where, like Imogen raised from the dead, she may be confronted by the reader in the enduring language of literature.

It is perhaps for this reason that Woolf changed her original plan and introduced Septimus as Clarissa's surrogate in death. To have had a single protagonist who was swallowed up in the darkness would have falsified her conception. She needed two protagonists, one who dies and another who dies with his death. Clarissa vividly lives through Septimus's death as she meditates alone during her party. Then, having died vicariously, she returns to life. She appears before her guests to cause, in Peter Walsh at least, "extraordinary excitement." Not only does Clarissa's vitality come from her proximity to death. The novel needs for its structural completeness two opposite but similar movements, Septimus's plunge into death and Clarissa's resurrection from the dead. *Mrs. Dalloway* is both of these at once: the entry into the realm of communication in death and the revelation of that realm in words which may be read by the living.

Though *Mrs. Dalloway* seems almost nihilistically to recommend the embrace of death, and though its author did in fact finally take this plunge, nevertheless, like the rest of Woolf's writing, it represents in fact a contrary movement of the spirit. In a note in her diary of May 1933, Woolf records a moment of insight into what brings about a "synthesis" of her being: "how only writing composes it: how nothing makes a whole unless I am writing. Or again: "Odd how the creative power at once brings the whole universe to order." Like Clarissa's party or like the other examples of building it up in *Mrs. Dalloway*, the novel is a constructive action which gathers unconnected elements into a solidly existing object. It is something which belongs to the everyday world of physical things. It is a book with cardboard covers and white pages covered with black marks. This made-up thing, unlike its symbol, Clarissa's party, belongs to both worlds. If it is in one sense no more than a manufactured physical object, it is in another sense made of words which designate not the material presence of the things named but their absence from the everyday world and their existence within the place out of place and time out of time which are the space and time of literature. Woolf's writing has as its aim bringing into the light of day this realm of communication in language. A novel, for Woolf, is the place of death made visible. Writing is the only action which exists simultaneously on both sides of the mirror, within death and within life at once.

Though Woolf deals with extreme spiritual situations, her work would hardly give support to a scheme of literary history which sees twentieth-century literature as more negative, more "nihilistic," or more "ambiguous" than nineteenth-century literature. The "undecidability" of *Mrs. Dalloway* lies in the impossibility of knowing, from the text, whether the realm of union in death exists, for Woolf, only in the words, or whether the words represent an extralinguistic realm which is "really there" for the characters, for the narrator, and for Woolf herself. Nevertheless, the possibility that the realm of death, in real life as in fiction, really exists, is more seriously entertained by Woolf than it is, for example, by Eliot, by Thackeray, or by Hardy. The possibility that repetition in narrative is the representation of a transcendent spiritual realm of reconciliation and preservation, a realm of the perpetual resurrection of the dead, is more straightforwardly proposed by Virginia Woolf than by most of her predecessors in English fiction.

JOHN BURT

Irreconcilable Habits of Thought in "A Room of One's Own" and "To the Lighthouse"

There are two varieties of Virginia Woolf studies. One variety, which includes the studies of Auerbach, Naremore, Leaska, and others, describes Woolf's technical experiments. The other, represented by Marder, Heilbrun, Showalter, and Bazin, describes her ideology. The two varieties do not, however, represent opposing schools of opinion, for the authors of each type, rejecting the distinction between form and content, generously tend to derive the other type's conclusions from their own premises. Woolf herself lends authority to this procedure, for she equates the modernist novel with the androgynous sensibility she advocates, and argues that the Edwardian realist novel's dogmatism and concern with purely external detail is symptomatic of the moral and artistic decrepitude of the partriarchy.

The equation of feminist content and modernist form is misleading, for it connects certain political ideas with formal principles within which those ideas cannot be argued with integrity. If the modernist novel, as Woolf insists, must not be tendentious, but must instead record the impressions that fall upon the mind like an "incessant shower of innumerable

From *English Literary History* 4, vol. 49 (Winter 1982). Copyright © 1982 by The Johns Hopkins University Press.

atoms," then advocacy, even of those values necessary for writing such a work, can have no place within its "semi-transparent envelope." Were Woolf to preach in *To the Lighthouse*, she would, apparently, flaw that novel no less than the narrator's outbursts, according to Woolf, flaw *Jane Eyre*. How is it, then, that *To the Lighthouse* can be, as it is, at the same time an example of a form that has renounced overt persuasion, and a powerful presentation of certain moral and political ideas that its author expects the reader to adopt? Form and content it seems, are not only to be distinguished, they are to be opposed.

Perhaps our mistake is to assume that form and content must be consonant with each other, when in fact their dissonance may reflect those contradictions that artists, like everybody else, must, and yet cannot ever, resolve. Phyllis Rose has lucidly argued that the androgyny Woolf advocates in *A Room of One's Own* is, essentially, Keatsian negative capability described in sexual terms. I will discuss the arguments of *A Room of One's Own* and the themes of *To the Lighthouse* as examples of negative capability in their own right, describing both the formal and the ideological contradictons within which Woolf lives and writes, and estimating what, as an artist, she gains by remaining within them.

I

A Room of One's Own is primarily about the effects of women's poverty upon their art, but it is also about growing uneasiness between the sexes. When Woolf describes an ideal future, in which imaginatively androgynous writers will restore the romance of the past in a more perfect form, the two concerns merge. They diverge, however, when she evaluates the past: describing the emergence of women writers, she sees the past as a sort of dark age from which society has been painfully emerging; describing the collapse of romance, she sees the past as a vanished Eden. Even the idea of imaginative androgyny serves to separate the two major concerns of the book when it is applied to past art, for we learn towards the end of the book that the androgyny of past male writers is a product of the very circumstances that produced the economic and artistic subjection of women.

The central argument of the book might be summarized in five theses:

1. Patriarchal society imposes economic and social restrictions upon women on account of its own need for psychological support.

2. These restrictions limit the experience upon which art depends, causing creative women to suffer and depriving the general culture of their contributions.

3. As the material condition of women has improved, women writers have emerged, and the integrity of their work, its freedom from the scars and kinks of personal limitations, has risen in proportion to their status.

4. The rise of women has deprived the patriarchy of its psychological support, causing uncomfortable relations between the sexes that reflect themselves in the limitations of contemporary art.

5. When the emancipation of women is complete, a more adequate sexuality and a more adequate imagination, marked by androgyny or sexual openness, must emerge.

This argument depends upon a progressive view of human history, and an optimistic view, or at least a not tragic view, of human nature. The unhappiness of past eras is the result of the errors of past generations, errors defined in such a way as to make them easy to correct. It is one of the curious features of Woolf's theory of the origin of the subjection of women that that subjection is not motivated by men's will-to-power over women but rather by men's doubts about themselves; it is the creation of weakness searching for succor, not of strength searching for a victim:

> Women have served all these centuries as looking-glasses possessing the magic and delicious power of reflecting the figure of man at twice its natural size. Without that power probably the earth would still be swamp and jungle. . . . For if she begins to tell the truth, the figure in the looking-glass shrinks; his fitness for life is diminished. How is he to go on giving judgment, civilizing natives, making laws, writing books, dressing up and speechifying at banquets, unless he can see himself at breakfast at twice the size he really is?

If there is bitterness in this passage, it is certainly not the bitterness one can find in *Three Guineas*. Contemptible as Woolf may find the pomposity she describes, she is more mocking than vituperative, and the sensitive egotists she describes seem more foolish than dangerous. If men oppress women not through joy of doing so but through weakness and self-doubt, we have no reason to suspect that progress is impossible, for we have no reason to suspect the men she describes of the bad faith that would make it so. Woolf's tone is critical, but also confident that the progress that such criticism is an attempt to bring about is not out of reach.

The underargument of *A Room of One's Own* presupposes a much less happy view of human nature and of history. This view is nowhere stated explicitly in the book, but the longing for the prewar era that colors the underargument is certainly a reaction against an unstated apprehension about human nature. As the critical tone of the major argument reflects optimism about the human prospect, so the nostalgia and tenderness of the underargument are signs of the half-hidden fear to which they respond. The underargument might be summarized as follows:

1. Men and women, before the war, could joyfully idealize each other.

2. This capacity for mutual joy accounts for the integrity, the imaginative life, of the art of the past, and can be identified with imaginative androgyny.

3. The war has destroyed this capacity entirely, but left us with a longing for it.

On the face of it, this argument, except for its mention of the war, seems to be simply a corollary to the argument concerning poverty and women. But to say that sexual uneasiness is caused by the lurid light in which men and women saw each other's faces in 1914 is very different from saying that this uneasiness is caused by the partial emancipation of women. For the slaughter at the Somme reveals far more than merely that Douglas Haig and his staff were ridiculous men of the sort Woolf satirizes above; the war reveals facts about human nature that make every hope about moral advancement and progress mere wishful thinking. These facts, and not the sexual uneasiness they cause, are the burden of the underargument.

If the mention of the war as a possible cause of sexual uneasiness is brief and seemingly offhand, the fact of the war's destruction shapes, implicitly, the most distinctive feature of the underargument, the positive tone of its description of the prewar era. Although the major argument's description of this era, as we have seen, is far from strident, nevertheless it is clear that the old order was riddled with folly, that the future would certainly bring improvement, and that the present, for all of its discomfort, is a necessary stage in the bringing about of that improvement. The underargument, in contrast, not only idealizes the past in general (the positive features of which it hints are lost forever) but also idealizes the very sexual transaction that was the source of the problems the major argument was intended to solve.

The scene Woolf describes by way of noting what the current age has lost—the scene that illustrates how male artists of the past came upon the openness to the feminine that gave their works imaginative life—is simply a slightly spruced-up version of the scene that summarized the origin of the subjection of women. Male writers turned to women for support, and

What they got, it is obvious, was something that their own sex was unable to supply; and it would not be rash, perhaps, to define it further, without quoting the doubtless rhapsodical words of the poets, as some stimulus, some renewal of creative power which it is in the gift only of the opposite sex to bestow. He would open the door of the drawing-room or nursery, I thought, and find her among her children perhaps, or with a piece of embroidery on her knee—at any rate, the centre of some different order and system of life, and the contrast between this world and his own, which might be the law courts or the House of Commons, would at once refresh and invigorate; and there would follow, even in the simplest talk, such a natural difference of opinion that the dried ideas in him would be fertilised anew; and the sight of her creating a different medium from his own would so quicken his creative power that insensibly his sterile mind would begin to plot again, and he would find the phrase or the scene which was lacking when he put on his hat to visit her.

The only difference between this scene, where a weary man is revivified by contact with the life of a woman, and the earlier scene, where an insecure man bolstered his morale by forcing a woman to reflect him at twice his actual size, is the tone of the narrator. For the events are identical. Through this presentation of its central transaction the underargument subverts the larger argument of which it is ostensibly a subsidiary part, and leads the book into a thicket of self-refutation from which there appears to be no escape.

What could have caused this reevaluation of the terms of the argument? What necessity compels Woolf not only to look with nostalgia and affection upon a past from which she and her whole society were trying to emerge, but also to idealize the very transaction that lay at the heart of the mistakes of that past? The sexual openness of the prewar years is never discussed as something present, but always as something lost. It is introduced, in the course of her description of the luncheon party she attended at Oxbridge, as a missing undertone:

> Before the war at a luncheon party like this people would have said precisely the same things but they would have sounded different, because in those days they were accompanied by a sort of humming noise, not articulate, but musical, exciting, which changed the value of the words themselves.

Woolf goes on to embody this murmuring in the love lyrics of Tennyson and Rossetti, lyrics the likes of which we no longer hear. The humming noise and the romance it represents are victims of the war. But, of course, they are not the only victims. For certainly the progressive argument, depending as it does on a sunny view of human possibilities, must also have died in the war. If Woolf does not say as much herself, it can only be because she sophistically displaces the war's destructive power from the progressive argument onto the idea of romance. Since the idea of romance and the possibility of androgyny seem to be related forms of imaginative openness, however, it is difficult to see what she gains by substituting a particular victim of the war, romance or androgyny, for the general victim, hope, unless it is enough that such a substitution gives the longing through which hope is to be rebuilt a particular and identifiable form.

The old order, destroyed by the war, then, is sacrificed in place of hopes that the war calls into question; and the value Woolf assigns to that order is its value as a sacrifice, a value created in retrospect by the destruction to which it is consigned. One of the elementary methods of surviving a catastrophe is to posit something valuable of which it has deprived us, so that by fixing our minds with longing upon what we have lost, we may give direction to our attempts to rebuild our lives. Destruction draws the sting from criticism of the old order, and the softening of criticism yields an ideal, even in that order's very shortcomings, that may guide us out of destruction. Only the need to answer the war's unspoken but looming objection could have necessitated such a radical reevaluation of the terms of Woolf's argument, could have led her to praise a transaction which she ought, by rights, to have criticized.

The reaffirmation of the values of the past that is so crucial to the underargument is a device to meet the danger posed to the book by the view of human nature that the war justifies. It is at the same time an ideal view of the human possibility, raised to meet the grave doubts about it that the war has caused, and a surrogate victim, which can be sacrificed in place of hopes about the future. The good Victorian past is a retrospective creation of the shadow of the war, just as the bad Victorian past is the creation of the sunlight of contemporary hopes. By idealizing the transaction that was the fundamental instrument of the subjection of women, Woolf takes back her argument in a limited way—and appeases the force of the unspoken argument of the war, which might otherwise have repealed a progressive essay entirely.

How the creation of the idea of lost romance might help a progressive view of history persist despite the war—by first displacing the war's destructive power, and then providing a focus for whatever regenerative powers we have at our command—might be summarized by means of a diagram:

Progressive argument
(Positive view of human nature)

Unstated total repeal of argument
(War makes a positive view of human nature impossible to believe)

Surrogate victim partially displaces repeal
(War makes romance impossible)

Shift of emphasis redeems surrogate victim
(The romance of the past is an ideal to be recreated)

Reaffirmation of progressive argument
(Romance will be recreated in a progressive way)

The introduction of the underargument allows the book to recover from the damage inflicted on it by the consciousness of the war, but the book continues to manifest the tension between criticism and nostalgia through which it recovered. This recovery does not take place by logical means—the progressive argument is repealed by the war as much at the close of the book as it was at the beginning—but it is too much to ask a book to argue a war away. It is enough if it can marshal those hopes and longings by means of which wars can be survived.

If A Room of One's Own recovers at all, then, it recovers through a brave sophistry. The two arguments of A Room of One's Own are not reconcilable, and any attempt to reconcile them can be no more than an exercise in special pleading. A Room of One's Own, however, is not an argument but, as Woolf proclaims in its opening pages, a portrayal of how a mind attempts to come to terms with its world. We find in the under-argument that the world is perhaps not a place with which anyone could come to terms. Yet Woolf does not abandon those progressive hopes that she had wished to see realized, for even if the world is what she fears it might be, she knows that to abandon even dubious hopes would be a form of death, and that to hold fast to them, even in the face of what she knows, is a form of courage. The central contradiction in A Room of One's Own is the result not of weakness but of honesty.

II

It is traditional for critics of To the Lighthouse to juxtapose lists of masculine and feminine characteristics (using the Ramsays as representatives of their sexes) and to postulate that Art is a mediator between them. But beneath the tension between men and women is a different tension that cannot be resolved or repressed but only lived. We see this tension most clearly when we try to reconcile the progressive judgments the novel forces us to make with the far different conclusions forced upon us with equal urgency by the dark events, the deaths of characters we have loved, that form the thematic and structural center of the novel.

Where *A Room of One's Own* presents successive arguments that run in opposite directions, *To the Lighthouse* presents characters whose natures demand to be seen simultaneously from opposite points of view. Mr. Ramsay, for instance, is a more or less tyrannical representative of the old order, and we see him time and time again demanding sympathy and support in ways that we recognize from *A Room of One's Own* as being the stuff of which the subjection of women is made. Critics traditionally have taken a rather dim view of him, and their view is the counterpart in this novel of the progressive argument of *A Room of One's Own*. But Mr. Ramsay is not to be summed up so easily, and it is not simply the complexity of a convincing character that accounts for this difficulty.

Woolf's original conception of *To the Lighthouse* apparently included a much harsher version of Mr. Ramsay. Her entry in *A Writer's Diary* for May 14, 1925, describes her original idea for the novel:

> This is going to be fairly short; to have father's character done complete in it; and mother's; and St. Ives; and childhood; and all the usual things I try to put in—life, death, etc. But the centre is father's character, sitting in a boat, reciting We perished, each alone, while he crushes a dying mackerel.

This Ramsay is more self-pitying, more violent, and less human than the one we actually meet in *To the Lighthouse*. His self-pity speaks for itself. His crushing of the mackerel, an apparently pointless act, deserves a closer look.

In 1925, after she finished *Mrs. Dalloway*, Woolf wrote a series of short stories that were collected and published in 1973 under the title *Mrs. Dalloway's Party*. In one of these stories, "The Introduction," we meet a character named Lily Everit, who seems to be a younger and more vulnerable Lily Briscoe. When the story opens, Lily is standing alone at Mrs. Dalloway's party, knowing that Mrs. Dalloway is about to "bear down on her" and introduce her to "the world." As she watches Mrs. Dalloway come towards her, she clasps to herself, "as a drowning man might hug a spar in the sea," an essay she has written on the character of Dean Swift. Lily is not eager to be pushed into this "world," or, more specifically, into the old sexual order, and she describes to herself the role Mrs. Dalloway wishes her to play, in a figure that recurs in the story:

> All made her feel that she had come out of her chrysalis and was being proclaimed what in the long comfortable darkness of childhood she had

never been—this frail and beautiful creature, this limited and circumscribed creature who could not do what she liked, this butterfly with a thousand facets to its eyes, and delicate fine plumage; and difficulties and sensibilities and sadnesses innumerable: a woman.

Mrs. Dalloway introduces the reluctant Lily to an arrogant young man named Bob Brinsley, in whose presence Lily fades. Her instinct, as she hears his monologue about his accomplishments and his belittling remarks about what he presumes to be hers, is to wish to destroy her essay, which earlier had been a bulwark she had opposed to "masculine achievement." As he rambles on about himself, Brinsley carelessly rips the wings off a fly. Lily reacts with a horror that completes her self-abasement and surrender; Brinsley's violence to the fly's wings shrivels the metaphorical wings upon her own back converting them into the "weight of all the world."

The connection between the sadistic destruction of a small creature and the subjugation of women by men that we find in "The Introduction" was apparently also supposed to be made in *To the Lighthouse*. Mr. Ramsay, who crushes a mackerel, was to be similar to Bob Brinsley, who tears the wings off a fly. But in the novel as it was finally written, this act is transferred to a comparatively minor character, Macalister's boy, who accompanies Mr. Ramsay, Cam and James on their trip to the Lighthouse in the last part of the novel. The act is still, perhaps, the climax of the book, but its meaning is vastly altered from Woolf's original idea of it.

The mutilation of the mackerel is described in a laconic paragraph enclosed in brackets—a paragraph like those that crop up in the "Time Passes" section of the novel. Like the parenthetical paragraphs of "Time Passes," it emphasizes the darkness and incomprehensibility of life we have seen hinted in *A Room of One's Own*. The scene interrupts and confirms the meditations of Lily Briscoe, who afterwards describes her state of mind immediately before as that of one who "steps off her strip of board into the waters of annihilation." On shore, working on her painting, Lily has begun to despair of making sense of her world, and she longs for Mrs. Ramsay, who has been dead for nearly ten years, to come back and give her the strength to struggle with life. She turns to Augustus Carmichael, an artist like herself, and, also like herself, someone rather out of the mainstream of sexual life, someone with whom she has a great unspoken affinity. Posing questions to him in her mind "about life, about death," she initiates a silent conversation with him that continues until the end of the book:

> What does it mean? How do you explain it all? she wanted to say, turning to Mr. Carmichael again. For the whole world seemed to have dissolved

in this early morning hour into a pool of thought, a deep basin of reality, and one could almost fancy that had Mr. Carmichael spoken, for instance, a little tear would have rent the surface pool. And then? Something would emerge. A hand would be shoved up, a blade would be flashed.

Mr. Carmichael's unspoken response to Lily's question would be that everything but art vanishes, and it is in art that meaning must be found. Lily, in turn, seems to answer that all she can find in her art is her pain. Yet despite this, Lily's vision does not fade, but intensifies and darkens in character, revealing the central fact upon which art is based, what it takes to make beauty roll itself up and make empty flourishes form into shape. The shift to the boat where Macalister's boy mutilates the mackerel is not a shift away from the impending vision but the realization of that vision—in a way it is his knife that is the knife of the vision, and the reader learns (if Lily herself does not since she doesn't see this scene) that the blade of the vision does indeed cut:

> Was she crying then for Mrs. Ramsay, without being aware of any un-happiness? She addressed old Mr. Carmichael again. What was it then? What did it mean? Could things thrust their hands up and grip one; could the blade cut; the first grasp? Was there no safety? no learning by heart of the ways of the world? no guide, no shelter, but all was miracle, and leaping from the pinnacle of a tower into the air? Could it be, even for elderly people, that this was life?—startling, unexpected, unknown? For one moment she felt that if they both got up, here, now on the lawn, and demanded an explanation, why was it so short, why was it so inex-plicable, said it with violence, as two fully equipped human beings from whom nothing should be hid might speak, then beauty would roll itself up; the space would fill; those empty flourishes would form into shape; if they shouted loud enough Mrs. Ramsay would return. "Mrs. Ramsay!" she said aloud, "Mrs. Ramsay!" The tears ran down her face.
>
> VI
> [Macalister's boy took one of the fish and cut a square out of its side to bait his hook with. The mutilated body (it was alive still) was thrown back into the sea.]

Only at this moment does Woolf abandon the narrative distance, the irony implicit in her multiple point of view narration, to join what she says in her own voice (within the brackets) to what she said (in indirect discourse) through Lily Briscoe. Woolf's parenthesis is the expression, even the fulfillment, of Lily's vision, as if the author took her cues from the character she has created rather than standing at a distance, evaluating and undercutting (as was her usual practice). Confronting the problem of the treachery and emptiness of life, Woolf and Lily are united in what my colleague Jonathan Freedman calls a "shared *cri de coeur.*"

The mutilation of the mackerel, which was originally intended to epitomize Mr. Ramsay and provoke the reader's hostility to him, instead becomes the symbolic center—shared by character, author, and reader— of grief over the death of Mrs. Ramsay. The concern of the novel shifts from criticism to mourning, and as it does so our view of the characters we have been predisposed to scorn, like our view of the prewar era in *A Room of One's Own*, changes in a way nothing in the original idea, no matter how subtle or three-dimensional, could have led us to expect. This radical alteration of the novel's intent runs parallel to the alteration of *A Room of One's Own* two years later, and can be attributed to the same cause, to the necessity of confronting that collection of unhappy facts I have called the postwar argument.

III

Life's violence and life's meaninglessness are the central subjects of *To the Lighthouse*, and those passages where life is most unflinchingly seen—Lily's vision, "Time Passes," Mrs. Ramsay's reveries as a "wedge-shaped core of darkness"—are its greatest artistic tours de force. But it is not enough merely to confront the two chief terrors of life: they must be mastered, or at least survived. As in *A Room of One's Own*, it is in the old order, even in its shortcomings, that Woolf seeks the means of survival. Chastened and frightened by what the war proves about life, she idealizes the very trans-actions between men and women at which she had set out to scoff, and treats them not as the follies of an unenlightened age but as the attempts of that age to hold off the destructive forces by which it was finally over-whelmed. She returns to the Ramsays and their marriage, not abandoning her criticism, but adding a sympathy that springs as much from need as from nostalgia.

For all of its manifest problems, the Ramsays' marriage is carefully arranged to allow them to shield each other's different vulnerabilities; and, strangely enough, it is by means of the very qualities that other characters criticize—the generosity that puts everyone in Mrs. Ramsay's debt, and Mr. Ramsay's bullying—that they are able to do so. Mr. Ramsay's fear is of aridity, and that fear takes two forms. First, he fears that he cannot live up to the demands of his heroic notions, that his most recent work of philosophy was not quite his best. This fear is compounded by the suspicion that the encumbrances of marriage and child-rearing have prevented him from doing the work he might have done had he remained single. Second, he fears that his efforts are not in the circle of life. Mrs. Ramsay—in a scene identical to that we saw both criticized and idealized in *A Room of One's Own*—seems able to respond to both fears, quieting his doubts and assuring him that he has not missed out on life.

Mrs. Ramsay, in contrast, fears the destructiveness and treachery of life, and she asks explicitly and apparently with authorial approval what was asked only implicitly in *A Room of One's Own*:

> How could any Lord have made this world? she asked. With her mind she had always seized the fact that there is no reason, order, justice; but suffering, death, the poor. There was no treachery too base for the world to commit; she knew that. No happiness lasted; she knew that.

Mrs. Ramsay's response to her uneasiness about life is to encourage people to take part in it; she seems to represent some of the very dangers she opposes: "There were the eternal problems: suffering; death, the poor. There was always a woman dying of cancer even here. And yet she had said to all these children, 'You shall go through it all.'" The concords that Mrs. Ramsay creates to meet life are of course themselves a part of life. Even the image Lily uses to describe the Ramsays' domestic happiness (which appears as she describes the freshness those around the Ramsays can feel after they have made up some difference between them) is disquietingly close to her image of life's terror, for the "blade in the air" she mentions is without doubt the blade that was thrust up in the course of her vision:

> All would be as usual, save only for some quiver, as of a blade in the air, which came and went between them as if the usual sight of the children sitting round their soup plates had freshened itself in their eyes after that hour among the pears and cabbages. Especially, Lily thought, Mrs. Ramsay would glance at Prue . . . assuring her that everything was well; promising her that one of these days that same happiness would be hers. She had enjoyed it for less than a year, however.

These sharp objects seem to cut two ways, representing at the same time how we enter life and how we counter life with means that are themselves a part of life.

Mrs. Ramsay's matchmaking protects her no more effectively than Mr. Ramsay's bluster protected him, and both activities are seen by the others as at the same time threatening and pathetic; but methods that do not allow them to protect themselves nevertheless do allow them, temporarily, to protect each other. Mrs. Ramsay's cultivation of life, as we have seen, subdues her husband's fears of lifelessness. Mr. Ramsay's uncompromising truthfulness subdues Mrs. Ramsay's fear of life's destruction as well.

Mr. Ramsay is well aware of what he calls his wife's sadness, and it seems to him that there is little that he can do about it:

> He could not help noting as he passed, the sternness at the heart of her beauty. It saddened him, and her remoteness pained him, and he felt, as he passed, that he could not protect her, and, when he reached the hedge, he was sad. He could do nothing to help her. He must stand by and watch her. Indeed, the infernal truth was, he made things worse for her. He was irritable—he was touchy. He had lost his temper over the Lighthouse. He looked into the hedge, into its intricacy, its darkness.

Mr. Ramsay shows a little more self-knowledge here than most readers (except Leaska) have given him credit for. It is a curious fact, however, that the harshness that he, along with most readers, condemns in himself is the very thing that protects his wife, for a moment, from life. The episode in which he expresses these doubts about himself is a case in point.

Mrs. Ramsay has just sent James to bed after telling him that they probably will not go to the Lighthouse the next day. When James departs she withdraws into herself and momentarily enjoys a delicious self-possession. She slips free of any particular time and place and becomes a "wedge-shaped core of darkness" that wanders throughout a world of shadowy suppositions, rather, as Auerbach has noted, like the author herself. Mrs. Ramsay becomes, as it were, a modernist narrator, an ally of the "little winds" of "Times Passes," and as she does so, she necessarily becomes subject to the nihilism that Auerbach notes as the universal concomitant of the modernist technique. The case of the narrator, for instance, exemplifies the danger of her method, for it is when she is most thoroughly free of the constraints of Realism—in "Time Passes"—that she most clearly identifies herself with that destructive and treacherous thing she refers to as "life," taking the point of view of an inhuman host of winds that replaces and destroys human observers:

> Almost one might have imagined them, as they entered the drawing room questioning and wondering, toying with the flap of hanging wall-paper, asking would it hang much longer, when would it fall? Then smoothly brushing the walls, they passed on musingly as if asking the red and yellow roses on the wallpaper whether they would fade, and, questioning (gently, for there was time at their disposal) the torn letters in the waste-paper basket, the flowers, the book, all of which were now open to them and asking, Were they allies? Were they enemies? How long would they endure?

The destructive events in "Time Passes," that, like the mutilation of the mackerel, occur inside parentheses apparently obtruding into the text, in fact fulfill tendencies long latent in the figures of the passages they conclude. Just as the mutilation of the mackerel fulfills Lily's vision, so the wartime deaths fulfill potentialities of the shadowy, siren-like lyric prose that they seem to interrupt:

> But slumber and sleep though it might there came later in the summer ominous sounds like the measured blows of hammers dulled on felt, which, with their repeated shocks still further loosened the shawl and cracked the tea-cups. Now and again some glass tinkled in the cupboard as if a giant voice had shrieked so loud in its agony that tumblers stood inside a cupboard vibrated too. Then again silence fell; and then, night after night, and sometimes in plain mid-day when the roses were bright and light turned on the wall its shape clearly there seemed to drop into this silence, this indifference, this integrity, the thud of something falling. [A shell exploded. Twenty or thirty young men were blown up in France, among them Andrew Ramsay, whose death, mercifully was instantaneous.]

Like the narrator's, Mrs. Ramsay's meditations darken in character, and she apprehends life's treachery. But just at this moment, Mr. Ramsay passes by her and reproaches himself with his inability to protect her, and as he resolves not to interrupt her, she, knowing that he wishes to shelter her, stands up and goes to him herself.

When she goes to him, she is of course responding to his fear that he is outside of life, but her doing so enables him to respond to her own fear. It is contact with her husband's different nature that frees her from her melancholy, just as his contact with her freed him from his aridity:

> His arm was almost like a young man's arm, Mrs. Ramsay thought, thin and hard, and she thought with delight how strong he still was, though he was over sixty, and how untamed and optimistic, and how strange it was that being convinced, as he was, of all sorts of horror, seemed not to depress him, but to cheer him.

Even the domineering natural to one who "never tampers with facts" is later pressed into service against life:

> "You won't finish that stocking tonight," he said, pointing to her stocking. That was what she wanted—the asperity in his voice reproving her. If he says it's wrong to be pessimistic probably it is wrong, she thought; the marriage [Paul's and Minta's] will turn out all right.

The effect of Mr. Ramsay's asperity is to draw his wife from her unhappy musings, to recall her from a world Woolf always describes in the subjunctive to a world for which only the indicative is appropriate. This movement is, as Hartman has noted, a return from Modernism to Realism. The narrator often makes the same return, and for the same purpose: much as Mr. Ramsay protects his wife from life by insisting that she confine herself to what he sees as the facts, so Woolf herself repeatedly (and not always using Mr. Ramsay as an intermediary) protects her novel from the darkness that is its subject and motive power by returning to the narrative present of a traditional realist novel. This is not to say that Woolf returns from dangerous speculations to safer facts, for the facts are the violent events described in the bracketed passages that interrupt and confirm her most baleful speculations. Woolf returns not to the facts, but to the fictional conventions of Realism, just as Mrs. Ramsay returns not to the truth—for that is precisely what she is afraid of—but to the sustaining ignorance about life that she finds in her husband's inability to surmise. If the excursions out of the realist narrative present embody the source of the novel's power, then the return embodies what control Woolf is able to exercise over that power, and the discontinuity of the novel's form is a consequence of the complexity of its purpose. Just as *A Room of One's Own* partially redeemed the Victorian past in order to shield itself from the war, so *To the Lighthouse* partially redeems the realist novel in order to shield itself from the consequences of its central perceptions.

To the Lighthouse survives by returning to the very things—the realist novel and the old order—it had set out to discredit. But it is neither a realist novel nor a work of reactionary nostalgia, for in that case it would be a novel about delusion, not about mourning. Just as the progressive and postwar arguments stand side by side in *A Room of One's Own*, modifying each other and holding each other in check, so two irreconcilable assessments of the past stand side by side here. The survival of the novel's progressive ideology, an ideology critical of Mr. Ramsay, performs for the novel a function analogous to that Mr. Ramsay himself performs for his wife: it attempts to restrain, perhaps even to harness, the dangerous power provided by too clear a perception of life. The progressive ideology, however complicated by life's violence and meaninglessness, does for the content of *To the Lighthouse* exactly what the redemption of the realist conventions does to its form.

The attempt to restrain the dangerous but essential forces that drive the novel results not only in the explicit opposition of Mr. and Mrs. Ramsay we have just seen, but also in the tensions between sympathetic and unsympathetic views of their marriage, between postwar and progressive habits of thought, and between realist and modernist forms of narration. The discontinuities within the content and the discontinuities within the form of *To the Lighthouse* are closely comparable and serve a common purpose: they allow the novel to pit a terrible life against the lifeless ability to master life.

To the Lighthouse is not an artifact, whose shape we can describe and whose meaning we can surmise, but a challenge to a continuous and difficult effort undertaken no less by the reader than by the author. It is not a thing, but an occasion; and to read it, we must partake of the author's effort to resist both those postwar habits that would devote it to death, and those progressive habits that would transform it from a work of art into a tract. We must resist, that is, the very destruction and aridity that the female and male characters, respectively, most fear. Woolf's concept of androgyny comes down to nothing more than this dual resistance. Whether her own resistance is successful we cannot say, for nothing succeeds until we can say "It is finished." Although Lily Briscoe may say this of her painting, Woolf can never say this of her novel. For it is in the nature of the effort it represents that it must not end.

ROBERT KIELY

"Jacob's Room":
A Study in Still Life

Near the beginning and again to-
ward the end of her career, Virginia Woolf created literary portraits, each
inspired by a man she had loved and associated with Bloomsbury and with
crucial moments in her life. Though one book is a novel and the other a
biography, the works invite comparison on several grounds: they are the
only two books by Woolf in which a male is the central figure; both repeatedly assert the impossibility of representing character accurately in
words and thereby undermine their apparent reason for being; both reveal
an interest in modern painting, evident in all Woolf's work but in these
cases more than usually intense and self-conscious; and from both narratives
the protagonist has somehow escaped. Jacob Flanders and Roger Fry are
not there. The easel is ready, the room has been prepared, but the model's
chair is empty. Instead of a fleshed-out portrait, what we find more nearly
resembles a still life, a painstakingly careful arrangement of objects within
a frame. As the arrangement differs in each book, so necessarily does the
nature and effect of the absence of the assumed central figure. . . .

The parallels between Jacob Flanders and Thoby Stephen are as
obvious as the fact that *Jacob's Room* is a work of fiction, not a biography.
The Cambridge education, love of literature, visit to Greece, intention to
study law, even the awkward good looks and the tendency to be tongue-
tied they have in common. Woolf once referred to her brother as "a

From *Modernism Reconsidered.* Copyright © 1983 by the President and Fellows of Harvard
College.

charming great inarticulate creature," in very much the same words that are applied in the novel to Jacob. But as Woolf knew, these traits and experiences did little to distinguish her brother or the protagonist of her first experimental novel from hundreds of other young Englishmen of their generation.

Many years after Thoby's death, Woolf wondered how he would have turned out, whether he might have been "Mr. Justice Stephen . . . with several books to his credit." For a biographer, the speculation seems idle; for a sister and an artist not at all. Woolf felt that there was much she had not known or understood about her brother. At first she appealed to his Cambridge friends for help. But information was not really what she wanted; as she was to say later, facts did not have the power to convey life or to allay the feeling that "the best in us had gone."

Left with the memory of an important but unclear presence and the anguish caused by absence, Woolf experienced a grief of a peculiarly frustrating kind. Her sense of loss was powerful, yet the more time went by and the more she reflected on it, though the feelings did not vanish, the object to which they referred seemed to lose whatever shape and solidity it had possessed. For the artistic sensibility, it must have seemed an almost too familiar Romantic dilemma: to be overcome by emotions without having ready at hand a clearly defined object to which they can be attached or a satisfactory verbal formula through which they can be expressed.

Two attempts at resolving this problem favored by Romantic writers were the mythic reconstruction of character into an immortal being of absolute worth and dispersal of emotion into a landscape transformed by an atmosphere of nostalgia and melancholy. Woolf had a tendency—one might say a genius—for the latter.

Jacob's Room shows her first prolonged experiment with another way to give form to the emotions and, in doing so, to hint at the life that had inspired them. It is also at this stage that her years of observing Vanessa and her painter friends at work and her exposure to the post-Impressionists through the influence of Roger Fry converged to give her a concrete analogue to the writer's craft that helped her to break away from certain literary preconceptions.

In an essay entitled "Life and the Novelist," Woolf observed that for the writer too there is a studio, a solitary room where life is "curbed," even "killed." As the painter's perceptions and memories are broken into components of color and shading, so the writer's are "mixed with this, stiffened with that, brought into contrast with something else." What emerges may be "stark" and "formidable" but it can be "enduring," "the bone and substance upon which our rush of indiscriminating emotions was founded." Woolf's artistic economy has much to do with Cézanne and little to do with Gaudier-Brzska and the Vorticists. Hers is a salvage operation, not an act of hostility. Her literary counterpart of *nature morte* begins in negation, not of life or the value of art, but of certain assumptions about the relation between the two. In dealing with her unfocused emotion, she suspends belief in the suspension of disbelief, pares down her materials, dismisses illusion. From her earliest references to *Jacob's Room*, she comments on what is lacking: "The theme is a blank to me; but I see immense possibilities in the form." And later, "Beauty . . . is only got by the failure to get it . . . by facing what must be humiliation—the things one can't do." When Lytton Strachey wrote to her praising the novel, she responded in a characteristic way, pointing to an achievement while acknowledging an apparent shortcoming: "Of course you put your infallible finger upon the spot—romanticism. How do I catch it? Not from my father. I think it must have been my Great Aunts. But some of it, I think, comes from the effort of breaking with complete representation. One flies into the air. Next time I mean to stick closer to facts."

By admitting at the outset that in planning *Jacob's Room* she had no theme in mind, that the work makes no claim to beauty or completeness of representation, Woolf does more than disarm her critics. She reveals a state of mind. Upon retiring to her solitary room to compose *Jacob's Room*, like the painter of a still life, she chose a subject—the education of a young man—familiar to the point of being a cliché; furthermore, like the painter whose subject is fruit or flowers, emblems of perishable beauty, she exposes the tension created by imposing an appearance of permanence on that which cannot be preserved; finally, and perhaps most importantly, she takes advantage of being able to compose twice. In contrast to the illusion created by much landscape and portrait painting it is apparent to a viewer of a still life that the painter has "set up" what he has painted and then painted it. There are two clearly visible arrangements. In a certain sense, all writers of fiction do this. But that Woolf was particularly conscious of doing it may well have set her on course not only for *Jacob's Room* but for the greater works to follow, in which the preoccupation with composition does not obscure the subject but becomes the subject while allowing a great deal else—beauty, for example, emotion, and even a theme or two—to slip between the crevices.

In allowing Jacob to be featureless or a blurred composite of the ways in which different people see him, Woolf may have confounded many of her first readers, but she seems to have discovered simultaneously her method and her subject. From the first scene on the beach when Mrs. Flanders gets up and prepares to leave, thereby spoiling the composition of Charles Steele's painting, the reader's attention is drawn to the experience, certainly not peculiar to artists, of trying to capture and frame that which keeps moving out of view. Like his mother and his friend Fanny, whose flashes of beauty cannot be caught by the painter Bramham, Jacob seems to defy the art of portrait painting. Mrs. Norman, his fellow traveler on the train to Cambridge, studies his features but only concludes that he appeared "out of place." Later, as he takes leave of the Durrants, another guest regrets his escape: " 'Not to sit for me,' said Miss Eliot, planting her tripod upon the lawn." Even Jacob's quiet reverie at the Acropolis is interrupted when he notices Madame Lucien Gravé trying to take a photograph of him: "Damn these women . . . How they spoil things." And once again he jumps out of the picture.

Those who had tried to capture Mrs. Flanders and Fanny were male painters, while it was more often women who wished to photograph, draw, or summarize Jacob; this difference not only suggests elements of sexual attraction, curiosity, and possessiveness in the artistic impulse but serves to remind us in Jacob's case, at least, that the refusal to be pinned down, which is his most consistent trait, is not a weakness in his character nor in Woolf's method, but an essential expression of his youth. Though Woolf recognized no theme as she planned *Jacob's Room*, it becomes apparent that her preoccupation with form and her refusal to aim for a "complete representation" coincided wih a fascination with youth and its effects on the lives around it. Woolf's novel is not a portrait of an artist or barrister as a young man because, though law and marriage could have been in Jacob's future, serious considerations of his future are among the many elements the artist eliminates from her canvas.

What is most attractive, puzzling, infuriating, and fundamental about Jacob and the fluid, almost casual fashion in which Woolf lets him escape categorization is just that: the refusal to settle down and take responsibility. Jacob has no character not necessarily because he is weak, stupid, spoiled, or selfish (though at times he seems to be all of these), but because he does not survive. In this he is like Rachel Vinrace in *The Voyage Out*. Yet his story, for all its underlying sadness, is unlike hers in its many moments of joy. Jacob's exits, his leaps to freedom, out of the train compartment, away from Professor Plumer's lunch party—"oh God, oh God, oh God!"—away from late-night philosophical discussions, out of bed with Florinda, out of London, out of Paris, out of Athens—all have about them the incomparable gusto and exhilarating sense of freedom possessed by the very young who do not yet have to choose.

The oppressiveness of *The Voyage Out* stems in part from the protagonist's sex, which prevents her, within the social conventions of the time, from exercising the temporary and illusory freedom so briefly but vigorously enjoyed by Jacob. Rachel's movement is not, like Jacob's, a series of leaps, one step ahead of those friends, relatives, or artists who are waiting nearby with a trap. She is trapped from the beginning. She moves from shelter to shelter without abandon and without apparent alternative. Jacob's death is one final surprising exit, one last abrupt departure accomplished with something midway between clumsiness and perfect style. Rachel's death is slow and lingering, a "drowning," a going under, a submission.

Like the fresh flower or fruit of a still life, the young Jacob is set up for admiration by the artist in full consciousness of the paradox of endowing his condition with an appearance of permanence. The death's head in the shape of a sheep's skull or the memory of a young father who had also quit the scene abruptly are never far from view. But for the most part Jacob seems to be miraculously unaware of and untouched by these reminders of decay, so obvious to the reader and to his middle-aged mother. Indeed, the various *memento mori* strewn about the beach and thoughout the text, which endow the book with pathos, also highlight the fragile and almost unbelievable innocence of the protagonist. Jacob basks in unawareness. To have made him knowing would have been to give him a character and a maturity of which Woolf seemed deliberately to wish to deprive him. It would also have provided a direct link with the reader that she seems not to have wished to forge. Like Cézanne's apples, Jacob is familiar, commonplace, undistinguished; and by virtue of his unconsciousness of time, he inhabits a realm the reader can imagine but not reach. In contemplating him, we contemplate a figure at once familiar and unfathomably strange.

Though a certain portion of Jacob's unconsciousness might be attributed to flaws in his character—insensitivity, egotism, absentmindedness—Woolf provides the reader with a number of messages about time's devastation structured in such a way that Jacob could not possibly have access to them. These messages are not embedded in sheep's skulls or gravestones, which any imaginative youth might interpret, but in brief collapsed biographical asides to the reader in which various minor characters' lives are foretold. For example, Mr. Floyd, the clergyman who proposed to Mrs. Flanders, went off to "Sheffield, where he met Miss Wimbush, who was on a visit to her uncle, then to Hackney—then to Maresfield House, of which he became the principal, and finally, becoming editor of a well-known series of Ecclesiastical Biographies, he retired to Hampstead with his wife and daughter, and is often to be seen feeding the ducks on Leg of Mutton Pond."

Similar brief biographical sketches are given of Sopwith, Professor and Mrs. Plumer, Erasmus Cowan, Miss Umphelby, Mrs. Pascoe, Florinda, Jinny Carslake, Cruttendon, and innumerable other characters in the novel. To list their names is to be surprised at how many there are and at how much trouble Woolf has taken over seemingly trivial details in the lives of these people, most of whom have relatively little to do with Jacob. It begins to be clear that the function of these fortune-teller's vignettes is not their direct relation to Jacob, but precisely that they contain information that Jacob cannot possess and will not live to learn or imitate. They provide illustrations, plainly visible to the reader, all but invisible to Jacob, of the way time confines and diminishes life. In painter's terms, they compose a background, a well-defined darkness, against which the vague outlines and ambiguous lights of the foreground are intriguing and increasingly beautiful.

The radicalness of Woolf's experiment seems all the more impressive when we remember that biography, even fictional biography, is nearly always linear, causal, and explanatory. The most common reason for writing biography is to explain how X became prime minister or Y a violinist. Both the information offered and the manner of its organization is determined, to a large extent, by the achievement (or interesting failure) that justifies the story in the first place. Since Jacob, like Thoby, did not live long enough to succeed or fail at anything important, the recorder of his life is free to arrange her materials in whatever manner she sees fit. Furthermore, since the whole idea of culmination is antithetical to her purpose, she does not assemble things so that they will point away from themselves, but, on the contrary, toward themselves and even toward the fact that their arrangement is arbitrary.

Like the painter of still life, Woolf makes no effort to conceal the fact that she is no neutral observer merely copying down what she sees and hears, but a highly active and intrusive organizer. All writers of fiction arrange twice: they establish an order, a sequence of events, a juxtaposition of moments; then they translate that order into language, give it a voice. What is so interesting about *Jacob's Room* is the care Woolf takes in making certain that the artificiality, the deliberateness of the process is noticed. She has no wish to cover her tracks, to naturalize. When, for example, she introduces Mrs. Flanders, before offering the usual biographical information, she shows an empty room: "Mrs. Flanders had left her sewing on the table. There were her large reels of white cotton and her steel spectacles; her needle-case; her brown wool wound round an old postcard. There were the bulrushes and the *Strand* magazines; and the linoleum sandy from the boys' boots."

There are a number of ways in which this material can be interpreted. One might go on about the solitude of the empty room, the signs of domestic activity, the economies and tastes of a family that is not rich, and so forth. Woolf undoubtedly expects this. But the repeated use of such descriptions—static, framed, complete in themselves, observed only by the narrator and reader—invites another kind of attention, one that does not yield meanings so much as recognitions. They stop us in our tracks and call attention to the discipline of discerning the inadvertent designs of particular lives.

Obviously, the designs and the images that constitute them are not independent of each other, yet the fact that their relationship is not simple, not indisputably significant, endows them with a special energy. Woolf's arrangement of Mrs. Flanders' belongings is neither pure abstraction nor complete meaning. It is enough of a set piece to call attention to itself as such, and yet its components lend themselves readily to being interpreted with reference to other elements in the book. The reader's freedom consists not in ignoring form or substance but in assessing them and their interconnection with epistemological intimidation. By being permitted to see the imposition of design so clearly, we feel free to imagine both the life it delimits and the life that escapes it.

Woolf's descriptions of Jacob's rooms are the major set pieces of the novel and the ones that best illustrate the artistry of confinement and release. Jacob's room at Trinity is first seen after he has settled in at Cambridge, but at the moment of the description, he, of course, is not at home: "Jacob's room had a round table and two low chairs. There were yellow flags in a jar on the mantlepiece; a photograph of his mother; cards from societies . . . notes and pipes." There follows a seemingly random list of some of Jacob's books—Dickens, Spenser, all the Elizabethans, Jane Austen "in deference, perhaps, to someone else's standard." The paragraph concludes: "Listless is the air in an empty room, just swelling the curtain; the flowers in the jar shift. One fiber in the wicker arm-chair creaks, though no one sits there."

Like the items on Mrs. Flanders' table, the objects in Jacob's room lend themselves easily to interpretations about the character of the young man who inhabits the space—his youth, masculinity, class, intellectual promise, literary taste. The final two sentences, however, with their emphasis on silence and emptiness, have an unusual and important effect. On one hand, they create a dramatic need, the need for an entrance, a gesture or voice to fill the void. On the other, they create a need for a key that might help to decode the signs that are so neatly but insignificantly placed about the room. For though youth, masculinity, and the rest are all apparent, the particular individual life that would give direction and specificity of meaning to these objects is missing. Once again, design and meaning are but loosely linked. As long as Jacob might come in, speak, strike a pose, the reader may be full of anticipation, but meanwhile he learns to make do with what is given.

The sudden elimination of that anticipation and the real force of "making do with what is given" constitute Woolf's presentation of Jacob's death. The final short chapter of the novel is full of exact repetitions of words and phrases from earlier sections. Though Bonamy remarks "Nothing arranged" on seeing letters strewn about, the chapter is the most carefully arranged in the book. The ram's skull, the high ceilings, the voice crying, "Jacob! Jacob!" the mother trying to make order out of confusion—all call attention to a formal symmetry even while delivering messages of grief. The most elaborate refrain echoes exactly the last two sentences originally used to describe Jacob's room at Trinity: "Listless is the air in an empty room, just swelling the curtain; the flowers in the jar shift. One fiber in the wicker arm-chair creaks, though no one sits there."

This time, of course, the design really is all there is. Jacob will not come in to pick up his letters and his life, to bring focus and meaning to the various traces of himself he has left behind. For the last time, the biographical, data-laden, knowable, summarizable Jacob has escaped. But is this escape, this absence, a failure in Woolf's art? On the contrary, it is her first important success. We know that Mrs. Flanders had "merchant of this city" inscribed on the gravestone of her husband, though that label had almost no bearing on his life or its meaning to her. One wonders what she might have come up with for Jacob; possibly, *pro patria mori*. Without ridiculing such branding, indeed filled with the ironic sense of its necessity for artists as well as for grieving survivors, Woolf calls our attention to the realities that make it inadequate. In a sense, not necessarily lugubrious, all efforts at capturing a life in words are like writing an epitaph or creating a literary *nature morte*. The achievement of *Jacob's Room* is that in conceding to Jacob's absence, in collaborating so ingeniously in his various vanishing acts, Woolf lets the individual go and, in the process, preserves and illuminates images of a wider common life.

GERALD LEVIN

The Musical Style of "The Waves"

Virginia Woolf is reported to have said that her books were conceived as music before she wrote them. A number of critics have tried to define their musical style—for example, Melvin Friedman, who shows that the "space-time dimension" of *Mrs. Dalloway* is used to counterpoint its themes, the musical style to be found in "the simultaneous presentation of several themes" and in imitation of the "circular movement" of sonata and fugue. Woolf's novel of 1931, *The Waves*, I shall try to show, is contrapuntal in the same way and at the same time advances beyond this conception. I shall suggest that the advance occurred probably under the influence of J.W.N. Sullivan's analysis in his 1927 book on Beethoven of the quartets, to which Woolf had been listening during the planning and writing of the novel. In some of its characteristics it even suggests the "pantonal" musical style perfected by Arnold Schoenberg in the 1920s, though there is no evidence of any influence or borrowing here.

Woolf's diary entry for December 22, 1930 shows that musical structure was on her mind as she approached the end of *The Waves*:

> It occurred to me last night while listening to a Beethoven quartet that I would merge all the interjected passages into Bernard's final speech, & end with the words O solitude: thus making him absorb all those scenes, & having no further break. This is also to show that the theme effort, effort, dominates: not the waves: & personality: & defiance: but I am not

From *The Journal of Narrative Technique* 3, vol. 13 (Fall 1983). Copyright © 1983 by *The Journal of Narrative Technique*. Eastern Michigan University.

sure of the effect artistically; because the proportions may need the intervention of the waves finally so as to make a conclusion.

The novel consists of a series of monologues of six friends, occurring at various times in their lives, beginning in childhood, and grouped into eight sections. In the ninth and final section, one of the six, Bernard, seeks to weave their various experiences and personalities into a final unity, as Woolf indicates in the diary. Introducing each section is a brief prose poem or interlude, in which the passing of time is marked and the sounds and rhythms of nature are described. These anticipate and counterpoint the human experiences and feelings that follow. Thus the third of the interludes ends with these words:

> The wind rose. The waves drummed on the shore, like turbaned warriors, like turbaned men with poisoned assegais who, whirling their arms on high, advance upon the feeding flocks, the white sheep.

And the fifth interlude ends with these:

> The waves fell; withdrew and fell again, like the thud of a great beast stamping.

There is a seventh character, the non-speaking Percival, and in the section immediately following we are told of his death in India, in a fall from a horse. The sounds of nature in the passages quoted are heard in this description of his death—the event which is the center of the novel:

> His horse stumbled; he was thrown. The flashing trees and white rails went up in a shower. There was a surge; a drumming in his ears. Then the blow; the world crashed; he breathed heavily. He died where he fell.

Visual images in this way join and are counterpointed with aural images to achieve a contrapuntal style. But Woolf's comment on Beethoven, in the diary, suggests that she was thinking about musical structure mainly as a thematic device and not as a "musical" rendering of sensuous experience, the conception and use of musical style we find in the poetry of Hopkins. The diary shows that her interest in Beethoven was long standing; in 1921, for example, she attended performances of the quartets in the course of a Beethoven festival in London. References to Beethoven increase from 1927 to 1930, thus the entry for June 18, 1927, in which Woolf records that she works on *The Waves* listening to Beethoven sonatas on the phonograph. It is impossible to know whether Sullivan's book, published in 1927, was the reason for her interest; Beethoven was much discussed by writers in these years—in 1927 notably by Sir Donald Tovey in his essay on Beethoven's art forms, in *Music and Letters*.

Woolf does not refer to the book directly in her diary or published letters, but she had known Sullivan as early as 1921, as her diary entry for December 18 of that year shows: "Sullivan is too much of the india-rubber faced, mobile lipped, unshaven, uncombed, black, uncompromising, suspicious, powerful man of genius in Hampstead type for my taste." She clearly disliked him, but probably respected him as a writer. Herbert Howarth has documented Sullivan's association with Huxley and other contributors to the Atheneum from 1919 to 1921, and his influence on Eliot.

Sullivan's book contains statements that suggest major themes of *The Waves*, in particular his discussion of the late quartets, specifically the B Flat Quartet, Opus 130, the Great Fugue, Opus 133 (originally the conclusion of the B Flat Quartet), and the C Sharp Minor Quartet, Opus 131. Sullivan's characterization of the Opus 130 fugue as the "reconciliation of freedom and necessity, or of assertion and submission," suggests the major theme of the final section, our "freedom" to experience the "eternal renewal, the incessant rise and fall and fall and rise again." Assertion and submission are key ideas in the novel, particularly in Bernard's assertion of the power of life—"Against you I will fling myself, unvanquished and unyielding, O Death!"—and they are for Sullivan essential to understanding the late quartets. These terms, he continues, "suggest the state of consciousness that informs the fugue, a state in which the apparently opposing elements of life are seen as necessary and no longer in opposition." His characterization of Opus 131 stresses its "mystical vision," a reality "where our problems do not exist, and to which even our highest aspirations, those that we can formulate, provide no key," a reality in which all "discords" are resolved. In general, Sullivan's characterization of the late quartets is fugal in conception:

> In these quartets the movements radiate, as it were, from a central experience. They do not represent stages in a journey, each stage being independent and existing in its own right. They represent separate experiences, but the meaning they take on in the quartet is derived from their relation to a dominating, central experience.

This passage describes exactly the structure of *The Waves*—the six characters also representing stages in a journey, their experiences interwoven and uniting in the consciousness of Bernard:

> Whatever sentence I extract whole and entire from this cauldron is only a string of six little fish that let themselves be caught while a million others leap and sizzle, making the cauldron bubble like boiling silver, and slip through my fingers. Faces recur, faces and faces—they press their beauty to the walls of my bubble—Neville, Susan, Louis, Jinny, Rhoda

and a thousand others. How impossible to order them rightly; to detach
one separately, or to give the effect of the whole—again like music. What
a symphony, with its concord and its discord and its tunes on top and its
complicated bass beneath, then grew up!

It is in this final meditation that Bernard identifies himself with Beethoven,
whose picture he buys in a silver frame: "Not that I love music, but because
the whole of life, its masters, its adventurers then appeared in long ranks
of magnificent human beings behind me; and I was the inheritor; I, the
continuer; I, the person miraculously appointed to carry it on."

Whether a literary style or representation of experience can be
musical or "fugal" in any exact meaning of these words remains a serious
question for criticism, and it was a question for Virginia Woolf. One difficulty is immediately apparent. Voices in the novel cannot be heard simultaneously, though images and phrases can pass from one monologue to
another. To quote Arnold Schoenberg, "the unity of musical space demands
an absolute and unitary perception." "The thing is to keep them running
homogeneously in & out, in the rhythm of the waves," Woolf writes in
another diary entry, "Can they be read consecutively? I know nothing
about that." An earlier entry suggests that she did associate propulsive
movement with fugal design: "How to end, save by a tremendous discussion,
in which every life shall have its voice—a mosaic [. . .] I do not know."
The style of *The Waves* is musical at least in the human and natural rhythms
it connects, as in Bernard's insight at the end:

> When the storm crosses the marsh and sweeps over me where I lie in the
> ditch unregarded I need no words. Nothing neat. Nothing that comes
> down with all its feet on the floor. None of those resonances and lovely
> echoes that break and chime from nerve to nerve in our breasts making
> wild music, false phrases. I have done with phrases.

The implication is that the musical experience is finally one of unresolved
dissonances. We have connection without consonance or resolution.

The general thematic structure presents an even more serious difficulty. In fugal style a single theme generates motifs heard throughout—
in different voices entering the fugue at the different moment and ending
in perfect accord. In *The Waves* we are given multiple voices, personalities,
attitudes and momentary consonance in Bernard's final affirmation, but a
single theme is never really "heard" throughout. It exists instead as an
idea—the tension between freedom and necessity, assertion and submission
noted earlier, and emerging in the final pages. Given this characteristic, a
better description of the musical style of the novel is "pantonal"—in which
the tonalities or six characters each becomes the thematic center at the

moment of expression but are absorbed into a whole which the novel discloses gradually.

Considered in this way, each character represents a phenomenal self that has a distinctive "tonality" and yet grows in experience. Thus Neville is precise, Susan jealous, Rhoda terrified, Jinny loving, Louis lonely, Bernard curious: these are their qualities in childhood. Toward the end Bernard restates these qualities in light of how they lived: "Louis was disgusted by the nature of the human flesh; Rhoda by our cruelty; Susan could not share; Neville wanted order; Jinny love; and so on." But the phenomenal self is not the only self. Alone, each responds in this distinctive way to experience; together, they move into potential communion. "But when we sit together, close," Bernard considers early in the novel, "we melt into each other with phrases. We are edged with mist. We make an unsubstantial territory."

For separation means the loss of the fully lived life, the possibility of which is present in Percival. Each is in some way aware of qualities in Percival that reveal their own; Louis intuits most that Percival has made each aware of what is particular in himself. Percival's later death awakens in them not only a sense of the finality of life but a power of feelings greater than each has previously known. Thus Rhoda fears the human touch and human cruelty but overcomes her fear momentarily in becoming the lover of the isolated and fearful Louis. She intuits that life remains unlived to the extent that others on whom our lives depend fail us; for they may die. That perception is shared by others. The symbol of the unlived life and the violence which can arrive unseen and unexpected is the dead man Neville heard about in childhood—the man found with his throat cut, under the apple trees.

Percival is sometimes apprehended through sounds of various kinds. For Louis Percival was "flowering with green leaves and was laid in the earth with all his branches still sighing in the summer wind." The "something stamping" that he has feared from childhood is the threat of extinction, even the death of nature. Rhoda seeks the meaning of Percival's death in the music of a quartet which states "what is inchoate" by giving feeling a structure. Percival's death—the dissolution of hard reality into abstraction and indistinctness—allows her to retreat into fantasy and engage in it fully. Music is, like the sea, the single experience (the fin, the wave) seen in distant water, general experience sustaining the individual, the patterns that define single sounds and tonalities, the solvent of single moments and experiences.

Each character finds his rapture in each separate perception of death, Bernard states at the end, and he finds his own momentary unity in merging their awareness in his own—unlike Rhoda who seeks a unifying pattern that obliterates personal distinctions and kills herself to find it. "All had their rapture," he states; "their common feeling with death; something that stood them in stead." Where others go to priests or poetry or friends, he goes to his heart, seeking "among phrases and fragments something unbroken—I to whom there is not beauty enough in moon or tree, to whom the touch of one person with another is all, yet who cannot grasp even that, who am so imperfect, so weak, so unspeakably lonely." He envisions finally the loss of self "weightless and visionless, through a world weightless, without illusion."

There is, then, a double awareness throughout the novel—of unity of feeling, "the swelling and splendid moment created by us from Percival," and of individual unhappiness and incompleteness. The whole novel suggests that only reconciliation with nature—in its aspect of change and death—can bring resolution. But, as we have seen, it is a spurious unity, an idea merely. In the final lines of the novel, Bernard chooses to accept death as necessary to this unification, but paradoxically he also desires to confront it, like Percival, "unvanquished and unyielding."

In the movement of these fragmented personalities toward everything different from themselves is to be discovered the "it" that Woolf refers to in her diary: the "astonishing sense of something there," the "sense of my own strangeness, walking on the earth"—indefinable yet discoverable in consciousness, in the process of living. The form of The Waves is the form of evolving consciousness out of silence, each character increasing in self-awareness of themselves and one another. As Bernard's final words on death show, experience is paradoxical. Separation from or denial of experience is extinction, a merging into clear sky, blue water. As objects of perception become distinct, like the waves they simultaneously become indistinct, then are lost. The edges of experience blur and feelings change. Consciousness is all that can be maintained.

These are the ideas and the form of experience captured by the musical style of the novel. The essential idea is that of music itself: the impulsion toward a unity achieved, the music resolving into silence and beginning again, Sullivan's "apparently opposing elements of life . . . seen as necessary and no longer in opposition." Yet, as we have noted, that unity is achieved in the consciousness of Bernard only. The unity of experience to which each character contributes is finally the sum of their perceptions and experiences, in Bernard's mind, never a merging or blending. The edges of their mutual experience remain blurred. Experience and feeling are to be understood rather as process, the musical equivalent of which is better described as "pantonal" than fugal.

In pantonal music, as Schoenberg formulated it in the 1920s and produced it, continuous variation replaces thematic repetition, essential to fugal style. It is the unbroken variation that gives the impression of ongoing process. More significantly, the thematic structure in pantonal music is identical with this variation.

We do not, in other words, hear a theme foreground as in tonal music, even in the fugue. Serving as the ordering principle, the tone row or series neither functions nor is heard as a traditional theme—though the basic row may be stated at the beginning of the work (as in Schoenberg's violin and piano concertos). Afterwards it occurs in the "mirror forms" of inversion in which the pitch relations are inverted (the second note for example falling a third if the second note of the basic set rises a third), of retrograde, in which the basic set is played back to front, and of retrograde-inversion. It is not an ordinary theme, we hear then. "The series is not a musical idea in the normal sense of that phrase," Charles Rosen states. "It is not properly speaking something heard, either imaginatively or practically; it is transmuted into something heard."

With the additional requirement that all twelve tones be heard before any one of them is heard again, the experience is not only one of continuous variation from the basic set but also one of delayed completion. Schoenberg thus refers to "the intention to postpone the repetition of every tone as long as possible." This postponement contributes also to the sense of ongoing experience or process. The music gives the effect, too, of total saturation and perpetual discovery. To quote Charles Rosen again, "The saturation of musical space is Schoenberg's substitute for the tonic chord of the traditional musical language. The absolute consonance is a state of chromatic plenitude."

These characteristics of pantonal music seem to me to correspond to those of Woolf's novel, in particular the impression it creates of continuous experience, each moment having the same value as every other. The unity of experience in both the novel and the pantonal composition remains the goal, perpetually sought and in the novel never quite achieved, much as the waves reach the shore and immediately disappear. Bernard's final meditation, with its acceptance of death and change and assertion also of the power of living, is the fullest approach to unity, but it is at the end only an approach—a challenge to Death itself.

This same sense of the fragmentary quality of life and at the same time of an underlying structure is contained in Sullivan's characterization of the late quartets, particularly the B Flat Major and the Great Fugue.

> Those faint and troubling intimations we sometimes have of a vision
> different from and yet including our own, of a way of apprehending life,

passionless, perfect and complete, that resolves all our discords, are here presented with the reality they had glimpsed. This impression of a superhuman knowledge, of a superhuman life being slowly frozen into shape, as it were, before our eyes, can be ambiguous.

This, I have tried to show, is the idea that possibly stands behind Woolf's theme of "effort, effort." Though the novel is fugal in the way suggested by the diary entry of 1930, Woolf was moving in a new direction of musical style. The moment of awareness represented in each section for each character is, in musical terms, a discrete tonal center, but without a fixed "background."

The novel moves overall through continuous variation, not through a repetition of experiences and perceptions, toward a final "resolution of forces"—without finally achieving it in actual experience. Even in the long concluding monologue which, in Bernard's words, seeks to "sum up," subjective and objective reality are indistinguishable. The purpose of musical style in *The Waves* is to maintain this sense of ongoing experience through a structure that seems never to end. "And in me too the wave rises," Bernard meditates in the concluding paragraph. "It swells; it arches its back. I am aware once more of a new desire, something rising beneath me like the proud horse whose rider first spurs and then pulls him back."

JUDY LITTLE

The Politics of Holiday: *"Orlando"*

In Virginia Woolf's novels the holi-
day context, removing characters as it does from the ordinary patterns of
behavior, provides an opportunity for a profound and extreme kind of
comedy, for a comedy of cultural mockery. Even the images which hold a
prestigious place in the "secular scripture" are mocked by the holiday consciousness. When the overturning of ordinary conventions, the overturning
typical of liminality, is defined in such an extreme context, when holiday
is a contemplative blank, then almost anything is fair game for mockery.
Rhoda in *The Waves* can speak of going through "the antics of the individual," i.e., of identity, of the ego. To the eyes that contemplate such
an unmarked world almost anything is possible; as Lily Briscoe perceived,
"anything might happen." If the norm is mysticism, the politics of holiday
may become radical indeed.

The holiday experience is ultimately a mystical one for Woolf's
characters, and perhaps for Woolf herself. In a very late memoir, she
decribes the vacations of her childhood, the family's annual sojourn on the
coast in Cornwall; those early summers, full of waves thudding and light
falling through window curtains, were "pure delight," and are perhaps linked
to "art, or religion." . . .

The semimystic life of a woman, as it developed into *Orlando* (1928),
became a semipicaresque, semibiographical fantasy of the life of a man,

From *Comedy and the Woman Writer: Woolf, Spark, and Feminism.* Copyright © 1983 by
University of Nebraska Press.

sixteen years old in the sixteenth century who retains his youth for decades, becomes a woman late in the seventeenth century (but still occasionally wears men's clothes for excursions into London's rougher areas), marries under pressure from the nineteenth century, has a child, and finally in the twentieth century wins a prize for a poem that has been in progress for over three hundred years. In March 1927, Virginia Woolf saw the projected book as one in which even her own style would be satirized: "Everything mocked," she said. A year later, as she finished the first draft, she called the book "a writer's holiday." It is in two senses a writer's holiday; it is a holiday for its author and for its main character, Orlando, who also is a writer and who mocks everything. Unlike Woolf, the character Orlando does not use her writing as a means of satire. Her slowly developing poem, "The Oak Tree," is apparently quite a serious work, but Orlando herself is a jester for all seasons, and Virginia Woolf's book is a burlesque of all genres—or at least, of many genres.

This holiday book is first of all a tribute to, and a caricature-biography of, Woolf's friend Vita Sackville-West; it draws upon the history of the Sackville family, its poets and diplomats, and it exaggerates the already large inventory of furnishings and staircases given in Vita's documentary book about the family home *Knole and the Sackvilles* (1922). But *Orlando* is a mock-biography, the narrator complaining frequently that Orlando's life simply refuses to become manifest in the mere facts, though these are supposedly the biographer's medium. Instead of the realistic and fully developed characters of a "novel," those in Orlando tend towards caricature and even allegory in the latter part of the book; this mode of characterization suggests the romance form which, as Northrop Frye notes, is a more "revolutionary" form than the novel, because the characters are not so thoroughly enmeshed in the social fabric of a single, stable, realistically portrayed society. Indeed the parodic history, the long time span of the action, sees its main character into and out of several revolutions and several distinct societies. In this respect *Orlando* demonstrates its affinity with the picaresque form, in which social institutions are attacked, the effect being, as Barbara Babcock notes, to remind us that norms are fictions and made by mere humans; further the picaresque hero is never reintegrated into society, in contrast to the novelistic hero, who in classic works is so integrated. Neither is Orlando integrated finally into society. She has a flexible and serviceable lack of commitment to the successively crumbling societies that she survives.

Although she tries to conform outwardly to each historical age and to the decorum and the codes expected of each sex, she becomes successively disillusioned with the values of each era and each sex. Finally shrugging off the last infirmity of noble mind, "gloire" (or "glawr" as her critic Nicholas Green pronounces it), Orlando recognizes that her imagination and its products are essentially a self-finding process. Ecstatically united with her "Captain self," allegorized in the irrepressible sea captain Marmaduke Bon-throp Shelmerdine, she evidently finds in him (herself) the "wild goose" of truth and imagination that she has been chasing. The end of the book is parodic mysticism: with the moonlit gleam of the jewels on her breast, Orlando guides Shelmerdine's plane towards her, and they are ecstatically united.

The androgynous Orlando is, appropriately, a vigorous countercul-ture of one. Her sexual versatility is an expression of a liminal androgyny, the symbolic sexual ambiguity characteristic of those undergoing ritual ini-tiations and often typifying those who belong to revolutionary or counter-cultural movements. Orlando's famous and often discussed androgyny implies wholeness, completeness, as many have observed; it suggests also, as Avrom Fleishman has pointed out, a special power similar to that imputed to initiates who participate in the transvestite rituals in many cultures. Orlando's androgyny further suggests the status of someone continually undergoing the liminal rituals of society, continually on the margins of life's major "stages" (to use Orlando's word), but never settling down into the conventions of any given society. Orlando remains in the liminal part of life's "passages"; indeed, the concept of a stable society in which such passages can be meaningful is itself mocked. Just when Orlando has under-gone initiation into the first passionate love of his life, the planet itself (or at least England) undergoes a major passage; the Great Frost is followed by a great flood, Orlando sleeps for seven days, and when he wakes, both he and history seem to have entered a new era. The violent, lusty gather-ye-rosebuds society has disappeared; the disillusioned and gloomy Orlando meditates on poetry. Or, much later, in the nineteenth century, in the era of large families, Orlando finally marries and has one child. Just about this time, the century turns, and instead of the childbirth ritual being the defining stage of her life, she is a twentieth-century woman, and public recognition of her poetry becomes the ritual milestone. Each time Orlando enters, metaphorically, the anthropological forest in order to receive an identity that will accord with social ritual, the ritual changes. She emerges from the liminal state only to find that the conventions have changed; she thus remains in a state of perpetual initiation, frequently making rather half-hearted efforts to conform to rules that wear out before she can fulfill them. So Orlando remains on continual holiday, in a civilization that is itself in a state of continual holiday, forever overturning itself and exposing its rituals and rules as obviously ephemeral.

Orlando's psychological relation to the historical periods through which she passes is hard to define exactly. She and any given historical milieu seem to reflect each other, and yet most readers agree with Orlando (and with Orlando's servants, who enthusiastically recognize and admire either him or her) that the main character does not change in any essential way; only Orlando's social behavior varies from age to age. The major joke of the sex change is that it makes little real difference in Orlando's character; by implication, most expressions of sex differences are cultural and not biological. The more Orlando changes, the more she stays the same. And yet the changes that she witnesses, and usually participates in, are major ones, not merely evolutions of manner but revolutions of basic norms and codes, those which, in the real, nonfictional world, are rooted in primary socialization; certainly the behavior of the sexes is so rooted. Orlando herself realizes this as she tries, on the ship, to adjust to the fact that sailors may drop off the rigging with excitement if she fails to keep her ankles covered. She realizes "for the first time, what, in other circumstances, she would have been taught as a child, that is to say, the sacred responsibilities of womanhood." We may theorize that Orlando was nurtured (as a boy?), was socialized into the values of some remote historical period (perhaps among medieval gypsies?), but in a fantasy such as this book is, we can see a Utopian psychology in operation. Because Orlando arrives as an adult on the scene of each new era, she escapes normal childhood socialization; she escapes the limited vision of "home," of the one childhood world, domestically and socially, which usually gives human beings their primary values and loves. Orlando's ancestral home perhaps symbolizes these pre-rational attachments, but even this home, this symbolic place of comfort, changes size and decor with each era and becomes emblematic of Orlando's capacity for change even at a basic level, at the level of what "home" means, of what psychological comfort and security mean. With an adult's judgment, not a child's dependent need, Orlando views each era, and is thus free to let go of illusion after illusion with a minimum of anguish and a maximum of growth and self-renewal.

Orlando's change of sex, important as it is, is only one of many changes; her discovery of the limited role allotted to women is only one of several major disillusionments. The feminist issues, prominent in this novel and in some ways parallel to those discussed in A Room of One's Own, are placed in the quite positive context of an ongoing process of personal and social evolution, an evolution which in this fantasy overturns stereotypical notions about sex roles as easily as stereotypical notions about the importance of personal fame or of social class. Because we have already seen her so readily and sensibly readjust to illusions about infatution, fame, and class, we are carried buoyantly onward by the momentum of suspended disbelief—and the momentum of the narrator's detachment and humor—when Orlando passes through the oppressive nineteenth century unscathed, having paid her dues to the "spirit of the age" by acquiring a wedding ring; she feels, however, as though she is crossing a border and carrying contraband, for she is a woman and yet she has smuggled a writer's mind into the nineteenth century.

In each era, Orlando is taken in by, or provisionally accepts, some prominent value or presupposition and then discards it, or at least views it in a qualified light. And this value is not always linked to sex role. Orlando must confront and overcome a desire for fame, both as a man and as a woman. His most troublesome challenge, after his beloved Sasha betrays him, is his commitment to "la gloire" of poetry and to his identity as a literary, artistic lord, writing in aristocratic ease on his vast ancestral estate. When this grandiose view of himself is destroyed by Nick Green's sharp satire on him, Orlando resolves to write only for himself in the future. With chagrin, he tears up a scroll on which he had fancifully appointed himself "the first poet of his race, the first writer of his age, conferring eternal immortality upon his soul and granting his body a grave among laurels and the intangible banners of a people's reverence perpetually." Orlando tears up his desire for fame as he tears up his presumptuous scroll with its aggressively redundant flourishes of Elizabethan style ("eternal imortality . . . perpetually").

Later, during a sojourn among gypsies, the female Orlando begins to lose another illusion, another false claim to identity and to self-esteem: her aristocratic family's proud ancestry. To her humiliation, the old gypsy Rustum points out that his family goes back two or three thousand years, his ancestors having built the pyramids. Back in England, Orlando meditates among the renowned bones of the family vault and again considers Rustum's humbling revelation. She decides that she is "growing up"; "I am losing my illusions," she says, "perhaps to acquire new ones." Her confidence about losing her great pride in her family's ancestry is a little premature, however, for she subsequently becomes rhapsodic about the grounds and grandeur of her huge home, and she decides Rustum was wrong.

In the nineteenth century—the century that launched a few women, such as the Brontës and George Eliot, into enduring fame—Orlando also gets her big break. Once again she confronts the illusion of fame. Orlando—

like Lily Briscoe—suspects, without apology or malice, that she is less than a first-rate artist. She is not fooled when Sir Nicholas enthusiastically compares her work to that of Addison and Thomson, and in the twentieth century, when her poem wins a cash prize, she laughs philosophically at fame. The poem becomes for Orlando more important than the prize, and the original real oak tree is more important than the poem "The Oak Tree." Orlando at age thirty-six and on the very brink of "the present moment," on the brink of reality without the illusions and assumptions of mere history which would limit that reality, drives quickly towards her ancestral home, calling upon all her past selves as she drives and seeking especially the "Captain self, the Key self." Arriving at the oak tree, she turns over her own history, recalling the illusions of fame and family: "What has praise and fame to do with poetry? What has seven editions (the book had already gone into no less) got to do with the value of it? Was not writing poetry a secret transaction, a voice answering a voice?" Then she once again hears the gypsy Rustum's voice taunting her about her pride in possessions, in race, in family heritage. Illusions, and memories of illusions, fall from her as she waits on the dark hill expecting the "ecstasy" of Shelmerdine's approach. With her brilliant jewels to guide it, his plane arrives, and he leaps to the ground while a valedictory wild goose hovers in tableau over his head. Appropriately, as Orlando's voice answers her voice, as the Captain self (or his image) arrives, as the psychological *meaning* of her poetry writing shakes itself free from the trammels of fame, family, adolescent infatuation, and the womanly eighteenth-century coyness and shyness, the midnight stroke of the present moment arrives. Orlando's history ends once the complex self, to which history has contributed, no longer depends on any particular historical emphasis or value, code of behavior, or ambition for its reality and sufficiency. The "present moment"—something impossible to isolate except in fantasy—is a suitable symbol for the condition of a self who is free of the major illusions of many eras and the major illusions and stereotypes of both sexes.

This ending, this solution, really takes Orlando's biography beyond biography and history beyond history. It implies transcendence, an inward turning, mysticism; it implies something serious in a book that began as comic. In this regard Virginia Woolf herself had some misgivings. After completing the book, she wrote in her diary: "The truth is I expect I began it as a joke and went on with it seriously. Hence it lacks some unity." Critics tend to agree with Woolf's perception of a change in tone as the concluding events are narrated. Jean Alexander asserts that satire is abandoned as Orlando moves towards the "exploration of the religious unknown in life," a direction that Woolf continues to pursue in *The Waves*. And Woolf indicated by a marginal note in her diary that she came to regard *Orlando* as "leading to *The Waves*." It is true that Orlando's finding of her self, her Captain self, is narrated in a kind of rhapsodic lyricism, but Woolf does not abandon comedy; a goose is not the most solemn image for truth, for some large discovery. The hints of comedy, even in the final events of the book, keep Orlando's vital and creative self where it has always been— in the liminal regions just outside of any congealed and solemn definition of what human society is, of what the sexes are, or of what a self is. The extravagant ecstasy of holiday prevails.

VIRGINIA BLAIN

Narrative Voice and the Female Perspective in "The Voyage Out"

Never was a book more feminine, more recklessly feminine. It may be labelled clever and shrewd, mocking, suggestive, subtle, "modern," but these terms do not convey the spirit of it—which essentially is feminine. That quality is of course, indescribable.
(*Times Literary Supplement* [April 1915])

A.J.: Virginia Woolf has said that it is fatal for anyone who writes to think of their sex.

S.B.: Nonetheless, Virginia Woolf thought a lot about her own sex when she wrote. In the best sense of the word, her writing is very feminine, and by that I mean that women are supposed to be very sensitive to . . . I don't know . . . to all the sensations of nature, much more so than men, much more contemplative.
(From Alice Jardine's interview with Simone de Beauvoir, transl. Ellen Evans, printed in *Signs: Journal of Women in Culture and Society*, 5 [1979])

It is reassuring and at the same time disappointing to find so experienced and profound a thinker about women as Simone de Beauvoir beginning to flounder as soon as she seeks to describe "feminine" writing in non-prescriptive terms. Of course, many would say

From *Virginia Woolf: New Critical Essays*, edited by Patricia Clements and Isobel Grundy. Copyright © 1983 by Vision Press Ltd.

that this is inevitable: exactly what they would have expected. Others, however, like the younger French feminist critic, Hélène Cixous, less afraid of being prescriptive, would argue that feminine or female writing has nothing to do with being more contemplative or sensitive to nature but must seek its own "body language," rejecting what she calls "phallogocentricism" in favour of a more appropriate morphological model.

It is not my purpose here to enter into an extended analysis of the current highly controversial "nature/nurture" debate about the true constitution of the feminine gender. However, it seems to me that the view Virginia Woolf puts forward in "Professions for Women," that our prime obligation in any such debate is to resist all attempts to contract its terms of reference, is one that still carries weight. "I mean, what is a woman? I assure you, I do not know. I do not believe that you know. I do not believe that anybody can know until she has expressed herself in all the arts and professions open to human skill." Although undoubtedly a feminist in the modern sense of the term, Woolf always remained adept at gracefully sidestepping the moment she felt herself being steered towards the limitation of any definitive standpoint. She certainly allowed herself a human inconsistency frowned upon by sterner theorists. ("If I were still a feminist . . . But I have travelled on" she muses in her diary entry for 17 October 1924—four years before the polemically feminist A Room of One's Own.) None the less, despite her resistance to marking out boundaries to female abilities and potentialities, her feminism was of the variety—once considered old-fashioned, now again, it seems, in the vanguard—that believes in "la différence":

> It would be a thousand pities if women wrote like men, or lived like men, or looked like men, for if two sexes are quite inadequate, considering the vastness and variety of the world, how should we manage with one only? Ought not education to bring out and fortify the differences rather than the similarities? For we have too much likeness as it is.

Such statements support de Beauvoir's insistence upon Woolf's gender-consciousness as a writer. Despite the arguments put forward in A Room of One's Own for an androgynous ideal, it remains true that Woolf's novels show a radical awareness of feminist issues, and that they take up the question of "what is a woman" from a perspective that aims to deconstruct the kind of masculine prejudices in Desmond MacCarthy's condescending praise of her for "courageously acknowledging the limitations of [her] sex." That is, from a perspective which is unashamed to be female, and which has as its ultimate goal the ability to take its own femaleness so much for granted that the issue of gender can be forgotten, as in the hypothetical case of Mary Carmichael in *A Room of One's Own*, who had "mastered the first great lesson; she wrote as a woman, but as a woman who has forgotten that she is a woman, so that the pages were full of that curious sexual quality which comes only when sex is unconscious of itself." As Woolf herself was the first to admit, she found female intellectual shame far easier to overcome in her own case than bodily shame, largely owing to the mixed advantages and disadvantages of her peculiar temperament and upbringing. But to give voice to an even intellectually unashamed female perspective meant giving voice to a new form of the novel, and it is these most tantalizing and nebulous aspects of novelistic form—narrative voice and perspective—that I shall chiefly be concerned to explore here.

In his recent essay on the narrative form of *Mrs. Dalloway*, Hillis Miller reminds us: "The most important themes of a given novel are likely to lie not in anything which is explicitly affirmed, but in significances generated by the way in which the story is told." In the terms of the present discussion, I would go further than this to argue that meaning can be no more and no less political than style, for in no other sense can a female perspective have meaning which escapes prescription. Style in Woolf's fiction is as much part of her "female perspective" as it is an expression of her aesthetic beliefs. Yet it is probably fair to say that she was less concerned with evolving a "feminine sentence" in the manner of a Dorothy Richardson who, having a dramatized first-person female narrator, used 'female' stream-of-consciousness, and more concerned, as she said herself, with "merely giving things their natural order, as a woman would, if she wrote like a woman." This is in key with her later brilliantly open-ended definition of novelistic form as "the sense that one thing follows another rightly." More specific, and so more useful for the present discussion, are her remarks in a review of Brimley Johnson's *The Women Novelists* (1918), about the very difficult question of the "difference between the man's and the woman's view of what constitutes the importance of any subject. From this spring not only marked differences of plot and incident, but infinite differences in selection, method and style"; "There is the obvious and enormous difference of experience in the first place; but the essential difference lies in the fact not that men describe battles and women the birth of children, but that each sex describes itself."

"Each sex describes itself": a remark with profound implications for Woolf's own art, and one which applies with particular force to her earliest novels. It is with the first three of these that I shall be most concerned here, for each in its own way is as experimental as any of the later fiction, in the sense that each is trying out means of breaking through the barriers of inherited male conventions towards the expression of an authentic woman's voice: not the voice of Everywoman so much as the voice of Virginia Woolf as subject-of-consciousness. Of course one must bear in mind in this context her Yeatsian quest for freedom from personality ("Sydney comes & I'm Virginia; when I write I'm merely a sensibility"). But as so many critics have remarked, there *is* a unique Woolfian voice belonging to her novels alone. She herself was quite aware of this quality and of its desirability; by the time she had finished *Jacob's Room* she felt she had found it: "There's no doubt in my mind that I have found out how to begin (at 40) to say something in my own voice." Her first two novels have commonly been held to be much less experimental than *Jacob's Room*, but in moving mountains the first efforts make least impression upon the onlookers, although in fact requiring more courage and vision than the last.

The mountain she was moving was of course the mountain of male prejudice. When she looked back for inspiration to earlier women writers, only Jane Austen and Emily Brontë seemed to have had the "genius [and] integrity . . . in face of all that criticism, in the midst of that purely patriarchal society, to hold fast to the thing as they saw it without shrinking . . . They wrote as women write, not as men write." Although Woolf admired Charlotte Brontë and George Eliot—the latter particularly, exerted a profound influence despite many surface differences—she felt that both of these writers had fallen foul of the current "man's sentence . . . unsuited for a woman's use." In a suggestively Beardsleyesque image, Woolf depicts Charlotte Brontë as one who "stumbled and fell with that clumsy weapon in her hands," while "George Eliot committed atrocities with it that beggar description. Jane Austen looked at it and laughed at it and devised a perfectly natural shapely sentence proper for her own use and never departed from it."

"Perfectly natural, shapely . . . proper for her own use": this statement, typically, pronounces eveything and nothing about "the" female sentence; her point being, of course, that there is no such thing. "Sentence" in this context takes on an almost metaphoric meaning, so that Woolf suggests that a writer needs, above all, the freedom to be his or her own creator in and of language. "I keep thinking of different ways to manage my scenes; conceiving endless possibilities; seeing life, as I walk about the streets, an immense opaque block of material to be conveyed by me into its equivalent of language" (November 1918). Exactly thirteen years later in another diary entry she wrote: "I think I am about to embody, at last, the exact shapes my brain holds. What a long toil to reach this beginning." In some senses all of Woolf's work can be read as a quest for an authorial

self, but the early work shows on its surface more of the signs of struggle
inherent in such a quest. The real bogey handed on to her from the nineteenth century, with which she engaged at this period in a life-or-death
combat, was the masculine voice of the omniscient narrator.

Jane Austen simply did not use the typically Victorian omniscient
narrator convention of Thackeray, Trollope and George Eliot; yet to imitate
her sentence would have been as pointless as to adopt George Eliot's heavy
disguise of a male persona. For an unspoken assumption among readers is
that the Victorian omniscient narrator *is* a male persona; female omniscience, in a patriarchal society with an androcentric religion, is a contradiction in terms. Under the conditions of this male-dominated tradition
which Virginia Woolf inherited, to adopt the all-knowing voice of omniscient narration was, in effect, to adopt a thoroughly masculine tone. It is
a measure of the miracle she wrought on behalf of her sex that by the time
she wrote *The Waves* she had created a linguistic territory in which a female
omniscient narrator could take voice and find the freedom in which to
remain sexually neutral. "I am the seer. I am the force that arranges. I am
the thing in which all this exists. Certainly without me it would perish. I
can give it order. I perceive what is bound to happen." As one of her more
peceptive commentators, J.W. Graham, has remarked of this passage from
the first holograph draft of *The Waves*, this "She . . . perceives what is
bound to happen: but she does not make it happen."

Graham speaks of the narrator in *Middlemarch* having "a form of
knowledge superior to [the characters]" whereas, "in contrast to this effect
of authorial omniscience, the narrative continuum that Virginia Woolf
sought to establish might be termed 'omnipercipience'." It is tempting to
take this view as further evidence for Woolf's success in dismantling the
kind of masculine prejudices endemic in the morally superior tone of the
typical Victorian narrator-persona and in creating a discourse which can
give voice to a morally neutral or unprejudiced female omniscience—or
more accurately, as Graham says, "omnipercipience." Of course *The Waves*
can in some senses be regarded as a special case, coming as the final ("six-
sided") flowering of her "androgynous" period of the late '20s, and in its
exploration of the idea of the androgynous mind even more of a *tour de
force* than *Orlando*. However necessary a path it was for her to have followed,
her later novels indicate the extent to which *The Waves* proved in this
regard to be a cul-de-sac. It seems to me that too much can be made too
easily of Woolf's so-called "androgynous ideal," and while we may not wish
to reduce it, as one critic does, to a "temporary metaphor, appropriate in
the context of an essay on women and fiction," we should perhaps remain

wary of pursuing it through her works with a kind of single-mindedness that was never exhibited by their author.

A discussion of the nature of narrative voice can usefully include extended analyses of passages from the works in question, but within the scope of this essay I can only offer some suggestions towards possible new lines of enquiry. If we now look at Woolf's first three novels while bearing in mind the especially problematical nature of the "I" for a female writer at the beginning of the twentieth century, it may help us towards a fuller appreciation of the genuinely revolutionary qualities they embody.

In a letter to Lytton Strachey written during the long composition of *The Voyage Out*, Virginia Woolf responds to his tales of the novel he will write with a characteristic blend of teasing affection and self-mocking envy: "Why do you tantalise me with stories of your novel? I wish you would confine your genius to one department, it's too bad to have you dancing . . . over all departments of literature . . . and now fiction." She then goes on to say: "A painstaking woman who wishes . . . to give voice to some of the perplexities of her sex, in plain English, has no chance at all." On one level, this clearly continues the tone of self-mockery, but its aptness to what she was in fact engaged upon in her first novel, giving "voice to some of the perplexities of her sex," lends it the deeper ring of truth. It is significant, too, that it is Strachey to whom she is writing in this disarmingly self-depreciating manner, since *The Voyage Out* can be read as an extended argument with those aspects of Bloomsbury most particularly represented by her earliest literary rival.

For while it is true that Bloomsbury was in many ways a strong liberating influence in Virginia Stephen's life, releasing her from the toils of respectable bourgeois hypocrisy associated with life at Hyde Park Gate, the double-edged characterization of the two Bloombury figures in *The Voyage Out*—St. John Hirst and Helen Ambrose—indicates the extent of their author's unease with some of the values they represent. Both appoint themselves as Rachel's educators; both regard their own attitudes to sexuality as uniquely untrammelled by conventional hypocrisy; both assume that women can have no equal share in male sexual enjoyment. When Rachel tries to explain to Helen her sense of fear and confusion at her own abruptly awakened sexual feelings after Richard Dalloway's kiss, Helen's response is dismissive.

> Men will want to kiss you, just as they'll want to marry you. The pity is to get things out of proportion. It's like noticing the noises people make when they eat, or men spitting; or, in short, any small thing that gets on one's nerves.

This is very similar to St. John's attitude to female sexuality: that it is virtually non-existent, and certainly has nothing to do with any notion of masculine pleasure or fulfillment. Here he talks to Hewet, who is beginning to fall in love with Rachel:

> "What I abhor most of all," he concluded, "is the female breast. Imagine being Venning and having to get into bed with Susan! But the really repulsive thing is that they feel nothing at all—about what I do when I have a hot bath. They're gross, they're absurd, they're utterly intolerable!"

This is a delightfully barbed parody of the narcissistic side of male homoeroticism; but one of its effects is to make more sinister the alliance between the female-despising Hirst and the strongly male-identified Helen. In a novel which is so largely concerned with the sexual initiation rites of a virgin girl, it is tempting to see in the characterization of these two Bloomsbury figures and their effect on Rachel a sharply personal reference to Woolf herself. However, more than enough has been written elsewhere about Virginia Woolf's relationships with her Bloomsbury friends, as well as with her father, mother, sister, brothers, half-sisters, half-brothers, brother-in-law, half-brother-in-law, to say nothing of husband, to make one almost begin to doubt whether any of her novels were "made up" at all. Louise De Salvo's account of the genesis of *The Voyage Out* seems to hint that the earlier version, *Melymbrosia*, is the better novel, because it bears a less disguised relation to Woolf's personal experiences. As a basis for evaluation this kind of reasoning is open to the objection that it refuses autonomy to the novel as fictional construct. *The Voyage Out* is not a disguised first-person novel, as such criticism implies. Although Rachel is seen from the inside, it is not her consciousness which frames the novel, but that of Woolf's narrator, whose gender-conscious ironies operate as a constant reminder to the reader of the existence of the sex-war as a kind of grim backcloth to the romantic love story.

Irony is of course an excellent substitute for masculinity when it comes to lending authority to a narrative voice, as women writers have always had reason to know. More assured in her later novels, as well as more anti-authoritarian, Woolf had less need of the interventions of an ironic narrator. Even in this novel, we find the poised witty voice of the opening—in tone a composite of Jane Austen and late George Eliot ("Each of the ladies, being after the fashion of their sex highly trained in promoting men's talk without listening to it"—to be gradually subsumed into the voices of the characters as the story draws further out from its solid anchorage in English literary tradition. It is too simple to say that the authorial voice becomes one with the heroine's: the perspectives are broader than any single viewpoint, as is beautifully illustrated by the final scene in which it is St. John Hirst, redeemed by his heroic perseverance on Rachel's behalf, who reverses her journey from this world into the unknown by coming back into the circle of light and warmth in the hotel from the darkness beyond.

One consequence of identifying Rachel Vinrace with her author has been a denigration of the novel as the product of a prudish mind. James Naremore, despite some excellent analysis of what he calls the "submission of the narrator's ego to the world she writes about," cannot resist chiding Woolf for being "manifestly prudish" in *The Voyage Out*. In a critic who is otherwise sensitive to what he terms "the generally erotic nature of her art," this misreading (as it seems to me) smacks of a blindness to the female perspective of this particular novel. Like De Salvo, he makes too close an association between the identities of author and heroine, and projects onto Woolf the nervousness about sexuality that is a characteristic of Rachel Vinrace. Virginia Woolf herself may or may not have been sexually nervous: the point I would wish to stress is that she is perfectly conscious, as author, of this quality in her heroine—it is not a case of an unconscious projection of her own secret fears.

Naremore quite rightly points to the evocative image of the old lady gardeners as one which contains overtones of both sexuality and death:

> millions of dark-red flowers were blooming, until the old ladies who had tended them so carefully came down the paths with their scissors, snipped through their juicy stalks, and laid them upon cold stone ledges in the village church.

But this is not a generalized image of a sex/death equation: it is specifically an evocation of female castrators at work, and as such carries a resonance not only in the scene where Rachel spies the old women decapitating live chickens behind the hotel, but also in the much later dream-image of her delirium: "Terence sat down by the bedside . . . Her eyes were not entirely shut . . . She opened them completely when he kissed her. But she only saw an old woman slicing a man's head off with a knife." This is a recurrent dream of hers, and, like the disgustingly oozy vaginal tunnel dream, represents an internalization by Rachel of certain male fears about women. (Particularly male homosexual fears—Terence's friendship with the homosexually-inclined St. John is left deliberately suggestive.) Naremore's misunderstanding of this important layer of meaning in the novel is underlined by the nature of his reference to Woolf's essay "Professions for Women," which he invokes in confirmation of his "author-as-prude" theory.

He cites a well-known passage from this essay in which Woolf confesses to having been unable, as a writer, to rid herself of inhibitions about "telling the truth about my own experience as a body," and in a footnote he quotes at length from another passage which develops the image of a woman writer as a girl fishing:

> letting her imagination sweep unchecked round every rock and cranny of the world that lies submerged in the depths of our unconscious being. Now came the experience that I believe to be far commoner with women writers than with men. The line raced through the girl's fingers. Her imagination had rushed away. It had sought the pools, the depths, the dark places where the largest fish slumber. And then there was a smash. . . . The girl was roused from her dream . . . she had thought of something, something about the body, about the passions which it was unfitting for her as a woman to say.

Certainly, this passage describes sexual inhibition in the writer as writer; but such inhibition could have other causes than prudishness. In fact, Naremore stops quoting at exactly the point where Woolf ascribes such a cause. She goes on:

> Men, her reason told her, would be shocked. The consciousness of what men will say of a woman who speaks the truth about her passions had roused her from her artist's state of unconsciousness. She could write no more. The trance was over. Her imagination could work no longer. This I believe to be a very common experience with women writers—they are impeded by the extreme conventionality of the other sex.

I should like to suggest that it is this very problem of a woman's disablement by fear of condemnation by the other sex, that is Woolf's subject in her first novel. For Naremore, like other critics, again too simply interprets Rachel's death. He assures us: "For Rachel . . . there does come an ultimate union with Hewet, which results indirectly in her death." "And ultimately, death has the power to bring about an intense communion; at the moment when Rachel dies, Terence feels that 'their complete union and happiness filled the room with rings eddying more and more widely'." Precisely: *Terence* feels—Terence, whose petty power struggle with Helen over the doctor ("Unconsciously he took Rodriguez' side against Helen") has led to a possibly fatal delay in obtaining more trustworthy medical help, and whose jealousy of Rachel's "otherness" gives credence to her delirious fears of "castrating," in the sense of emasculating, him:

> Terence . . . was looking at her keenly and with dissatisfaction. She seemed to be able to cut herself adrift from him, and to pass away to

unknown places where she had no need of him. The thought roused his jealousy.

"I sometimes think you're not in love with me and never will be," he said energetically. She started and turned round at his words.

"I don't satisfy you in the way you satisfy me," he continued. "There's something I can't get hold of in you. You don't want me as I want you—you're always wanting something else."

In this novel men and women are shown to share the fear that the other sex will use them, turn them into objects. But whereas men have an age-old common language in which to give voice to this fear, women have no such language. In Rachel, the fear becomes fatally internalized. Terence dismisses peremptorily and without compunction the most important thing in her life—her music: "that kind of thing is merely like an unfortunate old dog going round on its hind legs in the rain." Undertones suggesting Dr. Johnson's comment on women preachers reinforce his message here, and he remains quite insensitive to her anxiety at being exhibited as an object at the hotel tea-party after their engagement. The point is, of course, that there is no conceivable way for Rachel to object to any of this treatment, in terms a conventional male like Terence could understand, except by rejecting him outright. And rejecting a man one has attracted and to whom one has promised sexual fulfilment is in traditional male mythology tantamount to castrating him.

Despite some flaws in construction, this novel does not in my view read like the work of a writer projecting her own unconscious sexual timidity onto her heroine. Nor is it just another *Bildungsroman* detailing the metaphysical education of a heroine enacting Eliade's version of the heroic myth, who "returns to life a new man," as Avrom Fleishmann would have it. Some feminist critics have been equally guilty of ignoring the impact of the female perspective in this novel. Patricia Stubbs, for instance, futilely castigates Woolf for failing to create new feminist role models in her fiction, claiming that "she deliberately avoided [writing] at a conscious level about what it means to be a woman living in our society." "At a conscious level," does this mean, at the level of polemical assertion? Yet, if Hillis Miller is right, the most important themes of any novel lie not in its explicit affirmations, "but in significances generated by the way in which the story is told." If this is true of any novel it is surely true of *The Voyage Out*, which enacts precisely through its narrative strategies "what it means to be a woman living in our society" and which, as the remarkably polished first work of an extraordinarily sophisticated and self-aware mind, deserves to be taken more seriously in its own right as a voicing of "some of the perplexities of her sex."

" '[Gibbon] has a point of view & sticks to it' I said. 'And so do you. I wobble'." This snippet from a reported conversation with Strachey in 1921 once more disguises under disarming self-depreciation an important perception about the difference between Woolf's own writing and the arch-masculine style of a Gibbon or a Strachey. Her "wobbling" is her ability to undermine the very idea of any centralized moral standpoint, any authoritarian idea of "omniscience," by a strategy of continual modulation of tone of voice. This strategy she developed more fully in her middle period, but already in *The Voyage Out* she had taken up a distinctly combative posture toward the masculine intellectual world in general, and that of Bloomsbury in particular. By the time she wrote her next novel, *Night and Day*, she was prepared to take on the even more vexed question of woman versus family inherited from the Victorians. Here Bloomsbury was much more on her side, although the sex battle—or, more precisely, the battle for a hearing of the female view—still continues, endowing the fiction with its own intricate and comprehensive form.

ELIZABETH ABEL

Narrative Structure(s) and Female Development: The Case of "Mrs. Dalloway"

*I wish you were a Kangaroo and had a pouch for small
Kangaroos to creep to.*

—VIRGINIA STEPHEN to Violet Dickenson, June 4(?), 1903

*Our insight into this early, pre-Oedipus, phase comes to us as a
surprise, like the discovery, in another field, of the Minoan-Mycenean
civilization behind the civilization of Greece.*

—SIGMUND FREUD, "Female Sexuality," (1931)

We all know Virginia Woolf disliked
the fixity of plot: "This appalling narrative business of the realist," she
called it. Yet like all writers of fiction, she inevitably invoked narrative
patterns in her work, if only to disrupt them or reveal their insignificance.
In *Mrs. Dalloway*, a transitional work between the straightforward narrative
of an early novel like *The Voyage Out* and the experimental structure of a
late work like *The Waves*, Woolf superimposes the outlines of multiple,
familiar yet altered plots that dispel the constraints of a unitary plan, diffuse

From *The Voyage In: Fictions of Female Development*, edited by Elizabeth Abel, Marianne
Hirsch and Elizabeth Langland. Copyright © 1983 by the Trustees of Dartmouth College.
University Press of New England, 1983.

the chronological framework of the single day in June, and enable an iconoclastic plot to weave its course covertly through the narrative grid. In this palimpsestic layering of plots, Mrs. Dalloway conforms to Gilbert and Gubar's characterization of the typically female text as one which both inscribes and hides its subversive impulses.

The story of female development in Mrs. Dalloway, a novel planned such that "every scene would build up the idea of C[larissa]'s character," is a clandestine story that remains almost untold, that resists direct narration and coherent narrative shape. Both intrinsically disjointed and textually dispersed and disguised, it is the novel's buried story. The fractured developmental plot reflects the encounter of gender with narrative form and adumbrates the psychoanalytic story of female development, a story Freud and Woolf devised concurrently and separately, and published simultaneously in 1925. The structure of Woolf's developmental story and its status in the novel illustrate distinctive features of female experience and female plots.

Woolf repeatedly acknowledged differences between male and female writing, detecting the influence of gender in fictional voice and plot. While insisting that the creative mind must be androgynous, incandescent, and unimpeded by personal grievance, she nevertheless affirmed that differences between male and female experience would naturally emerge in distinctive fictional shapes. She claims,

> No one will admit that he can possibly mistake a novel written by a man for a novel written by a woman. There is the obvious and enormous difference of experience in the first place . . . And finally . . . there rises for consideration the very difficult question of the difference between the man's and the woman's view of what constitutes the importance of any subject. From this spring not only marked differences of plot and incident, but infinite differences in selection, method and style.

The experience that shapes the female plot skews the woman novelist's relationship to narrative tradition; this oblique relationship may further mold the female text. In a remarkable passage in A Room of One's Own, Woolf describes one way in which the difference in experience can affect the logic of the female text:

> And since a novel has this correspondence to real life, its values are to some extent those of real life. But it is obvious that the values of women differ very often from the values which have been made by the other sex; naturally, this is so. Yet it is the masculine values that prevail . . . And these values are inevitably transferred from life to fiction. This is an

important book, the critic assumes, because it deals with war. This is an insignificant book because it deals with the feelings of women in a drawingroom. A scene in a battlefield is more important than a scene in a shop—everywhere and much more subtly the difference of value persists. The whole structure, therefore, of the early nineteenth-century novel was raised, if one was a woman, by a mind which was slightly pulled from the straight, and made to alter its clear vision in deference to external authority . . . the writer was meeting criticism . . . She met that criticism as her temperament dictated, with docility and diffidence, or with anger and emphasis. It does not matter which it was; she was thinking of something other than the thing itself . . . She had altered her values in deference to the opinions of others.

Woolf explicitly parallels the dominance of male over female values in literature and life, while implying a different hierarchy that further complicates the woman novelist's task. By contrasting the "values of women" with those which "have been made by the other sex," Woolf suggests the primacy of female values as products of nature rather than culture, and of the named sex rather than the "other" one. No longer the conventionally "second" sex, women here appear the source of intrinsic and primary values. In the realm of culture, however, masculine values prevail and deflect the vision of the woman novelist, inserting a duality into the female narrative, turned Janus-like toward the responses of both self and other. This schizoid perspective can fracture the female text. The space between emphasis and undertone, a space that is apparent in Woolf's own text, may also be manifested in the gap between a plot that is shaped to confirm expectations and a subplot at odds with this accommodation. If the early nineteenth-century woman novelist betrayed her discomfort with male evaluation by overt protestation or compliance, the early twentieth-century woman novelist, more aware of this dilemma, may encode as a subtext the stories she wishes yet fears to tell.

Feminist literary criticism, Elaine Showalter states, presents us with "a radical alteration of our vision, a demand that we see meaning in what has previously been empty space. The orthodox plot recedes, and another plot, hitherto submerged in the anonymity of the background, stands out in bold relief like a thumbprint." The excavation of buried plots in women's texts has revealed an enduring, if recessive, narrative concern with the story of mothers and daughters—with the "lost tradition," as the title of one anthology names it, or, in psychoanalytic terminology, with the "pre-Oedipal" relationship, the early symbiotic female bond that both predates and coexists with the heterosexual orientation toward the father and his substitutes. Frequently, the subtleties of mother-daughter alignments, for which few narrative conventions have been formulated, are relegated to the background of a dominant romantic or courtship plot. As women novelists increasingly exhaust or dismiss the possibilities of the romantic plot, however, they have tended to inscribe the maternal subplot more emphatically. In contemporary women's fiction, this subplot is often dominant; but in the fiction of the 1920s, a particularly fruitful decade for women and women's writing, the plot of female bonding began to vie repeatedly with the plot of heterosexual love. Woolf, Colette, and Cather highlighted aspects of the mother-daughter narrative in works such as *My Mother's House* (1922), *To the Lighthouse* (1927), *Break of Day* (1928), *Sido* (1929), and "Old Mrs. Harris" (1932). In *Mrs. Dalloway*, written two years before *To the Lighthouse*, Woolf structures her heroine's development, the recessive narrative of her novel, as a story of pre-Oedipal attachment and loss.

In his essay "Female Sexuality," Freud parallels the pre-Oedipal phase of female development to the allegedly matriarchal civilization lying behind that of classical Greece, presumably associated here with its most famous drama; his analogy offers a trope for the psychological and textual strata of *Mrs. Dalloway*. For Freud conflates, through the spatial and temporal meanings of the word "behind" (*hinter*), notions of evolution with those of static position. Clarissa Dalloway's recollected development proceeds from an emotionally pre-Oedipal female-centered natural world to the heterosexual male-dominated social world, a movement, Woolf implies, that recapitulates the broader sweep of history from matriarchal to patriarchal orientation. But the textual locus of this development, to revert to the archaeological implications of Freud's image, is a buried *subtext* that endures throughout the domestic and romantic plots in the foreground: the metaphors of palimpsest and cultural strata coincide here. The interconnections of female development, historical progress, and narrative structure are captured in Freud's image of a pre-Oedipal world underlying the individual and cultural origins we conventionally assign the names Oedipus and Athens.

Woolf embeds her radical developmental plot in a narrative matrix pervaded by gentler acts of revision; defining the place of this recessive plot requires some awareness of the larger structure. The narrative present, patterned as the sequence of a day, both recalls the structure of *Ulysses*, which Woolf completed reading as she began *Mrs. Dalloway*, and offers a female counterpart to Joyce's adaptation of an epic form. *Mrs. Dalloway* inverts the hierarchy Woolf laments in *A Room of One's Own*. Her foregrounded domestic plot unfolds precisely in shops and drawing rooms rather

than on battlefields, and substitutes for epic quest and conquest the traditionally feminine project of giving a party, of constructing social harmony
through affiliation rather than conflict; the potentially epic plot of the
soldier returned from war is demoted to the tragic subplot centering on
Septimus Warren Smith. By echoing the structure of *Ulysses* in the narrative
foreground of her text, Woolf revises a revision of the epic to accommodate
the values and experience of women while cloaking the more subversive
priorities explored in the covert developmental tale.

A romantic plot, which provides the dominant structure for the
past in *Mrs. Dalloway*, also obscures the story of Clarissa's development.
Here again, Woolf revises a traditional narrative pattern, the courtship
plot perfected by Woolf's elected "foremother," Jane Austen. Woolf simultaneously invokes and dismisses Austen's narrative model through Clarissa's mistaken impression that her future husband is named Wickham. This
slight, if self-conscious, clue to a precursor assumes greater import in light
of Woolf's lifelong admiration for Austen and Woolf's efforts to reconstruct
this "most perfect artist among women" in her literary daughter's image;
these efforts structure Woolf's essay on Austen, written shortly after *Mrs.
Dalloway*. Woolf's treatment of the romantic plot in *Mrs. Dalloway* reveals
the temporal boundaries of Austen's narratives, which cover primarily the
courtship period and inevitably culminate in happy marriages. Woolf condenses the expanded moment that constitutes an Austen novel and locates
it in a remembered scene thirty years prior to the present of her narrative,
decentering and unraveling Austen's plot. Marriage in *Mrs. Dalloway* provides impetus rather than closure to the courtship plot, dissolved into a
retrospective oscillation between two alluring possibilities as Clarissa continues to replay the choice she made thirty years before. The courtship plot
in this novel is both evoked through memories of the past and indefinitely
suspended in the present, completed when the narrative begins and incomplete when the narrative ends, sustained as a narrative thread by Clarissa's enduring uncertainty. The novel provides no resolution to this
internalized version of the plot; the final scene presents Clarissa through
Peter Walsh's amorous eyes and allies Richard Dalloway with his daughter.
The elongated courtship plot, the imperfectly resolved emotional triangle,
becomes a screen for the developmental story that unfolds in fragments of
memory, unexplained interstices between events, and narrative asides and
interludes.

When Woolf discovered how to enrich her characterization by dig-
ging "beautiful caves" into her characters' pasts, her own geological image
for the temporal strata of *Mrs. Dalloway*, she chose with precision the

consciousness through which to reveal specific segments of the past. Although Clarissa vacillates emotionally between the allure of Peter and that of Richard, she remembers Peter's courtship only glancingly; the burden of that plot is carried by Peter, through whose memories Woolf relates the slow and tortured end of the relation with Clarissa. Clarissa's memories, by contrast, focus more exclusively on the general ambience of Bourton, her childhood home, and her love for Sally Seton. Significantly absent from these memories is Richard Dalloway, whose courtship of Clarissa is presented exclusively through Peter's painful recollections. Clarissa thinks of Richard only in the present, not at the peak of a romantic relationship. Through this narrative distribution, Woolf constructs two diversified poles structuring the flux of Clarissa's consciousness. Bourton is to Clarissa a pastoral female world spatially and temporally disjunct from marriage and the sociopolitical world of (Richard's) London. The fluid passage of consciousness between these poles conceals a radical schism.

Though the Bourton scenes Clarissa remembers span a period of several years, they are absorbed by a single emotional climate that creates a constant backdrop to the foregrounded day in June. Woolf excises all narrative connections between these contrasting extended moments. She provides no account of intervening events: Clarissa's marriage, childbirth, the move and adjustment to London. And she indicates the disjunction in Clarissa's experience by noting that the London hostess never returns to Bourton, which now significantly belongs to a male relative, and almost never sees Sally Seton, now the unfamiliar Lady Rosseter. Clarissa's life in London is devoid of intimate female bonds: she is excluded from lunch at Lady Bruton's and she vies with Miss Kilman for her own daughter's allegiance. Woolf structures Clarissa's development as a stark binary opposition between past and present, nature and culture, feminine and masculine dispensations—the split implicit in Woolf's later claim that "the values of women differ very often from the values which have been made by the other sex." Versions of this opposition reverberate throughout the novel in rhetorical and narrative juxtapositions. The developmental plot, which slides beneath the more familiar romantic plot through the gap between Peter's and Clarissa's memories, exists as two contrasting moments and the silence adjoining and dividing them.

Woolf endows these moments with symbolic resonance by a meticulous strategy of narrative exclusions that juxtaposes eras split by thirty years and omits Clarissa's childhood from the novel's temporal frame. There is no past in *Mrs. Dalloway* anterior to Clarissa's adolescence at Bourton. Within this selective scheme, the earliest remembered scenes become homologous to a conventional narrative point of departure: the description of formative childhood years. The emotional tenor of these scenes, moreover, suggests their representation of deferred childhood desire. Clarissa's earliest narrated memories focus on Sally's arrival at Bourton, an arrival that infuses the formal, repressive atmosphere with a vibrant female energy. The only picture of Clarissa's early childhood sketched in the novel suggests a tableau of female loss: a dead mother, a dead sister, a distant father, and a stern maiden aunt, the father's sister, whose hobby of pressing flowers beneath Littre's dictionary suggests to Peter Walsh the social oppression of women, an emblem of nature ossified by language/culture. In this barren atmosphere, Sally's uninhibited warmth and sensuality immediately spark love in the eighteen-year-old Clarissa. Sally replaces Clarissa's dead mother and sister, her name even echoing the sister's name, Sylvia. She nurtures Clarissa's passions and intellect, inspiring a love equal to Othello's in intensity and equivalent in absoluteness to a daughter's earliest bond with her mother, a bond too early ruptured for Clarissa as for Woolf, a bond which Woolf herself perpetually sought to recreate through intimate attachments to mother surrogates, such as Violet Dickinson: "I wish you were a Kangaroo and had a pouch for small Kangaroos to creep to." For Clarissa, kissing Sally creates the most exquisite moment of her life, a moment of unparalleled radiance and intensity: "The whole world might have turned upside down! The others disappeared; there she was alone with Sally. And she felt she had been given a present, wrapped up, and told just to keep it, not to look at it—a diamond, something infinitely precious, wrapped up, which, as they walked (up and down, up and down), she uncovered, or the radiance burnt through, the revelation, the religious feeling!—when old Joseph and Peter faced them." This kind of passionate attachment between women, orthodox psychoanalysts and feminists uncharacteristically agree, recaptures some aspect of the fractured mother-daughter bond. Within the sequence established by the novel, this adolescent love assumes the power of the early female bond excluded from the narrative.

The moment Woolf selects to represent Clarissa's past carries the full weight of the pre-Oedipal experience that Freud discovered with such a shock substantially predates and shapes the female version of the Oedipus complex, the traumatic turn from mother to father. As French psychoanalytic theory has clarified, the Oedipus complex is less a biologically ordained event than a symbolic moment of acculturation, the moment, in Freud's words, that "may be regarded as a victory of the race over the individual," that "initiates all the processes that are designed to make the individual find a place in the cultural community." For both women and men, this socialization exacts renunciation, but for women this is a process of poorly compensated loss, for the boy's rewards for renouncing his mother will include a woman like the mother and full paternal privileges, while the girl's renunciation of her mother will at best be requited with a future child, but no renewed access to the lost maternal body, the first love object for girls as well as boys, and no acquisition of paternal power. In *Mrs. Dalloway*, Woolf encapsulates an image of the brusque and painful turn that, whenever it occurs, abruptly terminates the earliest stage of female development and defines the moment of acculturation as a moment of obstruction.

Woolf organizes the developmental plot such that Clarissa's love for Sally precedes her allegiances to men; the two women "spoke of marriage always as a catastrophe." Clarissa perceives Peter in this period primarily as an irritating intruder. The scene that Clarissa most vividly remembers, the scene of Sally Seton's kiss, is rudely interrupted by Peter's appearance. Both the action and the language of this scene hint at psychological allegory. The moment of exclusive female connection is shattered by masculine intervention, a rupture signaled typographically by Woolf's characteristic dash. Clarissa's response to this intrusion images an absolute and arbitrary termination: "It was like running one's face against a granite wall in the darkness! It was shocking; it was horrible!" Clarissa's perception of Peter's motives—"she felt his hostility; his jealousy; his determination to break into their comradeship"—suggests an Oedipal configuration: the jealous male attempting to rupture the exclusive female bond, insisting on the transference of attachment to the man, demanding heterosexuality. For women this configuration institutes a break as decisive and unyielding as a granite wall. Clarissa's revenge is to refuse to marry Peter and to select instead the less demanding Richard Dalloway in order to guard a portion of her psyche for the memory of Sally. Woolf herself exacts poetic justice by subjecting Peter Walsh to a transposed, inverted replay of this crucial scene when Elizabeth, thirty years later, interrupts his emotional reunion with her mother by unexpectedly opening a door (in the granite wall?), asserting by her presence the primacy of female bonds. "Here is my Elizabeth," Clarissa announces to the disconcerted Peter, the possessive pronoun he finds so extraneous accentuating the intimacy of the mother-daughter tie.

Clarissa resists the wrenching, requisite shift from pre-Oedipal to Oedipal orientation, yet she submits in practice if not totally in feeling. The extent of the disjunction she undergoes is only apparent in the bifurcated settings of her history, the images reiterating radical divides, the gaps slyly inserted in the narrative. The most striking of these images and gaps concern Clarissa's sister Sylvia, a shadowy and seemingly gratuitous character, apparently created just to be destroyed. Her death, her only action in the novel, is recalled by Peter rather than by Clarissa and is related in two sentences. This offhand presentation both implants and conceals an exaggerated echo of Clarissa's split experience. A young woman "on the verge of life," Sylvia is abruptly killed by a falling tree that dramatically imposes a barrier to life in a gesture of destruction mysteriously associated with her father: "(all Justin Parry's fault—all his carelessness)." The shocking attribution of blame is only ostensibly discounted by parentheses: recall Woolf's parenthetical accounts of human tragedy in the "Time Passes" section of To the Lighthouse. The deliberate decision to indict the father contrasts with the earlier story, "Mrs. Dalloway in Bond Street," where Sylvia's death is depicted as a tranquil, vague event absorbed by nature's cyclical benevolence: "It used, thought Clarissa, to be so simple . . . When Sylvia died, hundreds of years ago, the yew hedges looked so lovely with the diamond webs in the mist before early church." The violence of Sylvia's death in the novel and the very incongruity between the magnitude of the charge against her father and its parenthetical presentation suggest a story intentionally withheld, forcibly deprived of its legitimate proportions, deliberately excised from the narrative yet provocatively implied in it, written both into and out of the text. This self-consciously inscribed narrative gap echoes the gap in Clarissa's own narrative, as the dramatic severance of Sylvia's life at the moment of maturity echoes the split in her sister's development. The pastoral resonance of Sylvia's name also implies a larger female story of natural existence abruptly curtailed. A related narrative exclusion suggests a crucial untold tale about Clarissa's relation to her mother, remarkably unremembered and unmentioned in the novel except by a casual party guest whose brief comparison of Clarissa to her mother brings sudden tears to Clarissa's eyes. The story of the pain entailed in this loss is signaled by but placed outside the narrative in the double gesture of inclusion and exclusion that structures Woolf's narration of her heroine's development. By locating the clues to this discontinuous narrative in the marginal moments of her text, Woolf creates an inconspicuous subtext perceptible only to an altered vision.

Woolf's discrete suggestion of an intermittent plot is politically astute and aesthetically adept. Her insight into the trauma of female development does subvert the notion of organic, even growth culminating for women in marriage and motherhood, and she prudently conceals her implications of a violent adaptation. The narrative gaps also challenge the conventions of linear plot and suggest its distorted regimentation of experience, particularly the subjective experience of women. These gaps, moreover, are mimetically precise: juxtapositions represent sudden shifts, silence indicates absence and loss. Perhaps Woolf's most striking achievement, however, is her intuition of the "plot" Freud detected in female development. Despite Woolf's obvious familiarity with the popularized aspects of Freudian theory, and despite the close association of the Hogarth Press with Freudian oeuvre, there can be no question of influence here, for Freud first expounded his view of a distinctively female development the year of *Mrs. Dalloway's* publication. Rather than influence, *Mrs. Dalloway* demonstrates the common literary prefiguration of psychoanalytic doctrine, which can retroactively articulate patterns implicit in the literary text. The similarities between these fictional and psychoanalytic narratives clarify the structure of Woolf's submerged developmental plot and the power of Freud's submerged demonstration of the loss implicit in female development.

Only late in life did Freud acknowledge the fundamentally different courses of male and female development. Prior to the 1925 essay entitled "Some Psychical Consequences of the Anatomical Distinction Between the Sexes," Freud clung, though with increasing reservations, to a view of sexual symmetry in which male and female versions of the Oedipal experience were fundamentally parallel. His growing appreciation of the pre-Oedipal stage in girls, however, finally toppled his view of parallel male and female tracks, inspiring a new formulation of the distinctively female developmental tasks. Female identity is acquired, according to this new theory, by a series of costly repressions from which the male child is exempt. The girl's developmental path is more arduous and bumpy than the boy's smoother linear route. For though the male child must repress his erotic attachment to his mother, he must undergo no change in orientation, since the mother will eventually be replaced by other women with whom he will achieve the status of the father; he suffers an arrest rather than a dislocation. The girl, in contrast, must reverse her course. Like the boy, she begins life erotically bonded with her mother in the symbiotic pre-Oedipal stage, but unlike him she must replace this orientation with a heterosexual attraction to her father. She must change the nature of her desire before renouncing it.

How, Freud repeatedly asks, does the girl accomplish this monumental shift from mother to father? Though the answers he proposes may be dubious, the persistent question indicates the magnitude of the event. The girl's entire sexuality is defined in this situation. She switches not only the object of her erotic interest, but also her erotic zone and mode, relinquishing the active, "masculine," clitoridal sexuality focused on her mother for the passive, receptive, "feminine," vaginal sexuality focused on her father. Freud goes so far as to call this change a "change in her own sex," for prior to this crucial shift, "the little girl is a little man." This comprehensive change in sexual object, organ, and attitude, the shift from pre-Oedipal to Oedipal orientation, inserts a profound discontinuity into female development, which contrasts with that of "the more fortunate man [who] has only to continue at the time of his sexual maturity the activity that he has previously carried out at the period of the early efflorescence of his sexuality." The psychosexual shift that occurs in early childhood, moreover, is often reenacted in early adulthood, for marriage typically reinstates a disruption in women's experience, confined until recently to a largely female sphere prior to the heterosexual contract of marriage.

The circuitous route to female identity, Freud acknowledged, is uniquely demanding and debilitating: "a comparison with what happens with boys tells us that the development of a little girl into a normal woman is more difficult and more complicated, since it includes two extra tasks [the change of sexual object and organ], to which there is nothing corresponding in the development of a man." No woman completes this difficult process unscathed. Freud outlines three developmental paths for women; all exact a substantial toll. If she follows the first, the girl negotiates the shift from mother to father by accepting the unwelcome "fact" of her castration, detected in comparisons between herself and little boys. Mortified by this discovery of inferiority, aware she can no longer compete for her mother with her better endowed brother, she renounces her active sexual orientation toward her mother, deprived like herself of the valued sexual organ, and accepts a passive orientation toward the superior father. Unfortunately, the girl's renunciation of active sexuality normally entails repressing "a good part of her sexual trends in general," and this route leads to sexual inhibition or neurosis, to "a general revulsion from sexuality." If she chooses the second path, the girl simply refuses this renunciation, clings to her "threatened masculinity," struggles to preserve her active orientation toward her mother, and develops what Freud calls a "masculinity complex," which often finds expression in homosexuality. Only the third "very circuitous" path leads to the "normal female attitude" in which the girl takes her father as the object of her passive eroticism and enters the female Oedipus complex. Curiously, however, Freud never describes this route, which turns out to be only a less damaging version of the first path toward inhibition and neurosis. To the extent that her sexuality survives her "catastrophic" repression of her "masculine" desire for her mother, the girl will be able to complete her turn to her father and seal her femininity by desiring his baby. "Normal" femininity is thus a fragile, tenuous proposition; no unique course is prescribed for its achievement. Freud's most optimistic prognosis assumes a doubly hypothetical, negative form: "If too much is not lost in the course of it [development] through repression, this femininity may turn out to be normal." The achievement of this femininity, moreover, is only the first stage, for the female Oedipus complex, like the male, must itself be overcome, and the hard-won desire for the father renounced and transferred to other men. Female development thus entails a double disappointment in contrast with the single renunciation required of men. No wonder Freud concludes the last of his essays on femininity by contrasting the youthful flexibility of a thirty-year-old male with the psychical rigidity of a woman the same age: "Her libido has taken up final positions and seems incapable of exchanging them for others. There are no paths open to further development; it is as though the whole process had already run its course and remains thenceforward insusceptible to influence—as though, indeed, the difficult development to femininity had exhausted the possibilities of the person concerned."

In *Mrs. Dalloway*, Woolf suggests the developmental turn that Freud accentuates in his studies of femininity. The narratives they sketch share a radically foreshortened notion of development, condensed for Freud into a few childhood years, focused for Woolf in a single emotional shift. Both narratives eschew the developmental scope traditionally assumed by fiction and psychology, committed to detailing the unfolding of a life, and both stress the discontinuities specific to female development. Woolf, moreover, portrays the sexual and emotional calcification that Freud suggests is the toll of "normal" development. Clarissa is explicit about her unimpassioned response to men, a response she perceives as a failure and a lack, a guarding of virginity through motherhood and marriage. Her emotional and physical self-containment is represented by her narrow attic bed, where she reads Baron Marbot's memoirs of the retreat from Moscow, a victory achieved by icy withdrawal. The association of her bed with a grave—"Narrower and narrower would her bed be"—links her adult sexuality with death. Yet, in a passage of extraordinary erotic writing, Woolf contrasts the description of the narrow bed with Clarissa's passionate responses to women, implying through this juxtaposition the cost of the pivotal developmental choice:

> Yet she could not resist sometimes yielding to the charm of a woman, not a girl, of a woman confessing, as to her they often did, some scrape, some folly . . . she did undoubtedly then feel what men felt. Only for a moment; but it was enough. It was a sudden revelation, a tinge like a blush which

one tried to check and then, as it spread, one yielded to its expansion, and rushed to the farthest verge and there quivered and felt the world come closer, swollen with some astonishing significance, some pressure of rapture, which split its thin skin and gushed and poured with an extraordinary alleviation over the cracks and sores! Then, for that moment, she had seen an illumination; a match burning in a crocus; an inner meaning almost expressed. But the close withdrew; the hard softened. It was over— the moment. Against such moments (with women too) there contrasted (as she laid her hat down) the bed and Baron Marbot and the candle half-burnt.

Woolf's language renders a passion that is actively directed toward women, and implicitly "masculine" in attitude and character, yet also receptive and 'feminine," epitomized in the image of the match in the crocus, an emblem of active female desire that conflates Freud's sexual dichotomies. The power of the passage derives in part from the intermeshed male and female imagery, and the interwoven languages of sex and mysticism, a mélange that recurs in Clarissa's memory of Sally Seton's kiss. Fusion—of male and female, active and passive, sacred and profane—is at the heart of this erotic experience. Freud's opposition of active, "masculine," pre-Oedipal sexuality to the passive, "feminine," Oedipal norm denies the basis for this integration. Clarissa's momentary illumination is enabled only by the sexual orientation Freud devalues as (initially) immature and (subsequently) deviant. Woolf's passage suggests the potential completeness Freud denies the pre-Oedipal realm and calls into question the differential of normal from aberrant sexuality. The stark contrast between the passionate moment and the narrow bed, another juxtaposition that conceals a schism between two radically different sexual worlds, subverts the opposition normal/abnormal. Woolf here elevates Freud's second developmental path over the costly route toward "normal femininity," as she valorizes a spontaneous homosexual love over the inhibitions of imposed heterosexuality.

As the passage continues, the gap between the sexual options emblematized by the moment and the bed evolves into the familiar split between Sally Seton and Richard Dalloway, the split that structures the developmental plot. The allegorical image of the bed leads to a more concrete description of Clarissa's reaction to her husband's return: "if she raised her head she could just hear the click of the handle released as gently as possible by Richard, who slipped upstairs in his socks and then, as often as not, dropped his hot-water bottle and swore! How she laughed!" The contrast between the passionate moment with women and the narrow marital bed becomes a leap from the sublime to the (affectionately) ridiculous. Opening with the conjunction "But," the next paragraph signals a turn away from mundanity back to "this question of love . . . this falling in love with women," inaugurating Clarissa's lengthy and lyrical reminiscence of Sally Seton. The opposition between Clarissa's relationships with men and women modulates to the split between her present and her past, her orientation and emotional capacities on both sides of the Oedipal divide. Woolf, like Freud, reveals the cost of female development, but she inscribes a far more graphic image of the loss entailed, questions its necessity, and indicates the price of equating female development with acculturation through the rites of passage established by the Oedipus complex.

These are radical claims, and Woolf suggests them indirectly. In addition to her use of juxtaposition as a narrative and rhetorical strategy, Woolf encodes her developmental plot through characters who subtly reflect Clarissa's experience. Perhaps most interesting of these is the infrequently noticed Rezia Warren Smith, wife of Clarissa's acknowledged double who has drawn critical attention away from the mirroring function of his wife. Rezia's life, like her name, is abbreviated in the novel, yet the course of her "development" suggestively echoes that of the heroine. Like Clarissa, Rezia finds herself plucked by marriage from an Edenic female world with which she preserves no contact. Her memories highlight the exclusively female community of sisters collaboratively making hats in an Italian setting that is pastoral despite the surrounding urban context: "For you should see the Milan gardens!" she later exclaims, when confronted with London's "few ugly flowers stuck in pots!" The cultural shift from Italy to England, like the shift from Bourton to London, locates this idyllic female life in a distant, prelapsarian era—before the war, before industrialization, before marriage. Marriage and war explicitly coalesce for Rezia as agents of expulsion from this female paradise: Septimus comes to Milan as a Birtish soldier and proposes to Rezia to alleviate his war-induced emotional anesthesia. Rezia's memories of Italy, a radiant temporal backdrop to her painful alienation in marriage and a foreign culture, provide a pointed parallel to Clarissa's memories of Bourton. And Rezia's final pastoral vision, inspired by the drug administered after Septimus's suicide, significantly begins with her sense of "opening long windows, stepping out into some garden," thus echoing Clarissa's first recollection of Bourton, where she had "burst open the French windows and plunged . . . into the open air." The death of her husband releases Rezia to return imaginatively to a past she implicitly shares with Clarissa: the female-centered world anterior to heterosexual bonds. After this moment of imaginative release and return, Rezia disappears from the novel, having accomplished the function of delicately echoing the bifurcated structure of the heroine's development.

The relation of Clarissa and Rezia exists only for the reader; the two women know nothing of each other. Woolf employs a different strategy for connecting Clarissa with Septimus, whose death severs the link between these female characters, releasing each to a new developmental stage, Rezia to return imaginatively to the past, Clarissa at last to transcend that past. Septimus's suicide enables Clarissa to resolve the developmental impasse that appears to be one cause of her weakened heart, her constricted vitality. Critics have amply explored Septimus's role as Clarissa's double. As important as this psychological doubling, however, is Woolf's revision of developmental plots, her decision to transfer to Septimus the death she originally imagined for Clarissa, to sacrifice male to female development, to preserve her heroine from fictional tradition by substituting a hero for a heroine in the plot of violently thwarted development, a plot that has claimed such heroines as Catharine Linton, Maggie Tulliver, Emma Bovary, Anna Karenina, Tess Durbeyfield, Edna Pontellier, Lily Bart, and Antoinette Cosway Rochester. By making Septimus the hero of a sacrificial plot that enables the heroine's development, Woolf reverses narrative tradition.

It is a critical commonplace that Clarissa receives from Septimus a cathartic, vicarious experience of death that releases her to experience life's pleasures more deeply. Woolf's terms, however, are more precise. The passage describing Clarissa's reaction to Septimus's suicide suggests that he plays a specific role in Clarissa's emotional development. Woolf composes this passage as a subtle but extended parallel to Clarissa's earlier reminiscence of her love for Sally and Bourton. The interplay between the language and structure of these two meditative interludes, the two major sites of the developmental plot, encodes Clarissa's exploration of a conflict more suppressed than resolved. By interpreting Septimus's suicide in her private language of passion and integrity, Clarissa uses the shock of death to probe her unresolved relation to her past. The suicide triggers Clarissa's recurrent preoccupation with this past, providing a perspective that enables her belatedly both to admit and to renounce its hold. On the day in June that encloses the action of Mrs. Dalloway, Clarissa completes the developmental turn initiated thirty years before.

Woolf prepares the parallels between the two passages by inaugurating both with Clarissa's withdrawal from her customary social milieu. The emotions prompting Clarissa's first meditation on Sally and the past are initially triggered by her exclusion from Lady Bruton's lunch. Woolf then describes Clarissa's noontime retreat to her solitary attic room as a metaphorical departure from a party: "She began to go slowly upstairs . . . as if she had left a party . . . had shut the door and gone out and stood alone, a single figure against the appalling night"; Clarissa is "like a nun withdrawing." Later that night, when Clarissa hears the news of Septimus's suicide, she does leave her party and retreats to an empty little room where "the party's splendor fell to the floor." The first passage concludes with her preparations for the party, the second with her deliberate return to that party. Within these enclosed narrative and domestic spaces, Clarissa relives through memory the passionate scene with Sally on the terrace at Bourton. The second passage replays in its bifurcated structure the male intervention that curtails the original scene. In this final version of the female/male juxtaposition, however, the emotional valences are reversed.

Clarissa's meditation on Septimus's death modulates, through her association of passion with death, to a meditation on her relation to her past. Woolf orchestrates the verbal echoes of this passage to evoke with increasing clarity the scene with Sally Seton. Septimus's choice of a violent, early death elicits in Clarissa the notion of a central self preserved: "A thing there was that mattered; a thing, wreathed about with chatter, defaced, obscured in her own life . . . This he had preserved." The visual image of a vital, central "thing" initiates the link with the earlier description of passion as "something central which permeated." The echoes between these passages develop through their similar representations of passion's ebb: "closeness drew apart; rapture faded, one was alone"; "But the close withdrew; the hard softened. It was over—the moment." As Clarissa implies that only death preserves the fading moment of passion, she prepares for her repetition of the *Othello* line that has signified her love for Sally Seton: "If it were now to die, 'twere now to be most happy." The metaphor of treasure which precedes this explicit allusion to the scene with Sally further connects Clarissa's response to Septimus ("had he plunged holding his treasure?" she wonders) with her memory of Sally's kiss as "a present . . . a diamond, something infinitely precious." Septimus's death evokes in Clarissa the knowledge of what death saves and what she has lost; her grief is not for Septimus, but for herself. Woolf weaves the verbal web between the two passages to summon once again the crucial scene with Sally on the terrace at Bourton, to enable Clarissa to confront her loss. Clarissa's appreciation of this loss, at last fully present to her consciousness, crystallizes in the contrast that concludes this segment of the passage: "She had schemed; she had pilfered. She was never wholly admirable. . . . And once she had walked on the terrace at Bourton."

With this naming of the original scene, Woolf abruptly terminates Clarissa's recollection, replaying with a brilliant stroke Peter Walsh's interruption, the sudden imposition of the granite wall. The masculine intervention this time, though, is enacted not by Peter but by Richard, and not as external imposition but as choice. Clarissa's unexpected thought of Richard abruptly and definitively terminates the memory of Sally, pivoting the scene from past to present, the mood from grief to joy: "It was due to Richard; she had never been so happy." The dramatic and unexplained juxtaposition encapsulates the developmental plot and the dynamics of its central scenes. This final replay of the developmental turn, and final microcosm of Woolf's narrative method, however, represent the abrupt transition positively. The joy inspired by Clarissa's thought of Richard persists as she celebrates "this having done with the triumphs of youth." Woolf does not fill in the gap splitting past from present, grief from joy. We can only speculate that Septimus's sacrificial gift includes a demonstration of Clarissa's alternatives: to preserve the intensity of passion through death, or to accept the changing offerings of life. By recalling to Clarissa the power of her past *and* the only method of eternalizing it, he enables her fully to acknowledge and renounce its hold, to embrace the imperfect pleasures of adulthood more completely. Through Septimus, Woolf recasts the developmental impasse in the general terms of progression or death. In the final act of the developmental plot, she qualifies her challenge to the notion of linear, forward growth.

Woolf signals the shift in Clarissa's orientation by concluding the interlude with Clarissa's reaction to the old lady across the way, an unnamed character who only functions in the novel as an object of Clarissa's awareness. The earlier meditative passage concludes with Clarissa's reflection in the looking glass; this one with an analogous reflection of a future identity. After Clarissa's thoughts shift from Sally and the past to Richard and the present, Woolf turns the angle of vision one notch further to open a perspective on the future. The old lady solemnly prepares for bed, but this intimation of a final repose, recalling Clarissa's earlier ruminations on her narrowing bed, carries no onus for the heroine, excited by the unexpected animation of the sky, the news of Septimus's suicide, the noise from the party in the adjacent room. Release, anticipation, pleasure in change, regardless of its consequences—these are Clarissa's dominant emotions. Her identification with Septimus and pleasure in his suicide indicate her own relief in turning from her past. The gulf between Clarissa and the unknown lady discloses the female intimacy forfeited to growth, yet Clarissa's willingness to contemplate an emblem of age instead of savoring a memory of youth suggests a positive commitment to development—not to any particular course, but to the process of change itself. The vision of the old lady simultaneously concludes the developmental plot and the depiction of

Clarissa's consciousness; the rest of the narrative turns to Peter and Sally. The developmental theme resides in the interplay between two interludes in the sequence of the day.

Freud's comparison of the pre-Oedipal stage in women to the Minoan-Mycenean civilization behind that of classical Greece provides a metaphor for the course and textual status of Clarissa's development. It also suggests a broader historical analogue to female development, though not an analogue Freud himelf pursues. Freud's psychoanalytic version of ontogeny recapitulating philogeny assumes a genderless (that is, implicitly masculine) norm: personal development repeats the historical progression from "savage" to civilized races. In *Mrs. Dalloway*, Woolf intimates more specifically that *female* development condenses one strand of human history, the progression from matriarchal to patriarchal culture implicit in Freud's archaeological trope. Woolf's fascination during the years she was composing *Mrs. Dalloway* with the works of Jane Harrison and the *Oresteia*, which traces precisely the evolution from Mycenean to Athenian culture, may have fostered this concern with the relation of gender to cultural evolution. The developmental plot embedded in *Mrs. Dalloway* traces the outline of a larger historical plot, detached in the novel from its chronological roots and endowed with an uncustomary moral charge.

Woolf assigns the action of *Mrs. Dalloway* a precise date: 1923, shortly after the war that casts its shadow through the novel. Through the experience of Septimus Warren Smith and the descriptions of soldiers marching "as if one will worked legs and arms uniformly, and life, with its varieties, its irreticences, had been laid under a pavement of monuments and wreaths and drugged into a still yet staring corpse by discipline," she suggests that the military discipline intended both to manifest and cultivate manliness in fact instills rigor mortis in the living as well as the dead. For women, the masculine war is disruptive in a different way. Woolf's imagery and plot portray the world war as a vast historical counterpart to male intervention in female lives. In one pointed metaphor, the "fingers" of the European war are so "prying and insidious" that they smash a "plaster cast of Ceres," goddess of fertility and mother love, reminder of the force and fragility of the primary female bond. Rezia's female world is shattered by the conjunction of marriage and war. The symbolic association of war with the developmental turn from feminine to masculine orientation will be more clearly marked in *To the Lighthouse*, bisected by the joint ravages of nature and war in the divisive central section. By conflating Mrs. Ramsay's death with the violence of world war, Woolf splits the novel into disjunct portions presided over separately by the mother and the father.

In *Mrs. Dalloway*, Woolf more subtly indicates the masculine tenor of postwar society. The youngest generation in this novel is almost exclusively, and boastfully, male: Sally Seton repeatedly declares her pride in her "five great boys"; the Bradshaws have a son at Eton; "Everyone in the room has six sons at Eton," Peter Walsh observes at Clarissa's party; Rezia Warren Smith mourns the loss of closeness with her sisters but craves a son who would resemble his father. Elizabeth Dalloway is the sole daughter, and she identifies more closely with her father than her mother (the plaster cast of Ceres has been shattered in the war). Male authority, partially incarnate in the relentless chiming of Big Ben, is more ominously embodied in the Doctors Holmes and Bradshaw, the modern officers of coercion. Septimus is the dramatic victim of this authority, but Lady Bradshaw's feminine concession is equally significant: "Fifteen years ago she had gone under . . . there had been no scene, no snap; only the slow sinking, water-logged, of her will into his. Sweet was her smile, swift her submission." The loose connections Woolf suggests between World War I and a bolstered male authority lack all historical validity, but within the mythology created by the novel the war assumes a symbolic function dividing a pervasively masculine present from a mythically female past.

Critics frequently note the elegiac tone permeating *Mrs. Dalloway*, a tone which allies the novel with the modernist preoccupation with the contrast between the present and the past. Nostalgia in *Mrs. Dalloway*, however, is for a specifically female presence and nurturance, drastically diminished in contemporary life. Woolf suggests this loss primarily in interludes that puncture the narrative, pointing to a loss inadequately recognized by the conventions of developmental tales. The most obvious of these interruptions, the solitary traveler's archetypal vision, loosely attached to Peter Walsh's dream, but transcending through its generic formulation the limits of private consciousness, is not, as Reuben Brower asserts, a "beautiful passage . . . which could be detached with little loss," and which "does not increase or enrich our knowledge of Peter or of anyone else in the book." Through its vivid representation of a transpersonal longing for a cosmic female/maternal/natural presence that might "shower down from her magnificent hands compassion, comprehension, absolution," the dream/vision names the absence that haunts *Mrs. Dalloway*. In the mundane present of the novel, the ancient image of the Goddess, source of life and death, dwindles to the elderly nurse sleeping next to Peter Walsh, as in another self-contained narrative interlude, the mythic figure of woman voicing nature's eternal, wordless rhythms contracts, in urban London, to a battered old beggar woman singing for coppers. The comprehensive, seductive, generative, female powers of the Goddess split, in the contemporary world, into the purely nurturant energy of Sally Seton and the social graces of the unmaternal Clarissa, clad as a hostess in a "silver-green mermaid's dress." The loss of female integration and power, another echo of the smashed cast of Ceres, is finally suggested in the contrast between the sequence envisaged by the solitary traveler and the most intrusive narrative interlude, the lecture on Proportion and Conversion, where Woolf appears to denounce in her own voice the twin evils of contemporary civilization. Rather than a sign of artistic failure, this interruption calls attention to itself as a rhetorical as well as ideological antithesis to the solitary traveler's vision. Sir Bradshaw's goddesses of Proportion and Conversion, who serve the ideals of imperialism and patriarchy, renouncing their status as creative female powers, are the contemporary counterpart to the ancient maternal deity, now accessible only in vision and dream. The historical vista intermittently inserted in *Mrs. Dalloway* echoes the developmental progress of the heroine from a nurturing, pastoral, female world to an urban culture governed by men.

One last reverberation of the developmental plot takes as its subject female development in the altered contemporary world. Through the enigmatic figure of Elizabeth, Woolf examines the impact of the new historical context on the course of women's development. Almost the same age as her mother in the earliest recollected scenes at Bourton, Elizabeth has always lived in London; the country to her is an occasional treat she associates specifically with her father. Elizabeth feels a special closeness to her father, a noticeable alienation from her mother. The transition so implicitly traumatic for Clarissa has already been accomplished by her daughter. By structuring the adolescence of mother and daughter as inverse emotional configurations, Woolf reveals the shift that has occurred between these generations. As Clarissa vacillates between two men, while tacitly guarding her special bond with Sally, Elizabeth vacillates between two women, her mother and Miss Kilman, while preserving her special connection with her father. Elizabeth's presence at the final party manifests her independence from Miss Kilman; her impatience for the party to end reveals her differences from her mother. The last scene of the novel highlights Elizabeth's closeness with her father, whose sudden response to his daughter's beauty has drawn her instinctively to his side.

The opposing allegiances of daughter and mother reflect in part the kinds of female nurturance available to each. Elizabeth's relation with the grasping Miss Kilman is the modern counterpart to Clarissa's love for Sally Seton. Specific parallels mark the generational differences. Miss Kilman's possessive desire for Elizabeth parodies the lines that emblazon Clarissa's love for Sally: "If it were now to die, 'twere now to be most happy" becomes, for Elizabeth's hungry tutor, "If she could grasp her, if she could clasp her, if she could make her hers absolutely and forever and then die; that was all she wanted." Sally walks with Clarissa on the terrace at Bourton; Miss Kilman takes Elizabeth to the Army and Navy Stores, a commercial setting that exemplifies the web of social and military ties. Miss Kilman, as her name implies, provides no asylum from this framework. Losing the female sanctury, however, brings proportionate compensations: Elizabeth assumes she will have a profession, will play some active role in masculine society. Woolf does not evaluate this new developmental course, does not tally losses and gains. If she surrounds the past with an aureole, she points to the future in silence. She offers little access to Elizabeth's consciousness, insisting instead on her status as enigma—her Chinese eyes, "blank, bright, with the staring incredible innocence of sculpture," her Oriental bearing, her "inscrutable mystery." Undecipherable, Elizabeth is "like a hyacinth, sheathed in glossy green, with buds just tinted, a hyacinth which has had no sun"; her unfolding is unknown, unknowable. Through the figure of Elizabeth as unopened bud, Woolf encloses in her text the unwritten text of the next developmental narrative.

The silences that punctuate *Mrs. Dalloway* reflect the interruptions and enigmas of female experience and ally the novel with a recent trend in feminist aesthetics. The paradoxical goal of representing women's absence from culture has fostered an emphasis on "blank pages, gaps, borders, spaces and silence, holes in discourse" as the distinctive features of a self-consciously female writing. Since narrative forms normally sanction the patterns of male experience, the woman novelist might signal her exclusion most succinctly by disrupting continuity, accentuating gaps between sequences. "Can the female self be expressed through plot or must it be conceived in resistance to plot? Must it lodge 'between the acts'?" asks Gillian Beer, the allusion to Woolf suggesting the persistence of this issue for a novelist concerned with the links of gender and genre. In her next novel Woolf expands her discrete silence to a gaping hole at the center of her narrative, a hole that divides the action dramatically between two disjunct days. *To the Lighthouse* makes explicit many of the issues latent in *Mrs. Dalloway*. The plot of female bonding, reshaped as the story of a woman's attempts to realize in art her love for an older woman, rises to the surface of the narrative; yet Lily's relationship with Mrs. Ramsay is unrepresented in the emblem Lily fashions for the novel, the painting that manifests a daughter's love for her surrogate mother as a portrait of the mother with her son. Absence is pervasive in *To the Lighthouse*. The gaps in *Mrs. Dalloway* are less conspicuous, yet they make vital and disturbing points about female experience and female plots. The fragmentary form of the developmental plot, where the patterns of experience and art intersect, conceals as insignificance a radical significance. The intervals between events, the stories untold, can remain invisible in *Mrs. Dalloway*—or they can emerge through a sudden shift of vision as the most absorbing features of Woolf's narrative.

Chronology

1882 Adeline Virginia Stephen born in London on January 25 to Leslie Stephen, statesman and man of letters, and Julia Duckworth Stephen. Her father had one (insane) daughter from a previous marriage, her mother three children from an earlier marriage; together they had four more children: Vanessa, Julian Thoby, Virginia and Adrian. Virginia educated at home by her parents.

1895 Julia Stephen dies; Leslie Stephen goes into deep mourning; Virginia has a severe mental breakdown. Household run by Julia's daughter Stella Duckworth, who postpones her marriage until Vanessa is old enough to take over.

1897 Stella Duckworth marries, becomes pregnant, and dies.

1902 Leslie Stephen knighted.

1904–05 Death of Sir Leslie Stephen in 1904. Virginia has a second mental breakdown, and tries to commit suicide by jumping out of a window. Vanessa, Thoby, Virginia and Adrian move to Bloomsbury. Virginia publishes first essays; soon becomes a regular book reviewer for the *Times Literary Supplement*. She also teaches at an evening college for working men and women.

1906 The four Stephens travel to Greece, where Vanessa and Thoby become ill; Thoby dies of typhoid fever at the age of 26.

1907 Vanessa Stephen marries artist Clive Bell; Virginia and Adrian room together near the Bells.

1910 First post-Impressionist Exhibition, engineered by Virginia's friend, critic Roger Fry. She later wrote that "in or about December, 1910, human character changed." Gradual gathering of "Bloomsbury Group," comprising such people as Lytton Strachey, Roger Fry, Duncan Grant, Desmond MacCarthy, John Maynard Keynes and E. M. Forster.

1912–15 Virginia Stephen marries Leonard Woolf on August 10, 1912. She has third mental breakdown, which lasts for three years. During this time she completes novel, *The Voyage Out* (originally titled *Melymbrosia*), but its publication is delayed by breakdown, and the war which is declared on August 4, 1914.

Finally published in 1915 by her half-brother, Gerald Duckworth. Woolf begins diary.

1917   The Woolfs buy a secondhand printing press, and set up the Hogarth Press in their basement. Later, the Press will publish Forster, Dostoevski, T. S. Eliot, Katherine Mansfield, Freud, Gorki and all of Woolf's novels and writings.

1918   The war ends, November 11.

1919   Publishes novel, *Night and Day*, with Gerald Duckworth; and collections of short stories with Hogarth Press.

1921   Publishes *Monday or Tuesday*, short fiction, with Hogarth Press. From this time, all her books will be published by the Press.

1922   Publishes *Jacob's Room*.

1925   Publishes *Mrs. Dalloway* and *The Common Reader*, a collection of essays. The Hogarth Press moves from the Woolfs' basement in Richmond to London.

1927   Publishes *To the Lighthouse*.

1928   Publishes *Orlando*, a fictional "biography" of Woolf's friend, and possibly, lover, Vita Sackville-West.

1929   Publishes book-length, feminist essay, *A Room of One's Own*.

1931   Publishes *The Waves*.

1932   Publishes *The Common Reader: Second Series*.

1933   Publishes *Flush*, a "biography" of Elizabeth Barrett Browning's spaniel.

1935   Produces *Freshwater, A Comedy in Three Acts* for her friends.

1937   Publishes *The Years*. Nephew Julian Bell killed in the Spanish Civil War.

1938   Publishes pacifist, feminist essay, *Three Guineas*.

1939   War declared on September 3; the Woolfs prepare to commit suicide if England invaded.

1940   Publishes *Roger Fry: A Biography*. Completes draft of *Between the Acts*. During Battle of Britain, London home destroyed by bombs.

1941   At the onset of another mental breakdown, which she fears will be permanent, Virginia Woolf fills her pockets with stones and drowns herself in the River Ouse on March 28, leaving suicide notes for her husband and sister. Her husband Leonard publishes various essays, short stories, letters and diaries of hers, as well as several autobiographies which detail their life together.

1969   Leonard Woolf dies.

Contributors

HAROLD BLOOM, Sterling Professor of the Humanities at Yale University, is the author of *The Anxiety of Influence, Poetry and Repression* and many other volumes of literary criticism. His forthcoming study, *Freud: Transference and Authority*, attempts a full-scale reading of all of Freud's major writings. A MacArthur Prize Fellow, he is the general editor of *The Chelsea House Library of Literary Criticism*.

REUBEN BROWER was Professor of English at Harvard University, and author of *The Fields of Light* and *Mirror on Mirror*.

ERICH AUERBACH was Sterling Professor of French and Romance Philology at Yale University. His books include *Mimesis, Dante: Poet of the Secular World* and *Scenes from the Drama of European Literature*.

GEOFFREY HARTMAN is Karl Young Professor of English and Comparative Literature at Yale University. He is the author of *Easy Pieces*.

FRANK D. McCONNELL is Professor of English at the University of California, Santa Barbara, and the author of books on H. G. Wells, Wordsworth and contemporary fiction, as well as studies of film and literature.

JAMES NAREMORE is Professor of English and Film Studies at Indiana University, and the author of *The World Without a Self: Virginia Woolf and the Novel* and *The Magic World of Orson Welles*.

PAUL WEST, novelist and critic, has taught at many universities, most recently at the University of Arizona as writer-in-residence. His many novels include *The Snow Leopard* and *Gala*.

HERMIONE LEE is Lecturer of English at the University of York. She is the author of studies of Philip Roth and of Elizabeth Bowen.

T. E. APTER is the author of *Fantasy Literature: An Approach to Reality* and studies of Woolf and of Mann.

PERRY MEISEL is Associate Professor of English at New York University. Besides *The Absent Father*, his study of Woolf and Pater, he is the author of a critical work on Hardy.

MARIA DiBATTISTA is Associate Professor of English at Princeton University. She is the author of *Virginia Woolf's Major Novels*.

E. L. BISHOP teaches English at the University of Alberta.

J. HILLIS MILLER is Frederick W. Hilles Professor of English and Comparative Literature at Yale University. His books include studies of Dickens and of Hardy, as well as *Poets of Reality*.

JOHN BURT is Assistant Professor of English at Brandeis University. His essay on *World Enough and Time* is included in *Robert Penn Warren: Modern Critical Views*.

ROBERT KIELY is Professor of English and American Literature and Language at Harvard University, and the author of *The Romantic Novel*.

GERALD LEVIN teaches at the University of Akron.

JUDY LITTLE, poet and critic, teaches at Southern Illinois University at Carbondale. She is the author of *Comedy and the Woman Writer: Woolf, Spark, and Feminism*.

VIRGINIA BLAIN teaches literature at Macquarie University in Sydney, Australia. She is the editor of *Mr. Sponge's Sporting Tour*, by R. S. Surtees.

ELIZABETH ABEL is Assistant Professor of English at the University of California, Berkeley, and the author of studies of Rhys, Lessing and Woolf, as well as the editor of *Writing and Sexual Difference*.

Bibliography

Adams, Kate. "Root and Branch: Mrs. Ramsay and Lily Briscoe in *To the Lighthouse.*" *San Jose Studies* 2, vol. 9 (1983):93–109.

Albright, Daniel. *Personality and Impersonality: Lawrence, Woolf, and Mann.* Chicago: The University of Chicago Press, 1978.

Alexander, Jean. *The Venture of Form in the Novels of Virginia Woolf.* Port Washington, N.Y.: Kennikat Press, 1974.

Apter, T. E. *Virginia Woolf: A Study of her Novels.* New York: New York University Press, 1979.

Barzilai, Shulamith. "The Knot of Consciousness in *The Waves.*" *Hebrew University Studies in Literature,* vol. 7 (1979):214–44.

Bazin, Nancy Topping. *Virginia Woolf and the Androgynous Vision.* New Brunswick, N.J.: Rutgers University Press, 1973.

Beja, Morris, ed. *Virginia Woolf: To the Lighthouse.* London: Macmillan & Co., 1970.

Bell, Barbara Currier. "*Orlando:* Mockery with a Grin or with a Vengeance?" *Modernist Studies,* vol. 4 (1982):207–17.

Bell, Quentin. *Virginia Woolf: A Biography.* 2 vols. New York: Harcourt Brace Jovanovich, 1972.

Bennett, Joan. *Virginia Woolf: Her Art as a Novelist.* 2nd ed., enlarged. Cambridge: Cambridge University Press, 1964.

Boone, Joseph Allen. "The Meaning of Elvedon in *The Waves:* A Key to Bernard's Experience and Woolf's Vision." *Modern Fiction Studies* 4, vol. 27 (1981–82):629–637.

Boyd, Mari. "The Art Theme in *Between the Acts.*" *Studies in English Literature,* vol. 59 (1983):49–64.

Brewster, Dorothy. *Virginia Woolf.* London: George Allen and Unwin, 1963.

Bulletin of the New York Public Library 2, vol. 80 (Winter 1977). Special Virginia Woolf issue.

Caves, Mary Ann. "Framing, Centering, and Explicating: Virginia Woolf's Collage." *New York Literary Forum,* vols. 10–11 (1983):51–78.

Clements, Patricia and Grundy, Isobel, eds. *Virginia Woolf: New Critical Essays.* Totowa, N.J.: Barnes & Noble Books, 1983.

Corner, Martin. "Mysticism and Atheism in *To the Lighthouse.*" *Studies in the Novel* 4, vol. 13 (1981):408–23.

Daiches, David. *Virginia Woolf.* 2d rev. ed. Norfolk, Conn.: New Directions, 1963.

DiBattista, Maria. *Virginia Woolf's Major Novels: The Fables of Anon.* New Haven: Yale University Press, 1980.

Dick, Susan. "The Restless Searcher: A Discussion of the Evolution of 'Time Passes' in *To the Lighthouse.*" *English Studies in Canada,* vol. 5 (1979):311–29.

Donahue, Delia. *The Novels of Virginia Woolf.* Rome: Bulzoni Editore, 1977.

Dowling, David. "Virginia Woolf's Own *Jacob's Room.*" *Southern Review* (Adelaide, Australia), 1, vol. 15 (1982):60–72.

Edwards, Lee R. "War and Roses: The Politics of *Mrs. Dalloway.*" In *The Authority of Experience: Essays in Feminist Criticism,* edited by Arlyn Diamond and Lee R. Edwards. Amherst: The University of Massachusetts Press, 1977.

Elert, Kerstin. *Portraits of Women in Selected Novels by Virginia Woolf and E. M. Forster.* Umeá: University of Umeá Press, 1979.

Farrell, Thomas J. "The Female and Male Modes of Rhetoric." *College English,* vol. 40 (1979):909–21.

Fleishman, Avrom. *Virginia Woolf: A Critical Reading.* Baltimore: The Johns Hopkins University Press, 1975.

Fox, Alice. "Virginia Woolf at Work: The Elizabethan Voyage Out." *Bulletin of Research in the Humanities* 1, vol. 84 (1981):65–84.

Frazer, June M. "*Mrs. Dalloway:* Virginia Woolf's Greek Novel." *Research Studies,* vol. 47 (1979):221–28.

Freedman, Ralph, ed. *Virginia Woolf: Revaluation and Continuity.* Berkeley: University of California Press, 1980.

Fromm, Harold. "Virginia Woolf: Art and Sexuality." *Virginia Quarterly Review,* vol. 55 (1979):441–59.

Frye, Joanne S. "*Mrs. Dalloway* as Lyrical Paradox." *Ball State University Forum* 1, vol. 23 (1982):42–56.

Gillespie, Diane Filby. "Virginia Woolf's Miss La Trobe: The Artist's Last Struggle Against Masculine Values." *Women and Literature* 1, vol. 5 (1977):38–46.

Gorsky, Susan Rubinow. *Virginia Woolf.* Boston: Twayne Publishers, 1978.

Graham, J. W. "Manuscript Revision and the Heroic Theme of *The Waves.*" *Twentieth Century Literature* 3, vol. 29 (1983):312–32.

Hafley, James. *The Glass Roof: Virginia Woolf as Novelist.* Berkeley: University of California Press, 1954.

Harper, Howard. *Between Language and Silence: The Novels of Virginia Woolf.* Baton Rouge: Louisiana State University Press, 1982.

Hasler, Jörg. "Virginia Woolf and the Chimes of Big Ben." *English Studies* 2, vol. 63 (1982):145–58.

Heinemann, Jan. "The Revolt Against Language: A Critical Note on Twentieth-Century Irrationalism with Special Reference to the Aesthetico-Philosophical Views of Virginia Woolf and Clive Bell." *Orbis Litterarum* 3, vol. 32 (1977):212–28.

Hessler, John G. "Moral Accountability in *Mrs. Dalloway.*" *Renascence,* vol. 30 (1978):126–36.

Hintikka, Jaakko. "Virginia Woolf and Our Knowledge of the External World." *Journal of Aesthetics and Art Criticism,* vol. 38 (1979):5–14.

Holtby, Winifred. *Virginia Woolf.* London: Wishart, 1932.

Hunting, Robert. "Laurence Sterne and Virginia Woolf." *Études Anglaises*, vol. 32 (1979):83–93.

Janardanan, N. "The Problem of Unity in Virginia Woolf's *The Years.*" *Journal of English Studies*, vol. 3 (1980):28–37.

Kaneuf, Peggy. "Penelope at Work: Interruptions in *A Room of One's Own.*" *Novel* 1, vol. 16 (1982):5–18.

Kapur, Vijay. *Virginia Woolf's Vision of Life and Her Search for Significant Form: A Study in the Shaping Vision.* Atlantic Highlands, N.J.: Humanities Press, 1981.

Kelley, Alice van Buren. *The Novels of Virginia Woolf: Fact and Vision.* Chicago: The University of Chicago Press, 1973.

Kenney, Susan M. "Two Endings: Virginia Woolf's Suicide and *Between the Acts.*" *University of Toronto Quarterly* 4, vol. 44 (1975):265–89.

Kenney, Susan M. and Edwin J., Jr. "Virginia Woolf and the Art of Madness." *Massachusetts Review* 1, vol. 23 (1982):161–85.

Kirkpatrick, B. J. *A Bibliography of Virginia Woolf.* London: Hart-Davis, 1967.

Leaska, Mitchell. *The Novels of Virginia Woolf.* New York: John Jay Press, 1977.

Lee, Hermione. *The Novels of Virginia Woolf.* London: Methuen & Co. Ltd., 1977.

Lewis, Thomas S. W., ed. *Virginia Woolf: A Collection of Criticism.* New York: McGraw-Hill Book Co., 1975.

Lilienfeld, Jane. " 'The Deceptiveness of Beauty': Mother Love and Mother Hate in *To the Lighthouse.*" *Twentieth Century Literature*, vol. 23 (1977):345–76.

Little, Judy. *Comedy and the Woman Writer: Woolf, Spark, and Feminism.* Lincoln: University of Nebraska Press, 1983.

Lorsch, Susan E. "Structure and Rhythm in *The Waves*: The Ebb and Flow of Meaning." *Essays in Literature*, vol. 6 (1979):195–206.

Love, Jean O. *Worlds in Consciousness: Mythopoetic Thought in the Novels of Virginia Woolf.* Berkeley: University of California Press, 1970.

———. *Virginia Woolf: Sources in Madness and Art.* Berkeley: University of California Press, 1977.

Lyons, Richard S. "The Intellectual Structure of Woolf's *Between the Acts.*" *Modern Language Quarterly*, vol. 38 (1977):149–66.

McLaughlin, Thomas M. "Virginia Woolf's Criticism: Interpretation as Theory and as Discourse." *Southern Humanities Review* 3, vol. 17 (1983):241–53.

McLaurin, Allen. *Virginia Woolf: The Echoes Enslaved.* Cambridge: Cambridge University Press, 1973.

Majumdar, Robin, *Virginia Woolf: An Annotated Bibliography.* New York: Garland Press, 1976.

Majumdar, Robin and McLaurin, Allen, eds. *Virginia Woolf: The Critical Heritage.* London: Routledge & Kegan Paul, 1975.

Marcus, Jane, ed. *New Feminist Essays on Virginia Woolf.* Lincoln: University of Nebraska Press, 1981.

———, ed. *Virginia Woolf: A Feminist Slant.* Lincoln: University of Nebraska Press, 1983.

Marder, Herbert. *Feminism and Art: A Study of Virginia Woolf.* Chicago: The University of Chicago Press, 1968.

Meisel, Perry. *The Absent Father: Virginia Woolf and Walter Pater.* New Haven: Yale University Press, 1980.

Miller, J. Hillis. "Mr. Carmichael and Lily Briscoe: The Rhythm and Creativity in *To the Lighthouse.*" In *Modernism Reconsidered,* edited by Robert Kiely, assisted by John Hildebidle. Cambridge, Mass.: Harvard University Press, 1983.

―――. "*Between the Acts:* Repetition as Extrapolation." In *Fiction and Repetition.* Cambridge, Mass.: Harvard University Press, 1982.

Modern Fiction Studies, vol. 18 (1972). Virginia Woolf issue.

Morris, Jill. *Time and Timelessness in Virginia Woolf.* Hicksville, N.Y.: Exposition, 1977.

Moss, Roger. "*Jacob's Room* and the Eighteenth Century: From Elegy to Essay." *Critical Quarterly* 3, vol. 23 (1981):39–54.

Naremore, James. *The World Without a Self: Virginia Woolf and the Novel.* New Haven: Yale University Press, 1973.

Nashashilsi, Pauline R. "Alive and There: Virginia Woolf's Presentation of Reality." *Dutch Quarterly Review of Anglo-American Letters,* vol. 7 (1977):184–99.

Novack, Jane. *The Razor Edge of Balance: A Study of Virginia Woolf.* Coral Gables: University of Miami Press, 1974.

Ohmann, Carol. "Culture and Anarchy in *Jacob's Room.*" *Contemporary Literature,* vol. 18 (1977):160–72.

Parkes, Graham. "Imagining Reality in *To the Lighthouse.*" *Philosophy and Literature* 1–2, vol. 6 (1982):33–44.

Pellan, Françoise. "Virginia Woolf's Posthumous Poem." *Modern Fiction Studies* 4, vol. 29 (1983):695–700.

Poole, Roger. *The Unknown Virginia Woolf.* Atlantic Highlands, N.J.: Humanities Press, 1982.

Poresky, Louise A. *The Elusive Self: Psyche and Spirit in Virginia Woolf's Novels.* Newark: University of Delaware Press, 1981.

Radin, Grace. *Virginia Woolf's "The Years": The Evolution of a Novel.* Knoxville: University of Tennessee Press, 1981.

Rantavaara, Irma. *Virginia Woolf's "The Waves."* Port Washington, N.Y.: Kennikat Press, 1969 (1960).

Richter, Harvena. *Virginia Woolf: The Inward Voyage.* Princeton: Princeton University Press, 1970.

Rose, Phyllis. *Woman of Letters: A Life of Virginia Woolf.* Oxford: Oxford University Press, 1978.

Rosenthal, Michael. *Virginia Woolf.* New York: Columbia University Press, 1979.

Ruddick, Lisa. *The Seen and the Unseen: Virginia Woolf's "To the Lighthouse."* Cambridge, Mass.: Harvard University Press, 1977.

Schaefer, Josephone O'Brien. *The Three-Fold Nature of Reality in the Novels of Virginia Woolf.* London: Mouton, 1965.

Schlack, Beverly Ann. *Continuing Presences: Virginia Woolf's Use of Literary Allusion.* University Park, Pa.: The Pennsylvania State University Press, 1979.

Spilka, Mark. "On Lily Briscoe's Borrowed Grief: A Psycho-Literary Speculation." *Criticism,* vol. 21 (1979):1–33.

———. "On Mrs. Dalloway's Absent Grief: A Psycho-Literary Speculation." *Contemporary Literature,* vol. 20 (1979):316–38.

———. "The Robber in the Bedroom; or, the Thief of Love: A Woolfian Grieving in Six Novels and Two Memoirs." *Critical Inquiry,* vol. 5 (1979):663–82.

Sprague, Claire, ed. *Virginia Woolf: A Collection of Critical Essays.* Englewood Cliffs, N.J.: Prentice-Hall, Inc., 1971.

Squier, Susan. "Mirroring and Mothering: Reflections on the Mirror Encounter Metaphor in Virginia Woolf's Works." *Twentieth Century Literature* 3, vol. 27 (1981):272–88.

Stewart, Jack F. "Impressionism in the Early Novels of Virginia Woolf." *Journal of Modern Literature* 2, vol. 9 (1982):237–66.

———. "Spatial Form and Color in *The Waves.*" *Twentieth Century Literature* 1, vol. 28 (1982):86–107.

Thakur, N.C. *The Symbolism of Virginia Woolf.* New York: Oxford University Press, 1965.

Trombley, Stephen. *All That Summer She Was Mad: Virginia Woolf: Female Victim of Male Medicine.* New York: Continuum, 1982.

Twentieth Century Literature, vol. 25 (1979). Virginia Woolf issue.

Virginia Woolf Miscellany, 1973–.

Virginia Woolf Quarterly, 1972–.

Vogler, Thomas A., ed. *"To the Lighthouse": A Collection of Critical Essays.* Englewood Cliffs, N.J.: Prentice-Hall, Inc., 1970.

Woodring, Carl. *Virginia Woolf.* New York: Columbia University Press, 1966.

Wyatt, Jean. "The Celebrations of Eros: Greek Concepts of Love and Beauty in *To the Lighthouse.*" *Philosophy and Literature* 2, vol. 2 (1978):160–75.

Zwerdling, Alex. "*Jacob's Room:* Woolf's Satiric Elegy." *English Literary History* 4, vol. 48 (1981):894–913.

Acknowledgments

"Something Central Which Permeated: *Mrs. Dalloway*" by Reuben Brower from *The Fields of Light: An Experiment in Critical Reading* by Reuben Brower, copyright © 1951 by Oxford University Press. Reprinted by permission.

"The Brown Stocking" by Erich Auerbach from *Mimesis: The Representation of Reality in Western Literature* by Erich Auerbach, translated by Willard R. Trask, copyright © 1953 by Princeton University Press. Reprinted by permission.

"Virginia's Web" by Geoffrey Hartman from *Chicago Review* 14 (Spring 1961), copyright © 1970 by Geoffrey Hartman. Reprinted by permission.

" 'Death Among the Apple Trees': *The Waves* and the World of Things" by Frank D. McConnell from *Bucknell Review* 16, copyright © 1968 by Bucknell Review. Reprinted by permission.

"Nature and History in *The Years*" by James Naremore from *Virginia Woolf: Revaluation and Continuity* edited by Ralph Freedman, copyright © 1980 by the Regents of the University of California. Reprinted by permission.

"Enigmas of Imagination: *Orlando* Through the Looking Glass" by Paul West from *The Southern Review* 3, vol. 13, copyright © 1977 by Louisiana State University. Reprinted by permission.

"*The Waves*" by Hermione Lee from *The Novels of Virginia Woolf* by Hermione Lee, copyright © 1977 by Hermione Lee. Reprinted by permission.

"An Uncertain Balance: *Night and Day*" by T. E. Apter from *Virginia Woolf: A Study of Her Novels* by T. E. Apter, copyright © 1979 by T. E. Apter. Reprinted by permission.

"Virginia Woolf and Walter Pater" by Perry Meisel from *The Absent Father: Virginia Woolf and Walter Pater* by Perry Meisel, copyright © 1980 by Yale University Press. Reprinted by permission.

"*Between the Acts*: The Play of Will" by Maria DiBattista from *Virginia Woolf's Major Novels: The Fables of Anon* by Maria DiBattista, copyright © 1980 by Yale University Press. Reprinted by permission.

"Toward the Far Side of Language: *The Voyage Out*" by E. L. Bishop from *Twentieth Century Literature* 4, vol. 27 (Winter 1981), copyright © 1982 by Hofstra University Press. Reprinted by permission.

"*Mrs. Dalloway:* Repetition as the Raising of the Dead" by J. Hillis Miller from *Fiction and Repetition: Seven English Novels* by J. Hillis Miller, copyright © 1982 by J. Hillis Miller. Reprinted by permission.

"Irreconcilable Habits of Thought in *A Room of One's Own* and *To the Lighthouse*" by John Burt from *English Literary History* 4, vol. 49 (Winter, 1982), copyright © 1982 by The Johns Hopkins University Press. Reprinted by permission.

"*Jacob's Room:* A Study in Still Life" by Robert Kiely from *Modernism Reconsidered* by Robert Kiely, copyright © 1983 by the President and Fellows of Harvard College. Reprinted by permission.

"The Musical Style of *The Waves*" by Gerald Levin from *The Journal of Narrative Technique* 3, vol. 13 (Fall 1983), copyright © 1983 by *The Journal of Narrative Technique.* Reprinted by permission.

"The Politics of Holiday: *Orlando*" by Judy Little from *Comedy and the Woman Writer: Woolf, Spark, and Feminism* by Judy Little, copyright © 1983 by University of Nebraska Press. Reprinted by permission.

"Narrative Voice and the Female Perspective in *The Voyage Out*" by Virginia Blain from *Virginia Woolf: New Critical Essays* edited by Patricia Clements and Isobel Grundy, copyright © 1983 by Vision Press Ltd. Reprinted by permission.

"Narrative Structure(s) and Female Development: The Cases of *Mrs. Dalloway*" by Elizabeth Abel from *The Voyage In: Fictions of Female Development* edited by Elizabeth Abel, Marianne Hirsch and Elizabeth Langland, copyright © 1983 by the Trustees of Dartmouth College. Reprinted by permission.

Index

A

A la recherche du temps perdu (Proust), 179
absolute subjectivity, 57
abstraction, 102, 109, 112–14
Aeschylus, 133, 153
affirmative movements, 44, 46–47, 49–50, 52
Albee, Edward, 84
Alexander, Jean, 228
"Allerseelen," 180–81
allegory, 147–48, 151–52, 224–25
anders-streben, 132
androgyny, 191–96, 206, 225–26, 232, 235
anthropomorphism, 108
Antigone (Sophocles), 139
art, 164, 167
    nature and, 46–49
Artaud, Antonin, 94
associationalism, 144
Auerbach, Erich, 203
Austen, Jane, 181, 234–35, 247

B

Babcock, Barbara, 224
Beckett, Samuel, 84, 90–91
Beer, Gillian, 263
Beethoven, Ludwig van, 215–18, 221
Bell, Quentin, 67, 167
Bennett, Arnold, 87
Bennett, Joan, 62
Bergson, Henri-Louis, 84
Between the Acts, 5–6, 41, 48–49, 70, 80, 82, 90, 111, 124, 129–30, 135–52
    allegory in, 147–48, 151–52
    characterization, 146, 148
    comical form, 144–45, 150–51
    Eros, 148–52
    historical pageant in, 137–38
    history in, 137, 140, 150–152

love, 141–42, 146, 148–49, 151
play of imagination, the, 144, 147, 152
plot, 151
satire and tragedy, blend of, 147, 150
time, aesthetic treatment of, 139, 144, 150–51
tragedy in, 144, 146, 150
transitions in, 41, 48
war, 141–46, 148–50
    love and hate, 141–46, 148–50
    sexual tragedy and, 142
Borges, Jorges Luis, 64, 90–91
Bostetter, Edward, 54
Break of Day, 246
Brewster, Dorothy, 55, 59
Brontë, Charlotte, 234
Brontë, Emily, 234
Brower, Reuben, 261
Buddenbrooks (Mann), 34

C

caricature, 224–25
Carroll, Lewis, 99
Cartesian Meditations (Husserl), 90
Cassirer, Ernst, 159–60
"Caterpillars of the Commonwealth Unite" (Leavis), 67
character, 105–17, 146–48, 219
Chaucer, Geoffrey, 131
Chekhov, Anton, 131
Chinese drama, 140
Cixous, Hélène, 99, 232
classical Greece, 246, 260
Coleridge, Samuel Taylor, 54, 132
comedy, 144–45, 150–51
communion, theme of, 22, 27, 33, 42, 45–52
conflict, 168
Congreve, William, 148
Connell, Evan S., 97

Conrad, Joseph, 169
consciousness, 86, 90
    multiple, 25–38
    subjective, 63
continuity, 22, 27, 33, 42, 45–52
Cortázar, Julio, 97
creation, 89, 93
Cymbeline (Shakespeare), 63, 186, 188

D

Dante Alighieri, 147
de Beauvoir, Simon, 231–32
de Man, Paul, 151
De Quincey, Thomas, 94, 132
De Salvo, Louise, 237–38
de Senancourt, Basil, 69
"Death of a Moth, The," 60
death, theme of, 175, 185–88, 190
dénouement, 150–51
deus ex machina, 149
dialectic, 48, 50
drama, 140–42

E

Eddington, Sir Arthur, 84
Einstein, Albert, 84
Eliot, George, 84, 234–35
    prescription for literary realism, 141
Eliot, T. S., 70, 73, 82
    on disassociation, 138
epistemology, 95
Eros, 148–52
être ensoi, 63
    see also Sartre
"Evening Over Sussex: Reflections in a
    Motor Car," 60–61
excursus, 30–33
Excursion, The (Wordsworth), 54
exlebte rede, 28–29
expressionism, 49, 52, 94

F

fascism, 76, 138–39
Faulkner, William, 45
female development, 244–64
female narrative, 244–48
female perspective, 231–41
"Female Sexuality" (Freud), 246
feminist literary criticism, 245
fictional voice, gender differences in, 244

Flaubert, Gustave, 34, 38
Fleishman, Avrom, 225, 240
*Forces in Modern British Literature 1885–
    1956* (Tindall), 95
Four Quartets (Eliot), 117
Freud, Sigmund, 148, 244, 246, 249,
    252–56

G

gestalt-narrative, 59, 61
Gide, André, 89
Graham, J. W., 235
Greeks, influence of, 133–34
Guiget, Jean, 59

H

Hamsun, Knut, 34
harmony, *see* rhythm
Harrison, Jane, 260
Hawkes, John, 216
Hilton, Walter, 56
Histoire (Simon), 97
history, 69–71, 82, 134, 196
Hitler, Adolf, 138
Homer, 32–33
Hopkins, Gerard Manley, 216
Hopscotch (Cortázar), 97
"How It Strikes A Contemporary," 131,
    133
Huizinga, Johan, 152

I

identity, repercussive, 92
illusion, 96
imagery, 106, 109–10, 112–15, 132
imagination, 83, 86, 91, 97–99
    human, 53
    romantic, 54
    space and, 43
    the artist and, 47
inner processes, 23–24, 27, 31, 33, 39
interpolation, 49–50
"Intimations Ode" (Wordsworth), 62, 64
"Introduction, The," 198–99

J

Jacob's Room, 90, 102, 111, 207–14, 241
    design and meaning, 214
    Roger Fry, influence of, 208
    still life and, 207–14

James, Henry, 44
    prose of, 45
James, William, 84
Jane Eyre (Brontë), 192
Jeans, Sir James, 84, 87, 95
Johnson, Brimley, 233
Jourdain, M., 87
Joyce, James, 87, 90, 103–04, 169
juxtaposition of images, 132

K
Keats, John, 192
"Kew Gardens," 154
Knole and the Sackvilles (Sackville-West), 224

L
language, 122, 133, 153–68, 255–57
Language and Myth (Cassirer), 159–60
Lawrence, D. H., 71, 125, 159
"Leaning Tower, The," 1, 129, 135
Leavis, Q. D., 67
"Life and the Novelist," 208
Locke, John, 144
logical conception, 159–68
love, 156–58, 161, 163, 165–66
    self-realisation and, 128
Lukacs, Georg, 142

M
MacCarthy, Desmond, 232
Mann, Thomas, 34
Marius the Epicurean (Pater), 2
"Melymbrosia," *see The Voyage Out*
Meredith, George, 133
metaphor, 7–18
    misused, 16–18
metaphorical conception, 159–60, 166–68
Middlemarch (Eliot) 235
Miller, J. Hillis, 151, 233, 240
mimesis, 49
mind, the, 89–93, 97, 99
"Modern Fiction," 85, 154
modernist novel, 191
moments of being, 154, 158–59
monologue intérior, 28
mortality, theme of, 75
mother-daughter alignment, 246, 249–53, 262

Moths, The, 55, 101
    see also The Waves
"Mr. Bennett and Mrs. Brown," 79, 83, 86
Mrs. Dalloway, 7–18, 44–45, 54, 63, 90, 109, 111, 116, 123, 126, 138, 169–90, 198, 243–64
    action of, 179
    communion in, 184–86
    constructive action in, 175, 182–83, 186, 189
    continuity, 45, 175, 181–82
    death, theme of, in, 175, 185–90
    doubling of Septimus and Clarissa, 2–3, 13–14, 186
    dramatic design, 7–16
    female development in, 244–57, 260–64
    language, 255–57
    metaphor, central, 7–18
    minds, relationship between, 170, 174–75, 185
    mysticism in, 255
    narrative
        past in, 170, 177–81
        repetition in, 169, 172, 190
        structure of, 244–54, 256–64
    narrator, 170–71, 177, 181
        universal mind of, 170, 173–174, 178, 188
    past and present, boundaries between, 176, 188
    plot, 244, 246–47, 252, 257–63
    plot developmental, in, 244–46, 248–50, 256–64
    psychological allegory, 250
    repetition, 187–88
        memory and, 170, 176–77
        of past, 170, 175–79, 185
    transitions in, 41, 172
"Mrs. Dalloway's Party," 198
Music and Letters (Tovey), 216
music, elements of in literature, 132
musical quality in writing, 168
Mussolini, Benito, 138
My Mother's House, 246
Mysterious Universe, The (Jeans), 84, 95
mysticism, 55–57, 223, 228, 255

N
Nabokov, Vladimir, 83, 88
Naremore, James, 238–39

narrative
    structure, 244–54, 256–64
    voice, 233–36, 241
narrator, 170–71, 177, 181, 188
    universal mind, 173–74, 178, 188
"Narrow Bridge of Art, The," 131
nature, 138
    art and, 46–49
    as symbol, 126
nature morte, 209, 214
Neutre (Cixous), 99
"New Criticism," 54
"new novel," 63
Night and Day, 90, 102, 111, 119–29,
        241
    love and self-realisation, 128
    nature as symbol in, 126
    romanticism, language of, 122
    self, 119–26
        society and, division between,
            119–26, 128
        suppression of, 121–27
    work, attitude towards, 123
        destruction of individuality,
            124
nihilism, 203
nouveau roman, 97
novel of silence, 165
Novel On Yellow Paper (Smith), 103–04

O

Oedipus complex, 249–50, 252–56
"Old Mrs. Dalloway," 246
"omnipercipience," 235
"On Not Knowing Greek," 135, 153
open-ended universe, 91
Oresteia (Aeschylus), 260
Orlando, 45, 49–50, 89–101, 116, 235
    androgyny, 225–26
    caricature and allegory, 224–25
    connectedness of things, 93
    creation of enigma, 93, 95
    expressionism in, 94
    holiday experience in, 223–25, 229
    illusion, 96
    mysticism in, 223, 228
    Ovidian metamorphoses in, 91
    prose of, 98
    random juxtaposition of items, 93
    relativism, 96–98

repercussive identity in, 92
social behavior in, 225–28
tone, change in, 228–29
universe, open-ended, 91, 92

P

painting, elements of in literature, 132
pantonal style, 215–21
past and present, 134
    boundaries between, 176, 188
Pater, Walter, 129–35
    Anders-streben, 132
    influence on Woolf, 2, 4–5, 129–35
    inscribed trace, 129
patriarchy, 76, 138, 191
"Patron and the Crocus," 164
phallogocentrism, 232
"Phases of Fiction," 129, 132
Planck, Max, 84, 89
Plath, Sylvia, 84
plot, 45, 49, 244–47, 252, 257–63
    character and, 45
Plotinus, 87
Plato (Pater), 133
Point Counterpoint (Huxley), 113
Points For a Compass Rose (Connel), 97
post-Renaissance culture, 134
pre-Oedipal relationship, 245–46, 250,
        252–54, 260
"Professions for Women," 232, 238
prose style, 44–46
    plot and, 45–46
Prometheus Unbound (Shelley), 56
Proust, Marcel, 34–35, 103–04, 176
psychological allegory, 250

R

Racinian theater, 140
radical character of human beings and
        things, 154
realism, 49, 52, 83
    constraints of, 203–05
    rejection of, 111–14
relativism, 96, 98
repercussive identity, 92
repetition, 105, 169–70, 172, 175–79,
        185–88, 190
"reverberation," 133
rhythm, 131–32
rhythmic prose, 104–05

problems of, 105–06, 110
Richardson, Dorothy, 233
Robbe-Grillet, Alain, 62–65
romanticism, language of, 122
Room of One's Own, A (Woolf), 6, 44,
    46, 49, 50, 81, 101, 129,
    191–206, 226, 232–33, 244, 246
    androgyny and, 192–95
    arguments of, 192–98
    habits of thought in, 191–206
    the war and, 193–97
Rose, Phyllis, 192
Rosetti, Dante Gabriel, 195

S
Sackville-West, Vita, 224
Sarraute, Nathalie, 62, 98
Sartre, Jean-Paul, 61, 181
Scale of Perfection (Hilton), 56
Schoenberg, Arnold, 215, 218
Science and the Modern World
    (Whitehead), 85
self, 119–27, 219
    reality and, 122, 128
    society and, 119–28
    suppression of, 72–73, 76, 121–27
Shakespeare, William, 5–10, 14, 18, 51,
    84, 97, 132–33, 139, 153
Shelley, Percy, 53–55, 62
Showalter, Elaine, 245
Sido, 246
Simon, Claude, 97
"Sketch of the Past, A," 134–35, 159
Smith, Stevie, 103–04
"Some Psychical Consequences of the
    Anatomical Distinction Between
    the Sexes" (Freud), 252
Speak, Memory (Nabokov), 88
Stars and Atoms (Eddington), 84
Steps Across the Frontiers (Heisenberg),
    98
Sterne, Laurence, 132, 144
stream of consciousness novel, 28,
    102–04, 109
structure, 215–18
Stubbs, Patricia, 240
subjection of women, 193–94, 196, 198
Sullivan, J. W. N., 215–17, 221
Suspiria de Profundis (De Quincey), 94
Swann's Way (Proust), 103–04

Symbolism (Whitehead), 84–85
Symbolism of Virginia Woolf, The
    (Thakur), 55
symbols, use of, 8–17, 126, 140

T
Tennyson, Alfred Lord, 195
Thakur, N. C., 55
theater, 140
"Three Guineas," 67, 72–75, 138–40,
    148, 193
time, treatment of, 30–36, 139, 144,
    150–51
Tindall, William York, 95
"Tlön, Ugbar, Orbis Tertius" (Borges),
    64
To The Lighthouse, 3–4, 19–40, 42–43,
    49–50, 52, 59, 79, 90, 101–02,
    108–11, 116, 131, 138, 143,
    191–206, 246, 251, 260, 263–64
    analysis of, 22–27
    Buddenbrooks, compared to, 34
    content and form, 192, 205
    continuity in, 22, 27, 33, 42
    destruction in, 199–203, 205
    excursus in, 30–33
    habits of thought in, 191–206
    Homer, compared to, 32–33
    imagination and space in, 43
    inner processes in, 23–24, 27, 31,
        33, 39
    Madame Bovary, compared to, 34,
        38
    motifs of, 22, 25, 43
    objective narration, lack of, 25–34
    progressive ideology in, 197, 201,
        205
    Proust, compared, to, 34–35, 176
    random moments transformed, 4, 39
    realist novel and old order, 198
    repetition of images and words in,
        8–18, 42
    subjection of women, 198–99
    tone, 25–28
    transitions in, 41
    Ulysses, compared to, 35, 38, 52
Tovey, Sir Donald, 216
tragedy, 144, 146, 150
transitions, 11, 14, 41–42, 45, 172
Tristam Shandy (Sterne), 144

Trollope, Anthony, 181
"tunnelling process," 179, 247
Turgenev, Ivan, 131, 134

U
Ulysses (Joyce), 52, 103–04, 246–47
"under-mind," 130–35
"under-texture," see "under-mind"
"Ur-Drama," 151

V
Virginia Woolf (Brewster), 55
voice, 133, 135
    see also narrative voice
Voyage Out, The, 49, 90, 122, 153–68,
    211, 236–41, 243
    communion with external, 156–58,
        162–63
    conflict, 168
    female perspective in, 237–41
    language, 153–68
        essence of words, 156–62, 66
        external reality and, 154, 161–
            62, 168
    love, necessity of, 156–58, 161,
        163, 165–66
    moments of being, 154, 158–59
    narrative voice in, 233–36, 241
    non-human realm, attraction of,
        157
    novel of silence, 165
    sexuality in, 237–41
    solace, 157
    symbol and meaning, 160
    word
        nature of, 168
        presentation of sensory
            experience and, 161–64
        vehicle for abstract thought,
            161, 163

W
Waste Land, The (Eliot), 70, 73
Waves, The, 5, 17, 49–51, 55–65, 90,
    101–17, 137–39, 143,
    215–23, 229, 235, 243
    abstraction in, 102, 109, 112–14
    anthropomorphism in, 108
    Beethoven and, 215–18, 221
    characters, phenomenal, 219

characters, treatment of, 56–61,
    105–17
    distinction through use of
        images, 106–08, 112
    language of, 107–08
gestalt-narrative, 59, 61
materialism, eradication of, 102
musical style of, 215–22
mysticism in, 55–57, 62, 64
pantonal style, 218–21
point of view, 102
repetition in speech, 105
rhythmic prose, 104–05
Schoenberg and, 215–21
structure, 215–21
Wells, H. G., 91
Wheeler, John, 86
Whitehead, Alfred North, 84–87
"Why War" (Freud), 148
Woman Novelist, The (Johnson), 233
women, subjection of, 193–94, 196, 198
Woolf, Virginia, see specific titles and
    subjects
Wordsworth, William, 54, 56, 60, 62,
    64, 176
"Writer's Diary, A," 101, 174, 179, 198

Y
Years, The, 67–82, 90, 112, 137–39
    action of drama, 139
    frustration, social and sexual, in,
        81–82
    history in, 69–71, 82
    marriage, 72–74
    nature in, 71
    patriarchy in, 76, 112, 137–39, 191
    Room of One's Own, compared to,
        81
    society, attitude towards, 67–68,
        71–74
    "soul," suppression of, 72–73, 76
    structure, 69
    unity, 68–70, 78–81
        compared with To The
            Lighthouse, 79
        from multiplicity, 68
        of public and private worlds, 68
    society and solitude, 78–80

Z
Zeitgeist, 85